D1328235

FODOR'S

ROCKIES & PLAINS

COLORADO
NEBRASKA
UTAH
WYOMING
SOUTH DAKOTA
NORTH DAKOTA
MONTANA

Colorado
Nebraska
Utah
Wyoming
South Dakota
North Dakota
Montana

ROCKIES &

Editorial Assistants: SPENCER SMITH
ADELA HORODECKI
DAVID LAHM
MELISANDE KOPP
ESTHER JOHNSTON
EDGAR NEEDHAM
LILLIAN KNAUS
MARILYN BIRKETT
DODIE GERSON
JARED WELCH
KATHERINE SPIELMANN

Illustrations: LYNN STURM
Symbols: LASZLO
Cover: JOEL SHUKOVSKY
Editorial Consultants: World Wide Information Services, Inc.

PLAINS

EUGENE FODOR
STEPHEN BIRNBAUM
ROBERT FISHER
EDITORS

STEWART UDALL
introduction

BILL HOSOKAWA
ROGER COX
CARRIE RODGERS
LOWELL JOHNSON
HARRY E. FULLER, JR.
BRUCE HAMBY
ROY PECK
LEAVITT F. MORRIS
JOHN R. MILTON
BILL OWEN
contributing editors

DAVID McKAY COMPANY, INC.—NEW YORK

Travel Books Edited by Eugene Fodor

1936 ON THE CONTINENT
1937 IN EUROPE
EUROPE IN 1938
MEN'S GUIDE TO EUROPE
WOMEN'S GUIDE TO EUROPE
FODOR-SHELL TRAVEL GUIDES. U.S.A. (8 volumes)

Area Guides, Revised Yearly

EUROPE
EUROPE UNDER 25
EUROPE ON A BUDGET
JAPAN
EAST ASIA
CARIBBEAN, BAHAMAS AND BERMUDA
SOUTH AMERICA
INDIA
MEXICO
ISLAMIC ASIA
SOVIET UNION

Country Guides, Revised Yearly

AUSTRIA	ISRAEL
BELGIUM AND LUXEMBOURG	ITALY
CZECHOSLOVAKIA	MOROCCO
FRANCE	PORTUGAL
GERMANY	SCANDINAVIA
GREAT BRITAIN	SPAIN
GREECE	SWITZERLAND
HAWAII	TUNISIA
HOLLAND	TURKEY
HUNGARY	YUGOSLAVIA
IRELAND	

CITY GUIDES: LONDON—ROME—VENICE—PEKING—PARIS—VIENNA

and the latest:

INDIAN AMERICA
EUROPE TALKING (A 19-LANGUAGE PHRASE BOOK)
WORLD CRUISING GUIDE.

MANUFACTURED IN THE UNITED STATES OF AMERICA

CONTENTS

GENERAL AND PRACTICAL INFORMATION

The *General and Practical Information* sections in this book contain detailed information on some or all of the following subjects: Facts and Figures, How to Get There, How to Get Around, Tourist Information, Seasonal Events, National Parks, State Parks, Camping Out, Trailer Tips, Farm Vacations & Guest Ranches, Historic Houses, Famous Libraries, Tours, Industrial Tours, Special Interest Tours, Gardens, Music, Stage & Revues, Nightclubs, Drinking Laws, Summer Sports, Winter Sports, Spectator Sports, Shopping, What to do With the Children, Indians, Photography, Quarries, Recommended Reading.

INTRODUCTION

Not only in films and TV, but in literature, the cowpoke has captured the public imagination. At one time, it took sixty-one pages to list the articles and books about the West in a publication of the American Historical Association, *Writings on American History*. Now, the Western History Association, established in 1962, publishes its own journal, *The American West*.

Nation Tilts Westward

This tremendous interest in the West continues. Frank Lloyd Wright, the famous architect, noted that millions of people were still pouring into that third of the nation lying between the Rockies and the Pacific Ocean. He called it the "Great Westward Tilt."

When I write of the Rockies and the Plains, I am speaking of Colorado, Wyoming, Montana, Utah, North Dakota, South Dakota, and Nebraska as well as my home state of Arizona and New Mexico. Actually, the eastern sections of Montana, Wyoming, Colorado, and New Mexico are considered in the Great Plains as well as in the Rocky Mountains—they overlap into two categories—geographically. The Great Plains have always had a proportionately larger rural and agricultural population than any other region in the nation, with the exception of the Great Basin in California. The Great Plains are a semi-arid land, which makes them strikingly different from the subhumid and humid land to the east and the arid land to the west. In the United States, first homesteaders, like the earlier mountain-plainsmen and cattlemen, were enticed by the vast and open grasslands. These treeless plains promised rich crops and grass fodder without the backbreaking and tedious tasks of grubbing stumps, digging roots, and burning slash.

The Great Plains in the early period was a man's country— more so than any other portion of the frontier. The men loved the Plains—the women were distrustful of the Plains. "Why there isn't even a thing that one can hide behind!" was one woman's pathetic exclamation.

As Walter Prescott Webb pointed out in his classic *The Great Plains:* "The loneliness which women endured on the Great Plains must have been such as to crush the soul, provided one did not meet the isolation with an adventurous spirit. The woman who said that she could always tell by sunup whether she should have company during the day is an example. If in the early morning she could detect a cloud of dust, she knew the visitors were coming!"

Today, the Rocky Mountain and Plains country man or woman

is completely American, but also unique. Great distances separate the populated areas. In some towns the high point in the year is a visit, or two, to anything remotely resembling a city.

It is a big country—this Rocky Mountains and Plains. It offers every bit of the world's scenery, from the highest mountains to the desert; from lush river valleys to high grass plains; from glaciers to hot springs. Perhaps the most important thing of all in this big place is its informality. In many ways the people who live here are like mountain and plains men and women of four generations ago.

A poet of whom I'm quite fond, Robert Frost, once wrote: "What makes a nation in the beginning is a good piece of ground." Three-fourths of my years have been spent in and about the West where there are still good pieces of ground. By edict of nature, nearly all of the West was, and always will be, different from the rest of the country. Daniel Webster called it a "wasteland"; Francis Parkman, "the great American desert." From the first, the West was destined to write a special chapter in our history. The Plains Indians, the vast prairies, the mighty massif of the Rocky Mountains, the parched deserts were all formidable barriers to settlement and migration. Its searing winds and harsh climate, its uncertain rainfall and thin soils made living a continual struggle.

Today, the flow of westward-bound Americans makes the great migrations of the pioneer period seem almost insignificant. The crack of a bull-whacker's whip and the creaking sound of a prairie schooner in the 1850's are in sharp contrast to the hum of a powerful engine as it propels its passengers comfortably in the same direction today.

The West—Still the Last Frontier

However, there is a common theme—call it what you will: Great Westward Tilt or Great Western Movement—the flow of American history has been westward in the pursuit of national and individual destiny. The last American frontier will always be the West. Generations were shaped by the forces which impelled them to shift the frontier farther West.

Americans who trek West, the pioneer or modern-day man, seek the same thing: economic opportunity, the climate, the spirit of adventure, or a desire to share in the bustle and vigor that have characterized western life. The major problems today are the same: the critical need for water, the sparse population in many areas, and the proper development of natural resources.

To some scholars the most distinctive feature of the American past was its three-century-long pioneering period. This pioneering experience seems to have endowed the American people with different characteristics and institutions than those of other peoples.

The frontier closed in 1890. A part of the American dream was over. Since then students of the West have been evaluating the days of the pioneers in relation to their own age. David Potter wrote that the moving frontier was one phase of the larger situation of opportunity and abundance which had marked the Americans as a "people of plenty." Self-reliance, courage, alertness, endurance, friendliness, informality are traits that emerged from the continuous cycles of land settlement.

"Americans are always moving on" was the opening line of Stephen Vincent Benet's unfinished heroic poem of the westward migrations, called "Western Star." Much of American literature has been dominated by this theme of restless movement on land or river or sea. Francis Parkman's *The Oregon Trail* was a stirring introduction to the West, along with other classics such as Walter Prescott Webb's *The Great Plains* and Bernard De Voto's *Across the Wide Missouri*.

To understand America you must see two aspects—that of restless mobility, and that of attachment to place, as emphasized by the regionalists and traditionalists. There is a double beat of migration and the sense of place. John Muir, the noted naturalist and wanderer in Yosemite, once wrote: "Climb the mountains and get their good tidings. Nature's peace will flow into you as sunshine flows into tree. The winds will blow their own freshness into you, and the storms their energy, while cares will drop off like autumn leaves."

The classical migration to the Western frontiers was perhaps the last spontaneous great migration in history. The explorers were followed by fur traders, followed by mountain men, ranchers, and miners, followed finally by farmers equipped with seed, cattle and implements. The later stages of this classical westward movement crossed the Great Plains and the mountain fastnesses of the Rockies and occupied the rich areas of the Pacific Northwest and California.

Not more than one out of twenty of those who took part in the Gold Rush to California found anything like success, yet we have forgotten the failures and remember only the big prizes.

By the 1850's the West was no longer quite the land of the unknown that it had been. Too many mountain men, too many settlers' parties, too many government survey teams had crossed the region to leave it a land of mystery. And yet, the West was so vast that there was always something new to be found. In 1858,

Lt. Joseph Ives led the first party into the bottom of the Grand Canyon. The fascinating reports of such expeditions were a part of the magnet that continued to draw men West.

In 1902, Owen Wister's *The Virginian* was published. The famous line, "When you call me that, smile," from the hero to the outlaw, is from this book. This work caused many an Easterner to forsake his hearth and travel West. Wister was Harvard-educated like his friend Theodore Roosevelt, to whom he dedicated his book. Wister's stories gave a true picture of a cowboy's life including the prototype of the brave cowboy who was soft-spoken with the women but a no-nonsense man with the outlaw.

After 1900, increasing numbers of Easterners ventured West to spend vacations. People have been venturing forth to the wild and woolly West ever since.

In 1908, President Theodore Roosevelt, who owned Elkhorn Ranch in the Bad Lands along the Little Missouri River in North Dakota, called a White House Conference to inquire into the state of the nation's natural resources. It was a landmark in the conservation history of the United States. It showed that the country knew little about its resources, and it excited public interest and action. Theodore Roosevelt set aside forest reserves, established five national parks, created bird and game preserves, promoted irrigation, and gave to the people their first real awareness of the need for conservation. T. R. gradually won the support of Western leaders, including lumber barons, for conservation.

Frederic Remington, the Western artist, was lamenting the passing of an era in 1905: "I knew the wild riders and the vacant land were about to vanish forever . . . I saw the living, breathing end of three American centuries of smoke and dust and sweat, and I now see quite another thing where it all took place, but it does not appeal to me." Remington in his paintings depicted the unfenced range, the stamina of cowboys, the courage of the people, and the dignity of free Indians.

The Idea for National Parks

It was another artist, George Catlin, who had the vision to understand the need to preserve this country's great natural treasures for the generations yet unborn. He had this realization in the 1830's "at a time when the plains seemed as unfathomable as the ocean, when pasture and grazing lands had no boundaries, and no one believed that the forests could be exhausted." In 1833, a prophetic passage of Catlin's was published in a New York newspaper, after he had traveled up the Missouri River into the heart of the Indian country in 1832.

Catlin suggested that the "looks and customs of the vanishing races of the native man in America . . . might in future be seen [by some great protecting policy of government] preserved in their pristine beauty and wildness, in a magnificent park, where the world could see for ages to come the native Indian in his classic attire, galloping his wild horse . . . amid the fleeting herds of elks and buffaloes. What a beautiful and thrilling specimen for America to preserve and hold up to the view of her refined citizens and the world, in future ages."

Catlin's progressive idea was considered by the Congress in 1864, when the Yosemite grant was made to the State of California. Yosemite is now a national park.

Another lively artist of the Western scene was Alfred Miller. In 1837 he joined William Drummond Stewart, a British army captain who was starting a trip to Oregon for the American Fur Company. Miller's brilliant pictures, particularly of the country west of the North Platte River and in the Rocky Mountains, have given us much of the most accurate documentation ever made of the early West, picturing the life of the Indians and the rendezvous with fur traders. Many of Miller's sketches and paintings were reproduced in Bernard De Voto's *Across the Wide Missouri*. In 1951, the University of Oklahoma Press published *The West of Alfred Jacob Miller* by Marvin C. Ross.

In 1871, the paintings and photographs of the geysers, great canyon, and waterfalls of the upper Yellowstone River, made by Ferdinand V. Hayden, helped persuade Congress to set aside the area as the country's first National Park.

Who were the people who went West? There were artists, the government survey teams in the decade of the 1870's, the writers, the fur traders. Then there were the English—remember that cowboy in Colorado?—the Irish, the Germans, and other nationality groups. The West was the frontier to them, it was no man's land, but to the Indians it was their ancient homeland.

The greatest number of prehistoric Indian remains are in the Southwest. Many are in the area around the Four Corners where the lonely desertlands of Arizona, New Mexico, Colorado, and Utah meet—the only spot in the United States where the boundaries of four states come together. Here, some time between the years A.D. 1 and 1300, an unusual Indian civilization flourished for a time, then mysteriously disappeared. The Four Corners region is one of fantastic buttes and mesas, gullies, and deep canyons through which rivers bend in wide S-curves. Utah's most famous national monuments (Arches, Rainbow Bridge, Capitol Reef, and Natural Bridge) are in the almost roadless country of southeastern Utah near Four Corners.

Utahans, it has been said, have always had a way of doing things different. All the conventions of Western life in Utah went haywire.

The particular quality of life in Utah is almost wholly Mormon, although the total church membership numbers perhaps only three-fifths of the population. In popular terms the West has always been independent—and Utah especially so, perhaps, a consequence of the strong-minded New Englanders who founded the Mormon Church. Historically, Utah has been a detoured country: the Oregon Trail went north of it; other cross-country travel, south of it. Canyonlands, the newest national park in the United States, is in Utah wrapped in serenity, waiting for discovery and appreciation by visitors.

Home of Many Nationalities

The Mormons are also an important part of the social structure of Wyoming—along with the cowboy who is the dominant figure in Wyoming folklore. During the period of free land and migration, Wyoming became the home of many nationalities— Italians and Greeks in mining, Scandinavians in logging, Mexicans and Russian-Germans in the beet-raising centers, Basques in the north-central part of the state, Chinese along the Union Pacific Railroad, together with Hungarians, Czechs, Slovaks, Danes, Englishmen, Irishmen, Estonians, and Japanese. These groups helped settle and build up Wyoming, and have become an integral part of its life.

Several Old-World cultural traits are preserved in the melting pot environment of Wyoming. The Italians have their celebrations; the Chinese have their Chinese New Year; the Greeks have an impressive funeral rite; and Pioneer Day is observed in Mormon communities to retell the story of the Great Trek to Salt Lake Valley in 1847. Wyoming has Grand Teton National Park, which includes part of Jackson Hole, winter feeding ground of the largest elk herd in America. The Grand Tetons themselves are the most spectacular peaks in the chain that forms our continental backbone.

The people who migrated to Colorado are similar to those who settled in Wyoming: Italians, Hungarians, Slavs, Orientals, the Chinese in the mines, Japanese on the farms. German-Russians were lured from the Volga by the introduction of sugar-beet culture, which they knew well; later, Spanish-Americans flooded in from the southern valleys and from Mexico to work the beet fields. The story of Coloradoans goes back even farther, of course, to the Indians of prehistoric times. Mesa Verde National Park is the most notable and best preserved prehistoric cliff dwelling in the United States. French voyageurs—hunters, trappers, and traders—also explored the northern streams of Colorado.

The magic cry "Gold!" was the signal for the great Colorado Pikes Peak rush of 1859, one of the great mass migrations of American history. Men of almost every nationality, occupation, and station in life swarmed into the Colorado mountains, and in their wake followed farmers, largely of European stock to settle in the fertile valleys, These are the Coloradoans.

The ethnic groups in Montana comprise descendants of the early French-Indian fur trappers; the English and Scotch who were usually the managers of the fur trade companies; the German and Irish who rushed to the Butte silver and copper ledges; and the Scandinavians who settled the dry-land sections after 1900. Today, persons of German extraction form the largest group, followed by the Norwegians and the English, Swedes, Irish, and Danes. Other nationalities include Poles, Czechoslovakians, Austrians, and Hungarians.

Germans were the first immigrants to arrive in any number in Nebraska and are now the largest group of foreign stock in the state. Many fled to America in 1848 following the political upheavals in Germany. They helped develop the sugar-beet industry. The Czechoslovak group, the next largest foreign stock group in Nebraska, has been understandingly interpreted in Willa Cather's books and hence made known to the country at large. Many of the early Slovak immigrants were of the "cottager" class and were first-rate farmers and hard-working people. They knew nothing of the isolated farmhouse, having lived in villages, so the frontier was a complete change for them and required great adaptability.

The Swedes and Danes came next to Nebraska and were well adapted not only to frontier life but to the climate as well. The Danes did much to advance progressive farming measures. The German-Russians were latecomers.

From territorial days until World War I a steady and evergrowing stream of immigrants poured into North Dakota from other states, Canada, and Europe. Although forty-two nations sent immigrants to the state, by far the greatest numbers came from northern Europe. Almost one-third arrived from Norway, while other countries, in the order of their contribution to the population, were Russia, Germany, Canada, Sweden, The Netherlands, Denmark, Hungary, Finland, Rumania, and Iceland.

The population of South Dakota remains preponderantly rural despite the steady but slow growth of urban centers. The bulk of the people are white, but there are many Indians living on or registered with eight reservations. The many nationalities represented among the people from the earliest days have produced a rural cosmopolitanism, with substantial contingents of Norwegians, Germans, Swedes, Russian-Germans, Danes, Czechs, Dutch, Canadians, and English.

These are Westerners all: the industrious Mormons; the Chinese in the mines; the homesteaders on their Nebraska claims; the cowboy who calls the West his home; the lumber- and cattlemen; the Indians, the Spanish, the Anglo-Americans—even the Eastern dude who loves the West and possibly feels like an old plainsman when out in the wide-open spaces—the big country.

A stirring epic is the story of America's westward movement. At heart it is the story of the men and women of all races and different origins and beliefs who helped shape the character of a nation. It grows more and more fascinating as it grows more and more remote.

FACTS AT YOUR FINGERTIPS

WHEN TO GO. This region, running from the Canadian border in the north to the northern borders of New Mexico and Arizona in the south, naturally has a great variation in temperature, and at all seasons. Generally speaking, there is plenty of sunshine, and the humidity is low throughout the region. This latter condition tends to cut down on discomfort in all but the highest temperature periods. Desert degrees sometimes soar to the 110–115 mark, while some nearby mountain summits wear their stoles of ermine-white snow year round.

There are travelers who find the desert areas of Colorado and Utah too hot in summer, while many others revel in the region's clear, hot days—its cool, cool nights. Visitors may, of course, plan off-to-the hills activities for the daytime hours, returning in the evening for a dip in that pool which is almost certain to be found at their hotel or motel.

From Thanksgiving to the middle of April there is some of the best skiing in the country at places like Aspen and Vail in Colorado and Alta and Snowbird near Salt Lake City. There is even year-round skiing on glaciers in Montana and Colorado.

Generally, average temperatures in winter are in the low 20's. Summer finds maximum temperatures in the mid-80's in the north to near 100 degrees in the south (in June, July, and August), with maximums in the 90's in surrounding months. But even in summer nights are cool, especially in the higher elevations.

PLANNING YOUR TRIP. Once you have decided where you are going, and when, it's time to get down to the details of hotel reservations and, if you are not traveling by car, ticket reservations. If you don't want to bother with reservations on your own, a travel agent can be of help. Using a travel agent, incidentally, won't cost you a cent, except for specific charges like telegrams. He gets his fee from the hotel or carrier he books for you. A travel agent can also be of help for those who would prefer to take their vacations on a "package tour"—thus keeping your own planning to a minimum; and in explaining the details of the "travel now, pay later" vacation possibilities offered by the nation's carriers. "Package tours" can also be great money savers, and tours of the fly/drive variety are extremely popular.

If traveling by auto, enjoy the family fun of jointly discussing and mapping your route. Or ask your auto club to do it for you. If you don't belong to an auto club, now is the time to join one. They can be very helpful about routings and offering emergency service on the road. If you plan the route yourself, make certain the map you purchase, or get from your local service station, is dated for the current year (highways and thruways are appearing and being extended at an astonishingly rapid rate). In addition, most states have their own maps, which pinpoint attractions, list historical sites, parks, etc. Write the *Tourist Information Dept., State Capitol Bldg.*, in the state or states you plan to visit for a copy of current maps. City chambers of commerce and the convention and visitors bureaus are also good sources of information.

Plan to board your pets, discontinue paper and milk deliveries, and tell your local police and fire departments when you'll be leaving, when you expect to return. Ask a kindly neighbor to keep an eye on your house or apartment; fully protect your swimming pool against intruders. Have a neighbor keep your mail, or have it temporarily held at the post office. Consider having your telephone temporarily disconnected if you plan to be away more than a few weeks. Look into the purchase of trip insurance (including baggage), and make certain your auto, fire, and other policies are up to date. Convert the greater portion of your trip money into travelers' checks. Arrange to have your lawn mowed at the usual times, and leave that kindly neighbor your itinerary (insofar as possible), car license number, and a key to your home (and tell police and firemen he has it).

PACKING. *What to take, what to wear.* Make a packing list for each member of the family. Then check off items as you pack them. It will save time, reduce confusion. Time-savers to carry along include extra photo film (plenty), suntan lotion, insect repellent, sufficient toothpaste, soap, etc. Always carry an extra pair of glasses, including sunglasses, particularly if they're prescription ones. A travel iron is always a good tote-along, as are some transparent plastic bags (small and large) for wet suits, socks, etc. They are also excellent, of course, for packing shoes, spillable cosmetics, and other easily damaged items.

Fun extras to carry include binoculars, a compass, and a magnifying glass—useful in reading those fine-print maps.

All members of the family should have a sturdy pair of shoes with non-slip soles. Keep them handy in the back of the car. You never know when you may want to stop and clamber along a rocky trail. Carry rain gear in a separate bag in the back of the car (so no one will have to get out and hunt for it in a downpour en route).

Women will probably want to stick to one or two basic colors for their wardrobes, so that they can manage with one set of accessories. If possible, include one knit or jersey dress or a pants suit. The general consensus among well-traveled women is that a full-skirted traveling dress will show less wear and wrinkling. For dress-up evenings, take along a couple of "basic" dresses you can vary with a simple change of accessories. That way you can dress up or down to suit the occasion. Remember also that nowadays pants are acceptable almost everywhere.

Be sure to check what temperatures will be like along the route. Traveling in mountains can mean cool evenings, even in summer—and so can traveling through the desert. An extra sweater is always a safe thing to pack, even if just to protect you from the air conditioning.

Men will probably want a jacket along for dining out, and include a dress shirt and tie for the most formal occasions. Turtlenecks are now accepted almost everywhere and are a comfortable accessory. Don't forget extra slacks.

Planning a lot of sun time? Don't forget something sufficiently cover-up to wear over swim suits en route to the pool, beach, or lakefront, and for those first few days when you're getting reacquainted with sun on tender skin.

 WHAT WILL IT COST? Two people can travel in this section of the U.S. for about $41.00 a day (not counting gasoline or other transportation costs), as you can see in the table below.

In some areas you can cut expenses by traveling off season, when hotel rates are usually lower. The budget-minded traveler can also find bargain accommodations at tourist homes or family-style YMCA's and YWCA's. Some state and federal parks also provide inexpensive lodging.

Another way to cut down on the cost of your trip is to look for out-of-the-way resorts. Travelers are frequently rewarded by discovering very attractive areas which haven't as yet begun to draw quantities of people.

Typical Expenses for Two People	
Room at *moderate* hotel or motel	$17.00
Breakfast, including tip	3.00
Lunch at *inexpensive* restaurant, including tip	3.00
Dinner at *moderate* restaurant, including tip	8.50
Sightseeing bus tour	5.00
An evening drink	2.50
Admission to museum or historic site	2.00
	$41.00

If you are budgeting your trip, don't forget to set aside a realistic amount for the possible rental of sports equipment (perhaps including a boat or canoe), entrance fees to amusement and historical sites, etc. Allow for tolls for bridges and superhighways (this can be a major item), extra film for cameras, and souvenirs.

Picnicking will not only cut costs, but will also save time and get you out of doors, away from the cars and highway. That beautiful scenery does not *have* to whizz by at 55 miles per hour. Many states have set aside picnic and rest areas, even along big highways and thruways, so finding a stopping place shouldn't be difficult. A number of restaurants have take-out service (you can pick up lunch at breakfast). So buy or assemble a picnic kit before you leave home. Include several Thermoses; it's a good idea to keep fresh water in one.

A plug-in water heater and a jar of instant coffee will, like picnics, serve a double purpose. They will take the gruff edge off any family member who is inclined to growl until a cup of the brew has been imbibed. And, if you're staying in a motel, you might buy some fruit and rolls or breakfast pastries the night before, thus saving on breakfast costs, and getting off-and-away that much sooner in the morning.

 HINTS TO THE MOTORIST. Shortly after you pass the ranger station a brief distance inside the comparatively new Canyonlands National Park in southern Utah, you encounter a sign, stuck in the sand. It reads: "Four-wheel drive vehicles only beyond this point." This is wild, rugged country, where you follow routes, not roads, through shifting sand, up trickling stream beds which can turn into raging torrents during a sudden storm, where the wheels of even four-wheel drive vehicles can sink hopelessly into the sand if they don't move along briskly, and where you climb a 27-degree face of sheer rock as part of getting over Elephant Hill. The Rockies and Plains area is the country of the Badlands of North and South Dakota, the mule-riding country of the Grand Canyon, the country of towering mountains interspersed with the broad flat spaces of the Plains—an area where the motorist can have virtually any driving experience he cares to meet. Yet this wild country is crisscrossed with modern highways which make driving a breeze.

On long, straight stretches of road across the Plains, on the Interstate, and on freeways, *highway hypnosis*—recognized by safety experts as contributing to many accidents—can be a problem. It results from steady driving over long distances at set speeds. Principal symptoms are drowsiness and the inability to concentrate on what you are doing. The cure: Vary your speed occasionally, stop to stretch your legs, have a cup of coffee or tea, take a little exercise, take a brief nap. The Interstate System of National and Defense Highways—a formidable name—is growing, and you will encounter it more and more in your travels. Driving such roads is decidedly different from driving old-style highways. The wise motorist studies in advance the exit and entrance points, lest he wind up beyond where he wants to go, or enters the highway headed in the wrong direction. When you enter a limited-access highway, be sure to allow plenty of space between you and the onrushing cars before you merge into the right lane.

DESERT DRIVING

You will encounter long stretches of desert driving in the southern portions of this area. Better cars, better roads, and more service facilities make desert driving less a hazard than it once was. The desert here won't resemble the sands of the Sahara. It will have considerable vegetation and rock outcroppings. A principal point to check before crossing the hot desert is your tires. Put them at normal driving pressure or slightly below. Heat builds pressure. If your car seems to be bouncing too readily, stop to let your tires cool. If you have a good radiator, don't worry about extra water, but keep an eye on the water gauge. Be alert for sudden sandstorms and rainstorms. If you have a car radio, keep it tuned to local stations for information about unusual road conditions. With all its dryness, the desert, in a flash flood, can be a death trap. In sandstorms, pull off the road and wait it out.

MOUNTAIN DRIVING

Unless you venture onto exotic mountain roads, you should have little trouble with mountain driving. Today's mountain roads are engineered for the ordinary driver. They are normally wide, well graded, and safe. Be especially wary of the speed limits posted for curves. Keep to the right. If your normal driving is at low altitudes, have a garage mechanic check your carburetor. It may need adjusting for mountain driving. Use your motor for downhill runs, second or low gear to save your brakes. If your car stalls, and your temperature gauge is high, it could mean a vapor lock. Bathe the fuel pump with a damp cloth for a few minutes.

If you get stuck—on Interstate, freeway, or country lane—use the universal rule of the road. Pull off the highway onto the shoulder, raise the hood, attach something white (a handkerchief, scarf, or a piece of tissue) to the door handle on the driver's side, and sit inside and wait. This is especially effective on limited-access highways, usually patrolled vigilantly by state highway officers. A speical warning to women stalled at night: Remain inside with the doors locked, and make sure the Good Samaritan is indeed what he seems. It is easier to find telephones along the major highways these days, since their locations are more frequently marked than they used to be. If you're an AAA member, call the nearest garage listed in your Emergency Road Service Directory. Or ask the operator for help.

PULLING A TRAILER

If you plan to pull a trailer (boat or house) on your holiday trip, and have never done so before, don't just hook up and set out. You need a whole new set of driving skills—starting, stopping, cornering, passing, *being* passed, and, most tricky of all, backing. Reading about it will help a little, but not much. Try to practice in an open field or empty parking lot, but, if this is not possible, take your maiden trip in light traffic. A few useful hints: In starting and stopping, do everything a little more slowly and gradually than is normal; in cornering, swing wider than usual, remembering the trailer won't follow exactly the rear wheels of the towing car. Too sharp a right turn will put your trailer wheels on the curb. In passing, remember you're longer than usual. Allow more safe distance ahead to pull back into the right lane. A slight bit of extra steering will help if you're *being* passed by a large truck or bus. In this situation, the trailer is inclined to sway from air currents. Don't worsen it by slowing down. It's better to speed up slightly. In backing, the basic technique is to turn the steering wheel in a way opposite to that in which you would want the car to go if you were driving it alone. From there on, it's practice, practice, practice. Most states have special safety regulations for trailers, and these change so frequently that the printed word fast becomes obsolete. If you plan to operate your trailer in several states, check with your AAA motor club, the police, or the state motor vehicle department about the rules. Also talk it over with the dealer from whom you buy or lease your trailer. Generally, speed limits for cars hauling trailers are lower, parking of trailers (and automobiles) is prohibited on expressways, and tunnels bar trailers equipped with cooking units which use propane gas.

PETS AND PACKING

Traveling by car with your pet dog or cat? More and more motels accept them but be sure to check before you register. Some turn them down, some want to look first, some offer special facilities—even a "doggy bag" for your pet's first meal. If it's a first-time trip for your pet, accustom it to car travel by short trips in the neighborhood. And when you're packing, include its favorite food, bowls, and toys. Your dog may like to ride with its head out the window. Discourage this. Wind and dust particles can permanently damage its eyes. Dogs are especially susceptible to heat stroke. Don't leave your dog in a parked car on a hot day while you dawdle over lunch.

One tip for frequent motel stops along the road is to pack two suitcases—one for the final destination, and the other with items for overnight stops: pajamas, shaving gear, cosmetics, toothbrushes, fresh shirt or dress. Put the overnight luggage into the trunk last, so it can be pulled out first on overnight stops. A safety hint: Don't string your suits and dresses on hangers along a chain or rod stretched across the back seat. This obstructs vision, and may cause an accident.

HOTELS AND MOTELS. *General Hints.* Don't be one of those travelers who persist in the practice of taking pot luck for lodgings. You'll probably waste a lot of post-sunset hours hunting for a place, and often won't be happy with the accommodations you finally find. If you are without reservations, by all means begin looking early in the afternoon. If you have reservations, but expect to arrive later than five or six p.m., advise the hotel or motel in advance. Some places will not, unless advised, hold reservations after six p.m.

If you are planning to stay in a popular resort region, at the height of the season, be kind to your nerves: reserve well in advance. Include a deposit for all places except motels (and for motels if they request one). Remember, too, that a city where you plan to stay—at any season—may be hosting a convention or special event. A number of chain or associated motels and hotels will make advance reservations for you at affiliated hostelries along your route.

A number of hotels and motels have one-day laundry and dry-cleaning services, and many motels have coin laundries.

Most motels, but not all, have telephones in the rooms. If you want to be sure of room service, however, better stay at a hotel.

Many motels have swimming pools, and even beachfront hotels frequently have a pool. Even some motels in the heart of large cities have pools. An advantage at motels is the free parking. There's seldom a charge for parking at country and resort hotels.

Hotel and motel chains. In addition to the hundreds of excellent independent motels and hotels throughout the country, there are also many fine establishments in both categories that belong to national or regional chains. A major advantage of the chains, to many travelers, is the ease of making reservations en route, or at one fell swoop in advance. If you are a guest at a member hotel or motel, the management will be delighted to secure you a sure booking at one of his affiliated hotels for the coming evening—at no telephone or telegram costs to you. Chains also usually have toll-free WATS (800) lines to assist you in making reservations on your own. This, of course, saves you time, worry and money. In some chains, you have the added advantage of knowing what the standards are, of being sure that you will have "quality-controlled" accommodations all the way. The insistence on uniform standards of comfort, cleanliness and amenities is more common in motel than in hotel chains. (Easy to understand when you realize that most hotel chains are formed by simply buying up older, established hotels, while most motel chains have control of their units from start to finish.) This is not meant to denigrate the hotel chains; after all, individuality can be one of the great charms of a hotel. Some travelers, however, prefer independent motels and hotels because they are more likely to reflect the genuine character of the surrounding area.

HOTEL AND MOTEL CATEGORIES

Hotels and motels in all the Fodor guidebooks to the U.S.A. are divided into five categories, arranged primarily by price, but also taking into consideration the degree of comfort you can expect to enjoy, the amount of service you can anticipate, and the atmosphere which will surround you in the establishment of your choice. Occasionally, an establishment with *deluxe* prices will only offer *expensive* service or atmosphere, and so we will list it as *expensive.* On the other hand, a hotel which charges only *moderate* prices may offer superior comfort and service, so we will list it as *expensive.* Our ratings are flexible and subject to change. We should also like to point out that failure to include certain establishments in our lists does not mean they are not worthwhile—many fine hotels and motels had to be omitted for lack of space. Conversely, a few establishments presently listed may be dropped in the future if better accommodations in their areas surpass the old hostelries in comfort, service, and atmosphere.

Although the names of the various hotel and motel categories are standard throughout this series, the prices listed under each category may vary from area to area. This variance is meant to reflect local price standards, and take into account the fact that what might be considered a *moderate* price in a large urban area might be quite *expensive* in a rural region. In every case, however, the dollar ranges for each category are clearly stated before each listing of establishments.

Super Deluxe: This category is reserved for only a few hotels. In addition to giving the visitor all the amenities discussed under the deluxe category (below), the super deluxe hotel has a special atmosphere of glamor, good taste, and dignity. Its story will inevitably be full of many historical anecdotes, and it will probably be a favored meeting spot of local society. If an American president or a foreign

25

princess comes to town, this hotel will probably shelter him or her. In short, super deluxe means the tops.

Deluxe: For a rough rule-of-thumb index, we suggest that the minimum facilities must include bath and shower in all rooms, valet and laundry service, suites available, a well-appointed restaurant and a bar (where local law permits), room service, TV and telephone in room, air conditioning and heat (unless locale makes one or the other unnecessary), pleasing decor, and an atmosphere of luxury, calm and elegance. There should be ample and personalized service. In a deluxe *motel,* there may be less service rendered by employees and more by machine or automation (such as refrigerators and ice-making machines in your room), but there should be a minimum of do-it-yourself in a truly deluxe establishment.

Expensive: All rooms must have bath or shower, valet and laundry service, restaurant and bar (local law permitting), limited room service, TV and telephone in room, heat and air conditioning (locale not precluding), pleasing decor. Although decor may be as good as that in deluxe establishments, hotels and motels in this category are frequently designed for commercial travelers or for families in a hurry and are somewhat impersonal in terms of service. As for *motels* in this category, valet and laundry service will probably be lacking; the units will be outstanding primarily for their convenient location and functional character, not for their attractive or comfortable qualities.

(Note: We often list top-notch ultra-modern hotels in this category, in spite of the fact that they have rates as high as deluxe hotels' and motels'. We do this because certain elements are missing in these hotels—usually, the missing element is service. In spite of automated devices such as ice-cube-making machines and message-signalling-buzzers, service in these hotels is not up to the standard by which we judge deluxe establishments. Room service is incredibly slow in some of these places and the entire atmosphere is often one of expediency over comfort, economy of manpower and overhead taking precedence over attention to the desire of guests.)

Moderate: Each room should have an attached bath or shower, restaurant *or* coffee shop, TV available, telephone in room, heat and air conditioning (locale not precluding), relatively convenient location, clean and comfortable rooms and public rooms. *Motels* in this category may not have attached bath or shower, may not have a restaurant or coffee shop (though one is usually nearby), and, of course, may have no public rooms to speak of.

Inexpensive: Nearby bath or shower, telephone available, clean rooms are the minimum.

Free parking is assumed at all motels and motor hotels; you must pay for parking at most city hotels, though certain establishments have free parking, frequently for occupants of higher-than-minimum-rate rooms. *Baby sitter* lists are always available in good hotels and motels, and *cribs* for the children are always on hand—sometimes at no cost, but more frequently at a cost of $1 or $2. The cost of a *cot* in your room, to supplement the beds, will be around $3 per night, but moving an *extra single bed* into a room will cost around $7 in better hotels and motels.

 DINING OUT. For evening dining, the best advice is to make reservations whenever possible. Most hotels and farm-vacation places have set dining hours. For motel-stayers, life is simpler if the motel has a restaurant. If it hasn't, try to stay at one that is near a restaurant.

Some restaurants are relatively fussy about customers' dress, particularly in the evening. For women, pants and pants suits are now almost universally acceptable. For men, the tie and jacket remains the standard, but turtleneck sweaters are becoming more and more common. Shorts are almost always frowned on for both men and women. Standards of dress are becoming progressively more relaxed, so a neatly dressed customer will usually experience no problem. If in doubt about accepted dress at a particular establishment, call ahead.

Roadside stands, turnpike restaurants and cafeterias have no fixed standards of dress.

If you're traveling with children, you may want to find out if a restaurant has a children's menu and commensurate prices (many do).

When figuring the tip on your check, base it on the total charges for the meal, not on the grand total, if that total includes a sales tax. Don't tip on tax.

RESTAURANT CATEGORIES

The restaurants mentioned in this volume which are located in large metropolitan areas are categorized by type of cuisine: French, Chinese, Armenian, etc., with restaurants of a general nature listed as American-International. Restaurants in less populous areas are divided into price categories as follows: *super deluxe, deluxe, expensive, moderate,* and *inexpensive.* As a general rule, expect restaurants in metropolitan areas to be higher in price, but many restaurants that feature foreign cuisine are surprisingly inexpensive. We should also point out that limitations of space make it impossible to include every establishment. We have, therefore, listed those which we recommend as the best within each price range.

Although the names of the various restaurant categories are standard throughout this series, the prices listed under each category may vary from area to area. This variance is meant to reflect local price standards, and take into account the fact that what might be considered a *moderate* price in a large urban area might be quite *expensive* in a rural region. In every case, however, the dollar ranges for each category are clearly stated before each listing of establishments.

Super Deluxe: This category will probably be pertinent to only one or two metropolitan areas. It indicates an outstanding restaurant which is lavishly decorated, which may delight in the fear it inspires among the humble. Frequently over-priced and over-rated, it will charge the customer at least $12 for soup, entrée, and dessert. The average price for the same is apt to be closer to $16.00, although some will run much higher than this. As in all our other categories, this price range does not include cocktails, wines, cover or table charges, tip, or extravagant house specialties. The price range here indicates a typical roastbeef (prime ribs) dinner. The restaurant in this category must have a superb wine list, excellent service, immaculate kitchens, and a large, well-trained staff.

Deluxe: Many a fine restaurant around the country falls into this category. It will have its own well-deserved reputation for excellence, perhaps a house specialty or two for which it is famous, and an atmosphere of elegance or unique decor. It will have a good wine list where the law permits, and will be considered the best in town by the inhabitants. It will have a clean kitchen and attentive staff.

Expensive: In addition to the expected dishes, it will offer one or two house specialties, wine list, and cocktails (where law permits), air conditioning (unless locale makes it unnecessary), a general reputation for very good food and an adequate staff, an elegant decor and appropriately dressed clientele.

Moderate: Cocktails and/or beer where the law permits, air conditioning (locale not precluding), clean kitchen, adequate staff, better-than-average service. General reputation for good, wholesome food.

Inexpensive: The bargain place in town, it is clean, even if plain. It will have air conditioning (when necessary), tables (not a counter), clean kitchen and attempt to provide adequate service.

BUSINESS HOURS AND LOCAL TIME. Time zones do not follow state lines throughout the Rockies and Plains states. All of Montana, Wyoming and Colorado are on Mountain Time, as are the western halves of South Dakota and Nebraska. All of North Dakota and the eastern halves of South Dakota and Nebraska are on Central Time. In Utah, the western third is on Pacific Time and the rest on Mountain Time.

SUMMER SPORTS. *Swimming* is invigorating in many of the lakes and reservoirs and relaxing in the hot springs pools found in Wyoming, Montana, Colorado and South Dakota. The Great Salt Lake offers something quite different, salt water that is more buoyant than the oceans. Water-skiing and sailing are popular on the larger lakes. Sailing is available on the lakes created by the many dams and on some reservoirs as well.

The many rivers and streams offer exciting possibilities for *canoeing, kayaking,* and *rafting.*

The Rocky Mountains offer ample opportunity for *hiking, backpacking,* and *mountain climbing* or *horseback riding.* Many areas are only accessible on foot or by horse.

Fishing in this area is very popular and the system of waterways quite extensive, and whether your pleasure is fly fishing the rivers and streams for trout or fishing the lakes for the larger walleye, bass, and northern pike, you're certain of great sport and much excitement.

In light of this area's western frontier heritage, it's not surprising to find that *rodeo* is the most pervasive of the spectator sports throughout this region. In general the season runs from late spring into early fall and whether it takes place in Nebraska, where rodeo was born, in Wyoming where Frontier Days attracts national champions, or at a small county fair, it's sure to be action-packed.

There are many fine *golf* courses throughout the area, such as the splendid layout at Jackson Hole in Wyoming. *Tennis* is also a popular sport, and courts are found at virtually every major resort or urban area.

WINTER SPORTS. *Skiing* is without a doubt the major winter sport of this area. New areas continue to be developed throughout the Rocky Mountains, especially Aspen and Vail in Colorado, and near Salt Lake City in Utah. Cross-country skiing, or *ski touring,* is becoming increasingly popular as both a means of escape from the cost of lift tickets and the ever-longer lift lines, and also as a means of enjoying the breathtaking scenery.

Each year, *snowmobiling* attracts more and more people who enjoy the thrill of speeding along snow-covered mountain trails or over open meadows. Many areas have organized rallies and races.

Ice skating on frozen lakes and ponds, or in year-round rinks, also has its share of enthusiasts.

Hunting for deer, antelope, elk, moose, and even bear brings hunters from all over into this area. There are also seasons for waterfowl, pheasant, quail, partridge, and grouse. In some cases, non-residents are permitted to hunt the less populous of these species only with bow and arrows.

ROUGHING IT. More, and improved, camping facilities are springing up each year across the country, in national parks, national forests, state parks, in private camping area, and trailer parks, which by now have become national institutions. This region of the country is particularly camping conscious.

Pack trips and backpacking are becoming increasingly popular, and there are, of course, many stalwart organizations throughout this region that can provide information and guidance. Check the various state chapters for specific names and areas.

Canoe trips and rafting adventures are also extrmely popular in this area, while it is also a particularly popular area for motor and mobile homes.

 TIPPING. These days, the going rate for tipping on *restaurant* service is 15%. For *bellboys, 25¢* per bag is usual. However, if you load him down with all manner of bags, hatboxes, cameras, coats, etc., you might consider giving an extra quarter or two. In many places the help rely on tips for a goodly portion of their income. So if you're staying in a *hotel or motel* more than a day, $1.00 per day should be left for the maid. If you are staying at an *American Plan* hostelry (meals included), $1.50 per day per person for the waiter or waitress is considered sufficient, and is left at the end of your stay. If you have been surrounded by an army of servants (one bringing relishes, another rolls, etc.), add an extra few dollars and give the lump sum to the captain or *maître d'hôtel* when you leave, asking him to allocate it.

Tipping at *counters* is not a universal practice. However, a number of customers do leave 25¢ on anything up to a dollar, and 10% to 15% tip in the *dining car* at each meal, and tip the *porter* (as you are leaving the train) 50¢ to 75¢ per person for each day spent on the train. Though many people are not aware of it, the 25¢ or 35¢ per bag you give the railway *station porter* is *not* a tip. At the end of the day he must hand in 25¢ or 35¢ for each bag he has carried, along with the stub of each luggage tag used. Therefore, his tip is only anything above 25¢ or 35¢ per bag. Best rule is probably to give him 50¢ per bag, and be grateful he was there to help you.

 HINTS TO HANDICAPPED TRAVELERS. Happily, more and more hotels and motels are becoming aware of those things which make traveling simpler for the handicapped. Two publications which give valuable information about motels, hotels, and restaurants (rating them, telling about steps, table heights, door widths, etc.) are *Where Turning Wheels Stop,* published by Paralyzed Veterans of America, 3636 16th St., N.W., Washington, D.C., 20010, and *The Wheelchair Traveler,* 22480 Cass Ave., Woodland Hills, Calif. 91364.

THE ROCKIES AND PLAINS

OLD WEST TRAIL

1. Boys Town, Joslyn Museum (Omaha).
2. Omaha Indian Reservation.
3. Winnebago Reservation.
4. Ponca State Park.
5. Old Dakota Territory Capital (Yankton).
6. Gavins Point Dam.
7. Lewis and Clark Reservoir.
8. Fort Randall Chapel Ruins and Fort Randall Dam.
9-11. Big Bend Dam, Crow Creek Indian Reservation, Farm Island State Park, State Capitol, Verendrye Monument at Fort Pierre, Oahe Dam (world's largest earthen dam).
12. Graves of Sitting Bull and Sacajawea.
13. State Capitol (Bismarck)
14. Fort Abraham Lincoln State Park.
15. Jamestown Dam.
16-18. Fort Totten Indian Reservation. Sully's Hill National Game Preserve, Burtness Scenic Highway.
19. Geographic center of No. America.
20. International Peace Garden.
21. Lake Metigoshe State Park.
22. Jet base, zoo.
23. Garrison Dam and Reservoir.
24. Old Fort Buford.
25. Theodore Roosevelt National Memorial Park (North unit).
26. Roosevelt N.M. Park (South unit).
27. Chateau de Mores.
28. Outdoor drama, "Old Four Eyes."
29. Makoshika State Park.
30. Fort Peck Dam.
31. Chief Joseph Battleground.
32. Old Fort Benton.
33. Russell Gallery.
34. State Capitol (Helena).
35. Lewis and Clark Caverns.
36. Virginia City, restored ghost town.
37. Site of 1949 earthquake.
38. The Museum of the Plains Indian.
39. Glacier National Park.
40. Flathead Lake.
41. U.S. Forest Service Smokejumper Center.
42. Big Hole National Battlefield.
43. First territorial Capital.
44. Custer Battlefield National Monument.
45. Missouri River Headwaters State Monument.
46. Beartooth Pass.
47-51. Old Faithful Geyser, Mammoth Hot Springs, Grand Canyon of the Yellowstone, Yellowstone Lake, Teton National Park.
52-54. Elk Refuge, Jackson Hole Wildlife Park, Togwatee Pass.
55. South Pass City, ghost town.
56. Atlantic City, ghost town.
57. Uranium Mill.
58. Wind River Canyon.
59. Hot Springs State Park.
60. Shell Creek Island.
61. Buffalo Bill Museum.
62-64. "City of Roses" (Lovell), Medicine Wheel, All-American Indian Days (Sheridan).
65. Buffalo herds.
66. Devil's Tower.
67. Scenic drive.
68-82. Black Hills Passion Play, Spearfish Canyon, Roughlock Falls, Homestake Gold Mine, Deadwood (historic town and museum), Mount Rushmore National Memorial, Pigtail Bridge. Norbeck Wildlife Preserve, Crazy Horse Monument, Sylvan Lake, Needles formation, Custer State Park (buffalo herds), Wind Cave National Park, Hot Springs, Rockerville (restored ghost town).
83. Badlands National Monument.

GREAT FALLS

MISSOULA

MONT.

⊕ Helena

BUTTE

LIVINGSTON

BILLINGS

MORAN

JACKSON

52-54

RIVERTON

OGDEN

Salt Lake City

PROVO

SALINA

UTAH

ST. GEORGE

CORTE

WOLF POINT
30
24
25
26
29
27
28
MILES CITY
Bismarck 13
14
21
20
22
16–18
23
15
94
N. DAK.

12

S. DAK.

9–11

SHERIDAN
SPEARFISH
BUFFALO
26
68–82
Pierre
25
27
23
24
25
8
7 6 5
4
LUSK
26
3
2
27
NEBR.
WYO.
88–90
SCOTTS BLUFF
1
OMAHA
92
23
OGALLALA
NORTH PLATTE
Lincoln
100 105
91
97–99
101 104
Cheyenne
94–96
KEARNEY
103
BEATRICE
25
102

Denver

COLORADO SPRINGS

PUEBLO

COLO.

84. Pine Ridge Reservation.
85. Roosevelt Reservation.
86. Chadron State Park.
87. Fort Robinson State Park.
88-90. Rawhide Pageant (Lusk), Spanish Diggings,
Fort Laramie National Monument.
91. State Capitol.
92. Overland Trail Museum, Scotts Bluff National
Monument.
93. Chimney Rock.
94-96. Lake McConaughy, Cowboy Capital of Nebraska
(Ogallala), Home of Buffalo Bill, Gothenburg
Pony Express Station.
97-99. Fort Kearney, Pioneer Village, House of
Yesterday.
100. State Capitol and University of Nebraska.
101. Atomic energy plant.
102. Homestead National Monument and Museum.
103. Brownville, early river town.
104. Arbor Lodge.
105. First town and first church in Nebraska.
(Bellevue).

COLORADO

COLORADO

Spacious Valleys, Towering Peaks

by

BILL HOSOKAWA, ROGER COX

and

CARRIE RODGERS

As a member of The Denver Post *staff since 1946, Bill Hosokawa has traveled extensively throughout Colorado. He is an associate editor of* The Post *and has also contributed to many national magazines.*

Roger Cox is a native of Grand Junction, Colorado, and is currently a freelance writer and editor in New York City.

Carrie Rodgers, a student at Colorado College, was chosen as one of Glamour Magazine's *top ten college girls of 1973. She has lived in Colorado all her life.*

Struggling westward across the Great Plains more than a century ago, a now-forgotten pioneer at the head of a wagon train gazed at the Colorado Rockies in the far distance. The morning sun glanced off the frosted peaks, vivid in the parched air, beckoning with promise of green forests, cool waters, and gold.

"The Shining Mountains," he muttered, half in awe at their beauty, half in exasperation at the massive granite stretched across the horizon.

Shining Mountains they have been ever since, dominating the Colorado scene as no other mountains dominate any state. The Rockies are the source of much of Colorado's wealth. They are the magnet that attracted a substantial part of the population, the spine that splits it economically, the barrier that blocked development and the resource that spurred it. Without the water stored through the winter in alpine snowbanks, the plains that make up half of Colorado would be little more than desert.

Approach Colorado today from any of the compass points—by air or rail or highway—and the part the mountains play in the state's way of life becomes quickly evident. The state is a perfect rectangle, nearly four hundred miles east to west, almost three hundred miles north to south. The foothills poke out of the plains along a north-south line about midway between eastern and western borders and then rise abruptly into mountains. Denver, sprawling on the plains, is only about fifty highway miles from the Continental Divide at Berthoud Pass. Most of the western half of the state is mountainous, broken by lush valleys and high plateaus. But even along the state's eastern fringe, where the rich Kansas and Nebraska prairie lifts imperceptibly into the dry High Plains, one need not drive far inside Colorado's borders to catch a view of the Shining Mountains.

The highways span the Continental Divide through a dozen high passes. But it is the airliner, racing at jet speed through the clear, thin skies, that provides the most awesome and meaningful sight of the Rockies—a tumbled, jumbled mass of forests, crags and icy peaks—stretching to the horizon. The great expanse of Colorado, eighth in size among the states, and the vastness of its wilderness (national forests cover one-fifth of the area), are impressively evident to the airborne traveler. Fifty-four of its peaks are 14,000 feet or higher; 1,500 are more than 10,000 feet tall.

Six major rivers rise in the Rockies. The Colorado and the Gunnison flow west, meeting at Grand Junction just before entering Utah; the Rio Grande southward; the Arkansas and South Platte wind eastward; the North Platte north into Wyoming. These rivers water nineteen states on their way to the sea, but before that, they make life possible on the Colorado plains, supporting cities and irrigating vast acreages of farmland and pasture.

While contemporary Coloradans seek the mountains for recreation, solitude or a livelihood, the first settlers stuck discreetly to the more hospitable low country. Folsom Man, 20,000 years ago, lived and hunted on the eastern plains. To mark his passing, he left exquisitely fashioned stone arrowheads, spear points and knives. The winds still uncover a few of these archeological treasures.

Four centuries before Columbus, cliff-dwelling Indians built and occupied multi-story apartment houses in the dry canyons of southwesternmost Colorado. No one is quite sure where they went, or why. The ruins of some of their homes are still preserved, most notably at Mesa Verde National Park where visitors may stroll along ancient trails and ponder over this lost civilization.

Less than a half century after Columbus stumbled on the New World, in 1541 to be exact, the Spaniard Coronado led an exploratory party north from Mexico in search of fabled Quivera and the Seven Cities of Cibola where the streets were allegedly paved with gold. Coronado found no gold, and no streets. The exact route of his march is unclear, but it is likely he cut across what is now southeastern Colorado. At least Coloradans like to think so.

As early as 1700, French voyageurs pushed into the Rockies in search of furs, leaving behind such durable names as Cache la Poudre for the river on whose banks they hid their surplus gunpowder. And the same year that a doughty bunch of discontented colonists assembled in Philadelphia to declare their independence from England, two Spanish friars in long robes, named Escalante and Dominguez, hiked from Santa Fe to the region of northwest Colorado before heading west.

Explorers, Then Trappers

Still, what is now Colorado was largely an uncharted and unknown wasteland when in 1803 it became a territory under the Louisiana Purchase. Shortly thereafter President Jefferson ordered Lieutenant Zebulon M. Pike to trot out and see what kind of a pig in a poke he had bought. Late in 1806 Pike reached the foot of the 14,110-foot peak named in his honor. Pike was an intrepid explorer but no mountain climber. He duly noted in his official report that it was unlikely the summit ever would be scaled. Each summer now, tens of thousands of visitors reach the peak in comfort, either by way of an automobile highway or a cog railway. And members of the AdAmAn Club, which gets its name from the fact it takes in a member each year, hike up Pikes Peak each New Year's Eve to shoot off fireworks trucked up before snow closes the highway.

Pike missed quite a sight by failing to climb the mountain. In 1893 a Wellesley College English professor, Katherine Lee Bates, was enjoying the view from the peak when the words that became "America the Beautiful" began to take shape in her head. "Oh, beautiful for spacious skies, for amber waves of grain," she wrote. "For purple mountain majesties above the fruited plain." And today, visitors gazing out over checkerboarded farmland and magnificent mountains unconsciously repeat her words.

American fur hunters followed Pike west; they traded with the Indians. The beaver they trapped in the aspen groves along mountain streams was in great demand for gentlemen's hats. But permanent settlers found little to bring them to Colorado, or to keep them there. The period of westward migration had begun, but the attraction lay elsewhere. The Santa Fe Trail cut south of Colorado, the Oregon Trail across Wyoming to the north where no mountains blocked the way. The trek to the farmlands of the Northwest, the Mormon migration to Utah and the California Gold Rush of 1849 largely bypassed Colorado.

The land that had been ignored was to have its day. In 1858 Green Russell, a Georgia prospector married to a Cherokee Indian, found small amounts of placer gold on the banks of Cherry Creek where Denver now stands. With memories of the California gold rush a decade earlier still fresh, fortune-hunters scrambled west to stake the likeliest claims. Now it was Pikes Peak or Bust, and many of the tenderfoot miners did go bust, for the sands were not nearly so rich as had been supposed. The hungry and disillusioned headed back to "the States," grumbling about the "Pikes Peak hoax." The hardy stuck it out and were rewarded in the spring of 1859 when John Gregory discovered rich gold deposits in a steep gulch forty miles west of the Cherry Creek settlements. This was to become the site of the twin towns of Central City and Blackhawk, called "the richest square mile on earth" until that title was wrested away thirty years later by another Colorado mining district, Cripple Creek.

Horace Greeley, then editor of the *New York Tribune,* was among the first easterners to reach Gregory's Gulch. He found some four thousand residents there, "including five white women and seven squaws living with white men." Half of the men had arrived within the week, with five hundred more coming in daily. Greeley reported everyone slept "in tents or under booths of pine boughs, cooking and eating in the open air." He wrote that there was gold to be found. Soon prospectors were pushing into the most isolated alpine valleys, washing the sands for gold, scarring the hillsides with painfully drilled holes.

Colorado's growth was swift and hectic. On Feb. 28, 1861,

Congress approved a bill to establish Colorado Territory and Colonel William Gilpin, a hero of the Mexican War, was appointed governor. The population at that time was established by a not altogether reliable census at 20,798 white males, 4,484 white females and 89 native to the territory—Cheyenne, Arapaho, Comanche and Kiowa on the eastern plains, the Utes in the western mountains. They soon made their presence known. Unhappy and restless as more and more whites came west, the Indians went on the warpath in 1864–65. The bloody uprisings were not finally put down until Federal troops were released for frontier duty at the end of the Civil War.

Young as it was, Colorado Territory had a key role in the Civil War. A motley volunteer army, quickly organized by Governor Gilpin, marched south to meet a Confederate cavalry force moving up from Texas under General Henry H. Sibley. They met at Glorieta Pass in northern New Mexico. The charging cavalry proved to be no match for the miner-army whose marksmanship had been sharpened in the mountains. Sibley's force was shattered and the gold fields preserved for the Union. Had the Confederacy seized Colorado gold, Jefferson Davis might have been able to shore up the South's economy.

Colorado derives its nickname "The Centennial State" from the fact that it became a state one hundred years after the signing of the Declaration of Independence. It was the thirty-eighth state.

Even before that time Coloradans were forced to recognize how the Rockies could block the state's development and had occasion to demonstrate their mettle. Denver's hopes of a place on a transcontinental railroad were crushed when the Union Pacific decided to lay its tracks along a relatively flat route through southern Wyoming. Denver business leaders determined that if the railroad wouldn't come to them, they would go to the railroad. They organized the Denver Pacific to connect with the U.P. at Cheyenne.

Nowhere is the indomitable spirit of early Coloradans displayed more dramatically than in the railrods they built—narrow-gauge lines that wound up and up and up over prohibitive grades into areas where the Iron Horse had no business going. Reaching far above timberline, operators of these lines faced crushing winter maintenance problems. Still, thanks to these railroads, inaccessible areas were opened for development, mining made feasible, towns were supplied and the state stitched together. Some of these lines have been converted to standard gauge, but most, alas, have been abandoned as mining dwindled or trucks took over.

One of the last passenger-carrying, narrow-gauge runs is operated by the Denver & Rio Grande Railroad between Durango and the old mining town of Silverton, in some of the state's most spectacular scenery. At the peak of the summer tourist season two trains, drawn by ancient but powerful steam locomotives, make the round trip daily. Another popular narrow gauge, the Cumbres & Toltec Scenic Railroad, runs a sixty-four-mile route between Antonito, Colorado, and Chama, New Mexico. The C&TS crests the summit of 10,015-foot Cumbres Pass, highest point reached in America by narrow-gauge rails.

In 1902, David H. Moffat, a Denver banker, organized a railroad to drive straight over the Rockies to the Pacific Coast. Corona Pass broke the railroad's back. The Continental Divide at this point is 11,680 feet above sea level. Winter storms made it impossible to maintain schedules. Finally in 1922 the State Legislature passed a measure setting up the Moffat Tunnel Improvement District. Bonds were issued and work started on a tunnel under the Divide. The bore is six miles long, took five years to complete, and cost $18 million. Taxpayers are still paying off the debt. Nonetheless, the tunnel finally gave Denver direct access to the sea. The old roadbed over Corona pass is open in summer to adventurous motorists willing to brave chuckholes, sharp curves and dust. The views are magnificent.

Gold and silver spurred the state's growth in the decades after statehood. Great silver strikes in Leadville, Aspen and Creede produced millions in new wealth. Between 1880 and 1890 Colorado's population doubled to 413,000. Then came the repeal of the Sherman Act in 1893, slashing the price of silver. Mines ceased operations and towns died overnight.

During this black period only the Cripple Creek gold fields kept the state's economy afloat. Discovered in 1890, this area just southwest of Pikes Peak produced some $400 miillion worth of gold before the richest lodes were played out. Texas Guinan began her career as an entertainer in Cripple Creek. Lowell Thomas spent his boyhood there. Jack Dempsey worked in its mines and fought for a $50 purse. Only summer tourists keep Cripple Creek alive today, but the proposed reopening of the long fallow mines may change the community's economy in the near future.

As mining dwindled, Coloradans realized their real wealth lay elsewhere. Farming—sugar beets, vegetable crops, melons, peaches, potatoes—was extended as irrigation projects made more water available. The plains yielded wheat and corn, and mountain pastures fattened growing herds of cattle and sheep. Manufacturing plants were established in the cities. At Pueblo, coal from Trinidad was used to smelt ores from Leadville and the now giant C.F.&I. Steel Corporation took shape. Mining equipment firms, first established to meet local needs, began to ship their highly specialized machinery to South America, Europe and Asia.

Meanwhile, the population grew steadily, even during the mining panics and the dust bowl years of the thirties when drought and wind devastated the southeastern corner of the state. Colorado's population topped one million for the first time in the 1930 census, boomed after World War II, and in mid-1966 was estimated at over two million.

These people make their livings in many diverse ways. Oddly enough, manufacturing and industry top the list, producing $2.5 billion a year. Agriculture and stock-raising are next, averaging $1.5 billion annually. Travel and tourism (cool summers, scenery, dude ranches, fishing, skiing) account for another $600 million, spent by some eight million visitors. The one-time kingpin of Colorado's economy, mining, runs a poor fourth with $400 million, about one-third of which is produced by oil.

The Soldiers Came Back

Three out of four Coloradans live in a string of cities stretched along the eastern foot of the Rockies, with Denver in the center. In fact, Grand Junction and Durango are the only communities west of the Divide to claim more than 10,000 residents. An estimated 1.2 million—more than half of all Coloradans—live in the Denver metropolitan complex.

The Denver of today is a far cry from the overgrown cow town of a generation ago. Thousands of servicemen who had trained during World War II at Lowry Air Base in Denver, Fort Carson near Colorado Springs and Camp Hale for mountain troops near Leadville, had fallen in love with the West, vowed to come back, and did. City-jaded Easterners sought and found breathing space in Colorado. Wealthy Texans bought into Colorado real estate, not without some hard feelings among fishermen who found favorite trout streams posted. Other new blood was attracted to the state by the expansion of oil, research and aerospace-oriented industries. These newcomers were responsible for profound changes in the state's intellectual climate and outlook.

The arrival of Palmer Hoyt from Portland, Ore., coincided wind outlook.

The arrival of Palmer Hoyt from Portland, Ore., coincided with the population influx. As editor and publisher of *The Denver Post,* the state's largest newspaper, Hoyt was as responsible as any one man for jolting Colorado out of its traditional provincialism. Perhaps it is significant that in 1964 Denver's airfield became an international airport, and that it has two sister cities, Brest, France, and Takayama, Japan.

Although Stetsons and cowboy boots can be seen on any downtown street, Denver's attitudes are as urbane and cosmopolitan as those of any metropolis. The big difference is the pace, which visitors quickly recognize as pleasantly less frenetic than that of the high-tension Eastern ulcer factories. Denver is also a young city, concerned with youthful activities. Particularly among secretaries and junior executives in the skyscraper offices, native Coloradans are scarce enough to be considered a rarity. Denver proper and Pueblo usually vote Democratic, but the Republicans are strong enough in the suburbs and the rest of the state to make virtually every election a ding-dong battle.

Seventeenth Street, Denver's banking, investments, insurance and transportation center, probably displays as many Ivy League suits per capita as Madison Avenue. But at the end of the day a Denver executive, instead of belting down a quick Martini before running for a train, hops into his car, drives to the suburbs in fifteen or twenty minutes, and sips his drink on the patio of his ranch-type home. For a night out, there's a choice of dining at any of several dozen excellent restaurants serving everything from authentic French and German cuisine to enchiladas, almond duck, sukiyaki and genuine Thai fare. True to Western tradition, however, most Denverites seem to prefer Colorado cornfed steaks or prime rib and tossed green salad.

In a great many instances it was the outdoors that lured the new Denverites to the West, and if anything, this interest seems to intensify rather than diminish after they arrive. The skiing season lasts for at least six months, and there is fishing the year around; in summer there is camping, boating, hiking, riding, driving, golfing and just plain mountain-admiring; in fall there is good hunting for both upland birds and big game. More and more city-dwelling Coloradans are buying mountain cabins, boats and campers.

However, like the tourists who demand hot showers, white linen and innerspring mattresses after a day of roughing it, Coloradans demand and enjoy the amenities of a sophisticated civilization. The Symphony, the Junior League Benefit, the Debutante Ball, the first night at Bonfils Civic Theatre are important events for ladies in furs and glittering jewels and their escorts in dinner jackets. Yet these same individuals support with equal enthusiasm the National Western Stock Show and Rodeo, where fat cattle and fearless cowboys vie for attention.

Not many years ago it could be charged with reasonable accuracy that Coloradans were a bit self-conscious about their isolation and inclined to be apologetic about their supposed lack of culture and horny-handed past. Not so today. By jet airliner they are less than two hours' flying time from the West Coast, three hours from the East. The Interstate system is rapidly shortening highway distances. Coloradans have made their pilgrimages to New York and San Francisco, to Paris and London and Rome, to Hongkong and Tokyo and Bangkok, and their collective verdict has been that travel is great but it's hard to beat Colorado. The state's adopted sons and daughters sing its praise loudest. Anyone who's lived in Colorado more than a year considers himself virtually a native—and talks as though he invented it.

GENERAL AND PRACTICAL INFORMATION FOR COLORADO

 FACTS AND FIGURES. Colorado gets its name from the Spanish for "red" or "muddy," referring to the Colorado River. Colorado's nicknames are *Centennial State* (because it entered the Union on August 1, 1876) and *Silver State*. The state flower is the Rocky Mountain columbine; state tree, the Colorado blue spruce; the state bird, the lark bunting; state animal, the Rocky Mountain bighorn sheep; the state motto is *Nil sine Numine* ("Nothing without Providence"); the state song is "Where the Columbines Grow." Colorado is in the mountain time zone. Its area is 104,247 sq. mi.; altitude, 3,350–14,431 ft. The state population (1971 estimate) is 2,313,000. Denver, Colorado's largest city, is the state capital.

The Continental Divide and the Rocky Mountains cut a north-south path down the center of Colorado, forming the headwaters of six great rivers· and dividing the state into the flat eastern region of the Great Plains and the high plateaus and deep gorges of the west. The mountainous western area contains some of the highest peaks in the country as well as some of America's finest resort areas. Cattle- and sheep-raising play a major role and, although the great days of gold and silver are over, mining remains important. The state is a leading source of molybdenum and uranium. Both agriculture and industry are hampered by lack of water—Colorado's biggest problem.

The climate is marked by sunny, pleasantly dry summers and cold winters, with little rainfall.

 HOW TO GET THERE. *By air:* Colorado is served by United, Trans World, Continental, Braniff, Frontier, Texas International, Western, North Central, and Aspen Airways on regular schedules into Denver's Stapleton International Airport. Colorado Springs, Pueblo, and Grand Junction also have major service.

By train: Amtrak has passenger service into Denver originating in Chicago or San Francisco. Connecting service into Grand Junction is available from the Denver & Rio Grande Western Railway.

By car: main highways into the state are I–25 from Wyoming in the north and New Mexico in the south; I–70 from Utah in the west and Kansas in the east; and I–80S from Nebraska in the northeast.

By bus: Greyhound and Continental Trailways both serve Colorado.

 HOW TO GET AROUND. *By air:* in addition to the major service into Denver, Frontier, Aspen Airways, and United provide air transportation within the state. Steamboat Springs-Hayden-Craig, Grand Junction, Aspen, Delta-Montrose, Gunnison, Cortez, Durango, Alamosa,

Lamar, Pueblo, and Colorado Springs are all served by one or more of these airlines.

By train: Denver & Rio Grande Western operates passenger service between Denver and Grand Junction.

By bus: Colorado Motorways, Continental Trailways, Denver-Boulder Bus Company and Greyhound serve Colorado communities.

By car: the major east-west route is I–70; from north to south on the Eastern slope take I–25, also known as the Valley Highway. US 50 and 550 serve the southwest corner and US 40 the northwest.

TOURIST INFORMATION. For specific information and descriptive brochures contact the Denver Convention and Colorado Visitors Bureau, 225 W. Colfax Ave., Denver 80202.

SEASONAL EVENTS. In *January,* there is the *Winter Skol Carnival* in Aspen and *ski races* throughout the state. Steamboat Springs, Leadville, and Crested Butte host *winter carnivals* in *February,* the *Roch Cup Races,* downhill and slalom, take place in Aspen, the Gunnison *Webster Players, Ltd.* give performances and Georgetown celebrates *Fasching,* nine days of German festivities at mid-month.

March brings *cutter races* to Steamboat Springs, *ski races* to various areas, and the *U.S. National Men's Curling Championships* to the Broadmoor World Arena in Colorado Springs.

The *Estes Park Hobby Show* and *Boulder Symphony Spring Concerts* open in *April. Easter Sunrise Services* take place at the Garden of the Gods near Colorado Springs.

May events include *rodeos, horse racing, golf tournaments,* Canon City's *Blossom Festival,* Aurora's *Pancake Festival,* Glenwood Springs' *Sportscar Rally,* the *opening of Trail Ridge Road,* Arapahoe Basin's *May Day Slalom,* the Alamosa Rail Fan Club's annual *narrow-gauge railroad trip,* and *horse shows* throughout the state.

Melodramas open in *June* in Cripple Creek, Cascade, Durango and various other towns; there are Colorado *Philharmonic Concerts* in Evergreen, *June Week and Graduation* ceremonies at the United States Air Force Academy in Colorado Springs, Grand Lake's *Sunrise Slalom,* Central City's *Opera and Drama Festival, water-skiing* tournaments, and the *Arkansas River International White Water Boat Race* at Salida (these are exciting kayak races while the river is at flood stage).

July has *stockcar races, rodeos,* and *horse shows* including the *National Arabian Horse Show* at Estes Park. Fourth of July activities abound, among them: the *Pikes Peak Hill Climb and Street Breakfast;* Breckenridge hosts *ski races* on a permanent snow field above the town; the *Koshare Indians* hold summer ceremonials at La Junta; Grand Lake has a *buffalo barbecue;* the *Aspen Music Festival* begins and runs through August; Boulder's *Shakespeare Festival* opens in Mary Rippon Theater; the "world's highest, longest, roughest, and toughest" race, the *Pack Burro Championship Race* over Hoosier Pass, takes place between Fairplay and Breckenridge; and the *Broadmoor International Theatre* at the Broadmoor Hotel in Colorado Springs brings in name entertainment through August.

In *August,* Grand Junction has *Intermountain Market Days;* Alamosa stages a *Kit Carson Riders Futurity Race and Derby;* Grand Lake has the *Shadow Mountain Sailboat Regatta;* Littleton holds the *National Little Britches Rodeo Finals;* the *Colorado State Fair* takes place at Pueblo; the *Pikes Peak or Bust Rodeo* is at Colorado Springs; and the *Navajo Trail Festival* in Durango includes a rodeo, square dancing, parade and horse racing.

The University of Colorado's *Big 8 football* season begins in *September.* Glenwood Springs has its annual *Art Festival,* and *Aspencades,* trips into the mountains to see the colorful changes autumn brings to the aspens, *rodeos* and *harvest festivals* are also common.

44

October has *Potato Day* in Glenwood Springs, the *Stone Age Fair* in Loveland, and the opening of the *big game hunting* season. Most of the states thirty-one *ski areas open* in *November. Goose hunting* season opens. Late in the month, Castle Rock has the *Christmas Star Lighting Ceremony. Hockey season* begins at the World Arena in Colorado Springs in *December.* Springfield has the *Annual Christmas parade;* La Junta the *Koshare Indians' Winter Night Ceremonial;* Central City the *Wintershire Festival of Christmas Lights;* and Beulah and Palmer Lake *Yulelog celebrations.* On New Year's Eve is the AdAmAn *fireworks display* on Pikes Peak.

NATIONAL PARKS. The Black Canyon of the *Gunnison National Monument* is probably the deepest, darkest, wildest and rockiest piece of real estate you will ever see. The Gunnison River has cut a narrow gorge, at times only forty feet wide, through nearly solid granite, to depths ranging from 1,730 feet to 2,425 feet. From the higher elevations it is possible to see the frothing white water below against a background of sunlight reflected from pink mica in the otherwise black walls. Legend has it that the canyon is so dark at the bottom and so narrow that it is possible in broad daylight to see the stars by looking straight up. Well-organized boat trips down the river and descents on Indian trails may be taken, but only experienced climbers should attempt any other route down the canyon. Some of the best fishing in Colorado is to be found on the Gunnison. The North Rim of the canyon is reached by gravel road east of Crawford on State 92. The South Rim is reached by US 50 to Montrose and then State 347 six mi. east. Park rangers have nightly programs during the summer. Campsites and picnic areas are available. Closed in winter by snow.

State 340 west from Grand Junction or US 70 from Fruita will lead into Rim Rock Drive of *Colorado National Monument,* 1,000 to 2,000 feet above the Grand Valley. Five-hundred-foot-high *Independence Rock, Window Rock,* the *coke ovens* and *Red Canyon* may be seen from lookouts along the 22-mile drive. Meadows of wildflowers and forests of juniper and pine surround the area. Wildlife, protected by the National Park Service, roam the area. Dinosaur beds are still being excavated here. Nearby, the largest flat-topped mountain in the United States, *Grand Mesa,* sprinkled with lakes and two miles high, may be reached on State 64. The Visitors Centers at park headquarters will acquaint the traveler with the area. Nightly programs by rangers during the summer. Campsites with excellent facilities and picnic areas are available. Well-marked trails for hikers are available.

Dinosaur National Monument, in the northwestern corner of Colorado, is reached from US 40 at Dinosaur, park headquarters. Much of the area's scenic beauty is a result of erosion by the Yampa and Green rivers. *Steamboat Rock,* carved out of layers of sandstone by the confluence of the Yampa and Green is now seven hundred feet above the river surface which once flowed over it. Its broad slab sides act as a sounding board for nearby *Echo Park.* Pictographs estimated to be 1,000 years old may be seen, as may archeologists removing the delicate bones of dinosaurs from their sedimentary storehouses. More than twenty skeletons have been reconstructed from bones taken from the huge quarry—deposited in the side of a hill some 100,000 years ago. The skeletons are housed in a museum reached through Jenson, Utah, twenty miles west of Dinosaur on US 40. Roads into the monument are often closed in winter due to snow. Campsites and raft trips are available in the area.

The only place in America where four states meet at one point is the junction of Arizona, New Mexico, Utah, and Colorado. The area is locally called "The Four Corners." *Hovenweep National Monument* is reached by a graded park road west of Cortez. The monument is a series of long-abandoned Pueblo settlements which punctuate the barren land and extend into southern Utah. The prehistoric

45

buildings, evidently built by a people similar to those who built Mesa Verde, are open for inspection. A ranger is on duty at Square Tower. Campsites and picnic areas are available. In rainy or snowy weather check in Cortez before attempting the dirt road.

Mesa Verde National Park will appeal to you in a different way from Rocky Mountain National Park. At Rocky Mountain you can glory in the natural beauty of canyons and outdoor wonders, but the wonders of Mesa Verde are man-made. Just as fossils tell us how plants and animals lived long ago, the ruins of these cliff cities tell us of a prehistoric civilization in Colorado very nearly a thousand years before the American Revolution. Since you are about to become a tourist-archeologist, some facts about Mesa Verde may help you. It is believed that about eight hundred years ago a severe and long drought forced the tribes which built Mesa Verde to leave their plateau for an area more favorable to agriculture. No one knows for certain who they were or to where they disappeared. *Mesa Verde* ("Green Tabletop") describes the general topography of the surface of the park, not the caves and canyons below. There are three general types of ruins open for inspection: pithouses, pueblos and cliff dwellings. The *pithouses* are shallow cliffings which were inhabited by one family. The *pueblo*, developed later, is a compound of several houses adjoining an open court. The pueblos form a village around the *kiva*, which was used for religious ceremonies. The *cliff dwellings* were built much later and offered excellent protection to their inhabitants. The *Cliff Palace* was built two hundred feet off the canyon floor and contains some two hundred rooms. The *Spruce Tree House* is relatively easy to enter and is one of the best preserved. It has 114 rooms and eight *kivas* and is not unlike today's apartment houses. No one may enter the fragile cliff dwellings unless accompanied by a park ranger. The ruins at the top of the mesa may be visited without a ranger.

The museum at Park Headquarters will add to the visitor's understanding of Mesa Verde and her people of long ago. Mesa Verde may be reached by car on US 160, thirty-eight miles west of Durango, then on twenty-one miles on park roads from the park entrance. Bus service from Spruce Tree Lodge is available for those who do not wish to drive their cars into the park; *Continental Trailways* has daily buses to Spruce Tree Lodge from Durango. *Frontier Airlines* serves Durango and Cortez ten miles west of Mesa Verde. A limited number of overnight accommodations are available at the park entrance, as are improved facilities for house trailers. A restaurant, service station, AAA road service, and tire agency are available. Evening campfire talks are given by park rangers and archeologists, and visiting Navahos from the neighboring reservation frequently demonstrate tribal dances and chants. Horseback trips through the area can be arranged at headquarters. Lodge is open May 15th to Oct. 15th.

Rocky Mountain National Park, with headquarters at Estes Park, is a huge family resort. The Chamber of Commerce in Estes Park has provided a variety of activities designed for young people, including a trout pond in which no one over 12 is allowed to fish. *Trail Rodge Road* (US 34) is a name which will give the word "breathtaking" a new meaning for the average traveler. The highest paved highway in the U.S., its fifteen miles of road above timberline, some at altitudes of 12,000 feet, look down on great sloping meadows of wildflowers. Slowly melting glaciers provide the water supply for a host of raging waterfalls, streams, and deep mountain lakes. On *Long's Peak* (14,255 feet), snowballs can be made in the middle of July, and *Iceberg Lake* really does have icebergs in it. At the western end of Trail Ridge Road is *Grand Lake,* which covers an area of 515 acres, and at 8,400 feet is the home of the highest yacht club in the world. All water sports are popular here, but be prepared for the icy waters of a lake whose depths have never been completely sounded.

Great Sand Dunes National Monument, located on State 150, thirty-six miles northeast of Alamosa, contains the highest naturally formed sand piles in the United States, some exceeding a height of eight hundred feet above the valley floor. The constant pressure of the wind sculpts the finely pulverized sand into a wonderland of hills, valleys and plains with the ease of a child playing on a beach, making this a National Monument which changes its face daily. During the day the dunes are visible for seventy miles, radiating a rosy warmth of sun on hot sand. The color and mood change with the angle of the sun, as lengthening shadows change the dunes to violet and mauve. The dunes also produce some of the greatest lightning displays in America. The combination of wind and heat rising from the thirty square miles of dunes creates titanic thunderstorms accompanied by extraordinary lightning bolts. The Visitors Center contains history and information on the area; campsites and picnic grounds are available, and a nature trail is marked for hikers.

Fossil Beds National Monument, one-half mile south of Florissant on County 1, is a 6,000-acre site once covered by a prehistoric lake. Thirty-five million years ago, erupting volcanoes filled the lake with ash and lava. Today perfectly detailed fossils of the insects, seeds and leaves of that period can be found in this area along with standing petrified Sequoia stumps.

 HOT SPRINGS. Colorado has a number of hot springs, among them *Glenwood Springs, Idaho Springs, Pagosa Springs, Hot Sulphur Springs,* and *Steamboat Springs,* all with facilities for enjoying the waters. Of these, Glenwood Springs is the most extensive with two outdoor pools, one of them two blocks long. Open all year, these are fed by natural warm mineral waters. *Hot mineral baths* are available at the Vapor Cave Baths and Health Spa.

 CAMPING OUT. Campers in Colorado will discover fully developed campsites in the state's eleven national forests, four national monuments, and two national parks, in addition to scores of state and local areas. Most are equipped for tents, trailers, and campers. Water, sanitary facilities and garbage disposal are available and many have swimming, boating, and fishing.

A Colorado Parks Pass, good for driver and passengers, is required for the state recreation areas. One-day pass is $1; annual pass $5. These are available from some parks and from most sporting goods stores. In addition, some parks may require a $2 campground fee.

Further information can be obtained from the Division of Game, Fish and Parks, 6060 Broadway, Denver 80216.

 TRAILER TIPS. In Grand Junction, one-half mile south of I–70 on exit 8 at 3238 F Rd., a KOA site has heated pool, sewer and electric hookups. Charge is $3 per night for two, 50¢ each additional person. North of Durango is the Ponderosa site off US 550. Fee is $1.25 per night for two including electrical hookup, 50¢ each additional person. Sewer, air-conditioning and electric heater hookups are also available at extra cost. In Estes Park, just across the road from Lake Estes on US 34, is a park offering water, electricity and sewer hookups. $3.50 per night for two, 50¢ for each additional. Seven miles north of Pueblo at I–25 exit 47 is the Buffalo Springs site with free dump station, electrical hookups, sewer, playground, country store, game room. Scenic view of Pikes Peak. $3.25 per night for two, 25¢ each additional person.

 FARM VACATIONS AND GUEST RANCHES. For the vacationer who likes to enjoy the great outdoors but still demands his creature comforts, Colorado has much to offer in the way of dude-ranch vacations. Reservations should be made well in advance.

The *C Lazy U Ranch*, seven miles northwest of Granby on State 125 and US 40, is one of America's finest, if not *the* finest, working guest ranch. This delightful ranch offers a variety of activities running from supervised programs for youngsters 5 to 12, to shuffleboard, skeet shooting, square dancing, lake and stream fishing, and barbecues, as well as the usual ranch activities. The C Lazy U is noted for its gourmet dining and the pleasant surprise of starting each day with a basket of fresh fruit in each room. The heated pool has a flagstone terrace adjoining a cocktail lounge with a panoramic view of the ranch. In winter, the ranch hosts appreciative, discriminating skiers.

Eleven miles northeast of Rifle on State 325, another working cattle ranch, the *CV Bar*, welcomes hungry, active tourists, as well as big-game hunters (in the fall) and hopeful fishermen. A heated pool and attractive lounge are available in addition to the usual activities; and this ranch welcomes children with special rates. Open June through October.

In south-central Colorado, on State 96 west of Pueblo, the *Don K Ranch* boasts its own ghost town. With the San Isabel Forest and the Sangre de Cristo Range to prowl, good food, heated pool, cocktail lounge, children's counselors, this may be the place for your Colorado vacation.

Adjoining Medicine Bow National Forest, on the Colorado-Wyoming line, *Focus Ranch*, while small, offers much. Excellent hunting and fishing, along with hay rides, square dancing, and swimming, plus the work of an active cattle ranch, are all available. Fourteen miles east of Slater on County 129.

Near Mesa Verde, adjoining the national forest, is *Lake Mancos Ranch*, located off US 160 from Mancos. In addition to the usual dude-ranch activities, and special fun for the children, this small, informal ranch offers a fall program of jeep trips into the mountains for picnics and viewing of the fall colors.

Ted Schafer's *Two Bar Seven Ranch* on the Colorado-Wyoming line, US 287, while small, has a host of various and unusual activities for guests. Probably the most popular and unusual is the annual trek from the ranch to Cheyenne via horseback and wagon for the annual *Cheyenne Frontier Days* celebration, which is held the last full week in July.

These are only a few of the dozens of good ranches in Colorado, both working and dude, that welcome visitors.

 MUSEUMS AND GALLERIES. The *University of Colorado Museum and Art Gallery* in Boulder is open to the public Mon. through Sat. 8 to 5, and Sun. and hols. 2 to 5. The *Natural History Museum* is quite extensive.

Central City's Opera House should be seen. The H. A. W. Tabor Collection is housed in the *Gold Mine Museum*. Open daily.

The *Colorado Springs Fine Arts Center* and *Taylor Museum* offer an unusual collection of southwestern United States primitive folk art and American Indian art. The building itself is an unusual piece of architecture. Open Mon. through Sat. 10 to 5, Sun. 1:30 to 5:30. The *National Carvers Museum* has permanent and changing exhibits of the work of nationally and internationally known carvers. Open 9 to 5; Apr. to Sept., 9 to 6, Sun. from 10:30.

Hagans Clock Manor Museum in Evergreen has a marvelous collection of clocks and music boxes. Guided tours, lectures, films, and programs presented. Small admission charge. Open Tues. through Sat. 10 to 4, evenings by appointment.

The *Hotel De Paris* and the *Hamill House,* both in Georgetown, are run for lovers of Victorian furnishings and architecture. Some of the best representatives of Victorian architecture in America are in this sleepy little mountain community. Both these museums are open daily in the summer and both charge a small admission fee.

Children will be enchanted with the *Buffalo Bill Museum* on *Lookout Mountain,* which contains items dealing with Cody's life and associates. Open daily, 8 to 6.

The *Colorado School of Mines* in Golden operates a geology museum which should be seen by anyone interested in minerals, fossils, rock, or ores. Open daily 8 to 5.

The *Colorado Railroad Museum*, the largest railroad display in the Rockies, is housed in an 1880-style railroad station. Open 9 to 7, June to Labor Day; rest of year to 5.

La Junta is the home of the *Koshare Indian Dancers* and their museum, located at *Otero Junior College*. This fascinating *Kiva* contains Indian art, handicrafts, and lore. Open 10 to 12, 1:30 to 5:30 and 7 to 9 daily in summer, 1:30 to 5:30 in winter.

H. A. W. Tabor left his mark on Colorado's cultural ways, and now Leadville has preserved and restored his last mine and the opera house he built for the town. Both the *Matchless Mine* and the *Tabor Opera House* charge small admission fees, but are worth the trouble to see. Tabor also built the opera house in Central City, used by the summer theater, and one in Denver which has since been destroyed.

The *El Pueblo Museum* in Pueblo features a full-size re-creation of El Pueblo Fort built in 1842, as well as history of the local steel industry. Open Tues. through Sat. 9 to 5, Sun. and hols. 12 to 5.

Trindad offers the *Baca House* and the *Bloom Mansion* for public visits. The Baca House is an 1869 adobe residence; the Bloom Mansion the 1882 baroque Victorian residence of a local cattle baron. Both open during the summer daily 9 to 5.

Nearly every town in Colorado has a museum of some sort, but particularly interesting is the *Cripple Creek District Museum*. The state historical society maintains a number of forts, monuments, residences, and sites throughout the state.

HISTORIC SITES. *Old Fort Garland,* on US 160, forty-seven miles west of Walsenburg, is a restored Army post that was once commanded by Kit Carson. Open daily 9 to 5. June 1 to Oct. 15. On US 85 south of Platteville is a reproduction of *Fort Vasquez,* a fur-trading post of the 1830's. *Pike's Stockade,* a moated log structure built in 1807 by Zebulon Pike, is on US 285 east of La Jara. Buffalo Bill Cody's grave is atop Lookout Mountain, west of Denver on US 40.

Mining played an important part in Colorado's history and more than three hundred *ghost towns* still survive today as remnants of the state's legendary past. The Central City-Black Hawk area was once known as the "richest square mile on earth" and the ghost towns of Nevadaville and Apex, and *Teller House* and *1878 Opera House* are reminders of the opulence that came and went. The "World's greatest gold camp" was at Cripple Creek-Victor where several excellent ghost towns survive. At the edge of Fairplay, one of Colorado's oldest cities, the 100-year-old town of South Park City has been reconstructed.

FAMOUS LIBRARIES. All the colleges and universities in the state have good libraries, open to the public, and the *Mineralogy Library* at the *Colorado School of Mines* in Golden is outstanding.

TOURS. *AA Sightseeing Tours* and *Continental Sightseeing Lines* in Denver and *Grey Line Tours* in Denver and Colorado Springs offer sightseeing tours around Colorado as well as locally. The *Burlington* and the *Denver & Rio Grande Western* railroads have tours, as do the *Greyhound Bus Company, Continental Trailways Bus Company* and *Colorado Motorways*. Many of the smaller cities and towns have *taxi companies* that will gladly take the tourist on a sightseeing trip in the local area. In the fall a number of *"Aspencades"* depart from various towns to view the spectacular colors of the changing leaves. Check with local chambers of commerce for exact dates and times. *Jeep tours* are popular in various parts of the state as a way to enjoy the mountains and get into

49

little-traveled areas in a manner more comfortable than on the back of a horse or by foot. Again, local chambers of commerce can help in arrangements.

INDUSTRIAL TOURS. The *Cudahy Packing Company,* 4801 Brighton Blvd., Brighton (tel. 623-5231), has a tour which children might enjoy. While in Climax be sure to see the *Climax Molybdenum Company's* mining operations. In Golden, the *Coors Brewery* (tel. 279-3311) has a plant tour. Loveland's *Great Western Sugar Company* offers tours through its plant, where locally grown sugar beets are processed. *Colorado Fuel and Iron Company* in Pueblo conducts tours of its steel-making operation.

SPECIAL INTEREST TOURS. The Durango to Silverton narrow-gauge railroad passes through spectacular Rocky Mountain scenery. First built in 1882 principally to carry precious metals out of the area, this rail line still uses steam locomotives. The train leaves Durango at 8:30 a.m. (a second train leaves at 9:30 from late June to Labor Day) and arrives at Silverton at noon. The return trip leaves Silverton at 2:05 p.m. (3:05 p.m.) and reaches Durango at 5:30 (6:30 p.m.) Trains run daily from late May to early Oct.

NIGHTCLUBS. The Broadmoor Hotel in Colorado Springs brings in "name" entertainment, particularly to their *Broadmoor International Theatre.* During the peak ski season, many of the Aspen clubs also have popular entertainers.

BARS. Because Colorado law requires that food be served where liquor is served, some of Colorado's best bars are also excellent eating places. *The Golden Bee,* at the Broadmoor Hotel in Colorado Springs, is an authentic replica of a 19th-century English pub. Central City boasts a wide variety of bars. The famous "Face on the Barroom Floor" is in the bar at *Teller House.* The *Red Ram Saloon* in Georgetown, and its Rathskeller, are well-liked.

DRINKING LAWS. Colorado Law requires that anyone purchasing hard liquor, wine, or "6%" beer must be *21 years of age.* Persons over 18 may purchase so-called "3.2" beer. Liquor may be sold until 2 a.m. Mon. through Sat. and until 8 p.m. on Sun. in places selling hard liquor and wine. The "3.2" beer may be sold until midnight, seven days a week. Drinks must be off the table at closing hour. Package goods are not sold over the bar, but may be obtained in package stores, open until midnight, Mon. through Sat. Colorado Law requires that any establishment serving liquor must also serve food, a law which is complied with in some pretty ingenious ways. Children may sit at a table if they are accompanied by an adult. Colorado operates under local option laws, so it is possible to find a few "dry" towns within the state.

MUSIC. Tops among the many musical activities outside of Denver is the *Aspen Music Festival,* held each summer with nationally known artists. The *Broadmoor Hotel* in Colorado Springs offers many fine performers in its International Center. Most Colorado cities and towns have local orchestras and bands which perform throughout the year, and the many colleges and universities in the state all feature musical events throughout the school term. Central City features two major operas each summer in the Opera House—these are performed by top-ranking artists. The *Little Kingdom of Gilpin* fairly resounds with music of one kind or another from dawn to the wee hours.

STAGE AND REVUES. Central City's *annual summer festival* includes the presentation of a major play with a broadway cast. Boulder has an annual *Shakespeare Festival*, the *Nomad Players* and the *University Theater* group. Other colleges and universities throughout the state have student theaters and often bring in outside talent to perform. Various towns throughout the state have melodramas which are presented with great glee, and much hissing at the villains and cheering of the heroes. The *Dark Horse Players*, of Estes Park, offer performances throughout the summer months. *The Koshare Indian Dancers* of La Junta present ceremonials throughout the summer on Saturday evenings. At Steamboat Springs, the world-known *Perry Mansfield Camp* presents a dance and drama festival in July and August The *Troupe of American College Players* in Grand Lake present a different show every night (theater in the round).

 SUMMER SPORTS. *Fishing:* 9,600 miles of unposted fishing streams and 2,850 cold-water lakes and reservoirs provide ample opportunity to catch the fabled Rocky Mountain trout. Rainbow, brook, native and brown trout are all famous for their fight, and while the fishing season lasts year round, the best months are July and Aug. A 10-day nonresident fishing license is $5, or $10 annually. They are readily available at sporting goods stores.

Hunting: more than 70,000 mule deer, 12,000 elk, 550 black bear are taken each year in Colorado. Antelope too are hunted.

There are seasons on pheasant, grouse, quail, ducks, Canadian geese, and ptarmigan, this last hunted above timberline. License fees and information about seasons can be obtained from the Department of Natural Resources, Division of Wildlife, 6060 Broadway, Denver 80216.

Water-skiing, swimming, boating, rafting, and *scuba diving* are popular throughout the state with numerous lakes and reservoirs open for use. Grand Lake is said to have the highest yacht club in America. *Tennis, golf, mountain climbing, rock hunting, hiking, horseback riding,* and even *panning for gold* are also possible.

WINTER SPORTS. Colorado has long been famous for its *skiing* facilities, and new improvements and areas are opened each fall. High elevations, low humidity, and well-planned slopes make for good skiing from November through May, with summer skiing on *St. Mary's Glacier.*

Arapahoe Basin, sixty-six miles from Denver on US 6, *Loveland Basin* and *Loveland Valley,* fifty-six miles west of Denver, on US 6, and *Berthoud Pass,* fifty-seven miles west of Denver on US 40, offer open slopes, high-speed lifts, and a variety of terrain. *Aspen, Buttermilk, Snowmass* and *Aspen Highlands* make up one of the largest ski complexes in the country—a full-blown resort town with accommodations running from luxurious to economical and food from hot dogs to gourmet dinners are available. The town is devoted to skiing and skiers, and its facilities are the best. *Winterskol,* in January of each year, turns the old mining town into one giant carnival. The *Broadmoor Hotel* has its own mountain and ski area, with snow machines in case nature fails to cooperate. *Crested Butte, Breckenridge,* and *Vail* are all areas with deluxe facilities for families. *Winter Park,* owned and operated by the City of *Denver* as part of its park system, grows yearly. The Denver & Rio Grande Western Railroad runs a ski train to *Winter Park;* the *Hochlandhof* lodge at the foot of the mountain is so charming that many people who do not ski take the train up, spend the day at the lodge enjoying the view, food, and drink, and go back to Denver with the train.

There is an ever-growing number of smaller, weekend areas ideally suited for the skiing family, and, while their facilities won't match those of Vail or Aspen,

51

they are adequate. Colorado ski areas are accessible by automobile, with the state highway crews doing an excellent job on the roads; bus service is available to the large areas; and the D&RGW train serves Winter Park. All areas have ski schools in operation and the cost of the lesson will be money well spent. Most areas have ski shops for the sale and rental of equipment.

Ice skating has grown in popularity in recent years in Colorado. The *Broadmoor* has a large indoor rink. Towns around the state have municipal ice rinks, and skates may generally be rented for a small charge.

SPECTATOR SPORTS. *Auto racing:* the famous Pikes Peak Hill Climb takes place July 4th outside Colorado Springs and, at the Continental Divide Raceways in Castle Rock, there is stock and sports car racing from May to Sept. *Greyhound racing:* from late Mar. to early June at Cloverleaf in Loveland, from early June to mid-Aug. at Pueblo Kennel Association in Pueblo, and during Sept. and Oct. at Rocky Mountain Kennel Club. *Horse racing:* at Uranium Downs from late June to late July in Grand Junction. *Rodeo:* although many communities have rodeos, some of the best known are the "Pikes Peak or Bust Rodeo" in Colorado Springs during the second week in Aug.; the Colorado State Fair and Rodeo in Pueblo beginning late Aug. Others take place at Craig, Montrose, Estes Park, Salida, Gunnison, Loveland, Canon City, Steamboat Springs, Boulder, Monte Vista, and Glenwood Springs.

SHOPPING. Colorado has more than its share of ordinary curio shops and souvenir counters, but it also has some different and interesting shops. Aspen's *Elli of Aspen* has a good collection of unusual sportswear, as does the *House of Ireland. The Arrow Shop,* Aspen, is an adventure in Western folklore, with Indian and Eskimo arts and crafts. *Terese David of Aspen* advertises "crazy clothes for matching people" and also has wonderful items for the "little people." Colorado Springs' *Broadmoor Hotel* has a branch of *Abercrombie and Fitch,* the delight of sportsmen the world over. *Gerry's Mountain Shop,* 821 Pearl Street in Boulder, supplies many expeditions in the mountain-climbing world. The *Pottery Parlor,* 534 Main Avenue, Durango, deals in pottery in all manner of shapes, sizes and colors.

WHAT TO DO WITH THE CHILDREN. Children in Colorado can find activities of all kinds and types to keep them busy. The *Cheyenne Mountain Zoo* in Colorado Springs will delight them. The *North Pole,* northwest of Colorado Springs, is the home of Santa's Workshop. A Wild West stagecoach, miniature train, Santa's car, and a magic-mine ride, plus doll-makers, puppeteers, magicians, glassblowers, gnomes, elves, and story book characters all make for enjoyment. *Ghost Town,* in Colorado Springs, caters to the imaginations of adults and children alike. Parks and museums throughout the state cater to children and attempt to make their visits both fun and educational. The national forests and monuments are made to order for children who love the outdoors, but it would be well to warn them about wandering off alone. The old mining towns, especially Central City and Leadville, will offer dozens of places for browsing, looking, and learning. Abandoned mines should not be entered, since the timbers are dry and could collapse; but many old mines have been safety-checked and may be entered with a guide, usually for a small fee. The *Garden of the Gods* and *Cave of the Winds,* both near Colorado Springs, offer unusual sights. Both wonderful for a day's excursion are the narrow-gauge railroad from Durango to Silverton and the *Cumbres & Toltec Scenic Railroad* from Antonito, Colorado, to Chama, New Mexico.

52

INDIANS. Colorado's history is inextricably bound to Indian culture and lore. Today the state has two reservations, the *Ute Mountain* and *The Southern Ute Reservations*, in southwestern Colorado. Nearly 1,000 Mountain Utes live on the reservations, which, while clinging to many ancestral traditions, have modern conveniences. Each summer the Utes stage their traditional *Sun Dance*. Visitors are welcome, but cameras are not allowed. The visitors are expected to view the dances with attention and respect. The Southern Utes hold their *Bear Dance* near Ignacio in May.

 PHOTOGRAPHY. In the high altitude and low humidity of Colorado, the air is clear and thin and there is an abundance of ultra-violet light which, though invisible, color film picks up as a blue haze. The use of a skylight filter cuts out these rays and your pictures will apprear normal. The light at these high altitudes is very bright, and pictures of sunlit scenes require ½ to 1 full stop less exposure than you would ordinarily use. If you can afford the extra cost in film of exposing ½ stop over and under in addition to what seems to be the correct exposure, you are nearly certain of getting a perfectly exposed photograph. Professional photographers often use this technique.

If your camera has interchangeable lenses, a wide-angle lens can capture not only the broad panoramic shots from the high peaks, but also insure that both the river and sky will appear in photos of the deep canyons.

 RECOMMENDED READING. Duncan Emerich's *It's an Old Wild West Custom* will give insight into some of the ways of the Westerner; *Timberline*, by Gene Fowler, is a delightful peek into the Denver of not-so-very-long-ago; Marshall Sprague's *Newport in the Rockies* tells of the life and times in Colorado Springs, and particularly of the Broadmoor Hotel; *Where the Old West Stayed Young*, a large, beautiful book by John Rolfe Burroughs, tells of the Brown's Park area; and *Stampede to Timberline*, by Muriel Sibell Wolle, tells of ghost towns and mining camps throughout the state.

EXPLORING DENVER

If you've had a long trip to Denver there's nothing more appropriate than a leisurely walking tour for getting the kinks out of your legs and to acclimate yourself to the mile-high air. The altitude doesn't bother most persons, but you may find yourself just a bit short of breath for a few days, so take it easy at first.

Best place to start is the Colorado Hospitality Center, at 225 West Colfax Avenue, just off the main business section and at the edge of the Civic Center complex. The Hospitality Center is housed in an attractive red sandstone and glass building immediately across the street from city hall (distinguishable by the clock tower and chimes), which Denverites call the City and County Building. Go in. You'll be welcomed by a pleasant young woman who can supply you with detailed maps, weather and road reports, the latest ski readings in winter and a list of local rodeos and other celebrations in summer. She can also tell you about accommodations, restaurant facilities, trailer camps, fish and game regulations, and a lot of other information to make your Colorado visit more enjoyable.

Now you're loaded down with literature and ready to begin your walk. Cross West Colfax toward the City and County Building, and be careful of the traffic. (It might be wise to point out here that many downtown Denver intersections have "Walk" and "Don't Walk" lights. When the "Walk" sign goes on, pedestrians are permitted to move in any direction, even catty-corner, while automobiles wait. You'll get used to it. Traffic Engineer Henry Barnes initiated the system in the late 1940's, and it worked so well he was rewarded eventually with the opportunity to solve New York City's traffic problems.)

Turn right, or west, toward the mountains. Adjoining the City and County Building, behind a wrought iron fence, is the United States Mint, where automatic machinery stamps out pennies, nickels, dimes, quarters and half dollars. This is also the largest depository of gold bullion—about six billion dollars—outside of Fort Knox, Kentucky. Summer tour hours are from 7:45 to 11 A.M. and 12:30 to 3 P.M. Regular hours are 9 to 11 A.M. and 1 to 2:30 P.M., Monday through Friday. The Denver Mint does not conduct tours for a two-week period at the closing of the fiscal year. Dates vary, but the mint tours generally cease for the final week of June until after the fourth of July. Tours start at the Cherokee Street entrance and no advance reservations are needed, although at the height of the summer tourist season, waits of an hour or more are not uncommon.

You'll hear the chatter of stamping machinery and the clatter of coins through the mint's open windows as you move on into the City and County Building. Denver's municipal affairs are conducted in this imposing, four-story, white granite structure faced with Doric columns. The mayor's office and city council chambers are here, as well as courtrooms and various city bureaus. Shortly before Thanksgiving each year, work starts on the lighting and decorating of Civic Center, a municipally financed project that has become a Denver tradition. In the weeks preceding and following Christmas, the streets are thronged each evening by those who have come to admire the display.

From the front steps of the City and County Building, take time to look out across the grassy mall, dotted with shade trees, that stretches eastward to the gold-domed Colorado State Capitol. The Capitol, constructed of Colorado gray granite, is a miniaturized version of the U.S. Capitol in Washington, D.C., and the mall is likewise a smaller version of the Washington mall. Fountains, a Greek Theater for public gatherings, and monuments to Denver

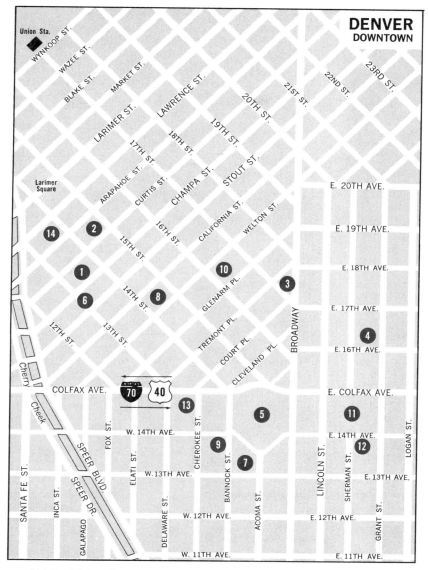

Points of Interest

1) Auditorium Arena & Theater
2) Brooks Tower
3) Brown Palace Hotel
4) Capitol Life Center
5) Civic Center
6) Convention Center, Currigan Hall
7) Denver Art Museum

8) Denver Post Building
9) Denver University Law Center
10) Masonic Temple Building
11) State Capitol
12) State Historical Museum
13) U. S. Mint
14) University of Colorado

and Colorado pioneers grace the mall, which is carefully tended and brightened in summer by extensive flower beds. To the left, in a classic colonnaded building, is the municipal body that holds Denver's life in its hands—the Board of Water Commissioners, charged with providing the city with a reliable supply of pure water from the vast mountain basins it taps.

Now, turn south along Bannock Street a half block to West 14th Avenue. Here on the corner is the University of Denver College of Law, part of the downtown campus of the privately endowed school. Next to it on the west, still across the street from the City and County Building, is a tall new structure decorated with colorful mosaic murals. This is Metropolitan State College, Denver's answer to the high cost of education beyond the high school level. Founded in the fall of 1965, it quickly won acceptance among students who for various reasons prefer to live at home while continuing with their schooling.

Now the route of our stroll turns east along 14th. On the other side of Bannock Street is the Denver Art Museum, noted for both its contemporary and traditional American and European exhibits. This new six-story building on the south side of the Civic Center is composed of more than one million specially designed, faceted-glass tiles. It also has an outstanding Oriental art collection, but perhaps it is best known for the encouragement it has given local painters, sculptors, and ceramicists with regional shows and sales. The museum is closed on Mondays.

Next to the museum complex, fronting on Broadway, is the $3 million Denver Public Library, where boys on roller skates work in the stacks, and paintings and records are loaned out as well as books. The Western History Department is considered one of the nation's best in this field. Priceless photo collections, Colorado newspaper files dating back to 1859, and rare volumes are available to the serious researcher.

Panorama of the Rockies

Proceed two blocks eastward along 14th, which now has become East 14th Avenue. On the right, at the two corners of Sherman Street, are the State Capitol Annex and the State Historical Museum. On the left is the massive, neo-classic Capitol. The museum, open daily, offers an insight into Colorado history with mementos of the bonanza mining years, dioramas of early-day Denver, artifacts of the Pueblo Indian culture, and even several mummified remains of Cliff-Dwellers.

The Capitol, completed in 1896, is typical of the porticoed and domed public buildings of that period; however, the dome, gilded with Colorado gold leaf at a cost of $23,000, is noteworthy as a tribute to the mining industry. The dome is floodlighted at night.

The thirteenth step of the western entrance to the Capitol is exactly one mile above sea level. A bronze plaque used to be mounted there, but it and its replacements kept disappearing and Colorado now frugally notes the elevation with a message chiseled into the stone. On a clear day (Denver also has a smog problem) a vast panorama of the Rockies is visible from this entrance. Heroic murals by Allen True depicting state history cover the main floor wall, and portraits of leading historical figures appear in the stained glass windows of the Senate chamber and under the dome. (Other murals by Allen True decorate the Telephone Building and the lobby of the Colorado National Bank in Denver.)

Capitol Hill, once the site of the luxurious homes of mining tycoons, is largely an apartment house area now. However, a dwindling number of mansions can be seen, and one of them, Molly Brown's House, is nationally known. This Victorian marvel at 1320 Pennsylvania Street was the home of Molly and her husband, James J. Brown, a wealthy mine owner. Molly was known for her flamboyant tastes and for the great heroism she displayed in the Titanic disaster. She became a famous folk heroine with the musical "The Unsinkable Molly Brown." The home is closed on Monday. The tour hours are 10 A.M. to 4 P.M., Tuesday through Saturday, and noon until 4 P.M. on Sundays.

Three short blocks east of Logan Street is the Episcopal Cathedral of St. John's in the Wilderness, at E. 14th Avenue and Washington Street. Built in the massive fifteenth-century Gothic style, the cathedral has some of the finest examples of English stained glass and German carved wooden figures in the West. This church's first home was a log cabin, built shortly after Denver was founded.

Now it is time to turn around and head back toward downtown Denver. Instead of retracing your steps, walk north one block to Colfax Avenue then turn left. At the corner of Colfax and Logan is the Roman Catholic Cathedral of the Immaculate Conception, a massive French Gothic structure with two lofty spires. A white Carrara marble altar, thirty feet high, and twenty-two stained glass windows designed at the Royal Bavarian Institute, grace the interior.

Time to think about lunch? You are now within a block or two of some of Denver's finest restaurants. At Colfax and Grant, only one block from the Cathedral and across the street from the Capitol, is the Quorum Room, operated by Pierre Wolfe, a

Swiss-trained Frenchman. On the next block, Sherman Street, are Le Profil (European style) and the Diplomat (American), both ranked high by gourmets. The Diplomat is closed on Sunday.

Or perhaps you'd prefer to stroll north on Sherman to 17th Avenue and turn left again, past the University Club to the Denver-United States National Bank Center on Broadway. Designed by the famous architect, I. M. Pei, this was the first of Denver's beautiful postwar buildings. A promenade, fountains and trout pools give a feeling of spaciousness.

Adjoining the Bank Center is the Cosmopolitan Hotel, with its Gun Room, noted for roast baron of beef, and Trader Vic's, a Polynesian restaurant.

The Brown Palace

Across from the Bank Center is Denver's most famous hotel, the venerable, gracious Brown Palace. The triangular brownstone structure is built around a lobby whose ceiling extends up the full eight stories of the hotel. This open lobby, gaily decorated at Christmas, is well worth a stop. Just off the lobby are the swank Palace Arms restaurant, and the Ship Tavern, where every chair is a captain's chair.

From the Brown, walk one block down 17th Street to Glenarm Place, stopping in mid-block to visit Kohlberg's, dealer in genuine Indian merchandise since 1888.

If you turn left on Glenarm and walk a half block you'll reach the thirty-story Security Life Building, whose Top of the Rockies restaurant on the top floor provides cocktails, lunches, dinners and an amazing view, although this one is from behind glass. Security Life also has an outside elevator. The glass isn't always spotless, but it's an exciting experience to watch Denver fall swiftly away as you scoot up the side of the building.

Whichever building you choose, the tour leads back to 17th Street, Denver's main shopping avenue. Turn left, toward Broadway. At the corner of Tremont Place, only a half block from the Security Life Building and on the same cross street as the Brown Palace, is Denver's largest department store, the May-D&F. It's an odd name, but a legitimate one. The "May" portion indicates it is one of the May Company chain, founded in the silver camp of Leadville by the pioneer merchant, David May. The "D&F" stands for Daniels and Fisher, a respected old Denver store that was absorbed by the May Company. Stroll through the store, then take the second-floor overpass directly into the lobby of the Denver Hilton Hotel. En route, in the passageway, you'll find Michelle's, an unusual coffee, pastry and ice cream shop patterned after a Mediterranean sidewalk cafe. It's an adventure to meet Michelle, which is the business name of John Michopoulos, one-time Greek fighter pilot turned confectionaire.

The Hilton is notable for its block-long lobby, a magnificent investment in space (as befits its role as a leading Colorado hostelry) in a time when architects and builders begrudge every square foot of non-revenue-producing area. An escalator takes you from the lobby to the ground-floor arcade. Now your walking tour is ended. The Hospitality Center is only a block away. But you haven't exhausted Denver's sightseeing opportunities by a long shot, and many of those remaining are "must-see's" by any standard.

Outside the Downtown Area

In east Denver, for example, there is the Denver Museum of Natural History in one corner of 640-acre City Park. Fossilized bones of prehistoric animals found in the Rocky Mountain region have been assembled into an outstanding display. Other exhibits show Rocky Mountain, Arctic, and South American animals and birds mounted in extremely lifelike natural habitat displays. The Denver Museum of Natural History also houses a planetarium that has programs going on all year. City Park itself has a large zoo, including a children's ranch zoo. In summer there are boating, free band concerts at night, and an electric fountain. Also in east Denver, adjoining Cheesman Park (where there is an exceptional view of the mountains), are the Denver Botanic Gardens, featuring a million-dollar conservatory for tropical flowers and plants.

In northeast Denver is the Mile High Kennel Club, where greyhounds race during a sixty-night season each summer. Even if you aren't interested in either wagering or greyhounds, you'll find the track is a gay, colorful, meticulously operated spot, visited by nearly ten thousand persons every evening and an important part of the Denver entertainment picture. (Persons under twenty-one are not admitted.)

And in southwest Denver, just outside suburban Littleton, is the Centennial Turf Club, offering a summer schedule of thoroughbred horse racing and an opportunity to try the pari-mutuel system while supporting efforts to improve the breed. Many of the horses that race here, incidentally, are Colorado bred.

To the northwest are two fine summer amusement parks, Elitch Gardens and Lakeside. Elitch's is famous for its formal floral gardens, the nation's oldest summer stock theater (with big-name

Broadway talent), and dancing with famous bands in an open-air ballroom. Lakeside also has a ballroom, speedboat rides, stock car races and a toy train that chuffs its way completely around Lake Rhoda. Farther west, at 17555 West 44th Avenue, is the Colorado Railroad Museum, calculated to make a rail buff's eyes mist with nostalgia. Steam locomotives of various sizes and vintages, railrod cars, narrow-gauge equipment, and many other displays of railroadiana have been assembled here by the Colorado Railroad Club. The club also schedules several outings by train each year, and this is the place to get information.

PRACTICAL INFORMATION FOR THE DENVER AREA

 HOW TO GET AROUND. *By bus:* the Denver Metro Transit operates the city's buses. Basic fare is 35¢. Buses run not only within Denver proper, but also out into the suburbs. Route and schedule information is available by calling 774-3111.

By taxi: cabs in Denver may be hailed or requested by phone. The basic charge is $1 for the first mile and 40¢ for each additional mile. Yellow Cab, 892-1212, is one of the major operators.

From the airport: taxi service to and from the airport averages $3.25 plus tip. Airport limousine service, which stops at the major hotels, costs $2.

TOURIST INFORMATION. For information and brochures about Denver contact the Hospitality Center, Denver Convention and Colorado Visitors Bureau, 225 W. Colfax Ave., Denver 80202.

 SEASONAL EVENTS. *January: National Western Livestock, Horse Show and Rodeo* takes place for nine days in mid-month. The *Western Annual Exhibition* at the Denver Art Museum opens and runs into *March.*

February: Garden and Home Show.

March: Denver Symphony has a series of free concerts.

April: Easter Sunrise services at Red Rocks. *Denver Bears* baseball season opens.

May: Lakeside Amusement Park, and *Elitch Gardens, Theatre and Bands* open to run throughout the summer. The Spring production of the *Denver Ballet* is offered mid-month. Thoroughbred and quarter *horse racing* at Centennial Race Track begins with pari-mutuel betting through mid-Nov.

June: Greyhound racing at Mile High Kennel Club throughout the summer with pari-mutuel betting.

July: The *All Colorado Art Show* at the Denver Art Museum, mid-month through Sept. *Denver Post Opera* performances are offered about mid-month. Free *band concerts* through Aug. take place in City Park.

September: Denver Broncos professional football season opens.

October: Early in the month is the *Larimer Square Oktoberfest.* The *Denver Symphony* and *Bonfils Memorial Theater* begin eight- and-nine month seasons.

December: Lights are turned on for the *Denver Civic Center Christmas Display.*

MUSEUMS AND GALLERIES. The *Denver Museum of Natural History* at City Park is one of the outstanding museums in the world. The "inhabitants" of this unique museum are shown in natural surroundings, whether they lived in prehistoric times or wander the world today. Open Mon. through Sat. 10 a.m. to 4:30 p.m. Sun. and hol. 12 to 5 p.m. The *Colorado State Historical Museum.* 14th and Sherman, covers Colorado from prehistoric times to today. Open 9 a.m. to 5 p.m. Mon. through Fri. 10 a.m. to 5 p.m. Sat., Sun., hol. The *Denver Art Museum,* 100 W. 14th Ave., includes a permanent collection of European, Egyptian, Greek and English works in the south wing; the *Schleier Gallery,* with its American collection; *Oriental Galleries,* with permanent collections on Asia; the *Living Arts Center,* with modern arts and designs, all at Civic Center; all are open Tues. through Sat. 9 a.m. to 5 p.m. Sun. and hol. 2 to 5 p.m.

HISTORIC SITES. Denver has unfortunately demolished many of her historic sites (the Mining Exchange Building, the Old Customs House, the Tabor Opera House, the Windsor Hotel) to make way for parking lots, but there are still a few to be visited. The "Unsinkable Molly Brown's" house, *The House of Lions,* while nowhere near as grand a palace as that depicted in the movie, is still standing on the east side of Pennsylvania St. between 13th and 14th, lions guarding the door. It is open for tours from 10 a.m. to 4 p.m. daily. Closed Mon. The *Governor's Mansion,* at 400 E. 8th Ave., a gift to the state from the Boettcher Foundation, is a 27-room Colonial structure with beautifully landscaped grounds. Tours are available on Tues. from 2 to 4 p.m.

FAMOUS LIBRARIES. The *Denver Public Library,* at 1357 Broadway and twenty branch locations, is the largest in the Rocky Mountain region. The Western History section is one of the finest in the country. Many programs and exhibits are presented for the public. Open Mon. to Thurs. 10 a.m. to 9 p.m.; Fri. and Sat. 10 a.m. to 5:30 p.m.; Sun. 1:30 to 5:30 p.m. Closed Sun. during June, July, and Aug.

TOURS. *AA Sightseeing Tours, Continental Sightseeing Lines,* and *Grey Line Tours* offer daily excursions around the city, as well as to the Denver Mountain Parks System, Estes Park, Pikes Peak, Mt. Evans, Central City, and the Air Force Academy, in the summer. "You haven't seen Denver until you've seen it with the Symphony Guides" is the motto of the *Denver Symphony Guild Tour Committee.* Its tours have proved to be extremely popular with local residents as well as travelers. Reservations should be made in advance through Symphony Guild Tours, Mr. Pitts, 2053 Clermont Street, Denver 80207.

INDUSTRIAL TOURS. The *Bowman Biscuit Co.,* 5000 Osage St., (433-6221), makers of crackers and cookies, will show you around its new, automated plant. *Denver Wholesale Florists,* 48th and Dahlia (399-0970), one of the largest, specializes in carnations. *Sunstrand Aviation,* maker of aerospace power systems, has a fascinating tour for space-minded people. At 2480 W. 70th Ave., (428-3636). The *Packaging Corporation of America,* 5501 Brighton Blvd. (288-2601), manufacturers of corrugated containers, has an interesting tour. The *Denver Post,* 650 15th St. (297-1437), conducts hourly tours showing how a metropolitan newspaper is published. *Rio Grande Railway Shops,* Burnham Shops, 8th Ave. at Osage St. (222-5333), have tours every thirty minutes, and special tours for children. Also, the *Gates Rubber Co.,* 999 S. Broadway (744-5394), gives tours upon request.

SPECIAL INTEREST TOURS. The *Denver Mint,* at Colfax and Delaware Sts. has tours during the summer from 7:45 to 11:00 a.m. and from 12:30 to 3:00 p.m., regular hours are 9 to 11 and 1 to 2:30 p.m., Mon. through Fri. children must be accompanied by an adult.

GARDENS. The *Denver Botanic Garden,* started only a few years ago, is one of the best in the western United States. A new and intriguing greenhouse has been built, and the offices and library are housed in one of Denver's finest old mansions. The garden also offers one of the best views of the mountains. Library and Garden House open from 9 a.m. to 5 p.m., Mon. through Sat. All the Denver parks have well-planned and cared-for flower displays, as does the Civic Center Complex.

MUSIC. Denver offers a variety of musical entertainment throughout the year. During the summer months outdoor band concerts are given nightly in City Park, with a background of changing fountain displays. *Red Rocks' Music Festival* during July and August, at Denver's outstanding mountain park, features nationally known talent. Throughout the year, various musical events are staged at the Denver Auditorium; and the *Denver Symphony,* under the baton of Brian Priestman, gives concerts twice a week in the winter to near sellout crowds, plus special youth concerts. A *businessmen's orchestra* performs regularly. Nightclubs around town bring in nationally known talent on a fairly regular basis.

STAGE AND REVUES. *Elitch Gardens,* a large amusement park at 38th and Tennyson St., is the home of America's oldest summer theater. A new production is mounted each week with nationally known stars. The *Denver Post's "opera under the stars"* is a yearly presentation of light opera or popular musicals, free to the public, usually late in July, at Cheesmen Park. The *Denver Civic Ballet,* an amateur group, performs throughout the year, with a major Christmas performance annually. Denver's beautiful *Bonfils Theater* presents several productions throughout the year. The drama department at the *University of Denver* presents an excellent selection of plays throughout the year with interesting and unusual settings. The *Denver Auditorium* plays host to a number of national companies of Broadway productions. Other "live" theaters are the *Trident* and the *Third Eye.*

NIGHTCLUBS. Denver offers a wide variety of nighttime entertainment. *Taylor's Supper Club,* at 7000 W. Colfax Ave., has been home for the Taylors for some fifteen years. The entertainment is good, and so is the food.

During the summer months *Elitch's* brings in theater productions and popular entertainers.

The *Warehouse Restaurant,* at 4444 Leseale Dr., brings in popular musical groups and nightclub entertainers as does *Marvelous Marv's* in Larimer Square.

Rock and other youth-oriented concerts generally take place in the *Denver Coliseum.*

BARS. The better bars in Denver are primarily either the hotel bars or the quiet bar-and-grill type. The city also abounds with entertainment bars and neighborhood taverns. The *Albany Hotel Bar* has been known for many years among the traveling public as always dispensing a stiff drink for a reasonable price. *The Gayety,* at 1643 Welton St., and *Shaner's* at 610 17th St., do booming luncheon trades with the local executives and are excellent places for good food and good drinks, rapidly served. Both are dimly lit, and one is not rushed in either establishment. The *Ship's Tavern* at the *Brown Palace Hotel* is a favorite with the newspaper world as well as the general public. The drinks are good, and the prime ribs cannot be beat. This is one bar where an unescorted woman may relax. It is a policy here that no male may join a woman or group of women once they are seated; a woman must meet her escort outside the tavern and be seated with him.

 SUMMER SPORTS. Denver has eighteen public *golf courses* and a number of excellent private clubs. The city parks have *tennis courts* and *swimming* pools. There are several *archery, trap,* and *rifle* ranges. *Boating* is possible on Sloans Lake, W. 26th Ave. at Sheridan Blvd., and at Cherry Creek Reservoir, ten miles southeast on State 83. Both have facilities for sail and power boats, and for water-skiing.

 WINTER SPORTS. *Skiing:* the closest ski area is just forty-four miles away, others are a bit further but still readily accessible, and now that the Eisenhower Tunnel is finished, many additional ski areas are within an easy drive of Denver. *Ice skating:* year-round skating is available at Denver University, or, in season, Court Place Plaza, downtown at 16th St. and Court Pl., and in the numerous lakes and ponds of the city's parks.

 SPECTATOR SPORTS. *Automobile racing:* Englewood and Lakeside speedways offer drag and sports car racing throughout the summer, and the Continental Divide Raceways is only a twenty-minute drive south. *Baseball:* the *Denver Bears* oppose American Association foes at the Denver Mile High Stadium during the summer. *Basketball:* the *Denver Rockets* of the American Basketball Association and the University of Denver basketball team. *Football:* the *Denver Broncos* of the National Football League. *Golf:* Denver hosts numerous golf tournaments during the summer months. *Hockey:* the *Denver Spurs* of the World Hockey League are popular as is the team from the University of Denver. *Horse and dog racing:* horseracing takes place at the Centennial Turf Club and greyhound races at the Mile High Kennel Club. *Rodeo:* the National Western Livestock, Horse Show and Rodeo is held in January at the Stockyards and the coliseum.

 SHOPPING. At the hub of the Rocky Mountain region, Denver has much to offer in the way of interesting and unusual shops. Some of particular interest to the traveler include *Kohberg's* at 211 16th St. across from the Hilton Hotel, with its own Indian silversmith; it is one of the most fascinating browsing shops around. Jewelry of distinctive design may be seen at *Donald Pick's*, in the Hilton Hotel. Mr. Pick is an authority on star sapphires. *Miller's Stockman Supply,* at 1350 Stout St., is one of the world's largest suppliers of gear and clothing for the stockman. In the *Cherry Creek Shopping Center* and the surrounding area are a number of notable shops, among them *Poco Imports,* 2617 East Third Ave. This is a charming, informal shop of Mexican imports. For the fashion-conscious male in the party, *Homer Reed, Ltd.,* 715 17th St., and *Robert Wilson's* at 1712 E. 6th Ave., are both interesting. The ladies will enjoy *Montaldo's,* 1632 California St., or *Cates First Avenue,* 105 Fillmore Street. Book lovers should visit *Fred Rosenstock's,* with one of the larger collections of Western Americana. Rosenstock also specializes in rare books. Skiers and sports enthusiasts will enjoy *Bob Kidders Ski Shop,* 1035 Cherokee St., and the *Aspen Leaf,* 221 Detroit St. A delightful boutique, *Amie's,* at the Hilton Inn, has many different items. Also at the Hilton Inn is *Joliffe's Oriental Art Shop.* Harry Hoffman's, at 18th and Glenarm Sts., one of the world's largest liquor emporiums, will interest many. *Cinderella City,* a super large shopping complex in Englewood, the western part of Denver, has a variety of types and sizes of shops, from the larger department stores to the smallest boutiques. *Larimer Square,* around 1430 Larimer St., houses some of the newest and most unique shops in Denver, from *Poor Richards Leather Shoppe* (with fine hand-crafted leathers) to bike shops, import shops from around the world, candle corners, and more.

WHAT TO DO WITH THE CHILDREN. A full day may easily be spent in *City Park*, with its zoo, children's zoo, and playgrounds. The *Denver Museum of Natural History and Planetarium* are in the park and should not be missed. Band concerts are given nightly in the summer months. *Congress Park* has a large outdoor swimming pool and *Cherry Creek Reservoir* offers boating, swimming, and water-skiing. *Elitch Gardens* has a delightful kiddieland, as well as the usual amusement-park attractions and beautiful flower gardens. *Lakeside Amusement Park*, with a huge indoor pool, stock-car races, speedboating and amusement rides, has long been a favorite with children. The Colorado *State Capitol, Governor's Mansion*, and *State Museum* are all interesting and open to the public. *Mile High Stadium*, home of the Denver Bears baseball team and the Denver Broncos football team, offers an evening of spectator sport whenever the teams are playing at home. The *Denver Public Library* and *Phipps Auditorium* often have films or lectures of interest to children. Young ladies will delight in the *Goodwill Industries Doll Museum*, and both boys and girls will enjoy the *Wax Museum*. Miniature golf in the summer will keep children busy at *Zeckendorf Plaza* at May-D&F. The *Colorado Railroad Museum*, in a depot-style building, houses many early Colorado railroad items. A trip to *The Fort*, an authentic reproduction of Bent's Fort, may be of interest—the children may try a piece of buffalo meat and browse in the trading post.

AROUND THE DENVER AREA

HOTELS AND MOTELS in Denver range from the old, established, world-famous Brown Palace through its sister lodgings in the deluxe and expensive categories, then on to the many fine hotels scattered along the metropolitan area's highways and side streets. Many of the latter are connected to national chain operations. Cost figures are generally for the minimum or moderate priced rooms, unless a range is indicated. Listings are in order of price category.

The price categories in this section, for double occupancy, will average as follows: *Deluxe* $26, *Expensive* $20, *Moderate* $16, and *Inexpensive* $12. For a more complete description of these categories, see the *Hotels & Motels* part of THE ROCKIES & PLAINS *Facts at Your Fingertips* at the front of this volume.

DENVER

The Brown Palace. *Deluxe.* Tremont and 17th Sts. Truly one of the world's fine hotels, with superb service, western hospitality, and tasteful decoration. Elegant dining in the *Palace Arms* or the *San Marco Room*, relaxed dining in the *Ship Tavern*, where prime rib reigns. Color TV, beauty and barber shops, drugstore. 825-3111

Cosmopolitan Hotel. *Deluxe.* Broadway and 18th Ave. In the heart of the entertainment and financial district, this large hotel provides TV, beauty shop, restaurant, cocktail lounge, entertainment. 623-2181

Denver Hilton. *Deluxe.* 1550 Court Pl. A large establishment with connecting bridge to *May-D & F* store. The block-long second-floor lobby is unusual. Five dining areas and cocktail lounge. Heated pool, saunas, color TV, barber and beauty shops, drugstore, airport bus available. In-building parking. 893-3333

Radisson Denver Hotel. *Deluxe.* 1790 Grant St. This enlarged hotel is located a short distance from the downtown area and features a sun deck and roof garden. Heated rooftop pool, TV. Dining room, coffee shop, cocktail lounge, barber and beauty shops, drugstore, free parking. *Playboy Club* on top floor. 292-1500

Regency Inn. 3900 Elati St. at W. 38th Ave. A large hotel in north Denver with color TV, two pools, saunas, exercise rooms, barber and beauty shops, restaurant and cocktail lounge. Free airport bus. 433-6131

Writers' Manor. *Deluxe.* 1730 S. Colorado Blvd. A large, modern motel with two heated pools, sauna, color TV. *The Tiffin Inn* serves excellent food and beverages. 756-887

Cherry Creek Inn. *Expensive.* 600 S. Colorado Blvd., 1 mi. north of Colorado Blvd. I–25 exit. This large motel offers a quiet, relaxed stay in southeast Denver. Color TV, heated pool, playground, barber and beauty shops, The *Red Slipper Room* is one of Denver's better eating establishments. 757-3344

Country Village Motor Inn. *Expensive.* 4700 Kipling St., on I–70 in Wheatridge. A large motel with spacious rooms, two heated pools, sauna, steam baths, exercise room, color TV, 24-hour cafe, cocktail lounge, entertainment. 423-4000

Four Winds Motor Hotel. *Expensive.* 4600 W. Colfax Ave., 3 mi. west on US 40. Medium-sized hotel in west Denver. Heated pool, color TV, nicely landscaped grounds. Dancing nightly, cocktail lounge, home of the *Captain's Table* restaurant. 244-8001

Holiday Inn-Central. *Expensive.* 1975 W. Bryant St. at W. 20th Ave. Near the Denver Bears Stadium, this circular building offers attractive rooms, heated pool, color TV, free coffee, rooftop restaurant, cocktail lounge. Free airport bus. 433-8331

Royal Inn of Denver. *Expensive.* 3270 Youngfield, 15 mi. northwest at I–70 exit 62 in Wheatridge. A medium-sized motel in a Denver suburb offering heated pool, indoor therapy pool, sauna, color TV, restaurant, cocktail lounge. Free airport bus. 238-7701

Sheraton Inn-Airport. *Expensive.* 3535 Quebec St. at Stapleton Airport. This modern hotel offers color TV, indoor heated pool, sauna, health club, restaurant and cocktail lounge. Free airport bus. 333-7711

Broadway Plaza. *Moderate.* Broadway at 11th Ave., 4 blks. south of State Capitol. In addition to attractive rooms, there are color TV, rooftop sundeck, free coffee. 24–hour cafe nearby. 266-3501

Continental Denver Motor Hotel. *Moderate.* Valley Hwy. at N. Speer Blvd. This large, easily accessible motel offers guests a large heated pool, color TV, barber, free coffee, good dining room, coffee shop, cocktail lounge, dancing. 433-6677

Denver TraveLodge. *Moderate.* Valley Hwy. at Speer Blvd. Small motel offers color TV, free coffee, sundeck. 24-hour coffee shop nearby. 458-5454

Kipling Inn. *Moderate.* 715 Kipling St., 9½ mi. southwest just off US 6 in Lakewood. This west Denver motel offers heated pool, color TV, playground, restaurant and cocktail lounge. Some units with kitchens. 232-5000

Quality Inn-Central. *Moderate.* 1840 Sherman St. A large motel within walking distance of downtown away from the traffic offering heated pool, color TV, restaurant and cocktail lounge. Covered parking. 244-4171

Ramada Inn-West. *Moderate.* 7150 W. Colfax Ave., 5 mi. west on US 40 in Lakewood. A large, well-run and pleasant member of the chain offering heated pool, sundeck, color TV, restaurant, cocktail lounge. Free bus to airport. 238-1251

Royal Host. *Moderate.* 930 E. Colfax Ave. Not far from downtown this motel offers comfortable rooms with refrigerators, outside, glass-enclosed elevator, color TV, free coffee. 24-hour restaurant nearby. 244-8081

American Family Lodge. *Inexpensive.* 5888 N. Broadway, 4 mi. north at I-25 exit 110. A good family motel with large, attractive rooms, TV, heated pool, playground. 892-5500

American Family Lodge-West. *Inexpensive.* 4735 Kipling St., 8 mi. west on

I-70 in Wheatridge. Large motel with heated pool, TV. 24-hour cafe opposite. 423-0800

Anchor. *Inexpensive.* 2323 S. Broadway, 4 mi. south on State 87. Small motel with TV, free coffee, pets, sundeck. 24-hour cafe nearby. 744-3281

DINING OUT. Denver is an eating-out town and offers much in the way of interesting and unusual fare. While there are many excellent restaurants serving international cuisine, those serving steak and lobster are particularly prevalent and popular. Most good restaurants prefer that reservations be made for dinner. Prices are for the medium-priced meals unless a range is indicated. For other worthwhile restaurants, check hotel listings. Restaurants are in order of price category.

Restaurant categories are as follows: *Deluxe* $9.50 and up, *Expensive* $6–$8.50, *Moderate* $4–$6, and *Inexpensive* $2–$3.50. These prices are for *hors d'oeuvres* or soup, *entré*

Editor's Choices

Rating restaurants is, at best, a subjective business, and obviously a matter of personal taste. It is, therefore, difficult to call a restaurant "the best" and hope to get unanimous agreement. The restaurants listed below are our choices of the best eating places in Denver, and the places we would choose if we were visiting the city.

CHATEAU PYRENÉES   Continental Cuisine
Elegant and authentic French cooking, with only one sitting each evening. Six courses are served, and there is a first class wine cellar to provide tempting libations. A normal meal here will take about three hours to consume. Average price for dinner (per person): $25.00. Interstate 25 at Yosemite Circle (west of Araphahoe Rd.), tel. 770-6660.

PALACE ARMS   Continental Cuisine
This is the choice of most of Denver's social lions, and a perennial winner of gastronomic awards. The decor is evocative of France, and the staff is all European. The food is carefully prepared, and the service is in the grand manner. Native steaks are also a specialty. Average price for dinner (per person): $13.50. 17th St. at Tremont Place (Brown Palace Hotel), tel. 825-3111.

EMERSON STREET EAST   Steak House
Top quality, Colorado-raised beef is the prime appeal. Draws a crowd interested in sports and sporting, and the actual Heisman Trophy (for individual football excellence) is on display. Average price for dinner (per person): $11.00. 900 East Colfax Ave., tel. 222-2888.

LAFFITE   Continental Cuisine
Located in Larimer Square, the now-restored district that housed the first businesses ever built in Denver. Continental specialties are complemented by excellent seafood and some Creole dishes. Dining on two levels, with mere mortals served in the main dining room, and the "jet set" in the special room in the basement. Average price for dinner (per person): $13.50. 14th & Larimer Streets, tel. 222-5811.

KYOTO
Japanese Food

Four chefs from Japan hold forth in the new Japanese center. Tatami rooms for those who care for authentic seating on the grass-matted floors, and also hibachi tables where you can eat where food is cooked. Average price for dinner (per person): $11.00. 19th & Lawrence Streets (Sakura Square), tel. 572-3441.

Other recommended restaurants:

FRENCH

Quorum. *Expensive.* 233 E. Colfax Ave. A favorite with the Capitol set across the street, Denver's award-winning restaurant features Neptune *mousseline, entrecote au poivre, tournedos,* and flaming desserts. Excellent cuisine and wine cellar. Open 11:30 a.m. to 2 p.m., 5:30 to 10:30 p.m.; Sat. 5:30 to 11 p.m.; Sun. 5:30 to 9 p.m. 244-8146

Top of the Rockies. *Expensive.* 1616 Glenarm Pl. in the Security Life Building. Following the breath-taking ride in a glass-enclosed elevator, the quiet charm of a French alpine village greets you. The view of the city and mountains from the thirtieth floor adds beauty to the charm of the restaurant. Specialties are Chateaubriand, flaming dishes. Dancing, entertainment, Tues. to Sat. Open 11 a.m. to 2:30 p.m., 5 to 10 p.m.; Fri. and Sat. to 11 p.m.; Sun. 11:30 to 2:30, 5 to 10 p.m. 825-3321

AMERICAN/INTERNATIONAL

Cafe Promenade. *Expensive.* 1430 Larimer St. In historical Larimer Square, this quaint and attractive restaurant features Continental cuisine with veal, lamb, and seafood especially prepared, and they do their own baking. Weather permitting, there is outdoor dining. Wine cellar open 9 a.m. to 11:30 p.m. Closed Sun. 244-4209

Jake's. *Expensive.* 3900 Elati St. at W. 38th Ave. in the Regency Inn Hotel. Elegant, candlelit dining. House specialties are beef Wellington, prime rib, Chateaubriand, lobster thermidor, house pastries. Open 11:30 a.m. to 2 p.m., 5:30 to 10:30 p.m.; Fri. and Sat. from 6 p.m. 458-6789

The Fort. *Moderate.* 17 mi. southwest just off US 285 near Morrison. Modeled after an early-day Colorado fur trading fort, this charming restaurant is set in the foothills overlooking Denver. Buffalo, elk, and beef steaks are charcoal-broiled Indian and trapper style. Open 5 to 10 p.m. 697-4771

Hungry Dutchman. *Moderate.* 7209 S. Clinton, ¼ mi. east of I–25 exit 89 in Englewood. Generous portions of good food in a Dutch setting. Specialties are prime rib, beef fondue, lobster and crab. Open 5:30 to 10 p.m.; Sat. 5 to 11 p.m.; Sun. noon to 9 p.m. 771-0285

Hungry Farmer. *Moderate.* 6925 W. Alameda, 1 mi. south of US 6 in Lakewood. Hearty farm food is served in a large barn. Prime rib, steak, barbecued ribs, chicken are only part of Granny's selection. Open 5:30 to 10 p.m.; Sat. 5 to 11 p.m.; Sun. noon to 9 p.m. 238-4321

Drumstick. *Inexpensive.* 6501 W. Colfax Ave., 3 mi. west on US 40. This good family restaurant serves chicken, shrimp, deluxe hamburgers. Daily specials including all-you-can-eat chicken 'n dumplins. Open 11:30 a.m. to 9:30 p.m. Also at: 7400 N. Federal Blvd., 428-3596; and 4095 S. Santa Fe Dr., 761-1513

STEAK HOUSES

Scotch-N-Sirloin. *Deluxe.* 1196 Grant St. in the Gotham Apartment Hotel. An intimate and romantic spot. They have steak, prepared in the manner of nine different countries. 266-3551

El Rancho Colorado. *Expensive.* 18 mi. west at I–70 exit 55A in Golden. In addition to steak and prime rib, they serve fresh, boned rainbow trout. The rustic atmosphere includes a terrace cocktail lounge with a fireplace called "The Forge." A charming restaurant in the heart of the mountains. Open 5 to 10 p.m.; Sun., noon to 8 p.m. 277-0666

Golden Ox. *Moderate.* 3150 E. Colfax Ave. Charcoal-broiled aged steaks are served here in a Western setting. This popular restaurant is open 11:30 a.m. to 10 p.m.; Sat. 5 to 11 p.m.; Sun. 4 to 9:30 p.m. 377-8894

North Woods Inn. *Moderate.* 6115 S. Santa Fe Dr., 12 mi. southwest on US 85 in Littleton. This locally popular restaurant serves steak, lobster, and logging camp food with their own sour dough bread. The decor is north woods. Open 5 to 10:30 p.m.; Sun., noon to 9:30. Closed Mon. from Sept. to May. 794-2112

SEAFOOD

Boston Half Shell. *Expensive.* 1020 15th at Arapahoe in Brooks Towers. In a rustic New England harborside decor, fresh seafood flown in daily is expertly prepared. Live Maine lobster is a specialty. Nightly entertainment in the piano bar. Open 11 a.m. to 11 p.m.; Fri. and Sat. to midnight; Sun. 5 to midnight. 825-4609

Fisherman's Cove. *Expensive.* 1512 Curtis St. Fresh- and salt-water seafood, flown in fresh daily, is served in an atmosphere that recaptures the 18th-century New England fishing village. Decor includes authentic antiques and artifacts of that era. Waterfall fills live lobster tank. Open 11:30 a.m. to 2 p.m., 5:30 to 10 p.m.; Fri. to 11 p.m.; Sat. 5:30 to 11 p.m. Closed Sun. 893-1325

POLYNESIAN

Trader Vic's. *Expensive.* Broadway and 18th Ave. in the Cosmopolitan Hotel. Polynesian, Cantonese, and Continental dishes are served in a South Seas decor. Exotic drinks are available from the bar. Jacket and tie. Open 11 a.m. to 1:30 a.m. Closed major hols. 623-2181

MEXICAN

La Bonita. *Inexpensive.* 1351 Court Pl. Authentic Mexican food in a charming restaurant decorated with murals that tell the history of Mexico. *Albondigas,* Mexican meatballs, are an unusual specialty. Cafeteria style at lunch, table service in the evening. Open 10 a.m. to 10 p.m.; Sat. from 11:30 a.m. Closed Sun. 543-9103

GERMAN

Alpine Village Inn. *Moderate.* 1150 S. Colorado Blvd. This small restaurant serves remarkable food amid a Bavarian decor that includes a waterfall and fireplace. Specialties are sauerbraten, roast caponette, steak. Special children's plates are available. Open 5 to 10 p.m.; Sun., noon to 8:30 p.m. Closed Mon. 756-3802

Bratskeller. *Moderate.* 1430 Larimer. Located in Larimer Square this Bavarian restaurant serves bratwurst, shrimp boiled in beer, shish kebab with a complete selection of imported beers, wines and liquors. Dining in an outdoor beer garden or indoors where there is an indoor-outdoor fireplace. Open 11 a.m. to 2 a.m.; Sun. 1 p.m. to midnight. 244-9645

JAPANESE

Fuji-en Sukiyaki House. *Moderate.* 930 Lincoln St. Authentic Japanese food and drink are served either at traditional low tables or at conventional tables and chairs. Specialties are sukiyaki, tempura, teriyaki and Japanese saki. Open 4 p.m. to 12:30 a.m.; Sun. 4 to 10 p.m. 266-2178

ITALIAN

Mario's. *Expensive.* 1747 Tremont Pl. While you enjoy fine Italian-American cuisine, "Mario's Singers" serenade you with their renditions of grand opera, light opera, and popular Broadway musical hits. A unique restaurant with an Italian cafe atmosphere. Open 5:30 p.m. to 2 a.m. Closed Sun. 825-4271

HUNGARIAN

The Golden Fiddle. *Expensive.* 3370 S. Acoma. Strolling violinists, continental specialties, wonderful Hungarian wines and authentic atmosphere make this an unusual and enjoyable place to dine. Reservations suggested. Open 5:30 to 10 p.m. Closed Sun. and Mon. 781-7819

EXPLORING COLORADO

Colorado is such a large state, with so many interesting attractions, that a visitor could spend two weeks driving through it and still not cover every area, or anywhere near all its important features. It takes more than a day just to drive through it: Julesburg in the northeastern corner (named for Jules Beni, the Overland Stage station agent whose ears were cut off by badman Jake Slade) is all of 591 highway miles across plains and over peaks from Cortez in the southwestern corner (Ute and Navajo country).

Three one-day trips with Denver for a base of operations, and one more ambitious circular trip around the state, have been planned. They have been designed to interlock so that, for example, the vacationer can leave our first tour at Granby and enter the circle tour after a short drive to Dillon.

Only two major sections of the state are missed in these tours. The first is the eastern plains, notably the agriculturally rich South Platte and Arkansas river valleys, with warm-water fishing, harvest festivals and pheasant hunting. The other is the sparsely populated northwest (trout fishing in the upper Yampa River and its tributaries, skiing at Steamboat Springs, deer and elk hunting, and Dinosaur National Park where one can watch paleontologists working to uncover dinosaur fossils).

A First Tour

Take the Valley Highway (I-25) north out of Denver. Turn off on the Denver-Boulder Turnpike, which is plainly marked, 3.5 miles north of the Denver city limits.

Approaching Boulder, the towering, tilted, slablike peaks on the left are the Flatirons. At their base, standing out like a medieval castle, is the new home of the National Center for Atmospheric Research. Nearby are the National Bureau of Standards Laboratories, for study of radio waves and cryogenics, the science of extremely cold temperatures. Boulder is the home of the University of Colorado, whose parklike campus and distinctive red sandstone buildings at the foot of the Flatirons make it one of the nation's most beautiful schools. Folsom Field,

69

where Big Eight Conference football games are played, seats 50,000. A spectacular side trip is a drive up Flagstaff Mountain for picnics and a view of Boulder and the plains.

Now you have a choice. You can continue north through Boulder fifteen miles along State 7 to Lyons. The road leads along the foothills with a broad panorama to the right of an agricultural plain dotted with irrigation reservoirs. Lyons, where much Colorado sandstone is quarried for use in patios and building, is also the entrance to the North St. Vrain Canyon, leading to Estes Park. This is a pleasant twenty-mile climb up relatively gentle slopes, much of it within Roosevelt National Forest.

Or, for a view of more unusual country, turn west in Boulder on State 119 for a sixteen-mile drive up Boulder Canyon to the rugged mountain town of Nederland. The last two miles wind along the edge of Barker Reservoir, deep, cold, and fair for fishing when full. Turn right at Nederland onto State 172, the Peak to Peak road. It winds through lodgepole pine forests, with startling views of the Continental Divide's rocky ridges. From Nederland it is forty-five easy miles to Estes Park by way of the tiny communities of Ward, Raymond, and Allenspark. Spur roads on each side of 172 lead to alpine lakes with picnic areas and hiking trails, and to slumbering old mining camps long abandoned to wind, weather and packrats. Don't be in a hurry to cover this stretch. Exploratory excursions along these side roads will prove rewarding. Of particular interest is Arapaho Glacier, the southernmost living glacier, which supplies a portion of Boulder's municipal water; it can be reached by a four-mile hike.

Rocky Mountain National Park

Only a tenderfoot looks for a park at Estes Park. "Park" is an old western term for a mountain valley, and this was Joel Estes' domain in 1860. When two other families moved in to share this huge, rugged hollow in the Rockies, Estes moved out, complaining of too many people. Estes Park is the gateway to Rocky Mountain National Park, a 405-square-mile reserve of towering peaks and untouched forests set aside for public amazement and enjoyment in 1915. The town of Estes Park has a year-round population of only about 1,500, but in summer tens of thousands of visitors flock to the resort hotels, dude ranches, motels and campgrounds in the area. An aerial tramway to the top of 8,896-foot Prospect Mountain offers a breathtaking view of the peaks and valleys. Boating and fishing on Lake Estes, scores of miles of riding and hiking trails, and hundreds of miles of trout streams are other attractions in this area. The summit of Longs Peak (14,256 feet) can be scaled via trail by most persons in reasonably good health, but its sheer East Face is one of the nation's most challenging climbs.

The wilds of Rocky Mountain National Park can be explored afoot at leisure, or one can drive through it over the nation's renowned Trail Ridge Road, skirting chasms a thousand feet deep, and winding over the windswept tundra above the timberline. Summer comes late to the high country, but brings with it a profusion of exquisite, tiny wildflowers. Near the top of Milner Pass, 10,758 feet high (where you cross the Continental Divide), is a museum of tundra ecology where the wonderfully diverse flora and fauna of this climatically inhospitable land are displayed. Trail Ridge Road is usually closed by snow in late October or early November and not reopened until Memorial Day, sometimes only after strenuous work by road crews, while young athletes celebrate the event by skiing on the snow at the top and on the icy water of Grand Lake at the western foot of the road. In midsummer, however, the country above timberline is delightfully cool after the heat of the plains. Grand Lake (8,380 feet) is considered the world's loftiest yacht anchorage.

It is sixty-two miles from Estes Park to the town of Granby, on the western side of the Divide. Allow yourself three hours for a leisurely drive, more if you can afford it. Three sizable lakes—Grand Lake, Shadow Mountain and Granby Reservoir— make the Granby area a recreation center. Dude ranches abound. The Colorado River and its tributaries provide first-rate trout fishing. The lakes have been planted with kokanee salmon, among other species, and they provide exciting fishing as well as a unique sport—snagging with treble hooks—during the early winter spawning season. Since the kokanee die, anyway, after they spawn, snagging is permitted to avoid wasting a food resource. Granby is also in the center of the Middle Park area, noted for its dude and cattle ranches and lumbering.

Turn east at Granby on US 40. It is an eighty-nine-mile drive back to Denver. The highway runs through vast hay meadows, past Fraser (where President Eisenhower liked to fish), the Winter Park ski development at the western mouth of the Moffat Tunnel, and up over 11,314-foot Berthoud Pass. There's another ski area at the summit and a chair lift that carries hardy tourists even higher in summer for some literally breathtaking views from atop the Continental Divide.

Once you've crossed Berthoud, it's only an hour's drive, all downhill, to Denver, by way of the old mining town of Idaho Springs, now a bustling resort town.

Drive west out of Denver on Alameda Avenue, past expanding housing developments and sprawling Denver Federal Center, a sword-to-plowshares operation where a World War II Remington ammunition plant has been converted into headquarters for major government agencies. The world-famous Bureau of Reclamation Laboratories test dam designs and train hydraulic engineers from all parts of the Free World. Alameda Avenue swings over the rock outcroppings known as the Hogbacks and opens up on Red Rocks Park, the outstanding feature of which is a 10,000-seat amphitheater between two towering red sandstone promontories. One, shaped like the prow of a giant liner, is called "Shiprock." The other is "Creation Rock." Silt deposits under a prehistoric sea formed the layers that went into these rocks; a cataclysmic upheaval forced the sea to retreat, shattering the rock formations and thrusting them upward. Erosion by wind and rain carved them into the fanciful shapes visible today. Many visitors find it well worth their time to park their cars and stroll into the amphitheater for a view of Denver in the distance, and to contemplate the immense forces that created this park. Easter Sunrise services are held here, and concerts are scheduled during the summer. The stage is one hundred feet wide and the acoustics are said to be ideal for musical productions.

First Territorial Capital

From Red Rocks Park, backtrack to the Hogback Road (State 26) and drive north a mile to US 40. This is a bit tricky here, so watch it. Bear right, downhill, on US 40, which takes you back toward Denver. Stay on the highway about a mile, then take the turnoff to the left toward Golden on County 93. The turnoff is plainly marked. Another mile takes you to four-lane US 6, and Golden is just a mile farther on. Here is the site of the first territorial capital, the Colorado School of Mines (where tomorrow's civil, mining, and petroleum engineers get a first-rate education), and the Coors Brewery, which is open for tours.

From Golden, return to US 6 for a thirteen-mile drive up winding Clear Creek Canyon. The highway crosses and recrosses a brawling mountain stream that, despite its name, is rarely clear. The road bores through some tunnels and clings to the creek bank at the foot of beetling cliffs. It is difficult to believe that the route follows the bed of a long-abandoned railroad.

The Old Opera House

At the fork, turn right onto State 119. Seven more miles of gentle climbing brings you to Blackhawk, which looks like a set from a Western movie. Turn left here on State 279. Central City is only a mile up this steep, twisting road, but it is a memorable ride. The earth on each side is cruelly gashed by the remains of gold mines. Victorian homes, many restored and used as summer residences, cling precariously to the hillsides. Once 15,000 persons lived in these two communities. Now the permanent residents number scarcely more than 350. But summer is a lively time. The Central City Opera House on Eureka Street, built in 1878 with granite walls four feet thick, is the home of an opera and play season. Artists from the Metropolitan and other leading opera companies fly out with their families to vacation and sing. The operas are followed by a Broadway hit play, often staged with the original cast. The Opera House, the Teller House Hotel completed in 1872 (President Grant slept here), and other historic buildings are preserved by Denver University. Along with Victorian furnishings, diamond dust mirrors and the like, the Teller House boasts a genuine *Face on Barroom Floor,* painted on the floor of the Gold Nugget Bar in 1936 as a prank by the late Herndon Davis. The face, of a dark and brooding beauty, is protected by plate glass.

The pavement ends at Central City (8,560 feet and cool even in midsummer), but the adventure is just starting. Continue up the Quartz Hill Road, usually kept in good shape, to Russell Gulch. Now begins a looping, twisting, seven-mile descent to Idaho Springs. Take it easy. It's not dangerous if you're careful, but it's a long way straight down if you should slip! The scenery, especially in fall when the distant hillsides are ablaze with golden aspen, is well worth the hairpin curves.

Idaho Springs, named for the hot springs known to the Indians and still used today, is the center of a once-rich mining district that has readjusted its sights to the tourist trade. Take the overpass that crosses US 6-40 and follow State 103 along Chicago Creek. Summer homes dot the area. The road climbs steadily through stands of lodgepole pine and aspen for fourteen miles, and suddenly there's gemlike Echo Lake, 10,600 feet above sea level. Camping and picnic facilities are available. Echo Lake is among the mountain parks maintained by the city of Denver, and trails lead to scenic vantage points looking both north and south along the Rockies.

America's Highest Road

Echo Lake is also the place that separates the men from the boys. The more adventuresome can turn off here to State 5, which twists and climbs another fourteen miles, past icy Summit

73

Lake (where sometimes a herd of mountain sheep frolics and distracts trout fishermen) to the very peak of Mount Evans, 14,260 feet high. This is the nation's highest automobile road. Despite the elevation, the trip is not difficult for experienced drivers. Refreshments and souvenirs are available at Crest House, while atop a rock pile a few feet away are the laboratories where cosmic ray and other high-altitude experiments are carried on. One of the thrills of a drive to the top is watching a summer thunderstorm taking shape and swirling and boiling over the forests far below. The altitude is not harmful to a person in good health, although exertion is difficult in the oxygen-thin air. Cars likewise will perform at less than usual efficiency. The road above Echo Lake is closed in winter by snow.

Those who prefer to view their mountains from a distance can skip the Mount Evans trip and continue on paved State 103. It climbs briefly, drops to cross 9,807-foot Squaw Pass, then descends in long, easy grades, with each turn opening on new mountain vistas. The end of the trail here is Bergen Park, another unit in the 20,000-acre Denver mountain parks system. A tiny community has grown up at this crossroads. One of the attractions is Clock Manor, an unusual museum of odd and wonderful timepieces.

Another three miles of driving returns you to US 40, which leads past Genesee, another of Denver's mountain parks. If you see a cluster of out-of-state automobiles parked at the edge of the highway, it probably means the buffalo and elk herds have come out of the timber and are grazing close by.

Don't be in too great a hurry now. The best is yet to come. Two miles farther, take a left turn onto State 68 to 7,500-foot Lookout Mountain, only two miles away. Buffalo Bill's tomb is located here, along with a museum containing Cody's guns, clothing, and mementos of his romantic career. If at all possible, plan to reach Lookout Mountain just before dusk. Watch Metropolitan Denver's lights wink on as darkness creeps across the plains—hundreds of thousands of lights stretching in every direction, criss-crossing a half mile below in a latticework of brilliance. The air will be cool and scented with pine, and Denver will offer you an unforgettable sight from this mountain lookout.

Although it is possible to return to US 40, the more interesting descent is down the seven-mile Lariat Trail, so named because the road twists like a rope. Each turn provides a view of Denver's lights from a different angle. At the foot of the mountain is Golden once again, and from here it's a twenty-minute trip back to Denver via US 6.

As he leaves Denver southbound on I–25, the traveler is tantalized by Pikes Peak, on the southern skyline like the Shining Mountain of old, first misty in the distance, then towering taller and taller as one approaches it. I–25, also called the "Valley Highway," swings across the fringes of downtown Denver, follows the course of the South Platte briefly before swinging southeast past two of Denver's largest industrial plants, the Gates Rubber Company and Samsonite Luggage Company. The six-lane freeway pinches down to five past the University of Denver stadium (the school no longer has a football team), and the comfortable upper-middle-class southeast Denver residential area. After several miles of apartment complexes the road gives way to rolling wheatfields and pastureland.

Thirty miles south of Denver is Castle Rock, seat of Douglas County, and a town that takes its name from a distinctive castle-shaped rock that rears behind the community. A rough road winds to the summit, where, on a clear day (and it's usually clear), one can see nearly two hundred miles in every direction. Indians and early explorers used it as a landmark.

The terrain rises almost imperceptibly over the next nine miles until the highway crosses the Palmer Lake divide south of Larkspur.

Air Force Academy

Pikes Peak is closer now, and so is the Air Force Academy, youngest and flashiest of the service schools. The entrance is plainly marked. Stop at the sentry box to pick up a map, then drive directly to the overlook for a general view of the main Academy buildings across the expansive intramural athletic fields. The academic area is not open to the public, but various other areas are. Everyday except Sunday and during the brief summer vacations when the cadets are visiting Air Force bases, the cadet corps assembles at 11:30 A.M. to march in formation to lunch at the dining hall. This is a solemn, stirring parade to martial music and a sight well worth seeing. Also open to the public is the many-spired glass and aluminum chapel, variously described as an accordian-like collection of wigwams and an inspiring contemporary cathedral. The best way is to see and judge the chapel's beauty for yourself. Fine roads through the 17,900-acre Academy grounds are open during daylight hours, and it is possible to drive through the reservation and join I–25 just north of Colorado Springs.

"Little Lun'on"

Colorado Springs is the state's second largest city, long famous as a watering place and summer resort. It was founded in 1871 by

General William Jackson Palmer, promoter of the Denver and Rio Grande Railroad. General Palmer, who made or unmade towns depending on where he built his railroads, was also prominent in the planning of Colorado Springs, which he determined would have a gracious and cultured atmosphere not unlike his home town of London. Thus its nickname "Little Lun'on," also attributable to its popularity with British visitors. Pikes Peak looms over the city. In fact, the mountain seems to rise right at the end of Pikes Peak Avenue in downtown Colorado Springs. (There are many places in Colorado with the name "Springs"—Pagosa Springs, Poncha Springs, Steamboat Springs, etc.—but only Colorado Springs is referred to as "The Springs.") Vacationers can spend days visiting the various attractions in this area. A few of the more notable are described in this chapter.

Garden of the Gods is an area of odd and unusual formations of bright sandstone hues. In summer, the Junior Chamber of Commerce sponsors chuckwagon dinners here three times a week. (Reservations necessary.)

In Colorado Springs proper is the Fine Arts Center, with an outstanding permanent collection of southwestern Indian, religious, and folk art, as well as contemporary American works. The Pioneer Museum has a fine collection of locally important historical mementos. The Van Briggle Pottery works offers tours of its plant, where art and garden pottery is created with locally mined clays.

Just south of Colorado Springs is the amazing *Broadmoor Hotel* complex founded by Spencer Penrose. This is a complete resort community in itself, with a luxury hotel, seven dining rooms, convention hall, 36-hole golf course, indoor and outdoor pools, year-round ice-skating rink, rodeo grounds, miniature railway, skiing slope in winter (with a snowmaking machine), carriage museum and zoo. The zoo is on the slopes of Cheyenne Mountain and ranks as one of the finest in the nation. Particularly outstanding is the primate house. High above the zoo, reached by a toll road, is the Shrine of the Sun memorial to Will Rogers. A granite tower, one hundred feet high, houses carillons. The interior walls are decorated with frescoes by the late Randall Davey. An observation balcony provides a sweeping view of Colorado's eastern plains.

Adjoining Colorado Springs on the west, along US 24, is Manitou Springs, a thriving tourist center. The mineral springs from which the community gets its name are still active. Tourist attractions, most of which charge fees, abound. Manitou Springs is also the terminal for the cog railway to the summit of Pikes Peak and the cable car system to the top of Mount Manitou. Don't worry about confusing the two: It costs $8.40 to rideup Pikes Peak, $1.50 to cog up Manitou Mountain. Pikes Peak offers three trips a day, at 9 A.M., 1 P.M. and 5:15 P.M. (the night special). It is advisable to have reservations at least one day in advance. The fee for children under twelve is $4.20; children under five ride free. For the Manitou Cog Rail the fee for children from five to eleven is 75¢. They are open from 10:30 A.M. to 9 P.M., and have runs every thirty minutes.

Driving up Pikes Peak

Four miles beyond Manitou Springs, up steep and historic Ute Pass, is Cascade, the cutoff point for the automobile highway up Pikes Peak. The climbing season usually starts in early June and lasts until the first weekend in October, although the season may be extended, weather permitting. The toll is $1.50 per adult, 25¢ for children six to eleven years old, and under five free. The road to the summit climbs 7,309 feet in nineteen miles. The Pikes Peak Hill Climb automobile races are held each July 4.

US 24 continues to climb gently to Woodland Park, center of an extensive dude ranch and recreation area. Seven miles farther is Divide, where the road forks. US 24 goes on into South Park. State 67, turning left, offers a leisurely eighteen-mile drive through hay meadows and pine groves on the "back" side of Pikes Peak until, at the crest of Tenderfoot Hill, the once fabulously rich Cripple Creek-Victor Gold Fields stretch before you. In summer Cripple Creek bustles with tourists, but when they are gone the basin is peopled by only a handful of residents, many of whom are natives of the area, living buoyed up by the hope that one day gold mining will become profitable again. There is increased talk of reopening several of the mines, so their hopes may soon be realized. The hillsides are dotted with the tailings dumps of abandoned mines and weather-scarred wooden buildings that seem to lean more precariously after every winter. Oldtime residents maintain a free museum, where one can get an accurate idea of what the area was like when twenty thousand persons worked, brawled, reared families, got drunk, became rich, or went broke in Cripple Creek and its satellite communities. (Cripple Creek and its sister ghost, Victor, can also be reached from Colorado Springs by the Gold Camp road, a gravel route that winds, twists and tunnels for thirty-six miles through wild, spectacular country over the abandoned roadbed of the Cripple Creek Short Line Railroad.)

Cripple Creek's liveliest attraction since the end of World War II is the Imperial Hotel, refurbished by Wayne and Dorothy

77

Mackin, where in summer a professional cast stages oldtime melodrrmas. (Reservations are advisable.)

US 85 is an alternate route into Denver from the south, generally following the course of the South Platte. West of the highway, across Plum Creek, almost hidden in the bottom growth, is Louviers, where Du Pont Powder Plant manufactures the dynamite used in mines and mountain construction work.

Fourth Tour—Circling Colorado

This 1,250-mile circular tour of Colorado, beginning and ending at Denver, is designed to take a minimum of four days and hit most of the state's interesting areas not covered in the three previous tours. The tour can be extended to five, six, or more days simply by lingering at places that appeal to the visitor and exploring attractions short distances off the tour route.

This tour starts by going southwest out of Denver on US 285, past Morrison (which is a stone's throw from Red Rocks Park; see *Second Tour*) and up the gash slashed by Turkey Creek into the dark granite foothills of the Rockies. Although the ridges tower high above the road, the highway is wide and the grade gentle. Generally, the route follows the old Denver-Leadville stagecoach route, on which travelers braved rutted trails, primitive accommodations and desperadoes to reach the silver diggings in the two-mile-high Leadville area. Later, the Colorado, South Park & Pacific Railroad followed much the same route in an ambitious if foolhardy effort to reach the coast by way of Leadville. (The dreams of these men were greater than their knowledge of railroad economics. To meet expenses, it was necessary to charge more to transport freight from Denver to Leadville than from New York to San Francisco by way of Cape Horn.) Only a few crumbling ties and rusting spikes, covered by underbrush, remain.

At Bailey, US 285 winds along the banks of the South Platte River. Near Grant, high on a hill to the right, stands the fifty-two-foot-tall glazed white statue of *Christ of the Rockies*. It stands guard over the Santa Maria Camp for Girls and is illuminated at night. Also near Grant, the 23.3-mile-long Roberts Tunnel under the Continental Divide discharges water collected on the Western Slope into the South Platte for eventual delivery to Denver homes and industries.

Favorite Mountain Scene

Sixty-five miles from Denver rises 10,000-foot Kenosha Pass, one of the state's lowest. The highway curves to open a

magnificent panorama of South Park. A lofty valley stretching forty miles to the south and west, almost table-top flat, rimmed by darkly wooded hills and snowcapped peaks, this view of South Park is the favorite mountain scene of many Coloradans in a state of superlative scenes. Several tributaries of the South Platte twist and loop over the park's broad hay meadows (the growing season is too short for other agricultural pursuits) and sleek Herefords and Black Angus cattle graze placidly on land that once heard the thunder of buffalo hooves.

Fairplay, eighty-five miles from Denver and at the western edge of South Park, is the valley's largest community, with a permanent population of fewer than six hundred. The town was named by men who settled the area in 1859 after having been chased out of the nearby Tarryall placer beds by other miners who resented competition. Near the center of Fairplay is a stone monument to "Prunes," a burro that mooched a living from the townsfolk for years after having labored several decades for a variety of prospectors. Local residents have also recreated an oldtime mining town called South Park City, where a visitor can see what frontier life was like more than a century ago.

The tourist may continue down South Park and over Trout Creek Pass thirty-four miles to Buena Vista, on the Arkansas River. The State Reformatory is at Buena Vista, at the base of the Collegiate Range, a string of 14,000-foot peaks with such names as Princeton, Yale, Harvard and Oxford.

Our tour, however, turns north (right) at Fairplay on State 9 toward 11,541-foot Hoosier Pass. Five miles beyond Fairplay is what remains of Alma, once a busy mining and placer site and one of the state's first gold camps. It was here that a dance hall girl, known only as Silver Heels, remained, when others fled, to nurse miners stricken in a smallpox epidemic. Eventually she too contracted smallpox. She survived, but her beauty was destroyed, and one night she slipped away unnoticed. According to legend a heavily veiled woman, presumably Silver Heels, returned to Alma from time to time to visit the graves of miners who died in the epidemic. A mountain northwest of Alma is named in her honor. A rough dirt road leads from Alma over 13,185-foot Mosquito Pass to Leadville, but this is not recommended for the average tourist.

Hoosier Pass over the Continental Divide cuts through the 14,000-foot peaks of the Park Range. A few miles north of the pass is Breckenridge, another old mining camp. An extensive ski and summer home development has been started here. In 1936, it was discovered that a strip of land surrounding Breckenridge had never been taken into the United States. Somehow, the various purchases and annexations had not included the area. The then governor, Ed C. Johnson, by proclamation claimed the land to be a part of the United States and Colorado.

Highway 9 follows the Blue River to Frisco and the Dillon Reservoir, an enormous lake filled for the first time in the summer of 1965. The water stored here is diverted from the Colorado River watershed to the state's eastern slope, flowing under the Continental Divide via the 23.3-mile Roberts Tunnel to Grant, on the way to Denver's mains. A massive earthen dam at Silverthorne holds back the water. The reservoir covered the site of the original town of Dillon, which was moved to a wooded point on the northern edge of the lake. Dillon Reservoir has become a center for boating and fishing, with extensive jeep and riding trails in the mountains surrounding it.

Our route turns left at Frisco onto US 6, along the rippling waters of Tenmile Creek. The seven-mile-long drive to Wheeler Junction is unusual—the massive rock walls that rise almost straight up in a sheer cliff are unlike most Colorado canyons, whose walls taper up in a sharp V.

The left fork of the highway at Wheeler Junction (State 91) leads to Leadville, a community of more than 4,800, two miles above sea level. During the late nineteenth century, when it was one of the world's richest silver producers, it had a population of some 30,000. The glory that was is preserved in places like the Hotel Vendome, Healy House Museum, and the Tabor Opera House. The greatest of the silver kings was H. A. W. Tabor, who built a multi-million-dollar fortune on a $17 grubstake, then died virtually destitute. The Tabor story is the basis for the American opera, *The Ballad of Baby Doe*, which was the name of Tabor's blond second wife. His divorce from his prim and proper first wife, Augusta, to marry Baby Doe, a divorcée herself, was a scandal that rocked both Colorado and Washington, where Tabor had gone as an interim senator. Tabor's last words of advice to Baby Doe were, "hold on to the Matchless," the mine which had made him as much as $100,000 a month. Baby Doe lived her last days as a recluse in a cabin at the Matchless, and she was found frozen to death there in 1935. The mine is preserved as a museum. Many residents of Leadville work at Climax, twelve miles away, where a mountain is systematically being cut down to produce most of the free world's molybdenum, a steel-hardening alloy. This is an area that shouldn't be missed if at all possible.

In the interest of conserving time, however, the tour turns right at Wheeler Junction, remaining on US 6. It leads over Vail Pass and down along Gore Creek to Vail Village, where an alpine ski town has sprouted along with condominium apartments and luxury homes. Fortunate is the visitor whose arrival coincides with the turning of the aspen, usually in mid-September. The lower reaches of the entire Gore Range seem to be orange and gold. The gondola ride to mid-Vail and the spacious lodge there provide an unforgettable vista, particularly if an early snow has frosted the high peaks.

Highway 6 continues westward past Eagle, the answer to a spotsman's dreams, with trout in the Eagle river, land elk and deer in the nearby hills. West of Eagle, the mountains give way to a high plateau. The Colorado and Eagle rivers meet at Dotsero, where two branches of the Denver & Rio Grande Railway come together for the run down spectacular Glenwood Canyon. Here the Colorado River has cut a 1,000-foot chasm between slate-colored cliffs. North of the Colorado lies the White River wilderness area, heavily wooded and virtually unscarred by roads. More than 900,000 acres are set aside in this preserve. Some of the state's best fishing—rainbow, German brown and brook trout that run uniformly more than two pounds each—is to be found in lonely lakes and rushing streams at the end of a fifteen-mile horseback trek. So isolated is the White River country that many longtime Coloradans have never set foot in it. Experienced packers are available as guides.

At the lower end of Glenwood Canyon is Glenwood Springs, principal supply point of a vast recreation area. Within Glenwood is a 600-foot-long swimming pool, open the year around, fed by hot and cold sulphur springs. Both Presidents Teddy Roosevelt and Taft vacationed here. The Roaring Fork, one of the outstanding fishing streams in a state of outstanding streams, enters the Colorado here.

Aspen Fund and Culture

Forty-two miles south of Glenwood Springs, via State 82, is famed Aspen, Colorado's top ski center and an old silver mining town that was transformed into a mountain cultural mecca by the money and vision of the late Chicago industrialist, Walter P. Paepcke. The summer Aspen Music Festival and School, and the Aspen Institute for Humanistic Studies, which sponsors lectures and seminars on a variety of significant subjects, are now widely known. Within a twenty-mile radius of Aspen are some twenty-five trout lakes and a thousand miles of trout streams, plus countless miles of hiking and riding trails. Mountains to challenge expert climbers are numerous, while thrill-seekers can ride sleds behind the Huskies of Toklat Kennels at Ashcroft or explore ghostly ruins abandoned to the elements when the silver petered out. Not far from Aspen, up the green and beautiful Crystal River Valley, is Marble, where stone for the Lincoln Memorial and the Tomb of the Unknown Soldier was quarried. Four huge ski developments—Aspen Mountain, Aspen Highlands, Snowmass and Buttermilk Mountain—offer hundreds of miles of ski runs of varying difficulty, and some of the lifts run in summer to take tourists to scenic lookouts. For the more adventurous driver, State 82 continues over 12,095-foot Independence Pass, graveled but rough, to Leadville.

The tour route, however, backtracks down to Glenwood Springs, and then via US 6, it proceeds twenty-six miles to Rifle. Rifle is at the edge of what undoubtedly is the world's greatest deposit of oil shale. Shale beds two thousand and more feet thick lie in mahogany-colored cliffs to the north and west of Rifle, extending into Utah and Wyoming. These deposits hold more oil than all the petroleum man has used since the beginning of time. Colorado's shale reserves alone are estimated at one trillion, four hundred billion barrels of oil. Scientists employed by both the government and private industry have been working out economical methods of extracting the oil from the rock.

Grand Junction—Uranium Capital

From Rifle, US 6 runs parallel to the Colorado River sixty-two miles to Grand Junction, largest city in western Colorado, with a population of approximately twenty thousand.

Grand Junction, which gets its name from the joining of the Colorado and Gunnison rivers, is a thriving transportation and shipping center. In the mid-fifties it boomed as the capital of the uranium rush. The boom has tapered off, but Grand Junction is still important as the location of the Atomic Energy Commission's raw materials (uranium) procurement office. A few years ago downtown Grand Junction merchants, in an effort to keep business from fleeing to suburban shopping centers, approved a mall-type shopping park along the main street. The experiment resulted not only in beautification of the downtown area, but was an economic success.

Ten miles west of Grand Junction is Colorado National Monument, twenty-eight square miles of weirdly eroded stone spires, canyons and fossil beds. Two to three hours spent in a circle drive along the canyon rims is time well invested.

Make sure your gas tank is full before taking US 50 southeast out of Grand Junction. Nine miles up the highway is the tiny crossing called Whitewater. Turn right here onto State 141, and prepare to enter some of Colorado's wildest, loneliest canyon country, an area largely overlooked by tourists. The highway, paved and well-maintained, stretches through sagebrush flats and dry washes for forty-four miles to Gateway, where it crosses the muddy, shallow Dolores River. For the next thirty-seven miles to Uravan, the road borders first the Dolores, and then the San Miguel (pronounced San M'gill hereabouts) rivers, leading past towering red sandstone cliffs, polished by wind and sand into monolithic slabs, and often into the shapes of ships and pyramids.

Back in 1881, gold-seekers found a soft yellow-orange ore near what is now Uravan. About its only use was for coloring pottery. In 1898, several tons of this ore was shipped to France and Mme. Marie Curie used it in experiments that resulted in the extraction of radium. For the next thirty years, ore from this region produced about half the world's radium supply. A mill was built at Uravan to process vanadium, a steel-hardener, from the same ores. During World War II, in the crash program to develop a nuclear bomb, the waste rock in the tailings piles at the Uravan mill was reprocessed to extract the suddenly precious uranium which had been thrown away. The mill, now operated by Union Carbide, extracts uranium from local ores and vanadium has become just a by-product.

Nineteen miles past Uravan, take the right fork to State 141 for the fifty-seven-mile drive to Dove Creek. This apparent wasteland, thoroughly explored for uranium and oil, has a strange, lonely beauty of its own, but you'll be glad to reach civilization once more at Dove Creek, center of a prosperous pinto bean-growing area. Total distance from Grand Junction to Dove Creek is 169 miles. Dove Creek was little more than a raw frontier until farmers from the dust bowl in eastern Colorado came in to conquer the arid flats. Zane Grey, the western author, lived for some years in Dove Creek.

You are back in the mainstream again. US 160 is a fast, smooth road to Cortez, thirty-seven miles southeast, trading center for sheep herders, cowmen, miners, prospectors, oilfield hands and residents of the Ute Mountain Indian Reservation. Cortez is the jumping-off place to Shiprock and the Navajo Indian country of New Mexico and to Monument Valley, Flagstaff, and the Grand Canyon in Arizona, by way of the new highway through the Four Corners. This is where Utah, Arizona, New Mexico and Colorado meet, the only place where four states come precisely together. With a population of close to seven thousand, Cortez is also the closest city to Mesa Verde National Park, the entrance to which is only ten miles to the east.

There is no other national park quite like Mesa Verde, which means "green table" in Spanish. The table is a plateau, rising fifteen hundred feet above the surrounding valleys. In canyons gashed into the plateau, an early tribe of Indians grew corn with water brought in by primitive irrigation systems, and built apartment-like dwellings under overhanging cliffs. One settlement, called Cliff House, has two hundred rooms on eight levels. A study of tree rings indicates the area suffered a severe drought in the thirteenth century and the Indians wandered away about the year 1276. Thanks to the dry air and the protection of the caves, many well-preserved swellings and artifacts were found by the first white men. The National Park Service has restored some of the ruins and conducts tours among them, with lectures about the people who lived in them seven hundred years ago. Visitors would be wise to visit the museum at park headquarters before joining the tours. The tours are free and start at frequent intervals during the summer season. Limited accommodations are available in the park. Well-marked automobile tours to various ruins are also available.

Spectacular Mountains

Thirty-six miles east of the park entrance is Durango, metropolis of southwestern Colorado, with a population of more than 12,000. Once a wide-open frontier town, Durango is a prosperous trading and tourist center. It is the home of Fort Lewis College, whose campus is atop a steep hill overlooking the city. Durango is at the base of the San Juan mountains, which many Coloradans consider the most spectacular in the state. Fishing, hunting and skiing are available within a few miles of downtown.

The best-known attraction here is the Rio Grande's narrow-gauge train to Silverton, a forty-five-mile trip up the gorge of Rio de las Animas Perdidas (River of Lost Souls), shortened by natives to the Animas River. Belching smoke and cinders, an ancient steam engine chuffs and puffs through thick forests and along steep cliffsides for an unforgettable ride into yesterday. Since capacity is about four hundred passengers (although two sections are run during the height of the season), it is wise to make reservations early. The trains leave at 8:30 and 9:30 A.M., climb nearly three thousand feet, and arrive at Silverton for a two-hour stop. The return trips start at 5:30 and 6:30 P.M., arriving in Durango about three hours later.

The time in Silverton is just long enough to lunch, stroll around the streets and peer into abandoned buildings and browse among the curio shops. If you don't find any agates on the Animas

River's gravel bars, there are numerous youngsters anxious to sell you specimens of iron pyrite, azurite, malachite, or quartz crystals for twenty-five to fifty cents. Although it once boasted 10,000 residents, Silverton now has considerably fewer than a thousand. It is the seat of San Juan County, which has the distinction of being so high and rugged that it has not one acre of farmland in it.

To save time, some visitors prefer to ride up on the train and be met at Silverton by a member of the party who has driven the fifty miles via US 550, continuing north without returning to Durango. (Those who make the round trip by train report the descent is just as interesting, and revealing of new sights, as the ascent.)

Highway 550 rises quickly from Silverton to 11,018-foot Red Mountain Pass (named for the reddish hue of the soil), strikingly beautiful in summer but impassable in winter. This is the "Million Dollar Highway," which follows a toll road route laid out by Otto Mears in the 1880's. The origin of the name is obscure. Some say it was so named because of the cost, while others contend it is because gold-bearing gravel was used before its value was discovered.

Beyond the pass is Ouray (pronounced U-ray), built in a mountain pocket a mile and a half above sea level. This is the heart of the "Switzerland of the Rockies." Within a fifteen-mile radius of Ouray are seventy-one peaks, seven of which are more than 14,000 feet high, and seventeen others that are more than 12,000 feet high. Nearby is the Camp Bird Mine where Thomas F. Walsh, father of Evelyn Walsh McLean, made his fortune. At one time it produced as much as four million dollars a year in gold. Ouray has piped water from a hot springs into a public swimming pool, and maintains a picnic area in Box Canyon, where Canyon Creek plunges down a dark, misty gorge. If you can spare the time, by all means take a jeep trip into the high country along trails calculated to frighten even a mountain goat. The paved highways are spectacular enough, but the high trails, which only a jeep can navigate, offer something totally different to appreciate in this area of rugged vistas.

From Ouray the highway descends gradually to Montrose, thirty-seven miles away, center of a farming, mining and stock-raising area. Fourteen miles outside Montrose is Black Canyon of the Gunnison National Monument.

From Montrose, turn east again on US 50. The road winds through the Gunnison Valley, a rich ranching area. A series of three dams, part of the Curecanti Project to harness the Gunnison, will drown out much of that river's famous trout fishing, but more than five hundred miles of other streams remain in the area. The town of Gunnison, home of Western State College, lies fifty-nine miles east of Montrose. Twenty-eight miles north of Gunnison is Crested Butte, once a dying mining town, now the location of a huge, luxurious winter sports center.

The tour continues sixty miles eastward of Gunnison along US 50 over magnificent, sweeping Monarch Pass (11,312 feet), where skiers find some of the state's deepest snows, to the crossroads of Poncha Springs, where dozens of hot springs bubble with water containing salts similar to those at Hot Springs, Arkansas.

You have a choice here. US 285 heads north to Buena Vista, South Park, and Denver. US 50 continues east to Canon City and Pueblo. (Canon City is the location of the state prison and the Royal Gorge, where the world's highest suspension bridge crosses the 1,000-foot-deep gorge of the Arkansas River.)

Let's go south, for in that direction lie some little-known facets of Colorado, and a culture whose roots reach back to the earliest settlers. Just south of gentle Poncha Pass begins the San Luis Valley, once the bed of an inland sea, and now the largest of Colorado's four high parks, each rimmed by mountain ranges, strung north to south across the state. As much as forty-five miles wide, the valley is more than one hundred miles long and extends across the border into New Mexico. On the east it is bounded by the stark Sangre de Cristo (Blood of christ) range, so named because of the ruddy sunset glow, and on the west by the western portion of the Rio Grande National Forest.

Shortly after entering the valley, US 285 curves west to Saguache (an Indian name, pronounced Sa-watch), remembered in Colorado history as the place where Alfred Packer was imprisoned while awaiting trial. Packer was found quilty of eating five companions to keep himself alive when trapped by deep snow in the mountains near Lake City.

The road, straight as a gun barrel, heads due south to Monte Vista through countryside dotted with artesian wells and richly productive of potatoes, alfalfa, wheat and malting barley.

Alamosa, seventeen miles beyond Monte Vista, is the valley's largest city, with 6,500 residents. It is a rail and shipping hub for lettuce, spinach, peas and other crops grown in the cool, high atmosphere, and the site of Adams State College. Some twenty-four miles south of Alamosa is the village of Manassa, immortalized by sportswriters of a generation ago as the birthplace of Jack Dempsey, the "Manassa Mauler."

Thirteen miles north of Alamosa is tiny Mosco, turning-off point for State 150, to Great Sand Dunes National Monument. Here, a thousand miles from any ocean, nature in a whimsical mood piled up restless sand dunes extending for some ten miles along the foot of the Sangre de Cristo mountains. The crests of the dunes rise to as much as six hundred feet above the valley floor.

The tour turns east at Alamosa onto US 160, skirting 14,317-foot Blanca Peak before reaching Fort Garland, twenty-six miles away. Fort Garland was manned by federal troops from 1858 to 1883, and Kit Carson was its commanding officer for a time. Some of the fort buildings have been restored, and a state museum displays mementos of Indian-fighting days.

I–25, a four-lane highway that runs virtually all the way from Cheyenne, Wyo., on the north, to the New Mexico border, skirts Walsenburg's eastern fringes.

The tour swings north from Walsenburg, forty-eight miles on I–25, to Pueblo. This is Colorado's third largest city, with a metropolitan population of more than 100,000. In under-industrialized Colorado, Pueblo is the center of the state's heavy industry. The Colorado Fuel and Iron plant produces steel, ingots, sheet, rails, and wire for the West's many needs, and many satellite industries have grown up alongside the steel mill. The demand for mill labor brought in people of many ethnic backgrounds, as a result of which Pueblo is probably the state's most cosmopolitan city. Pueblo is also the site of the state mental hospital, and is a trading center for the rich farm towns of the Arkansas Valley which strings out eastward to the Kansas border. Lakes, streams and guest ranches in the San Isabel National Forest are within a few miles of Pueblo. A large section of the flat, dry land between Pueblo and Colorado Springs, 43 miles to the north, is within the Fort Carson military reservation, used as an Army training site. I–25 provides fast, smooth access from Pueblo to Colorado Springs and to the terminus of the tour, Denver, 112 miles to the north.

AROUND THE STATE

HOTELS AND MOTELS. Accommodations in the non-ski resort areas of Colorado tend to be friendly and warm toward the motoring family. These operations depend heavily on summer revenue and will make every effort to make travelers comfortable. The ski area accommodations tend to be somewhat more expensive, and their bounty of powdery snow puts these hotels and motels in a "sellers' market"—especially during winter holidays.

The price categories in this section, for double occupancy, will average as follows: *Deluxe* $25, *Expensive* $20, *Moderate* $15, and *Inexpensive* $12. For a more complete description of these categories, see the *Hotels & Motels* section of THE ROCKIES & PLAINS *Facts at Your Fingertips* at the front of this volume.

ALAMOSA

Alamosa Inn. *Moderate.* On US 160 at 285. Heated pool, saunas, TV, dining room and cocktail lounge. 589-2567

ASPEN

The Applejack Inn. *Expensive.* 311 W. Main St. Small with indoor heated pool, recreation balconies, sun deck. Free continental breakfasts. 925-7650

Aspen Inn. *Deluxe.* 701 S. Mill St. A motel in downtown Aspen. Sitter list, heated pool, lawn games, skiing, health club, restaurant, bar, entertainment. 925-3462

Aspen Meadows. *Deluxe.* On 8th St. at west edge of town. This small inn offers chalet accommodations with central building containing all hotel services, plus health center, saunas, steam baths, tennis courts, swimming pool, cocktail lounge, and the excellent *Copper Kettle* restaurant. 925-3426

Pomegranate Inn. *Deluxe.* 2 miles west on State 82. Rooms with fireplaces, suites, heated pool and therapy pool, ice cream parlor, billiard room. 925-2700

The Smuggler. *Moderate.* 101 W. Main St. A charming, small inn. Attractive units, larger ones have living areas. Lounge with beautiful fireplace and coffee bar. Afternoon tea served in winter. Heated pool. Home of the *Little Calico Kitchen.*

The Villa of Aspen. *Moderate.* On State 82. A friendly lodge with huge stone fireplace, complimentary continental breakfast, Heated pool, children's play area, outdoor barbecue, courtesy car. Baby sitters available. 925-3451

Maroon Creek Lodge. *Expensive.* 2½ mi. southwest on Maroon Creek Rd. At the base of Aspen Highlands ski area. Early American decor in units containing living room, kitchenette, bath and one or two bedrooms. Heated pool, sauna. Spectacular view. 925-3491

The Prospector. *Expensive.* E. Hyman at S. Monarch. A small, long-established, informal place with beautiful grounds. Complete breakfast is included in daily rates. Heated pool. 925-3634

BOULDER

Golden Buff Motor Lodge. *Expensive.* 1725 28th St. Established motel convenient to University of Colorado campus. Large, well-decorated rooms, heated pool, putting green, color TV. 442-7450

Harvest House Motor Hotel. *Expensive.* 1345 28th St. A large, modern high-rise motel with beautifully landscaped grounds, excellent dining facilities, cocktail lounge, swimming pool, tennis courts. Try the Champagne Sunday Brunch. 443-3850

Holiday Inn of Boulder. *Expensive.* 800 28th St. Large national chain motel. Pool, dining room. 443-3322

Royal Inn of Boulder. *Expensive.* 770 28th St. Across from University of Colorado. Restaurant, bar, pools, attractively furnished rooms, private patios. 449-3800

Crestwood. *Moderate.* 2800 Baseline Rd. Heated pool, TV, playground, cafe nearby. 442-3927

University Inn. *Moderate.* 1632 Broadway. Small, pleasant motel. Heated pool, TV. Near downtown Boulder. 442-3830

BRECKENRIDGE

Inn at Breckenridge. *Expensive.* 600 S. Ridge St. In the heart of the Breckenridge ski area, this lodge offers excellent dining room, cocktail lounge, heated pool, tennis courts, badminton, and archery. Summer activities. 453-2378

BRUSH

Thunderbird Motor Inn. *Moderate.* 1 mi. north on State 71. Color TV, heated pool, pets, cafe, oversize beds. Dancing nightly. 842-5146

Empire Motel. *Inexpensive.* 1408 Edison. Small motel with heated pool, large shaded lawns. Miniature golf next door. 842-2876

BUENA VISTA

Sumac Lodge. *Moderate.* On State 24. Pond, mountain view, shaded lawn, coin laundry. 395-8111

Topaz Lodge. *Moderate.* On State 24. Small, friendly lodge plans scenic drives for travelers on request. TV, cafe nearby. 395-2430

BURLINGTON

Chaparral Motor Inn. *Moderate.* ½ mi. north on State 385. Heated pool, playground, pets limited, color TV. 346-8306

Ramada Inn. *Moderate.* 450 S. Lincoln. Color TV, heated pool, pets, cafe, bar, dancing, entertainment. 346-5555

CANON CITY

Royal Gorge. *Expensive.* 1925 Fremont Dr. Heated pool, TV, pets, cafe, bar. Attractive rooms, free airport bus. 275-3377

El Camino. *Inexpensive.* 2980 E. Main St. Attractive motel with TV, playground, cafe ½ mi. 275-9986

J's Motel. *Inexpensive.* 1620 Main St. Nice rooms, new restaurant. 275-3306

COLORADO SPRINGS

Antlers Plaza. *Deluxe.* Pikes Peak Ave. at Chase Stone Center. Located in the heart of downtown Colorado Springs. A new luxury, 15–story complex complete with lounge, coffee shop, and specialty dining room. Rooftop heated pool, color TV, bar, dancing, entertainment. Barber and beauty shops; golf, tennis privileges. 473-5600

Broadmoor. *Deluxe.* 5 mi. south on US 85, 87, then west on State 122. This distinctive, world-famous resort is set on 5,000 acres. A center for large convention groups, facilities include color TV, two large heated pools, saunas, four dining rooms, bars, barber, beauty and other shops. Recreational facilities include golf, tennis, riding, skiing, ice rinks, boats, squash, handball, skeet, scuba. Entertainment, dancing, movies. 634-7711

Dravo Manor Motor Hotel. *Expensive.* 1703 S. Nevada. A small, well-kept motel with heated pool, color TV, restaurant, bar. 632-2663

Holiday Inn-Central. *Expensive.* 8th and Cimmaron Sts. Large motel with heated pool, color TV, restaurant, bar, dancing, entertainment. 473-5530

Palmer House. *Expensive.* I–25 at Fillmore St. exit. Large, beautifully planned motel with spacious rooms, heated pool, TV, restaurant, cocktail lounge, dancing, entertainment. 636-5201

89

Dale Motel. *Moderate.* 620 W. Colorado Ave. Small motel. Tour service for the area. Large, comfortable rooms, heated pool, TV. 636-3721

Imperial "400." *Moderate.* 1231 S. Nevada. Modern, small chain motel with heated pool, color TV, cafe nearby. 634-1545

Mayfair Hotel. *Moderate.* 120 E. Platte Ave. Facing Acacia Park. Spacious, well-furnished rooms, scenic tours arranged. TV, free coffee, free parking. 634-5552

Ponderosa Motel. *Moderate.* 5700 N. Nevada. Large, modern motel with heated pool, TV, playground; cafe not far. 636-5271

Sunset. *Inexpensive.* 1802 E. Platte Ave. Small motel with TV, cafe 1 blk. 633-4665

CORTEZ

Sands of Cortez. *Moderate.* 1100 E. Main St. Heated pool, color TV, playground, pets, restaurant and lounge. 565-3761

Turquoise. *Moderate.* 535 E. Main St. Color TV, heated pool, restaurant and cocktail lounge. Free airport bus. 565-3778

CRAIG

Cosgriff. *Inexpensive.* 110 E. Victory Way. Pleasant rooms with TV, dining room and cocktail lounge. Close to City Park. 824-6505

CRESTED BUTTE

Crested Butte Lodge. *Deluxe.* 2½ mi. north off State 135. Heated pool, sauna, playground, pets limited in this luxurious modern lodge. Summer activities as well as skiing in winter. 349-5362

Matterhorn Inn. *Expensive.* 3¼ mi. off State 135. Pleasant rooms off central halls. Restaurant and cocktail lounge. Closed Apr. to June. 349-5332

CRIPPLE CREEK

The Imperial Hotel. *Inexpensive.* 123 N. 3rd St. A relic of the 1891 Gold Rush—beautifully restored and great fun. The Imperial Players present an authentic melodrama in the *Gold Bar Room Theater.* Open June to Sept. The dining room is excellent. Cocktail lounge. 689-2291

DILLON

Lake Dillon Condotel. *Moderate.* Lodge Pole Rd., on Dillon Reservoir. TV, free coffee, limited pets, therapy pool, pool table. Cafe nearby. Some units with kitchennettes (priced higher). 468-2409

Ptarmigan Lodge. *Moderate.* 3 blks. south of US 6. Color TV, free coffee, sitter list. Cafe adjacent. 468-2341

DURANGO

General Palmer House. *Moderate.* 567 Main Ave. A gay '90's relic, restored, modernized and a delight to stay in. TV, small pets, cafe, bar. D & RGW narrow-gauge railroad depot adjacent. 247-4747

Strater Hotel. *Moderate.* 669 Main Ave. Small, modern, nice rooms. All public rooms are in gay '90's decor. Delightful cocktail lounge, good dining room. *Diamond Belle Bar,* melodramas in the *Diamond Circle Theater* during summer. 247-4431

Silver Spruce. *Inexpensive.* 2929 N. Main Ave. TV, pets, cafe 2 blks. Small, comfortable motel. 247-2202

EMPIRE

Hotel Splendide. *Moderate.* On Sunny Ave. A luxurious restoration of an 1870 mining-town hotel. Very small but with an unusually good dining room and intriguing bar. 569-8870

ESTES PARK

Hobby Horse Motor Lodge. *Expensive.* 1800 Big Thompson Hwy. Medium-sized motel with large, well-landscaped grounds. All units have mountain views and are nicely furnished. Heated pool, sun decks, playground, TV. Cafe ¼ mi. 9–hole golf course adjacent. 586-3336

Lake Estes Motor Inn. *Expensive.* 1650 Big Thompson Hwy. Medium-sized, with three heated pools, playground, horses available, pleasant rooms. 586-3386

Trail Ridge. *Moderate.* 1701 Moraine Ave. 1½ mi. southwest on State 66. Comfortable motel with heated pool, TV, restaurant and cocktail lounge. 586-4585

Triple "H." *Moderate.* 1800 Big Thompson Hwy. Small motel with TV, sundeck, shuffleboard. Cafe adjacent. Closed Oct. to mid-May. 586-4533

FORT COLLINS

Holiday Inn. *Moderate.* 3 mi. east on State 14. Chain member with heated pool, color TV, restaurant, cocktail lounge, entertainment, beauty shop. Free airport bus. 484-4660

University Motor Inn. *Moderate.* 914 S. College Ave. Opposite Colorado State University with heated pool, color TV, cafe. 484-1984

FORT MORGAN

Park Terrace Motor Hotel. *Moderate.* 725 Main St. Small with cute rooms, heated pool, coffee shop. 867-8256

GEORGETOWN

Georgetown Motor Inn. *Moderate.* On east edge of town, I–70 exit 43. Alpine inn in a scenic, historic location. Heated pool, good Alpine restaurant, cocktail lounge. 569-2292

GLENWOOD SPRINGS

Holiday Inn. *Expensive.* 2 mi. west at I–70 exit. Chain member with color TV, heated pool, saunas. Restaurant, bar, entertainment, dancing. 945-8551

Hot Springs Lodge. *Moderate.* Center on I–70. Large motel with comfortable rooms, 2-block-long hot-spring pool, terrace dining, playground, sportswear shop, cocktail lounge. 945-6571

Denver. *Inexpensive.* 7th and Cooper Sts. Friendly, informal atmosphere with TV, pets, restaurant, cocktail lounge. 945-6565

GRANBY

El Monte Lodge. *Moderate.* ½ mi. west on US 40. TV, heated pool, playground, pets limited. Restaurant and cocktail lounge. 887-3348

GRAND JUNCTION

Holiday Inn. *Expensive.* 755 Horizon Dr. off I–70 near airport. A large member of chain with comfortable rooms, suites available. Portable bar, meeting facilities, heated pool, sauna, lounge. 243-6790

Bar-X Motel. *Moderate.* 1600 North Ave., ½ mi. northeast on US 6, 24. Modern, with spacious grounds; across street from golf course. Heated pool, color TV, restaurant, bar, free airport bus. 243-1311

El Palomino. *Moderate.* 2400 North Ave., 1½ mi. northeast on US 6, 24. Opposite shopping center; color TV, heated pool, playground, free coffee, shuffleboard, picnic area. Pleasant rooms. 242-1826

American Family Lodge. *Inexpensive.* 721 Horizon Dr., 3½ mi. north at I–70 airport exit. Attractive rooms, heated pool, TV, playground, pets. Cafe opposite. 243-6050

Holiday. *Inexpensive.* 1460 North Ave., on US 6. Color TV, limited pets, free coffee. Cafe adjacent. 242-5747

GRAND LAKE

Daven Haven Lodge. *Moderate.* ¼ mi. south of Main St. Small summer resort on the shores of Grand Lake. Private beach, boats, water-skiing, miniature golf, shuffleboard, badminton, heated pool. Cocktail lounge and two dining rooms. Excellent family place. 627-3381

91

Riggs AA. *Inexpensive.* 2 blks. west on State 278. Playground, pets, free coffee, cafe nearby. Closed Nov. to Apr. 627-3344

GREELEY

Inn Towne. *Moderate.* 1803 9th St. Comfortable motel. TV, free coffee, kitchen units available. Cafe 3 blocks. 353-0447

Sundown. *Inexpensive.* 2131 8th Ave., 1 mi. south on US 85. Two blocks from University of Northern Colorado. TV, free coffee. Cafe opposite. 352-9261

Tomichi Village. *Moderate.* 1 mi. east on US 50. Large motel with heated pool, cocktail lounge, and restaurant. 641-1131

Western Motel. *Moderate.* 411 E. Tomichi, center of town on US 50. Near Western State College. Small motel with heated pool, restaurant, and cocktail lounge. 641-1722

IDAHO SPRINGS

Peoriana Motel. *Inexpensive.* 1 mi. east on US 6, 40. Small, a favorite of skiers, has large, well-furnished rooms, color TV, cafe nearby. 567-2021

LAMAR

El Mar Motel. *Inexpensive.* 1210 S. Main St. Small, modern with TV, heated pool, cocktail lounge and restaurant. 336-4331

LEADVILLE

Silver King Motor Inn. *Moderate.* 2020 Poplar St. TV, sauna, pets, restaurant and cocktail lounge. 486-2610

Timberline. *Inexpensive.* 216 Harrison Ave. Small, comfortable motel with TV, cafe nearby. 486-1876

LONGMONT

Lamplighter. *Moderate.* 1642 N. Main St. Comfortable motel with indoor heated pool, TV, free coffee. 776-7620

Bar-C. *Inexpensive.* 1524 N. Main St. Small motel with TV, limited pets, free coffee, cafe nearby. 776-7856

LOVELAND

King's Court. *Moderate.* 928 Lincoln St. Small motel with heated pool, TV, free coffee, nicely landscaped grounds. Cafe 3 blocks. 667-4035

MESA VERDE NATIONAL PARK

Far View. *Moderate.* At Navajo Hill, 15 mi. from park entrance. Private balconies provide a magnificent view of the canyon. Camping sites and trailer facilities are available. Cafeteria. Summer reservations advisable. Closed Oct. 15 to May 15. 529-4421

MONTROSE

Red Arrow. *Expensive.* 1 mi. east on US 50. Attractive rooms in this motel with heated pool, color TV, playground, free coffee, sundeck. Cafe nearby. 249-9641

Black Canyon Motel. *Moderate.* 1 mi. east on US 50. Small, with well-furnished rooms, heated pool, TV, playground, pets, restaurant next door. Free airport bus. 249-3495

Lazy I G Motel. *Moderate.* 1 mi. east on US 50. Very small, has deluxe rooms, heated pool, TV, free coffee, playground. Manager knows area and happily helps tourist, arranges hunting, fishing, jeep trips. 249-4567

OURAY

Box Canyon. *Moderate.* 1st St. and 3rd Ave. At the mouth of the canyon with a spectacular view. TV, playground, pets, free coffee. Cafe nearby. 325-4551

Ouray Chalet. *Inexpensive.* On US 550, State 789. Small motel with sundeck, free coffee. Cafe nearby. 325-4331

PAGOSA SPRINGS

Spring Inn. *Moderate.* 2 blks. south of US 160. Very small inn with mineral water baths, delightful rooms, cocktail lounge and restaurant, TV, pets. 968-2287

PUEBLO

Holiday Inn. *Expensive.* 4001 N. Elizabeth. A large chain member. Heated pool, restaurant and cocktail lounge. 543-8050

Pueblo West Inn. *Expensive.* 201 McCulloch Blvd. Very attractive motel with color TV, heated pool, restaurant and cocktail lounge. 18–hole golf course, tennis courts, heliport. 547-2111

Ramada Inn. *Expensive.* 2001 N. Hudson Ave. Motor hotel with heated pool, good dining room, cocktail lounge, color TV, playground, beauty shop, free airport bus. 542-3750

Rambler. *Moderate.* 4400 N. Elizabeth St. Heated pool, TV, 24–hour cafe nearby. 543-4173

Town House. *Moderate.* 8th St. at Santa Fe Ave. Medium-sized with heated pool, color TV, dining room, coffee shop, cocktail lounge. 543-6530

SILVERTON

Grand Imperial Hotel. *Moderate.* 1219 Main St. A Victorian hotel, recently restored, features TV, restaurant, beauty shop, movies; jeeps available. Closed Oct. to May. 387-5527

STEAMBOAT SPRINGS

Holiday Inn. *Expensive.* 3 mi. east on US 40. Two stories, very attractive with some balconies. Heated pool, color TV, kennel, sauna, restaurant and cocktail lounge. 879-2250

Ptarmigan Inn. *Expensive.* 2 mi. east on US 40. This very attractive motel has a view of Mt. Werner. Heated pool, sauna, restaurant and cocktail lounge. 876-1730

Western Lodge. *Moderate.* 1122 Lincoln Ave. Opposite the park, heated pool, TV, free coffee. Cafe nearby. 879-1050

Bristol. *Inexpensive.* 917 Lincoln Ave. Small hotel with TV, free parking, pets. Cafe nearby. 879-1400

STERLING

Sterling Motor Lodge. *Inexpensive.* 731 N. 3rd St. TV, playground, pets limited, free coffee, 24–hour cafe nearby. 522-2740

TRINIDAD

Country Club Motor Inn. *Deluxe.* 1100 Country Club Dr. Small motel, nice rooms with oversize beds, heated pool, color TV, *Martha Lee Restaurant,* cocktail lounge, playground, beauty and barber shops. 846-2215

Ramada Inn. *Expensive.* 702 W. Main St. Small chain member, delightful rooms, heated pool, cocktail lounge, dining room, coffee shop, TV, weekend entertainment. 846-2271

Main Street. *Inexpensive.* 616 E. Main St. Small motel with TV, free coffee. Nearby cafe. 846-2229

VAIL

Christiania-at-Vail. *Deluxe.* On Hanson Ranch Rd. Small, friendly, informal lodge at the foot of the mountain. Heated pool, sauna, limited pets, free coffee. Restaurant nearby. 476-2261

Gasthof Gramshammer. *Deluxe.* 3 blks. south of I–70 in Vail Village. Tyrolean lodge owned by Vail's professional racer and his wife. Cocktail lounge, bar, and excellent dining room. Closed Easter to June 15. 476-5626

The Lodge at Vail. *Deluxe.* 2 blks. south of I–70. Splendid Alpine lodge, Bavarian *Rathskeller,* cafeteria, sauna, cocktail lounge, heated pool, TV, ice skating. 476-5011

Vail Village Inn. *Deluxe.* 1 block north of I–70. Large motor inn with unique architecture, heated pool, dining room with excellent food, coffee shop, cocktail lounge, fireplace lounge, sundecks, TV. 476-5622

WALSENBURG

Country Host. *Moderate.* 1¾ mi. north at jct. State 69. TV, playground, limited

pets, free coffee, trailer park available. Cafe adjacent. 738-2900

WINTER PARK

Winter Haven Lodge. *Deluxe.* 2½ mi. west on US 40 in Hideaway Park. On a modified American plan. TV, free coffee, free bus to ski lifts, good for couples and skiing groups. 726-5353

YOUTH HOSTELS. Denver has both a *YWCA* and a *YMCA* with resident and transient facilities. At the major *ski* areas in the state a number of dormitory-type accommodations are available at an inexpensive rate. *Hotels and motels* throughout the state, and particularly in college towns, offer lower rates to groups. *Fraternity and sorority houses* on most college campuses are open in summer months, and members from other schools may be able to stay in them if they're not filled with summer-school students.

DINING OUT. Dining out in Colorado towns can be great fun for the traveling family. Many of the smaller towns have different or unusual restaurants featuring local specialties, such as fine Mexican food. Prices are for the medium-priced items on the menu. For other worthwhile restaurants, check the hotel listings. Restaurants are in order of price category.

Restaurant categories are as follows: *Deluxe:* $9.50 and up, *Expensive:* $6–$8.50, *Moderate:* $4–$6, and *Inexpensive:* $2.50–$4. These prices are for *hors d'oeuvres* or soup, *entrée,* and dessert. Not included are drinks, tax or tips. For a more complete explanation of restaurant categories, refer to THE ROCKIES & PLAINS *Facts at Your Fingertips* at the front of this volume.

ASPEN

Copper Kettle. *Deluxe.* 535 E. Deane Ave. Consistently named one of America's best restaurants, and with good reason. Each night authentic dishes from a nation or area are featured. Other choices are offered, but no one really orders them—the specialties are too good. This establishment should not be missed by anyone who truly enjoys good food. Cocktail Lounge. Reservations. *Prix fixe.* Open 6 to 10:30 p.m. 925-3151

The Crystal Palace. *Deluxe.* 300 E. Hyman Ave. This should be seen—it's Victoriana gone crazy. Where else can you find wrought-iron bedsteads used as room dividers or fireplace mantels as a bar. The *prix fixe* dinners and entertainment are good, too. Cocktail lounge. Open 8 p.m. for dinner, show at 9:30 p.m. 925-1455

Golden Horn. *Expensive.* 400 E. Cooper at Mill St. Austrian cuisine. Efficient, unobtrusive service, warm decor, sparkling crystal, and a magnificent Caesar salad are only a few of the attractions of this charming room. Cocktail lounge, entertainment. Reservations. Open 6 to 10 p.m. 925-3373

Guido's Swiss Inn. *Expensive.* 403 S. Galena St. A Swiss chalet at Ajax Mountain with much to offer. If you are a cheese fondue fan, by all means order it here. Cocktail lounge. Open 11:30 a.m. to 9 p.m. Closed Apr., May, Nov. 925-7222

The Red Onion. *Expensive.* 920 E. Cooper Ave. A mining-day saloon, in fact the only one in town still operating at its original location. The saloon remains as it was in 1892, but the dining room is contemporary. Gourmet dinners and charcoal-broiled steaks are specialties. Cocktail lounge, entertainment. Open 11:30 a.m. to 2 p.m., 5:30 p.m. to 3 a.m.; Sun. to 10:30 p.m. 925-7001

Skiers Chalet Steak House. *Moderate.* Aspen St. at #1 lift. Good for families, this candlelit restaurant overlooks the town and mountain. Charcoal-broiled steaks are featured. Open 5:30 to 10 p.m. 925-3381

BOULDER

Catacombs. *Expensive.* 2115 13th St. in the Boulderado Hotel. This delightful restaurant in downtown Boulder is popular locally. Prime ribs are the specialty served in a candlelit atmosphere. Cocktail lounge. Open 11 a.m. to 2 a.m.; Sun. and hols., 4 p.m. to midnight. 449-4818

Flagstaff House. *Expensive.* On Flagstaff Mountain. Continental American menu including prime rib, filet à la Wellington, Alaska king crab. Own bread. Cocktail patio. Overlooks city, mountains. Open 5 p.m. to midnight. 442-4640

Greenbriar. *Expensive.* Jamestown Star Rte., 8 mi. north on US 36 at jct. Lefthand Canyon Rd. Continental and American menu features veal Oscar, beef Wellington, shrimp Provençale, live Main lobster, San Francisco French bread. Own desserts. Charming Old World atmosphere, book-lined walls. Chef owned. Cocktail lounge. Jacket and tie. Open 5 to 10:30 p.m.; Sun. 4 to 10 p.m.; hols. noon to 10 p.m. 442-9531

Red Lion Inn. *Expensive.* Boulder Canyon Rd., 4 mi. west on State 119. Continental and American menu includes prime rib, elk, antelope, duck à l'orange. Cocktail lounge. Jacket and tie. Open 5:30 to 10:30 p.m.; Fri. and Sat. 5 to 11 p.m.; Sun. 5 to 10 p.m. 442-9368

Roman Arches. *Moderate.* 5364 Arapahoe Ave. Continental cuisine includes lasagna, manicotti. Great family restaurant. Own baking. Cocktail lounge. Open 11 a.m. to midnight. 447-2495

Tico's. *Inexpensive.* 1101 Walnut St. Mexican and American menu. Own desserts. Cocktail lounge. Open 11 a.m. to 2 a.m.; Sun. 3 p.m. to midnight. 449-6661

BRECKENRIDGE

The Parlour Steak House. *Expensive.* 208 N. Ridge St. Charming, century-old house; intimate candlelit setting. Excellent food. Specialties include escargots, veal, lamb, steak, artichokes. Reservations required. Open 5 to 10 p.m.; summer from 6 p.m. 453-9990

Briar Rose. *Moderate.* 109 E. Lincoln. Charming 1890's decor on the site of an old mining boarding house. Specialty is prime rib. Cocktail lounge. Open 5:30 to 10 p.m.; Sat. from 4 p.m. 453-9948

CANON CITY

Sali's Club Paradise Restaurant. *Moderate.* 141 S. 9th St. Known for its homemade pastas, this quiet restaurant specializes in excellent Italian cooking. Children welcome. Open 11 a.m. to 11 p.m.; Sun. noon to 8 p.m. 275-7221

CENTRAL CITY

Black Forest Inn. *Expensive.* ¾ mi. east on State 279 in Black Hawk. A picturesque chalet with beer garden, Bavarian atmosphere. Authentic German dishes expertly prepared. Elk, venison, pheasant, and other native game featured in the fall. Open noon to 10 p.m. Closed Mon. and Jan. to Feb. 582-9971

Teller House Eureka Room. *Expensive.* 110 Eureka St. Laden with romance and history, the Teller house has been restored to its former splendor. Open during summer months. Cocktail lounge. Teller Bar with "Face on the Bar Room Floor." Entertainment. Open 4 to 9 p.m. Closed Mon. 582-5201

Johnson's Smorgasbord. *Moderate.* 121 Main St. on State 279. The only restaurant in town open year round. Elaborate smorgasbord plus cocktails, or enjoy your choice of sandwiches or full-course dinners from a varied menu. Open 7 a.m. to 10 p.m. 582-9966

COLORADO SPRINGS

Broadmoor Hotel Dining Rooms. *Deluxe* to *Moderate.* In the Broadmoor Hotel. There are a number of fine restaurants in this complex: the *Broadmoor Tavern*, the *Tropical Garden Room*, the *Main Dining Room*, the *Lake Terrace Lounge*, the *Penrose Dining Room* (atop the hotel), and the *Golden Bee*, an English pub of the 19th century that was brought over and rebuilt. Check with the hotel for the various hours. 634-7711

Red Cloud Inn. *Expensive.* 10 mi. west at US 24 Topeka Ave. exit in Cascade. Specializing in Swiss and American food this restaurant features prime rib, flaming Chateaubriand, king crab legs. Own baking. Early western memorabilia including Baby Doe Tabor's velvet-covered piano. Jacket and tie. Open 6:30 to 9:30 p.m. Closed Sun. and Jan. to Feb. 684-9915

Flying W Ranch. *Moderate.* 6100 Wilson Rd. A truly Western dinner, served on tin plates by lantern light on picnic tables. Children's plates. Western entertainment follows dinner. This is a working cattle and horse ranch. Reservations required. Dinner served from 4:30 to 7:30 p.m. 598-4000

Stagecoach Inn. *Moderate.* 702 Manitou Ave., 4 mi. west on US 24 Business in Manitou Springs. In an early American decor, chicken, prime rib, rainbow trout are featured. Own baking. Open 11:30 a.m. to 9:30 p.m. 685-9335

The Village Inn. *Moderate.* 217 E. Pikes Peak Ave. Located in a beautiful old church, this restaurant serves consistently good food, from a versatile menu. Cocktail lounge. Open 11 a.m. to 8:30 p.m. 633-8619

Mission Bell Inn. *Inexpensive.* 178 Crystal Park Rd. in Manitou Springs. Locally popular Mexican restaurant in a Spanish decor. Open 5 to 10 p.m. Closed Mon. 685-9089

CRESTED BUTTE

The Steak House. *Moderate.* ½ mi. northwest on Slate River. This restaurant has a rustic decor and looks out on the butte. The very limited menu includes only mahi mahi broiled in sherry sauce, chicken, and steak. Open 6 to 9 p.m. Closed Easter to June 15, Oct. to day before Thanksgiving. 349-5250

DURANGO

Chez Louis. *Expensive.* 819 Main St. French and American menu including coq au vin, escargots, rack of lamb. Open 11:30 a.m. to 11 p.m. Closed Sun. and Labor Day to May. 247-5005

Grand Palace. *Moderate.* 557 Main St. Located in 19th-century surroundings in Rio Grandeland, the Rio Grande Railroad's recreation of an early-day frontier town. Distinctive service and fine food. Cocktail lounge. Open 6 a.m. to 10:30 p.m. 247-2018

ESTES PARK

Old Plantation. *Moderate.* 128 E. Elkhorn Ave. Yankee pot roast, baked chicken, rainbow trout are specialties. Own pastries. Open 11:30 a.m. to 8:45 p.m. Closed Oct. to May. 586-2800

The Range Restaurant. *Moderate.* 1560 Big Thompson Hwy. This fairly large restaurant encourages family dining. Many little touches add to your comfort. Prime ribs are the specialty. Cocktail lounge. Children's menu. Open 6 a.m. to 9 p.m. Closed Oct. 16 to May 1. 586-9941

FORT COLLINS

Black Knight. *Moderate.* 3905 S. College Ave. In a Medieval decor, this restaurant serves prime ribs, Black Forest pie, and other savory dishes. Wed to Sat. there is also entertainment. Open 11:30 a.m. to 2 a.m.; Sat. from 5 p.m. 484-3830

GEORGETOWN

Red Ram. *Moderate.* 606 Alpine St. This Victorian establishment in downtown Georgetown has a saloon with tables around a balcony, and a small delightful dining room featuring German and Austrian food. The saloon is said to be the oldest in Colorado. The stone-walled *Rathskeller* is candlelit and a favorite with skiers and the college crowds. Entertainment, reservations. Open 11 a.m. to 9:30 p.m.; Sat. and Sun. 11 a.m. to 10 p.m. 569-2565

Silver Queen. *Moderate.* 500 6th St. French and American menu whose specialties include veal, Dover sole, langoustine. Jacket and tie. Open 11:30 a.m. to 2 p.m., 6 to 9 p.m. 569-2961

GLENWOOD SPRINGS

Buffalo Valley Inn. *Moderate.* 3½ mi. southeast on State 82. In a rustic, early western setting, including paintings by a noted Western artist, Jack Roberts, steaks and ribs are prepared over an old-time applewood cooking pit. Children's menu available; small bar; reservations advised summer ski seasons. Open 5 to 10 p.m.; Sun. 4 to 10 p.m. Closed Thurs. 945-7220

GOLD HILL

Gold Hill Inn. *Expensive.* In Gold Hill, follow Sunshine Canyon Rd. out of Boulder. The specialties here combine French and American cuisine. Superbly prepared foods, including the bread, are served in the delightful mountain scenery of the hills above Boulder. Open 6 to 10 p.m. Closed Mon. 443-6461

GRAND JUNCTION

Cafe Caravan. *Moderate.* 105 W. Main St. Features general menu and smorgasbord. Cocktail lounge, occasional entertainment. Open 5 a.m. to 10 p.m. 242-2661

GREELEY

Garden Kitchen. *Moderate.* 119 18th St. Pleasant restaurant specializing in Chinese dinners. Own rolls and pastries. Open 6 a.m. to 9 p.m. 353-5544

LOUISVILLE

Colacci's. *Inexpensive.* 810 Main St. While this restaurant makes its own pasta and sauces, it's also known locally for steaks and shrimp. Cocktail lounge. Open 9 a.m. to 10 p.m.; Fri. and Sat. to 11 p.m.; Sun. to 8 p.m. 669-9979

LYONS

Black Bear Inn. *Expensive.* 42 E. Main St. This predominantly German menu features sauerbraten, schnitzels, own cheesecake, apple strudel, chocolate cake. Charming candlelit decor has entertainment on weekends. Open 11 a.m. to 3 p.m., 5 to 10 p.m. 823-6812

La Chaumiere. *Expensive.* 8 mi. northwest on US 36. This *prix fixe* French menu offers three entrees which change daily. The chef recites the menu. The view of the mountains, the intimate atmosphere, and the excellent food and wine combine to make this a thoroughly pleasant place to dine. Open 5:30 to 9 p.m.; Sat. from 6 p.m.; Sun. and Hols. 1 to 7 p.m. Closed Jan. and Feb. 823-6521

MONTROSE

Country Diner. *Moderate.* 1 blk. north of Ute Museum on Chipeta Ave. This restaurant does its own baking and specializes in steak. An excellent place to take the family. Open 5 to 8:30 p.m. Closed Sun. and Mon., and Dec. to Mar. 249-5866

OURAY

1876 Gourmet. *Expensive.* 545 Main St. An International menu that changes daily. Own baking. Weathered beams and paneling from a 100-year-old mine and period lamps make up the charming decor. Cocktail lounge. Open 6:30 to 9:30 a.m., 5 to 9:30 p.m. Closed Oct. 15 to Apr. 26. 325-4361

PUEBLO

Furphy's. *Expensive.* 8th St. at Santa Fe Ave. in Town House Motel. This locally popular restaurant features a Victorian decor and prime rib and live Maine lobster. Cocktail lounge. Open 6:30 a.m. to 9:30 p.m.; Fri. and Sat. to 10 p.m.; Sun. 7:30 a.m. to 8 p.m. 545-6993

Top o' the Town. *Expensive.* 4201 Elizabeth St. Specialties are prime rib, steak, seafood. This locally popular restaurant is open 4:30 to 10 p.m. Closed Sun. 544-4596

SALIDA

The Spa. *Moderate.* 415 Rainbow Blvd. A restful, quiet dining room with a glorious view of the surrounding mountains. Specialties are steak and trout with children's plates. Own baking. Open 6 a.m. to 10 p.m., winter to 8 p.m. 539-6532

SILVERTON

Grand Imperial. *Moderate.* 1219 Main St. International dishes are the specialties here with half-price children's plates. Salad bar, own baking. Cocktail lounge. Open 7:30 a.m. to 2 p.m., 6:30 to 10 p.m. Closed Oct. to May. 387-5527

STEAMBOAT SPRINGS

The Gallery. *Expensive.* Atop Storm Meadow Athletic Club. This Continental and American menu is served amidst beam ceilings and paintings. Specialties include charcoal-broiled steak, beef Wellington, live lobster, shrimp Donatello. Open noon to midnight; ski season from 8 a.m. 879-0239

VAIL

Gasthof Gramshammer. *Expensive.* 3 blks. south of I–70 in Gasthof Gramshammer. Continental menu whose specialty is antelope rahm-schnitzel. Children's plates are available. Tyrolean atmosphere. Open 11:30 a.m. to 3 p.m., 6 to 10 p.m. Closed Easter to June 15. Also *Antlers Room* in winter. Features rack of venison, elk steak Hubertus, pepper steak à la francaise. Open 6 to 10:30 p.m. 476-5626

Lord Gore. *Expensive.* Hanson Ranch Rd., ½ mi. southeast of I–70. In an elegant atmosphere, beef, veal and wild game are featured. Cocktail lounge. Open 6 to 10 p.m. Closed Wed., May, Oct. 476-3443

Red Lion Inn. *Expensive.* 3 blks. south of I–70. Continental and American menu featuring trout, prime rib, crab legs. A candlelit, Tudor decor with terrace dining in summer. Open 11:30 a.m. to 4:45 p.m., 6 to 10 p.m. Closed Oct. 15 to Nov. 15. 476-5740

UTAH

UTAH

The Outdoor Amphitheater
by
HARRY E. FULLER, JR.

Harry Fuller has lived in Salt Lake City for thirteen years, where he is an editorial writer for the Salt Lake Tribune.

There is a sort of topographical symmetry to Utah. Almost 85,000 square miles in area, this 45th of the 50 states, squatting in the Rocky Mountain Great Basin, is divided down the middle by a huge, jutting spine—the Wasatch Range, looming to rugged peaks between 9,000 and 12,000 feet high. On either side a wrinkled, mostly arid landscape slopes away to the lower elevations. The western flank is almost completely wrapped in desert, picturesque at dawn or dusk, but hostile and harsh in the sun's punishing glare. The state's eastern shoulder is at least relieved by powerful waterways, principal among them the Green and Colorado Rivers. But even these alternately cascading and drifting waters pass through occasionally barren desolation.

Prominent landmarks of water distinguish the state's northern and southern extremes as well. Not much more than thirty miles below the Idaho border is the familiar natural wonder, Great Salt

101

Lake. The ghostly remnant of an even greater inland sea—Lake Bonneville—Great Salt Lake is still approximately thirty miles wide by seventy-five miles long. It is hospitable to sailing, a bouyant brand of swimming and, at the Bear River drainage, duck hunting.

More to the north and east, Bear Lake, fresh water and a favorite of boaters, dips its southern two-thirds from Idaho into Utah at Rich County.

On Utah's southern rim, man has created new and immense Lake Powell, 180 miles long, deepening and reaching out behind Glen Canyon dam astride the Colorado River.

Utah is as varied as it is large—parched desert and snow-capped mountains; hard-rock plateaus and green-carpeted valleys; dry gullies and roaring-water gorges; sand dune windrows and rippling expanses of cooling lakes. Through reclamation and cultivation much has been artifically enhanced, even while being exploited.

Exploitation of the land has been an absolute necessity for Utah to support permanent communities. At that, growth has been slow and often hesitating. The state is littered with shards of abandoned town sites. In 1972, Stephen L. Carr compiled a book that listed and described over 150 ghost towns languishing throughout Utah. It confirms a considerable background of pioneer trial and error. Steadily, however, Utah has developed into a single, elongated urban center embracing Salt Lake City, surrounded by thinly populated areas with residents depending for livelihoods on agriculture, mining, light manfacturing, oil production or an accelerating tourist trade.

It's not always love at first sight between Utah and its newer arrivals. The state lacks a cultural profusion found in older, more heavily populated regions of the U.S. Beyond that, community life in Utah manifests a definite insular quality. The power and presence of the Mormon Church, with few exceptions, strongly influences politics, government and social standing. This, quite naturally, affects non-Mormons in ways ranging from mild amusement to angry resentment. To get the feel for Utah "atmosphere," it's essential to understand some of the state's quite unique history.

Out of the Mainstream of American History

Utah is, not by original plan but rather by consequence of violent events, headquarters and sacred home of the Church of Jesus Christ of Latter-day Saints. The church, a Christian denomination, blossomed 150 years ago in New York, the gospel revelation announced by a prayerful young man named Joseph Smith, Jr. With a loyal following, he first moved west, settling in Kirtland, Ohio. The next move was to Jackson County, Missouri, and finally to a place called Nauvoo, Illinois. Surmounting constant difficulty, Smith managed to build a thriving community at Nauvoo, but at the expense of so much local enmity that a mob murdered him in a jail where he and other church leaders were being held. Smith's life ended prematurely, but his vision survived to inspire yet another migration, this one the most successful and significant.

Led by a colonizing genius, Brigham Young, the Latter-day Saints packed what they could into wagons and escaped their tormentors, seeking a haven isolated from those not of their creed. This turned out to be the Great Salt Lake Valley, at the foot of the Wasatch Mountain Range. In 1846, the time of their advance party's arrival, the area was actually Mexican land. Through man-fashioned irrigation, effective organization, back-breaking toil and unshakable faith, the pioneers, as they have since been reverently titled, made the harsh surroundings livable.

Descendants of those original settlers, and there are thousands, consider the memory of the dedication and sacrifice of their forebearers to be a consecrated legacy. Utahans aren't always alert to the tangible remains of pioneer times. Irreplaceable hundred-year-old church buildings have been blithely razed. It's more the spirit of devoted perserverance that is lodged firmly in the Mormon heart. This helps account for a particular brand of conservatism or provincialism.

Modern Mormonism

Actually, modern Utah has abundant reason to be, for its small population, uncommonly cosmopolitan, even sophisticated. Its education level per capita is a national leader. From the beginning, Utah was a melting pot. Brigham Young dispatched missionaries throughout likely places in Europe as well as the U.S. to spread the glad news of a blessed Zion in the American West. And scores answered. Immigrating across the seas they eagerly joined homegrown converts. To this day the church maintains a foreign language capability at its Salt Lake City offices that surely rivals the United Nations'.

Most good church members are well traveled beyond the average. As young people, they are called to the missionary field, spending at least two years tending church business, preaching the gospel somewhere other than Utah, as often in England, Germany, Scandinavia, France and Italy as along the Eastern or

Western seaboard or among the Polynesian or Japanese islands. Yet with all these eye-opening influences, Utah's Mormon majority can still identify with views formulated in the nineteenth century.

This includes adherence to the concept that life is a literal struggle between divinity and evil; that while God leads the truly devout, Satan guides the footsteps of the wrong-doer. Also, individual dependence on public assistance deprives the individual of the opportunity to choose, as a matter of judgment, a correct or mistaken path. Church policy condemns abortion as it does murder and all ordinary crime. It stresses self-reliance, although from Brigham Young's day, it has also operated a church welfare program as an interim help for the unfortunate.

As an article of faith, practicing church members abjure liquor and tobacco. Among the bitterest battles waged statewide during recent years were those over what degree Utah would permit liquor to be sold publicly. A referendum held in 1968, asking whether mixed drinks could be sold in licensed outlets, went down to crushing defeat after a campaign that nearly polarized the entire state population.

Does this mean Utah is a collection of close-minded, parochial blue-noses? Not at all. In the first place, approximately 40 percent of the state is non-Mormon. Beyond that, however, while most adherents to the state's principal institution abide strictly by doctrine bequeathed from their elders, they can also be disarmingly tolerant. LDS thinking is neither slavish nor monolithic. Church members are united behind established precepts, but that doesn't prevent them from differing among themselves on politics, economics, social theory or even theology.

Stodginess is not a principal Utah characteristic. Rather an active interest in entertainment has produced the likes of the late jazz great Red Nichols, the Osmond Brothers, along with actresses Maude Adams, Laraine Day and Fay Dunaway. Sports are almost an obsession, especially basketball, which the Mormon Church encourages with a competitive program organized in full LDS thoroughness. National caliber athletes have come from Utah, including former boxing champion Gene Fullmer, world record co-holder in the discus, L. Jay Sylvester, professional football linemen Merlin and Phil Olsen and New York Mets outfielder George Theodore. Enthusiasm for dancing since pioneer days provided instrumentalists a pay day in Utah long after America's big band era ended.

Other pioneer preoccupations are shared today by most Utahans, Mormon and non-Mormon. One is transforming drab desert into grassy vale. Water originally diverted from highland streams for nurturing crops now pours onto suburban lawns so every growing season will adorn yards in emerald green framed by flourishing flower beds.

A Modern Theocracy

Still, the difference between being Mormon and non-Latter-day Saint, or Gentile, in Utah is, if sometimes only subtle, always basic. In his 1957 Frederick William Reynolds lecture at the University of Utah, English Professor William Mulder, himself a Utah Mormon, explained: "Utah was a land where the Mormons at last could be the original settlers, keeping the outsider in the decided minority. . . . It was a Bible commonwealth, making no distinction between temporal and spiritual affairs under the strong central direction of the great colonizer as President of the Church and for ten years as Governor of the Territory (Brigham Young)."

And Leonard J. Arrington, recently named LDS Church historian, wrote in his 1958 book, *Great Basin Kingdom,* that: "The establishment of God's Kingdom on earth, according to Mormon belief, required equal attention to the temporal and spiritual needs of man. . . . Economics, and secular policy in general, were thus placed on a par with—or incorporated in—religion. . . . Of the 112 revelations announced by Joseph Smith, 88 dealt partly or entirely with matters . . . economic in nature. . . . There is no doubt of the Mormon teaching that religion was concerned with the everyday duties and realities of life, and that church leaders were expected to minister not only to the spiritual wants of people, but to their social, economic and political wants as well."

These scholars were writing about early Mormon history. But while attitudes and policy have altered considerably with conditions, the pervasive effects of that deep-down Mormon belief has not disappeared in Utah.

Through its banking affiliate, Zion's First National, the church stays deeply in the state's economic mainstream. It retained control of Utah-Idaho Sugar Company after the Federal Trade Commission forced Henry Havemayer to break up the American Sugar Refining Company in 1914. In the seventy years after 1900, the church helped promote and finance insurance companies, textile mills, hotels, an airline, hospitals, radio and television stations, aggregating an investment said to total well over $200 million by the '60's.

Non-Mormons have had successful political careers in Utah. But not many. They include but two governors, Simon Bamberger, 1917–21, who was Jewish, and J. Bracken Lee, 1949–57, from a Protestant background. No member in Utah's congressional delegation during modern times has been anything but a nominal or devout LDS member. The State Legislature, with 27 senators and 75 representatives, is considered 90 percent Mormon. Generally, it's considered extremely difficult for a Gentile to win statewide, and many district-wide, offices in Utah elections.

Political competition is brisk between traditional Republican and Democratic parties. The Democrats hold a registration edge, which may seem anomolous in a fundmentally conservative state, but Utah brand Democratic persuasion isn't the orthodox liberalism the party represents elsewhere.

In 1972, a Democrat, Calvin L. Rampton, shattered Utah political tradition by winning re-election to the governor's office for a third consecutive term. Until then, several men had served two straight terms as governor, but none three. Many observers argued Utah voters considered the two term limitation, although no a law, fundamental custom. Governor Rampton proved them wrong. An especially popular governor, he also had the good fortune to reach office during one of Utah's most prosperous periods. Personality—not charisma, but the individual characteristics displayed—count for a great deal in Utah elections.

Utah voters pride themselves on going to the polls, but are also apt to say, "I vote for the man, not the party." This has resulted, recently, in a Democratic governor and a Republican-controlled State Senate and Democrat-controlled House of Representatives.

For years, Utah has had one Democrat and one Republican in the U.S. Senate, while regularly replacing those holding the state's two House seats. Consequently, the state has, occasionally, had helpful seniority in the Senate, but seldom in the House.

Utah needs effective representation in Washington, D.C., because the state's land area is over 60 percent federally owned. A large portion is uninhabitable or used for grazing, but under the circumstances, Utah's development and growth has been even more impressive.

One hundred and twenty-five years after the first Mormon settlers camped in the Great Salt Lake Valley, Utah the state has become a prosperous, forward-looking enterprise. Residents don't yet number much more than 1 million, and over half cluster in a narrow urban corridor running about forty miles north and south of Salt Lake City. Few pockets of chronic poverty exist and confidence in the future seldom lags. Economic fluctuations experienced in the past have been evened out by a diversifying industry. Mining and agriculture are increasingly complemented by light manufacturing, service trades of every description and a technological capacity germinated by participation in America's space and missile development. Tourism recently became the state's second ranked income producer.

An Outdoor Paradise

An old-timer, making conversation while riding the Germania chair lift at Alta's famed ski resort, pointed to the headwall looming high above "Ballroom" run and said: "One day we skied here in early morning, went back to Salt Lake City (only twelve miles below in the valley) and played several sets of tennis. That afternoon we played eighteen holes of golf and that night we camped in Provo Canyon after doing some fly-fishing in the evening along the Provo River." It was a triumphant account of some rather unusual exertion, but it was not unbelievable.

That versatile day outdoors is quite credible. It reflects, without exhausting, Utah's vast recreational inventory. The man in the chair lift could have added that his group ate lunch while sailing on Great Salt Lake. Or he could have said the next day they struck camp and drove north out of Provo Canyon on US 189 for daybreak horseback riding near Park City and later indulged in some water-skiing at Rockport reservoir fifteen more miles north.

Still, such travels would not have included the state's five spectacular national parks, two national recreation areas, seven national monuments, five national historic landmarks or one high mountain wilderness area. It would, however, have touched two of the state's nine national forests, one of forty-three state parks, one of fourteen ski areas and two of seventeen major reservoirs or lakes. Utah, from end to end, is a sportsman's smorgasbord.

Tennis courts dot each public park, municipal golf courses regularly decorate the landscape, including one state course at Wasatch State Park near Midway in Summit County. Mountain streams feed river systems famous for angling or white water boat floating.

Amazingly, 150 years after the mountain men stalked its northern slopes and 125 years after Mormon settlers started founding permanent communities, Utah is still being "discovered," by its own residents as well as by its visitors.

GENERAL AND PRACTICAL INFORMATION FOR UTAH

UTAH FACTS AND FIGURES. Utah is named for the Ute Indians, and means "hill dwellers." Its nickname is *Beehive State.* The sego lily is the state flower; the blue spruce, the state tree; the California gull, the state bird and the elk, the state animal. "Industry" is the state motto. "Utah, We Love Thee" is the state song.

Salt Lake City is the state capital. By the most recent figures population is 1,059,273.

The promised land of the Mormons is a country of rugged mountains, salt deserts, fertile valleys, eroded rock and rich mineral wealth. Mountains cover much of the eastern and central portions of the state, and in the southeast is the dramatic landscape of the Colorado Plateau—cut by canyons, gorges, mesas and buttes. In the west, beyond the Great Salt Lake, are the mud and salt flats of the Great Salt Lake Desert. Mining and light manufacturing lead the state's economic activities. Agriculture is important as well, while tourism has lately become the second best income producer. Utah's climate is dry, with hot summers and cold winters, except in the southwestern corner, where temperatures usually remain moderate in winter. Heavy mountain snowfalls supply spring, summer and fall water needs.

 HOW TO GET THERE. *By car:* I–80, probably the most heavily traveled transcontinental highway, passes through Salt Lake City. From the north I–80N runs southeast through Salt Lake from Portland, Oregon. I–15 comes from the Los Angeles area through Cedar City, Utah, and up to Salt Lake.

By air: Salt Lake City is the major terminal. Among the long-distance carriers serving it are United, TWA and Western.

By train: Amtrak's *Rio Grande Zephyr* runs from Denver to Ogden, Utah, about 30 mi. north of Salt Lake City. From Ogden you can catch a bus to Salt Lake.

By bus: Trailways and Greyhound are the major carriers to Utah (Salt Lake City is the busiest terminal) but the region is also served by numerous other lines including Crown Transit, Linea Azul, Sun Valley and Bremerton-Tacoma.

 HOW TO GET AROUND. *By car:* The Interstates (I–70 and I–80 eastwest, and I–15 north-south) are the primary means of communication where there are long distances between towns. State roads crisscross the rest of the state except in truly desolate areas like the Great Salt Lake Desert to the west of Salt Lake City.

By air: From Salt Lake City, Hughes Airwest flies to Cedar City, in the southwest part of the state; and Frontier flies to Vernal in the northeast. There is also charter service from Salt Lake City to local airports near Zion, Bryce and Canyonlands National Parks.

By train: Ogden is on the Amtrak line, but there is no intrastate service.

By bus: All the major cities and towns in Utah have good bus service. Trailways, Greyhound, Sun Valley and Mid-Continental are some of the carriers.

TOURIST INFORMATION. Detailed information about anything in the state may be obtained from the Utah Travel Council, Council Hall, Capitol Hill, Salt Lake City 84114. Tel. (801) 328-5681.

 SEASONAL EVENTS. Utah keeps busy year round with entertainment, cultural, sporting and festival events. As with most states, winter month attractions are mostly indoor, of a cultural nature and not quite as plentiful as spring, summer and fall activities. The more urban the setting, the more versatile the annual events calendar.

January: In Salt Lake City, the drama season is still in full swing, with productions at *Promised Valley Playhouse, Theatre 138* and the *Glass Factory.* The American Basketball Assn. *Utah Stars* are in mid-season at the Salt Lake City Salt Palace, as are the Western Hockey League *Golden Eagles.* At Park City, the *Silver Wheel Theatre* presents old-fashioned melodrama. Winter resort specials include the *Color Country Winter Classic* at Brian Head ski area and the *Snow Cup Race* at Alta. Tremonton usually schedules the *Bear River Cutter Races*–horses pulling chariots on ice runners—during January.

February: *Kingsbury* and *Babcock Theatres* at the University of Utah usually present drama and music performances during the month. These will probably include a Ballet West performance. Park City's ski resort will hold the *Canada-American-Lowell Thomas Classic* and the *Dave Novelle Memorial Dual Slalom.* Both are ski races. Pro basketball and hockey will continue in Salt Lake City.

March: Special events centers at University of Utah in Salt Lake City, Utah State University, at Logan, Weber State University, Ogden, and Brigham Young University, Provo, usually hold public programs varying from concerts to pop artists. The *Mormon Festival of Art* is usually conducted at Brigham Young University. Basketball and hockey near season's end in Salt Lake City.

April: *Springville Museum of Art,* Springville, holds its annual national art exhibit. *Utah Symphony* and *Ballet West* spring gala at Utah State University. The annual *jeep safari* rendezvous in Moab—bring your own jeep. Brian Head Ski Resort holds its spring fiesta, while Alta stages a national gelande—*ski ramp jumping*–at its famed ski area. The *Dixie College Rodeo* is held at St. George.

May: *Golden Spike Celebration* at Brigham City; *Smithfield Health Days,* Smithfield; *Black and White Days,* Richmond; *Cache Dairy Festival,* Logan; annual *Ute Indian tribal bear dances* at Whiterocks; *Green River Friendship Cruise,* 180 miles from Green River to Moab.

June: The *Lagoon* amusement park opens for the summer season near Farmington. The Salt Lake City municipal band starts its Sunday concerts in Liberty Park. At Moab, the *Canyonlands Festival and Rodeo* is presented, while at Bluff an annual *Indian Days* festival is held. Rodeos at Price, Lehi and Pleasant Grove are usually produced during June. As is the *Dinasaurland Art Festival* at Vernal. *Saratoga Amusement park,* near Lehi, opens for the summer.

July: Annual celebrations are in high gear. *Bridger Days* at Hyrum; *Freedom Festival,* Provo; *Mormon Miracle Pageant,* Manti; *Old Capital Days,* Fillmore; *Ute Stampede,* Nephi; *Annual Utah Shakespearean Festival,* Southern Utah College at Cedar City; *Days of '47 parades,* Orem; *Ute Indian tribal sun dances,* Whiterocks.

August: *County fairs* are prevalent, in Heber City, St. George, Salt Lake City, Logan, Tremonton, Nephi, Parowan, Farmington, Manti. Park City usually holds its annual art festival and speed trials get underway at the Bonneville Salt Flats. Swiss Days, Heber City, which can also be scheduled the first week of September, usually cap August.

September: Park City stages an outstanding Labor Day program including mining skill contests and rugby matches. Later in the month a *Rugby Challenge Cup* tournament is played at Park City. *Peach Days Art Festival* at Brigham City and the *Cache Valley Threshing Bee,* featuring old-fashioned steam-driven machinery, is held at College Ward. Salt Lake Public Library holds a fine arts festival.

October: *Utah Stars* basketball and *Golden Eagles* hockey starts another season. The *Hansen Planetarium* in Salt Lake City also launches a new season. Annual ram sale and harvest festival is held at Spanish Fork.

November: *Golden Spike livestock show,* Ogden; Christmas parades in Cedar City and Ogden. College and university football games conclude at University of Utah, Utah State University, Weber State College and Brigham Young University.

December: An international *Christmas celebration* is held at Ogden's municipal gardens, *Utah Symphony* and *Ballet West* launch season in Salt Lake City. The Salt Lake Oratorio Society's annual performance of "The Messiah" is performed in the Salt Lake City Tabernacle. Temple Square, Salt Lake City, is decorated in thousands of Christmas lights. On Saturdays, cutter races are held at Tremonton.

NATIONAL PARKS. The five national parks in the state of Utah offer much in the way of outdoor living for hardy travelers who enjoy roughing it. *Bryce Canyon National Park* is located in the southwest part of the state. Its multicolored layers of limestone and clay produce a quilted effect that is enhanced by the rays of the sun. Bryce Canyon itself is particularly impressive, as are Yellow Creek, Willis Point and Rainbow Point. There are 20 miles of roads in the park, but some sections are accessible only on a mule or horse. For those without cars, the park provides transportation at a nominal charge. The Rim Road trip will cover most points of interest. In addition to a hotel and lodge the park has improved camp sites. Camping is limited to 14 days. Bryce Canyon also has a well-organized museum with lectures and illustrations explaining the origins of its outstanding features.

At *Zion National Park*, the emphasis is also on natural beauty. But while at Bryce most of the viewing is down, at Zion it is up. At the entrance visitors pass between two enormous colored monoliths, indicating what is to come. After entering the "gate," visible in the distance is the famous Bridge Mountain, so named because of a natural rock bridge high on the crest. Past this is a succession of rainbow-hued rock formations including Streaked Wall and the Mountain of the Sun. Driving north to the road's end leads to the Great White Throne and The Organ. The green, wooded canyon and murmuring river combine with majestic temples and towers to make this a magnificent showcase of natural splendor. Hiking trails lead to such places as Emerald Pool and the Hidden Cave. Swimming in the Virgin River is an unforgettable experience. A hotel, cabins and campsites offer accommodations for extended stays. Many Jeep camp tours are available for a good, close look at Utah's newest National Park—*Canyonlands.* They can be engaged at Moab, Blanding or Monticello. This park is divided roughly into the Needles Section at the southern end and the Island in the Sky at the northern end. Between the two are fascinating formations in The Maze, Land of Standing Rocks, Doll House, Salt Creek, Horseshoe Canyon and White Rim. In the south lies Chesler Park, a secluded valley completely ringed by fingers of rock jutting skyward.

Arches National Park, north of Moab, has five distinct sections, all unique in geology and scenery. The Windows Section is centrally located, Courthouse Towers is in the southern end, Klondike Bluffs at the northernmost point and Devils Gardens and Delicate Arch fill the rest of the northern section. The park gets its name from the 89 erosion-formed natural arches scattered around its interior.

Stone portals and bridges are found in *Capitol Reef National Park,* a slender stretch of sightseeing country about midway between Bryce and Canyonlands. It also contains petrified forests and artifacts left by pre-Columbian Indians of the Fremont culture. It is named for the gigantic, domed formations, capped with white sandstone and resembling the nation's capitol. They are part of the Waterpocket Fold, a 100-mile-long bulge in the earth's surface that contains depressions eroded in the rock and capable of holding thousands of gallons of rain water. In the north end, on cliffs behind the peach orchards at Fruita, are petroglyphs carved by ancient Indians. Outlaws, including the infamous Butch Cassidy, knew the area as a perfect hideout.

In addition to the national parks, Utah has seven national monuments. On State Route 14, near Cedar City, is *Cedar Breaks National Monument,* red and white colored rock country decorated with a profusion of wild flowers in season. Near Point Supreme are full service camp facilities, an information center and a museum explaining the various natural surroundings.

Dinosaur National Monument is particularly fascinating. East of Vernal in northeastern Utah, the area has supplied the largest collection of prehistoric vertebrates in the U.S. Entire skeletons have been excavated intact by several

110

archeological institutions. Some are kept at a small museum in the monument for visitors to inspect. Many canyons remain unexplored, but it's possible to ride big rubber rafts on safe guided trips through such perilous-sounding places as Split Mountain Canyon and Whirlpool. Cave dwellers have left crude pictures in the monument caves.

Natural Bridges National Monument takes its name from three rock bridges visible from White Canyon. In cave dwellings, open to the public, a fine, sweeping view of the area is possible. This monument is in southeastern Utah, approachable on U-95 or U-261 off U.S. 163.

On the Navajo Indian Reservation is *Rainbow Bridge National Monument*. It features a fantastic natural bridge which is now only a quarter mile away from the rising waters of Lake Powell. Eventually, as the reservoir water reaches maximum levels, boats will be able to move even closer.

Timpanogos Cave National Monument, in north-central Utah, east of Lehi in American Fork Canyon, features sidewall scenes of white and pink crystals enclosing stalagmites and stalactites shimmering in artificial lighting. The caves are open from May to October. Picnic facilities lie nearby, along with a convenient grocery store.

Newly established *Golden Spike National Historic Site*, at Promontory in Northern Utah, marks the completion point of America's first transcontinental railroad. It includes replicas of the two steam engines that met nose to nose in 1869 when driving the final "golden" rail spike was celebrated. A museum at the site also tells the country's cross-nation railroad story.

STATE PARKS. There are 25 state parks in Utah, the largest are Snow Canyon, Dead Horse Point and Wasatch Point.

Snow Canyon (5,688 acres), near St. George in the southwest corner of the state, is formed by a large gorge cut out of multi-colored sandstone. There are facilities for both recreational vehicles and tents. Open all year.

Dead Horse Point (4,627 acres) is an area of deep gorges and mesas. Dead Horse Point itself rises about 2,000 feet above the Colorado. Located southwest of the town of Moab. There are tent and recreational vehicle spaces and flush toilets. Open all year.

Wasatch Mountain (22,000 acres), near Heber City southeast of Salt Lake City, has trailer hookups, tent spaces, fishing and hunting. There is a golf course nearby. In Heber City is the Wasatch Mountain Railway which chugs along a 3-hour trip through Heber Valley, Provo Canyon and Bridal Veil Falls.

FARM VACATIONS AND GUEST RANCHES. There are not as many guest ranches in Utah as in some of the other "Old West" states, but the ones here have some of the most spectacular scenery in the country. *Triple R Farms* in Payson, about 50 miles south of Salt Lake City, has all the ranch activities and animals. This and most guest ranches are great places for children.

Bottle Hollow at For Duchesne is owned and operated by Ute Indians. You can take it easy around the modern lodge and pool or take guided trips into the Green River Wilderness.

On the Navajo Reservation in the Monument Valley area is *Gouldings Trading Post and Lodge*. You can take guided jeep tours through this almost unbelievable country of towering mesas and pinnacles and precipitous gorges.

MUSEUMS AND GALLERIES. *Paiute Indian Museum*, Public School Administration Building, Cedar City, has a collection of many items reflecting the life of the Paiute Indians. *Southern Utah Museum of Natural History*, College of Southern Utah, is open daily and features

111

collections and exhibits of Utah's relationship with studies in such fields as anthropology, biology and geology. *Worthens Store of Ten Thousand Stones*, Fremont, has an excellent geological collection from around the world. *Man and His Bread Museum*, Logan, in the library of the Utah State University, traces the history of agriculture from origin of man to the present. Closed Sunday. *Pioneer Museum*, Provo, contains a particularly extensive assortment of pioneer utensils, tools and weapons used in the early West. No charge, closed weekends. *Pioneer Village*, Salt Lake City, includes reconstructed buildings from several previous periods in U.S. history, complete with furnishings and, in the case of stores, original inventories. Open all week. March through September. *Golden Spike National Monument* museum at Promontory tells the story of America's first transcontinental railway. *Utah Field House of Natural History*, Vernal, features displays telling the state's geologic and human history, from prehistoric to modern times. Open afternoons all summer. No admission charge.

Art exhibits may be seen at the *Salt Lake Art Center*, near the University of Utah Campus, Salt Lake City. Closed Mondays and holidays. *Fairbanks Gallery of Sculpture*, Fairview, is open during the summer. Admission free. The *Springville Museum of Art*, Springville, Utah County, is Utah's most well-known art center. Outdoor art festivals are held annually at many of Utah's resort areas. Park City closes its Main Street for such an occasion, usually sometime in August.

HISTORIC SITES. Utah is a perpetual history lesson, with special locations to underline the text. St. George has the first Mormon temple built in Utah as well as Brigham Young's winter home, now a state park museum. Other pioneer homesteads are preserved in the area, particularly the *Jacob Hamblin Home* at Santa Clara.

The oldest House, the *Miles Goodyear Cabin*, is on display in Ogden. Built around 1841, the log-hewn house was used by the first white family settling permanently in what became Utah.

The town of Fillmore is the original Territorial Capital and retains the 1855 building that accommodated the state's first legislative sessions. It's now a museum.

Salt Lake City is packed with historic reminders. Prominent among them are *Lion House*, Brigham Young's office, and *Beehive House*, right next door, which was one of his homes. Also, there's "This Is the Place" monument, the *Daughters of the Utah Pioneers Museum* and *Council Hall*. The last two are on Capitol Hill. The *Salt Lake City and County Building*, on Washington Square, is an original and still used for local government purposes. The inside has been extensively remodeled, the second-floor walls are lined with vintage photographs and blueprints.

Ghost town prowling has become a popular Utah pastime, principally because there are so many abandoned settlements throughout the state and because it's another enjoyable way to see the countryside. Stephen L. Carr, in a 1972 publication, listed 150 ghost towns marking Utah's landscape. A good many are deserted mining camps, but some are former agricultural centers. Among the more interesting are Mercur and Ophir in Tooele County; Rockport, Summit County; Blacks Fork, Summit County; Rainbow, Uintah County; Scofield, Carbon County; Latuda, Carbon County; Eureka, Juab County; Mamoth, Juab County; Spring City, Sanpete County; Frisco, Beaver County; Cove Fort, Millard County; Osiris, Garfield County; Silver Reef, Washington County. In Pine Valley, Washington County, due north of St. George, stands a dignified old two-story church, a magnificent example of meeting house construction common a century ago. But standing as it does, isolated, yet still useful, it is one of rural Utah's most poignant sights.

TOURS. Few tours are confined to the state itself. But many companies that conduct tours of the region include trips into Utah. Those services operating within the state generally restrict themselves to particular areas and cover certain attractions rather than the full locale.

Gray Line Motor Tours conducts many short trips in and around Salt Lake City. These are perfect for seeing a great deal in a short time. The company also runs shuttles to Alta and Snowbird ski resorts up Little Cottonwood Canyon out of Salt Lake City. Gray Lines offers tours to Bryce Canyon National Park, Zion National Park and Cedar Breaks National Monument, as well as a Canyonland tour.

Continental Trailways schedules three-day tours from Salt Lake City to Zion National Park, Bryce Canyon National Park and Cedar Breaks National Monument. Also, a five-day tour including Grand Canyon, to the north rim. These tours are available from June 1 to Sept. 1.

With the construction of two high dams, one in Utah, the other just below the border in Arizona, more lake water is provided for several boat tours. Such trips are offered on Flaming Gorge Reservoir behind Flaming Gorge Dam by Hatch River Expeditions. Similar outings are available at Lake Powell behind Glen Canyon Dam, at Page in Arizona.

For the intrepid, white-water river running on the Green and Colorado Rivers is conducted by *Hatch Expeditions* in Vernal and *Tag-a-Long Tours* in Moab.

Silver Sands Beach, on Great Salt Lake, offers a boat cruise on the lake, including a dinner ride in the evenings.

INDUSTRIAL TOURS. Although famed for its natural beauty, Utah accommodates considerable industry. Many plants are open to visitors. While most of the following firms are pleased to welcome tourists, it is suggested they be notified before a planned arrival.

Several food processing places are open to public view. *Winder Dairy*, Salt Lake City, offers tours to those over six years old. These include milk, cheese and bread production, not animal herds. *Hi Land Dairy* of Salt Lake provides a milk processing tour. *Snelgrove Ice Cream Co.*, Salt Lake City, offers tours of an ice cream plant and the *Salt Lake Donut Co.* permits public inspection of its product in the making, any weekday before 4 p.m. *The Macaroni and Noodle Co.* in Kearns, Salt Lake County, is an LDS Church operation, using volunteer workers, and welcomes visitors.

Anyone interested in building material manufacture is invited to tour the *Otto Buehner Co.*, or *Buehner Block*, in Salt Lake City.

Utility tours are limited to those conducted by *Utah Power and Light Co.* at Castle Gate, Carbon County; *Orem*, Utah County; and the *Gadsby Plant* in Salt Lake City. *Young Electric Sign Co.* demonstrates glass blowing and neon sign manufacturing.

Mode-O'Day dress factory, Salt Lake City, demonstrates methods of cutting, assembling and sewing wearing apparel on Thursdays only. Saturday, at noon, *Wells Tannery*, Salt Lake City, conducts tours of the leather processing plant.

The Doll Hospital, Salt Lake City, has a fine display of dolls, varying in age, size and life-like appearance.

MUSIC. The Tabernacle on Temple Square in Salt Lake City is home of the *Utah Symphony* and the world-famous *Mormon Tabernacle Choir*. The Choir can be heard on Thursday evening rehearsals or on Sundays for the formal performance. The Tabernacle is also host to visiting symphonies during the year.

113

DRINKING LAWS. Utah's liquor control laws beg the visitor's indulgence. Beer is the only alcoholic beverage served in all public bars. And it is the 3.2 variety. Certain licensed restaurants also serve 2-ounce "mini-bottles" of the most commonly preferred cocktail or highball liquor. But they can only be ordered with food. That applies to wine as well. Private clubs, however, can serve mini-bottle mixed drinks whether food is also served or not. Some private clubs aren't overly careful in verifying the membership of their customers and all have liberal guest privileges. The difficulty is finding these oases without a local resident as guide. Almost all public eating and drinking establishments permit customers to carry their own liquor to the table or bar. This has earned collective state restrictions on the subject the title of "brown bag laws." And remember, in public restaurants, waiters and waitresses aren't permitted to fetch, open or mix mini-bottles. That all must be done by the customer. Mix will be served, however, and most good restaurants will chill wine brought to the establishment. Retail liquor is only sold in state stores or package agencies. The legal age is 21 and, for the most part, strictly enforced.

SUMMER SPORTS. Utah is a wonderland for outdoor recreation, a land of wide-open spaces, magnificent scenic variety and matchless natural wonders. Tennis and golf courses seem to be everywhere and for hardy individualists, possibilities for fishing, hunting, camping, hiking, horseback riding, swimming, water-skiing and boating abound.

Generally, Utah's *fishing* season starts the Saturday closest to June 1 and runs through November. However, some 200 waters are open year round. The state's most popular and regularly caught fish is the rainbow trout. Frequently taken from many waters are brook, native cutthroat, brown, Kokanee salmon, Mackinaw or lake trout, grayling, largemouth and white bass, channel catfish and walleyed pike.

Two large man-made lakes furnish spectacular opportunities for anglers— Flaming Gorge in northeastern Utah and Lake Powell in south-central Utah. The state has several streams, running through high mountain country and down along valley floors, joining sizable rivers, and all are sport for fishermen. These include the Provo, Weber and Logan Rivers; streams in Big Cottonwood Canyon, the High Uintah Mountains and most of the state's national forests. Non-resident licenses good for a year cost $15. A five-day adult tourist license is $5, a two-day tourist license, $2.50. Non-residents under 12 may fish without a license provided they are accompanied by a licensed angler and their catch is counted in the adult's daily limit.

Limits are: trout, salmon, 8 fish, except in some counties a bonus of 6 cutthroat and/or brook trout; grayling, 8 fish; Bonneville cisco, 50 fish, Bear Lake only; black bass, 10 fish; white bass, no limit; crappie, 10 fish, but in Lake Powell, no limit; walleyed pike, 6 fish except in Provo River, where the limit is 2; whitefish, 10 fish; channel cat, 4, except in Utah Lake and Willard Bay, where it is 16 fish. All other species, no limit.

Trails are excellent for *hiking* in Utah's national forests for short trips or several weeks backpacking. Long pack trips are advised to use guide services on the Colorado Plateau and High Uintahs Wilderness Area. An especially memorable hike is the 20-mile walk through Zion National Park's Virgin Narrows. This can be done in a day, but is better appreciated if planned for an overnight camp in the deep crevice of a canyon. Most of the walk is through the Virgin River water, which seldom reaches above waist height on an average adult. The hike starts several miles below Navajo Lake in the Dixie National Forest and concludes at the Bottom of a foot path in Zion National Park. Guide information at the park is available for this spectacular hike.

River running is a fast growing lure in Utah. These trips, in large, unsinkable rubber rafts, carry thrill enthusiasts through rough water on the San Juan, Green and Colorado Rivers. Charter arrangements can be made at Moab, Green River, Bluff and Mexican Hat. Boating, both water-skiing and sailing, can be enjoyed on Utah's several man-made reservoirs and lakes. In addition to Flaming Gorge, Lake Powell, Great Salt Lake, Bear Lake and Utah lake, there are Strawberry, Pineview, Scotfield, Deer Creek, Rockport, East Canyon, Otter Creek, Steinaker and Bottle Hollow Reservoirs.

There are 45 public *golf courses* in operation around Utah. Many are nestled in unique mountain or desert settings. The state maintains one, at Wasatch Mountain State Park, near Midway in Wasatch County.

Hunting is widely practiced in Utah, whether for deer, elk, antelope, jack rabbits, badgers, woodchucks and gophers or quail, pheasant, chukar partridge, ducks and geese. The large mule deer has been stocked around the state wherever browse and competition for the range allows. For years the annual harvest, attracting hunters from throughout the west, has averaged 100,000 deer. A non-resident big game license costs $50 for one deer, either sex.

Quail is best hunted in Washington County and the Uintah Basin while ringnecked pheasants can be found throughout central Utah during a short season in early November. Marshes along lakes and rivers are usual ambush sites for ducks and geese. Non-resident waterfowl and game bird licenses cost $20. Minimum age for hunting big game is 16, for waterfowl and game birds, it's 12.

 WINTER SPORTS. Utah's mountain winters are long, snow-covered and, though cold, often sunny for extended periods. The official state guide book lists 14 *ski resorts* in Utah, but not all excel. Those most likely to have ample, skiable snow on open slopes suitable for beginner as well as expert are Alta, Brighton, Solitude, and Snowbird near Salt Lake City; Park City and Park City West, in Summit County; Beaver Mountain, 27 miles east of Logan; Nordic Valley, 17 miles east of Ogden; Snow Basin, 19 miles east of Ogden; and Brian Head, 29 miles east of Cedar City. Overnight accommodations range from non-existent, at Snow Basin, to modest, at Brian Head, to limited, at Brighton, to adequate and comfortable, at Alta, to new and plush, Snowbird, to village size, Park City. Snowmobiling is catching on in Utah's snow country. It is allowed in certain areas of local canyons and on Salt Lake City's Mountain Dell Golf Course in Parleys Canyon. One of the state's finest public ice-skating rinks is at Salt Lake County's Salt Palace arena in downtown Salt Lake City.

SPECTATOR SPORTS. The American Basketball Association Utah Stars play at the Salt Palace in Salt Lake City, as do the minor league hockey team the Golden Eagles. The University of Utah in Salt Lake City, Brigham Young in Provo and Weber State in Ogden have full athletic schedules.

EXPLORING UTAH

Salt Lake City serves three essential purposes. First, and eternally foremost, it is the headquarters—the Mecca, the Vatican, the Jerusalem—of an international religion: the two-million-member Church of Jesus Christ of Latter-day Saints. Next, but not necessarily in that order, it is Utah's economic drive wheel. Finally it is the state's capital city. From any direction, the setting is impressive.

Approached from the west, Salt Lake City is seen as an urban ribbon, expanding gently and steadily up the jagged mountains that loom over the puny buildings below. From the north, there's the impression of a brick, steel and concrete wave washing into a protective cove formed by high, rocky headwalls. From the south the same suggestion of a gigantic, unbreachable wall is perceived, but it seems, this time, to be protecting a vast settlement, rolling beyond the northern horizon.

The view from the east is what most early pioneers encountered in their first introduction to a home in Utah, or as they knew it, the Territory of Deseret. The sight is much more spectacular today. The scene is a valley, hemmed on the opposite side by another ridge of low mountains—the Oquirrhs—running southward, interrupted on the north by the glinting Great Salt Lake. In the immediate foreground are gathered homes, churches, schools and shopping centers of a thriving metropolis. Farther to the right, on a prominent hill, stands the Christopher Wren-style state capitol building and, just below it, downtown Salt Lake City. Rising like a single, white-ribbed column is the sparkling new Mormon Church Building, the fourth "skyscraper" built recently at the head of State and Main Streets. The other three, University Club, the Kennecott Building and ZCMI center, have, along with the 30-floor church office building, given the city a high-rise skyline it previously lacked. They have also sharpened a local debate over developments that are drastically altering the city's former unique appearance.

The Pioneers' Progress

When the first Mormon refugees from midwestern persecution emerged from the mouth of Emigration Canyon, they glimpsed a valley stark and intimidating. Few trees shaded the land, the sun beat down unchallenged on the earth. Indeed, the ground was too hard for growing ample crops. Yet, these indomitable folk stayed. They constructed aqueducts and diverted water from the mountain streams. They organized the toil that lay ahead, they heeded commands issued by their leader, Brigham Young, they trusted the Lord's word as revealed to them by their martyred prophet, Joseph Smith, Jr., and they prevailed.

Salt Lake City proper has, in the past decade, lost population, but in the manner of other U.S. urban centers: people have moved to new, outer residential areas. The metropolitan area has constantly grown until it numbers more than a half-million.

In 1847, Brigham Young and his followers laid out their city by plotting a four-square grid oriented east-west and north-south.

SALT LAKE CITY

Points of Interest

1) Beehive House
2) Brigham Young's Grave
3) Brigham Young Statue
4) Cathedral of the Madeleine
5) City County Building
6) Council Hall
7) Fine Arts Museum
9) Geology Museum
9) Hansen Planetarium
10) Memory Grove
11) Mormon Temple
12) Pioneer Museum
13) Promised Valley Theater
14) Saint Mark's Cathedral
15) Salt Palace & Civic Auditorium
16) Seagull Monument
17) State Capitol
18) Tabernacle & Assembly Hall
19) Utah State Historical Society
20) Wax Museum

They made the streets 132 feet wide with 20-foot sidewalks, and 10-acre blocks about 650 feet to the side. Then they lined the residential streets with trees and irrigated the pavement by streams of clear water flowing in the gutters. The spaciousness has been preserved and recently enhanced when the city government required all downtown commercial signs to be flush against their buildings. This is actually the first step in a comprehensive downtown redevelopment project called "The Second Century Plan." At fruition it will incorporate numerous concepts more compatible with modern city planning. For now, Salt Lake City depends on the airiness of its wide streets along with accelerated renovation and new construction for a persistent sense of dynamism.

The newer residential neighborhoods are scattered along the series of "bench land" terraces several hundred feet above the city. Almost every lot has a view and the danger is that too much slope will be converted to home sites, preventing natural absorption needed for flash flood rain storms. Salt Lake City's normal weather pattern is seasonal in the familiar fashion. Temperatures can rise into the hundreds during summer months and plunge to near zero during winter. But conditions can also turn perverse, with sudden showers dropping several inches of rain in a few hours. Dan Valentine, humor columnist for the daily *Salt Lake Tribune,* once wrote: "Utah has two seasons: winter and August." The exaggeration was apt enough. Some years, wet, cool springs can last through June, when it suddenly turns uncomfortably hot. And fall has been known to return, accompanied by snow, in early September. But the quirky and extreme weather seldom lasts. Fall is usually beautiful, with warm days and cool nights. A normal spring is about the same, but clothed in blossoms bursting from bushes and fruit trees. Summer's heat is at least "dry," with little relative humidity. Brisk canyon winds can, however, make the dryness a discomfort rather than a relief.

The Temple Square

Salt Lake City's greatest single attraction for visitors is the Temple Square area. This is the sacred ground of Mormonism. Here, on two ten-acre blocks flanking Main Street, in the middle of town, are the central religious shrines of Latter-day Saint worship. The Temple block, on the west, is surrounded by a 15-foot-high adobe wall. On the grounds stand the Temple, Museum, Tabernacle, Assembly Hall and Visitors Center. Parking around the square is reserved for tourists from out of state.

Just inside the South Temple St. gate a public museum welcomes visitors. It includes primitive hand-made furniture, tools, agriculture implements and clothing from Utah's pioneer past. In one glass case is a wooden-cogged "roadometer" used to measure mileage on the long march across the Great Plains. The second-floor Indian Room displays artifacts left by Utah's prehistoric occupants, such as mummies, effigy jars, dippers, baskets and a variety of pipes.

Guided tours are offered on the Temple grounds every half-hour. On the itinerary is the Tabernacle, which houses the famous Temple Square pipe organ and from where Sunday Tabernacle Choir concerts are broadcast. This is an elongated structure with rounded ends that resembles a grounded dirigible. It is actually 250 feet long and 150 feet wide. Its vaulted self-supporting roof is 70 feet from the floor. Completed in 1867, the building can seat over 5,000 and is used for the church's biannual conferences. It also has served many years as a cultural center, where the Utah Symphony presents its season and visiting concert artists have performed.

As an auditorium, the building is known for its remarkable acoustics, although you can get an argument from different performers about whether the sound-carrying qualities are really helpful. In any case, no listener misses much. The choir, 375 mixed voices, was organized in the early 1850's and can be heard during its Thursday evening rehearsals as well as on Sundays, when the formal program is presented in its entirety.

South of the Tabernacle is Assembly Hall, a gray, granite structure seating 2,000, which also doubles as a lecture hall and place of worship. Facing the hall's east entrance is the Sea-gull Monument, said to be America's only historic monument to birds. It commemorates "The Miracle of the Gulls." In 1848 swarms of crickets descended from the mountain slopes to devour the pioneers' crop, the food that would protect them from famine the following winter. All eradication methods were insufficient and after the Mormons turned to prayer, flocks of sea-gulls appeared from the west, gorging themselves on crickets and rescuing the situation from certain disaster. Sea-gulls instantly earned an honored place in Mormon tradition.

Temple Square also holds monuments to the martyred Joseph Smith, the prophet, and his brother Hyrum, and the Three Witnesses Monument, with bronze bas-relief of the trio who testified that an angel showed them the golden plates from which the Book of Mormon was translated. A pedestaled statue of Brigham Young stands outside Temple Square, at its southeast corner, in the intersection of Main St. and South Temple St.

Overawing all else in Temple Square is the Temple itself. Although there are six other LDS temples in Utah, the Salt Lake City version has a majesty and singularity about it denied the others. Its architectural style is imprecise. Some have called it "Mormon Gothic," and the appearance is not dissimilar from Europe's Middle Ages cathedrals. And yet it departs from that design, too. In any case, the building was dedicated in 1893, exactly forty years to a day after ground was broken for the foundation. Granite for its 167-foot-high walls was quarried from the nearby mountains and first dragged by oxen and mules to the building site. Later, rails were used for transportation. At each end of the 163-foot-long, 100-foot-wide edifice rise three spire-tipped towers, the highest, 204 feet in the air, centered above the east façade. Balanced on that point is a gilded statue of the angel Moroni, heralding toward the east with a long-stemmed trumpet. According to Joseph Smith, it was Moroni, pronounced Mo-rown-eye, who led him to the golden plates engraved with hieroglyphics described as "Reformed Egyptian." Smith testified that with heavenly aid he was allowed to translate the record into English. Two years of laborious writing became the Book of Mormon. By 1830, Smith had six followers and the beginning of the Church of Jesus Christ, which eventually lengthened into the Church of Jesus Christ of Latter-day Saints.

Mormon History

The Book of Mormon is a fascinating work, purporting to be a history of Israelite wayfarers who reached the American continent about 600 B.C. They are supposed to have multiplied and moved into North, Central and South America. War developed between two nations, the Nephytes and Lamanites, until the latter completely destroyed the former about 400 A.D. The surviving Lamanites are considered by LDS members to be ancestors of present-day American Indians. Mormon was the Nephyte prophet who abridged and summarized the historic account divinely revealed to Joseph Smith.

Latter-day Saints belief isn't grounded exclusively in the Book of Mormon. They accept the Bible as the Word of God, as far as it has been "correctly interpreted." Mormon theology is outlined in 13 Articles of Faith and much of their moral teaching is found in the supplemental Word of Wisdom and Pearl of Great Price. The Doctrine and Convenants also contains Prophet Smith's later revelations. From the Word of Wisdom Mormons take their instruction against alcohol, tobacco, coffee, tea and other strong stimulants. Some argue it has become too central a dogma with the church, out of proportion with the Prophet's intention; that such counsel was meant only as sound advice on moderation. In this connection, it's often pointed out that Joseph Smith took wine just prior to his martyrdom in an Illinois jail. But stout Mormon adherents denouce a tippler as vigorously as they might an apostate. Simply put, the LDS people stress personal cleanliness, inside and out; that the body should be spared the ravages of excessive smoking and too much alcohol. Medical science doesn't refute the concept.

While all other buildings on Temple Square are open to the public, particularly the new Visitor Center at the northwest corner, the Temple is not. It is consecrated to Mormons in good standing only, where sacred rites, such as marriages, and other devotional work are performed. Mormons don't attend communal worship services in their Temples. These take place in neighborhood Ward and Stake Houses, which, in Salt Lake City, seem to dot every fourth or fifth street corner.

At the corner of South Temple and State Street are two buildings which originally served as office and residence for the church's second prophet, Brigham Young. They are the Lion House, his headquarters, and the Beehive House, appropriately named for the quarters he shared with his 26 wives and 56 children, at least some of them. Polygamy, of course, was the stigma that caused early Mormons their deepest trouble. It wasn't practiced by every LDS male, but, nonetheless, it had the first prophet's blessing, who said God willed that men take more than one wife. The indulgence had its practical value in the early days when husbands often died on the difficult way west and widows arrived in Utah without immediate prospects of support for themselves or their children. Still, America couldn't accept polygamy, even if—or perhaps especially if—it was approved by a Christian denomination. Congress denied Utah statehood until polygamy was purged and in late 1890, Church President Wilford Woodruff, Brigham Young's successor, issued a manifesto removing plural marriages from Mormon sanction. Statehood followed, but along with perpetual prosecution of polygamous elders who could not or would not accept the prophet's word. A splinter group still practices plural marriage in and around Utah. One investigator claimed during the 1960's there were 30,000 polygamists in Utah. What the figure may be now is only a guess. One thing is certain, plural marriage is enough to earn instant excommunication from the central LDS Church.

Brigham Young had other homes in Salt Lake City. One is preserved at the city's largest public park—Liberty Park, a grassy, tree-filled greensward that features a small amusement park and

Tracy Aviary, a colorful collection of birds and some animal life. The park also has its complement of tennis courts.

Salt Lake City has other parks. Pioneer Park, initially a gathering place for new arrivals, has a vintage steam engine donated by the Union Pacific. And Jordan Park is the location of the International Peace Garden, which has known times of neglect.

Capitol Hill

Salt Lake City is the state's capital city and Capitol Hill is worth a visit. It is reached on State Street, moving under restored Eagle Gate, marking the original entrance to Brigham Young's northside estate. On the hill, city dwellers used to gather wood from the prophet's grounds. Now forty acres are carefully landscaped around the granite and marble statehouse and office building. Completed in 1914, the copper-domed Capitol was designed for largely ceremonial uses, although it contained chambers for two houses of the bicameral legislature, the five-member State Supreme Court and the governor's office. Extensive interior remodeling has made space for administrative agencies. Expanding state government also led to construction in the late 1950's of an office building, north, across a plaza, from the older structure. The capitol first-floor hallway is lined with showcases exhibiting the qualities of every Utah county, mostly by region. Though sometimes slightly outdated, the displays are accurate enough to be edifying.

A favorite attraction is the original Mormon Meteor, the piston-driven car in which Ab Jenkins set endurance records at the Bonneville Speedway some thirty years ago. The speedway is about 120 miles west of Salt Lake City and in the Great Salt Lake Desert. It still hosts drivers and their crews attempting to set every imaginable land speed mark, in rocket cars, stock engine vehicles and motorcycles. The activity grows brisk toward summer's end, when the salt flats have dried to a table-top firmness, and continues until weather conditions force a halt, usually by November.

Skiing Around Salt Lake City

A central exhibit in the Capitol display consists of a large relief map of the state, shaped by the U.S. Forest Service. The mountain terrain around Salt Lake City stands out conspicuously, indicating why, in 1962, the city was selected as this country's nominee for the 1964 winter Olympics. Skiing is the area's chief winter pastime. East from the city, up two adjacent canyons are four ski areas that rival any in the U.S. for snow depth and consistency. Big Cottonwood Canyon leads to Solitude and Brighton. Little Cottonwood Canyon, a few miles farther south, trails up the mountain side to Snowbird and famed Alta. All operate a complex of chair lifts, but Snowbird features an aerial tramway that ferries skiers and sightseers to the top of 11,000-foot-high Hidden Peak. The trip takes about six minutes, and each of two cars carries 125 passengers in warm, dry enclosures. Snowbird is a year-round resort, with a village consisting of hotel, restaurant and condominium accommodations. It hosts conventions throughout most of the year.

On the east side of the mountains, Salt Lake City residents have been skiing at Park City for the last several years. Originally a mining town, Park City made a comeback from "ghost" status when its recreational potential was discovered. Developers have since filled vacant property with new condominium groupings, close to skiing in winter and golf courses and tennis courts in summer. Downtown Park City has retained much of its old mining character. As a "Gentile" town, Park City differs markedly from other Utah communities. Its streets are two-lane, it has more former saloons on the Main Street and its past is charred by horrendous fires that repeatedly leveled homes, stores, bars, churches and schools. Most of the mine owners, who took their riches from hills around Park City, lived in Salt Lake City. Today, remaining homes built by these mineral kings can be seen lining South Temple Street east of Brigham Street. One, belonging to the Thomas Kearns family, was eventually deeded to the state and served as the governor's mansion until it was turned into office and library for the Utah Historical Society.

"This is the Place"

South Temple is a good street to follow east from downtown. It leads to the University of Utah, laid out on a fine vantage point from which to view the city below. The campus, 482 acres large, was animated by a massive building program during the 1960's. New structures and landscaping created a particularly engaging combination at the institution's southern half, which embraces pleasant walkways and fountains. The north half is older, the original campus, but well cared-for and a portal to nostalgia. It also contains a highly regarded Museum of Natural History, housed in the university's former library. Guided tours are available. The school of architecture maintains a Fine Arts Museum and, year round, the school's various theaters and auditoriums produce drama, ballet, popular music festivals and classical recitals. Ballet West, a professional troupe supported by the intermountain region, is home-based at the university. On the campus edge, the Art Barn provides new showings of contemporary paintings, drawings, photography, sculptures and industrial art about every three weeks. The university's teaching hospital is nationally acclaimed, the only one between Denver and the West Coast. Its researchers have excelled in bone, blood and organ transplant work. Experiments with creating an artifical heart have attracted considerable scientific attention to the university's medical research program. And federal funding. The University Hospital and Medical Center is almost ninety percent federally financed. The campus has always been aware of the U.S. Government. At its back is the 9,000-acre Fort Douglas Military Reservation, complete with barracks, officers quarters and parade grounds. Much was declared surplus by the Pentagon and has been applied for by the state, to serve the university and other purposes. One of the other uses will be to enlarge Pioneer Monument State Park, which is south of the university and approximately at the spot where Brigham Young is supposed to have uttered his famous line, "This is the place," after emerging from Emigration Canyon overlooking Salt Lake Valley.

More precise historians quote Brigham as actually saying: "It is enough. This is the right place. Drive on!" And he knew exactly where he was going. That had been decided after advanced parties reported back about the prospects near the Great Salt Lake. In any case, the park has a "This is the Place Monument," a stone shaft and flanking extensions decorated by bronze figures of such early area explorers as Jim Bridger, Father Escalante and General John Fremont. Nearby stands a visitors center with murals telling the story of the Mormon migrations. Opposite the monument is Salt Lake City's Hogle Zoological Gardens, a small, but well-stocked, neatly kept zoo. There are picnic grounds along a slender stream in the canyon mouth, too

Below the zoo, south on Wasatch Boulevard, is a shopping center fairly typical of many that dot neighborhoods in the Salt Lake Valley. At least five are indoor "shopping malls," the most unique located at 7th East and 5th South. It is called Trolley Square because it is in converted bus line barns dating back to 1908. Tastefully remodeled for functional purposes, this shopping mall boasts fifty tenants, ranging from specialty stores, snack bars and a farmers market to restaurants and craft shops. Four small, but comfortable theaters operate in one building. The location is marked by a gold-painted and iron-ornamented water tower. Light bulb trimming gives the tank and its embellishments a special night-time appearance. Trolley Square is an extraordinary example of commercial recycling.

America's First Department Store

The newest enclosed shopping complex is downtown Salt Lake City's ZCMI Center. The initials stand for Zion's Cooperative Mercantile Institution, which means more in history than in the present. It was Brigham Young's answer to storekeepers who seemed to be profiteering among the early, struggling Mormon settlement in Salt Lake Valley. He simply put the Church in the retailing business and neutralized the competition. As it evolved, ZCMI is claimed by some to be America's first department store. Whatever the fact on that score, ZCMI is Utah's leading department store today and its new downtown building devoured the old structure, which was actually a collection of stores at the corner of Main Street and South Temple. Retained, however, as part of the new building's façade, is the cast-iron front that decorated ZCMI's Main Street entrances for decades. Another compromise between old and new can be seen on 1st South between Main and West Temple Streets. This short block was "renovated" in 1970, given new sidewalks, a median strip planted with seedling trees and stone benches at the corners. Yet the street lighting shines from vintage candelabra lamp posts, deliberately installed to retain a dated, but ageless, ingredient. This street leads to the new Salt Lake County civic auditorium, called the Salt Palace. It seats 14,000 in the main area and has smaller meeting and exhibition rooms, as well as a little theatre.

Advent of the Salt Palace has transformed the city's downtown west side. A restaurant and specialty shop compound, entitled Arrow Press Square, blossomed in aged, rejuvenated brick buildings opposite the Salt Palace on West Temple. Three new hotels were constructed in the immediate vicinity. All in all, the effect has been a wholesome one. In addition, the Salt Palace attracted an American Basketball Association team, the Utah Stars, which during its first year in Salt Lake City won the ABA championship. A minor league hockey team, the Golden Eagles, shares the arena through the winter season, a member of the Western Hockey League. The building's versatility accommodates circuses, track meets, concerts and rodeos. It has become the modern home of the Pioneer Days rodeo.

Pioneer Day

July 24 is Pioneer Day, a state holiday in Utah. It commemorates the day in 1847 when the first Mormon pioneers reached their promised land, and in Salt Lake City it is preceded by a full week of activity. On the 24th, an enormous parade, featuring floats, marching bands, men's and women's horse brigades, clowns and dignitaries galore, files down Main Street, then to Liberty Park. In 1970, President Nixon attended the rodeo that July 24th. The city has recurrently hosted U.S. Presidents, almost steadily since World War II.

It may be, as some have suggested, that a national politician knows the value of paying a courtesy call on the favored city of a two-million-member organization. And in fewer places is there more ingrained respect for the U.S. presidency, no matter who holds it. Joseph Smith taught that America's constitutional form of government was divinely inspired. Beyond this, nevertheless, few cities rise above the nationwide urban monotony and represent a distinctive personality quite the way Salt Lake City does. People, whether President or plain traveler, need no other reason than their curiosity for inspecting this "City of the Saints" firsthand.

The Lake Itself

Two landscape imprints indelibly associated with Salt Lake City and Utah deserve special mention. One, of course, is Great Salt Lake. The other, Kennecott Copper Corp.'s mammoth open pit mine.

Great Salt Lake is indeed a natural wonder. Approximately 1,500 square miles in area, it is the nation's largest inland sea. Twenty-five percent saline, the lake is five times saltier than any ocean. Utah's relationship with the lake has changed through the years, just as the waterline has fluctuated.

Except for a species of tiny shrimp, no fish live in Great Salt Lake, so it had little practical value to the pioneers. Eventually, wood-hauling stern-wheelers plied its waters. Some were converted to early-day cruise ships. Lakeside resorts, dance halls and amusement parks have been operated around Great Salt Lake's eastern and southern shores through the years, but all have either burned or been abandoned. The last, giant Saltair, with its Arabian Nights-inspired pavilion, disappeared in flames during 1972. It had been closed since the mid-'50's.

Although the state created a park on Antelope Island in Great Salt Lake, east of Layton on State 127, high waves repeatedly washed out the road. Until funds are appropriated for firmer roadbed work, park improvements will be delayed. That leaves only one public access to the lake and its beaches. It is at Silver Sands, west of Salt Lake City on US 40. The area is leased from the state by private operators, so there is a charge for entering. If a pungent odor fills the air, it is not from sewage or industrial waste, it is the smell of dead brine shrimp washed up on the nearby shore. It's true, swimmers can bob on the lake surface "like a cork," without any effort. But some bathers suddenly discover they are allergic to salt in such concentrated solution. The reaction is a stinging sensation over that part of the skin immersed in the water. By all means shower under available fresh-water tanks after leaving the lake water.

Minerals Around Great Salt Lake

For years sodium chloride, common table salt, has been taken from the lake. Lately, other minerals, long known to be suspended through Great Salt Lake in measurable but elusive quantities, are being extracted. And the bed is being explored for oil.

In any case, Great Salt Lake is always a magnificent sight at sundown when clouds are also hugging the western horizon.

Kennecott's copper mine lies up Bingham Canyon. But it is visible from miles away as a tan and gray terracing on the face of the Oquirrh Mountains, sloping to Salt Lake Valley's western floor. Mining and its associate industries, smelting and refining, have, off and on for at least one hundred years, been a key factor in Utah's economy. Which is ironic because Brigham Young disdained the activity as too transitory and a magnet to unsavory types. He wanted his settlements snug to the ground, engaged in farming and farm-related industry. But it was too easy to find mineral deposits in such mountainous surroundings and a Mormon-baiting U.S. Army officer, Colonel Patrick E. Connor, dispatched federal troops to Salt Lake City in 1862, and he actively encouraged his men on prospecting expeditions. They found gold and silver, which produced other discoveries of zinc, silver-lead, coal and copper. Ore from Bingham Canyon was taken to Colonel Connor by an apostate Mormon, George Ogilvie. The colonel's assayer confirmed a rich lead and silver content, putting Bingham Canyon firmly in the nation's mining history. Low-grade copper, scattered finely through the ground, was eventually dug from the canyon; but not until the turn of the century, when mining engineer Daniel C. Jackling developed an economical metallurgical process, did the metal become a significant state resource. Since then, it has been Utah's most consistently important mineral product. Approximately $130 million worth of copper has been extracted annually from the Kennecott pit. The deepening, stair-step excavation can be viewed from an enclosed overlook, which features an amplified recorded message about the mine's past, present and future.

Jedediah Smith's Trail

In 1826, Jedediah Strong Smith, a mountain man known more for exploration than fur-trapping, hiked what is now Utah from north to south. He hugged the western flank of the Wasatch, searching for better beaver-snaring territory. Smith and his party had a desperate time of it—they nearly starved. Today, travelers following an equivalent route not only eat well, they linger at countless restful, scenic and thought-provoking intervals.

Jed Smith entered Utah through Cache Valley in the northeast corner. That probably would be done now on US 91 or 89, both rolling south from Pocatello. Or on US 30, which becomes State Route 30, from Rock Springs, Wyoming, on the east. Except for extensive cultivation, the country retains much of the naturalness encountered by fur-tracking wanderers over 150 years ago.

US 89, east of Logan, carries motorists through highland beauty in the Cache National Forest. Logan Canyon is particularly fascinating, with two glacial lakes—Tony Grove and White Pine—both reached by paved road or foot-path. The Jardine Juniper, said to be the oldest tree in Utah—over three thousand years withstanding wind, cold and sun—is also in Logan Canyon. US 89 nudges alongside Bear Lake, enjoyably frequented by water-skiers, sailing craft, fishermen and scuba divers. Bear Lake is acquiring an increasing assortment of condominium resort developments. It has had for years a state park on the western shore and the principal adjacent town is hundred-year-old Garden City.

Logan, at the junction of US 91 and 89, is the commercial hub of northeastern Utah. It is the location of Utah State University, originally limited to agricultural and forestry studies, which currently offers other courses as well as recurrently nationally ranked football and basketball teams. Logan also has one of Utah's four Mormon temples, a stone-hewn structure, finely landscaped and flower decorated during summer months.

Nine miles south and sixteen miles east of Logan, through Hyrum on State 101, a rare encounter is staged every winter. The Utah Wildlife Division has established, at a place called Hardware Ranch, an elk feeding station. The animals, mostly cows and an occasional lame bull, congregate in the snow to survive on daily alfalfa handouts. Visitors are transported into the midst of the herd by horse-drawn sleighs. It's a singular experience, mingling with five hundred seldom-seen creatures, approachable only because of their hunger.

Another entry to Utah known by the mountain men is along the present Interstate 80. It leads, after a junction at Echo, forty-three miles beyond Wyoming, to either Ogden or Salt Lake City. The I-80N branch traverses stunning Weber Canyon on its way to Ogden. Near Morgan, the super highway gives travelers an opportunity to view Devil's Slide, two parallel slabs of limestone twenty feet apart and forty feet high sticking to the mountain side. It helped conjure many Indian legends.

The Coming of the Railroad

Ogden, thirty-three miles north of Salt Lake City, is Utah's second largest city with 126,000 residents. It was also planned by Brigham Young, but, after the arrival of transcontinental rails in 1868, Ogden gained the reputation as a railroad town. It was, during those track-laying days, a brawling, free-for-all hot spot, causing the Mormon population considerable unease.

Now, the city is a quieter commercial and industrial center, beneficiary of a new church temple and home of Weber State College, a four-year vocational and liberal arts school. With the help of an active industrial development program and several federal installations—Hill Air Force Base, an Internal Revenue Service computer center, and Regional Forest Service office—Ogden continues growing. The Browning brothers, inventors of automatic weapons, were from Ogden. The John M. Browning Armory and Firearms Museum displays eighty-six original and production models of Browning rifles, pistols and machine guns.

On I-15, northwest from Ogden, in an especially tranquil setting, is Brigham City, given a space-age boost by missile industry firms located nearby. Via Brigham City, on State 83, motorists can visit one of Utah's latest National Historic Sites—the Golden Spike site at Promontory. It features a tourist center and replicas of two engines used during the driving of the last spike which completed America's first transnation railroad. During summer months the 1869 ceremony is reenacted at the Golden Spike National Historic Site as the finale to a film, narration and tour of the museum.

The Northern Tier

Doubling back, through Brigham City toward Ogden, travelers can encounter a collection of bird management areas around bays on the east-central portion of Great Salt Lake. At Willard Bay

State Park, summer regattas for both power and sail boats are held annually.

Utah's northern tier fluctuates dramatically, from the Great Salt Lake Desert on the western hand and the High Uintas Wilderness Area on the east. This magnificent slab of the Uinta Mountains, the only continental range running east and west, contains Utah's loftiest point—Kings Peak, 13,528 feet high. It is also preferred terminal for backpackers and campers. Mirror Lake resort touches the wilderness area at its eastern extremity and can be reached on U–150 as soon as the road is cleared of snow, sometime in late spring. Uinta mountain lakes and streams are a hardy fisherman's challenge.

Fishing in northeastern Utah can be successful without being strenuous, especially at Flaming Gorge Reservoir in the Flaming Gorge National Recreation Area, around and behind Flaming Gorge Dam. This is a delightful outdoor offering tucked into the northern and most eastern corner of Utah, approximately seventy-five miles due north from Vernal. Previously a hunter and fisherman rendezvous, Vernal has lately become the center for oil field development. The area has another distinction— prehistoric fossil remains at Dinosaur National Monument, twenty miles east of Vernal, where visitors can actually watch workmen patiently unearth bones of long-extinct giant reptiles. At Vernal, the state maintains the Field House of Natural Science, an exhibit of local geological features, prominent Utah scenes—not always up to date—and ancient Indian artifacts. This is Indian country.

The main highway between Vernal and Salt Lake City is US 40, which passes through the Uintah and Ouray Indian Reservation. The principal towns along this stretch are Roosevelt and Duchesne, but about seven miles east of Roosevelt is a modest experiment in contemporary Indian self-sufficiency. The Bottle Hollow Resort, a motel complex built alongside a 450-acre reservoir, is owned and operated by the Ute Indian Tribe. It derives its name from a previous custom of locals pitching empty liquor bottles into a natural depression in the brush dotted landscape between settlements at Roosevelt and Ft. Duchesne. The resort advertises ceremonial Indian performances and has a trading post dealing in native artwork and craft specialties.

On farther, closer to Salt Lake City, US 40 passes two more large fishing holes, Starvation and then Strawberry Reservoir, impounded sources of irrigation water also stocked with trout. Beyond, at Heber City, a left turn off US 40 leads to Provo along US 189. A right turn, staying with 40 to I–80, leads to Salt Lake City. Delaying at Heber City isn't a bad idea.

Heber is a familiar Mormon name, but the place could have easily been called Basel or Tavaness, anything from the Swiss foothills, as this is what the Heber Valley resembles. And it did to the Mormon converts from Switzerland who settled there. Directly west lies 22,000-acre Wasatch Mountain State Park, a hiking, camping and picnicking wayside that includes a 27-hole golf course nestled in a crisp Alpine setting.

Railroad Run

During summer months, a steam engine recalled from railroading's smoke-puffing past hauls a four-car coach-load from Heber City to Bridal Veil Falls in Provo Canyon. The round trip meanders through meadowland, along streams and reservoirs while penetrating a mountain pass. It's a quaint way to sightsee.

Bridal Veil Falls is a double cataract that splashes in steep descent down Provo Canyon's sheer mountain walls. It's viewable from alongside US 189, if that's the route selected out of Heber City. Provo Canyon is one of the principal passes slicing through the Wasatch Range and, most of the way, it follows Provo River, a premier trout stream. Also off US 189 in Provo Canyon is Sundance Resort, a development led by film actor Robert Redford. It features skiing during the winter and camping or horseback riding through the other seasons.

US 189 is an old, narrow road, but preferred by conservationists attempting to prevent a planned widening and straightening project. Whatever the outcome, the highway will still lead to Provo, Utah's second largest city.

Provo and BYU

Located at the foot of 11,000-foot-high Provo Peak, the city is typically Mormon, with clean, wide streets and well-tended landscaping. It is a combination farming, education and industrial center. The Mormon Church's biggest and best college campus graces Provo—Brigham Young University. Handsome and sprawling after a massive 1960's construction program, BYU, or "The BY," as it is colloquially called by many Utah admirers, attracts a 25,000-member student body from LDS families throughout the U.S. and foreign countries. Its rigid, and obeyed, code of conduct rivals its nationally ranked basketball teams for far-flung recognition. While some campuses were burning during the turbulent '60's, BYU was receiving endowments from non-Mormon benefactors who appreciated its constant orderliness. BYU administrators make a point of avoiding federal financing.

A U.S. Government decision to scatter basic industry during World War II gave the area around Provo a steel mill. Now owned and operated by the Columbia-Geneva Division of the U.S. Steel Corp., the mill has provided steady employment for over thirty years. Also persistent air pollution. Protecting air and water has been a problem in this area.

Utah Lake, twenty-three miles long north to south and ten miles wide, ripples just west of Provo. It is Utah's largest fresh-water lake. And while much is fit for boating, fishing and water-skiing, parts are termed a health hazard by state officials. The culprit is sewage, being treated, but not under full control before it finds the lake. A wise swimmer looks first for posted warnings. The situation hasn't discouraged Saratoga, a lakeside amusement park that attracts sizable crowds all summer long.

Just south of Provo, on US 89, lies Springville, also called Art City. The honorary title goes with Springville's Art Museum, which contains an acclaimed collection of paintings and sculpture. In April, the permanent display is enhanced with an annual exhibit by nationally known artists.

To the north, near Lehi, is Timpanogos Cave National Monument. Located in American Fork Canyon, the cleverly lighted caves were formed by a now-vanished underground river. The monument visitor center is open from May to October and the setting is spectacular. The cave is at the head of a long, uphill walk not recommended for the aging or infirm.

Gateway to Southern Utah

Provo could be considered the gateway to Southern Utah, the point from which the state gradually changes, becoming less populated, not as arable, with but a few exceptions, non-industrialized, and cross-cut by geologic extremes.

Brigham Young intended for the Mormons to be fully self-sufficient so that never again could they be easily uprooted and driven from their land. To this end he regularly sent immigrant groups streaming downstate with instructions to farm and create industry wherever possible. His expectations weren't always fulfilled, but the strength of his resolve is reflected in two early temples built in southern Utah. Provo only recently acquired a temple. Manti, 176 miles south of Salt Lake City, has had one since the late 1800's. It's said Brigham Young was particularly concerned about the region around Manti because an Indian chief had asked him to send white men bearing the Christian teaching. Be that as it may, settlements waxed and waned through the area during the pioneering era. To an extent that Fillmore, opposite Manti, on the west side of the Valley Mountains and farther south, was at one point competing with Salt Lake City for designation as state capital. It still retains the old territorial statehouse as a museum. Fillmore, named after the 13th President of the U.S., had a population numbering slightly under 2,500 in 1970. The largest city in south-central Utah is Richfield, about 4,400 strong on US 89, surrounded by sections of the Fishlake National Forest. It's also a jumping-off place for Capitol Reef National Park. The eighty-mile drive on State 24 provides a sudden and startling introduction to Utah's Colorado River canyon country. Crossing open, wind-weathered Awapa Plateau to a height of 8,410 feet, the highway drops into an attractive valley at the head of east-flowing Fremont River. Then, beyond Torrey, the descending roadway enters an arid land of rocks, buttes, mesas and gorges striped with brilliant colors. On the left is Waterpocket Fold, a 150-mile line of red, yellow and brown cliffs, several hundred feet high, capped by pinnacles and white capitol-like domes.

Colorado River Canyon Country

Sixty-one square miles in area, Capitol Reef National Park includes twenty-mile stretches of the cliff. The road moves along the base, encountering spurs and graded trails leading to impressive Grand and Capitol Gorges, Chimney Rock, Hickman Natural Bridge, petrified forests and Indian petroglyphs engraved on stone 1,200 years ago.

The Capitol Reef escarpment marks the southern boundary of Wayne Wonderland, a desert region of canyons, basins and sheer cliffs, the most awesome work produced by natural upheaval and erosion. Here stand Cathedral Valley, Walls of Jericho, Hoodoo Arch and the surrealistic Valley of the Goblins. Ask about road conditions before exploring these sites in standard model cars.

After departing the park, State 24 winds to Hanksville, the now-renowned Robbers Roost headquarters, made newly famous by the film "Butch Cassidy and the Sundance Kid." Yes, they were actual early-day Utah outlaws and this was their hideaway country. It is, today, a well-traveled way toward Lake Powell and the Glen Canyon National Recreation Area. Southeast from Hanksville, State 95 drops to a junction with State 276, which finally reaches Bullfrog Basin at lakeside. There are marinas and overnight facilities at the basin.

An alternate course follows State 95 to a river crossing at Hite. As long as the road is passable, this way leads to Natural Bridges National Monument, three gigantic rock spans and cliff ruins in tranquil high desert, dotted by piñon and juniper growth. East and north lies a section of the Manti-La Sal National Forest, and directly east a fork in State 95 leads to either Blanding, north, or Bluff, south. Blanding is larger, 2,250 people, and closer to Monticello, which is the actual center of the region's tourist activity. But Bluff is the more interesting, a tiny community with a dramatic past. It is the first white settlement in southeastern Utah, an oasis reached in 1879 by a Mormon party after an epic winter trek across the canyon harshness. From Bluff it's possible to boat through whitewater rapids of the San Juan River to Mexican Hat, named for a nearby sombrero-shaped rock. Also north on State 261 outside Mexican Hat, the nine-mile sidetrip to an overlook above the Goosenecks of the San Juan is worth taking. The river has carved a narrow canyon, 1,200 feet deep, in a sequence of horseshoe bends. Water must flow six miles to proceed one.

East of Bluff are the widely scattered prehistoric ruins of Hovenweep National Monument. The two Utah sections are reachable by partly paved, partly graded roads. South from Mexican Hat, on US 163, travelers enter the northern rim of the 25,000-square-mile Navajo Indian Reservation, largest in the U.S. Here, on the Utah-Arizona border, is awesome, incredible Monument Valley. Mile after mile, the pavement passes huge red sandstone buttes, pillars, columns and needles soaring more than one thousand feet above the wide desert floor. The unforgettable shapes have been given such names as Totem Pole, Castle, Stagecoach, Brigham's Tomb and Mitten Buttes. Indians still spend summers amid these wonders, living much as their ancestors did centuries ago. The Navajos have created Monument Valley Tribal Park, taking in 96,000 acres. It offers an observation building, Indian crafts center, campgrounds, fourteen miles of passable roads and trips to remoter sections in special big-wheeled vehicles.

Returning through Monticello, US 163 meets Moab, another tourist base camp. The Old Testament name is misleading these days. Moab bustles, often with Hollywood film companies, shooting outdoor scenes on location. They headquarter in Moab and search surrounding terrain for likely background to go with westerns, desert dramas and, yes, Biblical enactments. Scenes from "The Greatest Story Ever Told" were shot outside Moab. The desired "authenticity" isn't difficult to find.

In the 1950's, Moab enjoyed a different kind of drama. Uranium was discovered nearby and, while it lasted, the mining and prospecting was frenetic. Located above the confluence of the Green and Colorado Rivers on the Colorado, Moab makes the most of its river country. Various boat tours are available at the landings, including a night ride that takes sublime advantage of shapes formed on gorge walls with high-powered flood lights.

Arches and Towers

Crossing the Colorado, US 163 passes Arches National Park, featuring a fifty-three-square-mile area with rock spires, pinnacles and narrow fins pierced by 88 naturally formed openings. One is a 291-foot bridge, the largest known natural arch. Paved roads reach the finest specimens, but some walking is necessary to see rock-formed skyscrapers of Park Avenue, Landscape Arch, The Devil's Garden and whimsical Delicate Arch. Called Schoolmarm's Britches by local cowhands, the last is the most beautiful and remarkable of the bunch. Rising more than one hundred feet high, it stands alone and unsupported in a setting of slickrock domes, with the gorge of the Colorado River and the 12,000- to 13,000-foot peaks of the La Sal Mountains in the distance.

Castleton Towers and Fisher Towers are two other areas of unique rock formations northeast from Moab. They can be visited by a black-topped road through the multi-hued Colorado River gorge.

Canyonlands National Park envelopes the confluence of the Colorado and Green Rivers and exhibits the greatest variety of rock sculpture found anywhere on earth. Elevations range from 3,700 feet in the depths of Cataract Canyon to over 6,000 feet on the plateau rims. Between both a half-billion years of the planet's life is apparent in countless folds, warps, shifts and tilts. Canyonlands, established as a national park in 1964, is still fairly untamed. The more intrepid visitors can explore it satisfactorily on Jeep roads, but other autos are advised to proceed with advance knowledge about conditions ahead. Local pilots have offered sightseeing flights over the area and information on such possibilities is available at the Arches Visitor Center.

For a less expensive bird's-eye view of the Canyonlands region, a black-topped county road leads west from US 163, north of Moab, to Dead Horse Point State Park, a magnificent overlook on the Colorado gorge. Also, a graded road veers away from the Dead Horse Point approach southwest across the plateau to appropriately titled Island in the Sky, ending at Grand View Point. This jutting promontory provides a giddy, 2,500-foot-high view of the merging Colorado and Green Rivers.

US 163 continues north to I–70, built through country never before crossed by road or trail. Scenery this opened up is typical of the entire area. The 235-mile trip from here to Salt Lake City is usually made on US 50-6, branching north from I–70, through

Green River and Price. At Green River, the annual Friendship Cruise is annually launched in late May. Power boats of every description, conveying groups that vary from sightseers to fishermen to outdoors enthusiasts to purely revelers, compose the armada. Their destination is Moab, which is usually reached the second day out, total elapsed time depending on the boatman's skill and sobriety.

Price and Helper are centers of Utah's coal-mining industry. That industry has suffered economic ups and downs with the coal market and as a consequence the Price-Helper area shows scars of hard times past. Most Utah miners came from non-Mormon stock and the coal communities are no exception. They evidence a firm individuality verging on truculence toward the predominantly LDS settlements. In the past, Price was known to openly defy state laws restricting liquor sold in bars. A former mayor, J. Bracken Lee, who subsequently became a two-term Utah governor and then mayor of Salt Lake City, once arrested state liquor control officers in Price, claiming they had no jurisdiction interfering with municipal matters. Price is also the home of Eastern Utah College, formerly Carbon College, a two-year state institution.

Further South

Southern Utah is, for its population, particularly blessed with state colleges. Others, besides EOC, include Snow College at Ephraim and Southern Utah College at Cedar City. The Cedar City campus has developed as a center for arts instruction. This extends through painting, metal work and drama. Utah's summer Shakespearean Festival is held on the college campus every year in July.

Cedar City, on I–15, 260 miles south of Salt Lake City, is also a recreation and tourist center. It reclines on the western edge of the Dixie National Forest and is within eighteen miles of Cedar Breaks National Monument. Farther east, on State 14, then north on US 89, Bryce Canyon National Park drops away in a multi-hued extravaganza. One of Utah's newest ski resorts, Brian Head, is less than a two-hour drive, depending on road conditions, from Cedar City. The facility, with chair lifts rising above 10,000-foot elevations, is a favorite with skiers from Nevada, Arizona and even California.

Zion National Park is located directly south of Cedar City, off I–15 and then along state routes that take motorists through small prim Mormon settlements neamed Toquerville, LaVerkin and Virgin. A tranquil, wooded camping site east of Cedar City off State 14 is Navajo Lake. The lake is cold enough for good trout fishing and big enough for boating. The area around it is being "found," and fast acquiring vacation cabin sites. Another rediscovery is taking place at St. George in southern Utah.

St. George has Dixie State College and was a favorite wintering retreat for Brigham Young. His two-story house, an echo from New England, has been restored as a Utah State Park museum. Lately, condominium developers have done well at St. George, with accommodations for retirees, weekend recreation seekers and tourists traveling at a leisurely and stylish pace. The permanent community, 8,000 at the latest census, started with a cotton mission sent to the Virgin River Valley by Brigham Young in 1861. The pioneers endured considerable hardship, but managed to succeed. Utah's first Mormon temple, white stucco surrounded by desert palms, was erected at St. George in 1871. Early vineyards once produced quality Utah wine around St. George until a burst of abstinence wiped the industry out.

North of town rise the cool, forested Pine Valley Mountains, topped by 10,325-foot-high Signal Point. Five miles west from St. George is Dixie State Park at Santa Clara, featuring the formidable rock-fortress home built in 1862 by Jacob Hamblin, an outstanding Mormon explorer and missionary to the Indians. No one was more familiar with the obscure trails of southern Utah. Hamblin devoted almost half a century to keeping the peace between Indian tribes and white settlers. He died in 1886 while on the run from officers arresting polygamists. Southwest from Santa Clara, the highway passes through the Shivwits Indian Reservation, winding over the Beaver Dam Mountains as high as 4,800 feet.

An eastward route from St. George leads past Zion National Park on State 15 to a junction with US 89 on its way south to Kanab. Kanab has been called "Hollywood's backyard" because of the countless outdoor films photographed in its vicinity. The credits run from the early "Drums Along the Mohawk," to the more recent "Planet of the Apes." Parry Lodge in Kanab was made famous by the interviews with movie stars conducted there. Scenery around Kanab is literally "too magnificent to be real." The Moqui Indian caverns are located five miles north of town, displaying the largest fluorescent mineral exhibit in the United States. Immediately south of Kanab, the small Kaibab Indian Reservation hugs the state line in Arizona. The settlement, accessible from US 89 after that highway exits Utah, is exactly 305 miles beyond Salt Lake City and 71 miles away from the north rim of Grand Canyon.

AROUND THE STATE

 HOTELS AND MOTELS in Utah are relatively inexpensive. Their highest rates will be in effect for the "in-season" period which, according to the locale, is either ski time (November through April) or the summer months that bring tourists to the National Parks and forests lands. These are the rates we have used to compile our categories.

Based on double occupancy, the rate categories for Utah are: *Deluxe* over $27, *Expensive* $22-27, *Moderate* $16-22 and *Inexpensive* under $16.

For a more complete explanation of hotel and motel categories, refer to ROCKIES AND PLAINS *Facts at Your Fingertips* at the front of this volume.

ALTA

Alta Lodge. *Deluxe.* State 210 in Little Cottonwood Canyon. This ski resort has a variety of accommodations and prices—call for rates or package plans. Meals are served in the cafe and dining room and there is a package store. After skiing enjoy a game of ping-pong, pool, sit by the fireplace or read in the library. 742-3500

Rustler Lodge. *Expensive.* State 210. Offering everything from dormitory-style rooms to suites as well as family rates and ski package plans, this ski lodge has a cafe, bar, and package store; also saunas and a recreation room. 742-2200

BEAVER

Beaver TraveLodge. *Moderate.* 650 N. Main St. (US 91). Within a block you'll find a coin laundry and a cafe open 24 hours. Rooms have dressing areas, color TV, and phones: local calls free. 438-2409

Paice. *Moderate.* 161 S. Main St. (US 91). Attractively landscaped with a heated pool, the Paice also has color TV and free coffee in the rooms. A cafe open until midnight and a coin laundry are nearby. 438-2438

Sleepy Lagoon. *Moderate.* US 91. The small pond helps create the restful atmosphere suggested by the motel's name. Inside you will find attractive rooms and dressing areas. The motel also offers a heated pool while a cafe and laundromat are within a half mile. 438-5681

BLANDING

Cliff Palace. *Inexpensive.* 123 S. Main St. (US 163). Large, comfortable rooms and convenient at-door parking. The cafe one and a half blocks away is open until 10 p.m. and a coin laundry is also nearby. 678-2252

Gateway. *Inexpensive.* 88 E. Center St., 1 blk. N on US 163. The local cafe is directly opposite and the coin laundry is just down the street. Some rooms are better than others. Pets are allowed. 678-2618

BLUFF

Mokee. *Inexpensive.* US 163, 1 mi. S of town center. Although the rooms are not of uniform quality, you will enjoy the calm atmosphere and the beautiful cliff view. There is an adjacent cafe. 672-2217

Recapture Lodge. *Inexpensive.* US 163, ¼ mi. S of town center. If you are interested in exploring, geologist-guided trips and river trips are available here. Closer to home, use the heated pool or the shaded grounds for lawn games. A cafe and launderette are nearby. 672-2281

BRIGHAM CITY

Red Baron. *Moderate.* 1167 S. Main St. (US 89). They have a heated pool, will allow some pets. Their cafe opens 6 a.m.; it's 10 blocks to a laundromat. 723-8511

Westward Ho. *Moderate.* 505 N. Main (I-15). Adjacent to a city park and playground, this motel offers color TV and free continental breakfast in the summer. A cafe open from 5 a.m. to 5 p.m. and a coin laundry are less than two blocks away. 723-8594

BRYCE CANYON

Bryce Canyon Pines. *Moderate.* State 12, 6 mi. NW of Bryce Canyon Nat'l Park entrance. For children this motel offers free pony cart rides and horseback tours for adults in the summer. The rooms are furnished in a rustic, early American style but are uneven in quality. 834-9280

Pink Cliffs. *Moderate.* State 12 at State 22, 2 mi. N of Bryce Canyon Nat'l Park entrance. Besides cafe, coin laundry, and beauty shop, Pink Cliffs also has a trailer park. If you are flying, use the free airport bus. 834-5355

Ruby's Inn. *Moderate.* State 12, 1 mi. N of Bryce Canyon Nat'l Park entrance. Ruby's has a cafe, laundromat and a pool table. Some rooms are off central halls and are quiet and comfortable. 834-5341

CEDAR CITY

Astro. *Moderate.* 323 S. Main St. (US 91). For relaxation the Astro provides a heated pool, sauna, and color TV. The rooms have free coffee and queen-size beds. Cafe and coin laundry are close by. 586-6557

Cedar Crest. *Moderate.* 583 S. Main St. (US 91, I–15). Golfers will appreciate the putting green and 9–hole course and there is a playground for children. A cafe open 24 hours and a coin laundry are within 2 blocks. 586-6534

El Rey. *Moderate.* 80 S. Main St. (US 91, I–15). After a long drive, the El Rey's therapy pool and sauna may be just what you're looking for. There is also a heated pool and every room has color TV. 586-6518

Knell. *Moderate.* 190 S. Main St. (US 91, I–15). In the unusually attractive rooms you'll find free morning coffee and

color TV. Some pets are allowed. 586-6566

Zion's. *Moderate.* 222 S. Main St. (US 91, I–15). Zion's offers somewhat lower rates from November to March. They allow some pets and offer color TV and free coffee. A cafe and launderette are within easy walking distance. 586-9487

COALVILLE

Moore. *Moderate.* 90 S. Main (I–80). For $2 extra you get a kitchen with your room. Or, you can eat at the cafe half a block away. A playground is on the premises and a public pool and coin laundry in the next block. 336-5991

DUCHESNE

Gateway. *Moderate.* US 40. For those who want to stay awhile, the Gateway has weekly rates in its older rooms. A $5 deposit is required; you get large beds, color TV, and a cafe and a nearby laundromat. 738-2491

Ells. *Inexpensive.* US 40. If you're traveling in the summer you may appreciate the refrigerator available with some rooms. A cafe open until 10 p.m. and a laundromat are within easy reach. 738-2433

FILLMORE

Fillmore. *Moderate.* 61 N. Main (US 91). A family of 6 may have a room for $22. Across the street is a 24-hour cafe and less than a mile down the road is a coin laundry. 743-5454

Paradise Inn. *Moderate.* 800 N. Main (US 91). The rooms fulfill the promise of the motel's name with their decor, dressing areas, and oversize beds. For entertainment, watch color TV or use the heated swimming pool. The cafe is open from 6 a.m. to 10 p.m.; a coin laundry is a mile distant. 743-6895

GARDEN CITY

Bear Lake Motor Lodge. *Moderate.* State 30. This motel features rooms you can feel at home in, color TV and a cafe. If you are down to your last clean shirt, a laundromat is 3 miles away. 946-3271

GREEN RIVER

Green River. *Expensive.* I–70. Your children and pets can amuse themselves in the playground while you swim in the pool. Afterwards, drop your laundry into the coin machines two blocks away and then proceed to the nearby cafe, open until 10 p.m. 564-3234

Sleepy Hollow. *Inexpensive.* US 6, 50. Guests at Sleepy Hollow can be energetic by playing tennis in the adjacent city park. The motel is also near a cafe and a coin laundry. 564-3436

HEBER CITY

Green Acres Lodge. *Moderate.* 989 S. Main St. (US 40). For those arriving late, or getting up early, there is a 24–hour cafe nearby. Ten blocks away you'll find a coin laundry and the lodge itself has a playground and heated pool. 654-2202

Homestead. *Moderate.* US 40, 5 mi. W of town center. Reservations are necessary to stay at this resort-type motel which has 2 heated spring-fed pools, pony rides, tennis, a putting green, horseback riding, and bicycles. You may also play volleyball and ping-pong or just enjoy the lovely grounds and duck ponds. 654-1102

Wasatch. *Inexpensive.* 875 S. Main St. (US 40, 189). Since this motel's heated pool is open to the public, you have a chance to meet some of the town's residents. Volleyball and picnicking are available too, as well as ping-pong. You'll find a cafe a block away and a coin laundry a little further on. 654-2123

Hilton. *Inexpensive.* 516 N. Main St. (US 40). Trailer parking is available here as well as a picnic table, outdoor grill, and playground. A cafe and coin laundry

are close by. This is a small motel, only 11 rooms. 654-0956

Bar-M. *Inexpensive.* US 40, 189. Bar-M welcomes children and pets and has a playground for them plus a heated pool for adults. A cafe is across the street, a launderette just down the block. 654-0722

KANAB

Parry Lodge. *Moderate.* 89 E. Center St. (US 89). Until 10 p.m., room service provides liquor, wine, and beer. In the summer don't miss the melodramas performed on the covered patio or shady lawn. Other features are a heated pool, coin laundry, and specially arranged tours. 644-2611

Red Hills. *Moderate.* 125 W. Center St. (US 89). You can get a tan at Red Hills by using the sundeck and heated pool. In the shade watch color TV or sip a soda in the nearby cafe. Coin laundry 4½ blocks away. 644-2675

Four Seasons. *Moderate.* 36 N. 300 West (US 89). The rooms here are especially spacious and well-appointed. After a swim in the heated pool, watch color TV or stop in at the cafe only a block away. 644-2635

K. *Inexpensive.* 330 S. 1 East (US 89). The K is a small motel with trailer facilities and boat parking. The owners keep a sitter list and provide a playground and pool. 644-2611

Coral Sands. *Inexpensive.* 36 S. 1 East (US 89). If your children prefer not to sightsee, the motel provides a babysitter list. The rooms are large and a cafe and laundromat are conveniently near. 644-2616

LOGAN

Alta. *Moderate.* 51 E. 5 North (US 89). Here you'll find a playground for children and a cafe and coin laundry nearby. But more important, you won't have any trouble getting to sleep because this motel rates as more than usually quiet. 752-6300

Baugh. *Moderate.* 153 S. Main St. (US 89, 91). If you're on a honeymoon, ask for the bridal suite. Enjoy the heated pool, sundeck, and spacious grounds. Some rooms have a fireplace and dressing room. 752-5220

MEXICAN HAT

Canyonlands. *Inexpensive.* US 163. Large families (5 to 7) get a good rate here—$18. Pets are allowed and a cafe and coin laundry are near by. 2230

San Juan Trading Post. *Inexpensive.* US 163. Did you forget your toothpaste or razorblades? Befitting its name, the Trading Post sells sundries. The cafe serves until 9:30. 2130

Note: Telephone calls to Mexican Hat must be placed through an operator.

MOAB

Green Well. *Expensive.* 105 S. Main St. (US 163). Maybe it's just the color of the upholstery, but some motels have an indefinable aura of quality. This is one. It offers color TV, a heated pool, a cafe, and a launderette 10 minutes away. 259-6151

Moab TraveLodge. *Moderate.* 550 S. Main (US 163). Not only is the cafe open until 10 p.m. but liquor is available after 4 p.m. The rooms are appealing to a weary traveler as are the color TV and heated pool. 259-6171

Apache. *Inexpensive.* 166 S. 4 East (US 163). Since some of the local scenic tours might be too rugged for small children, the Apache provides a list of babysitters. It also has parking for self-contained trailers and a heated pool. 259-5727

Canyonland. *Inexpensive.* Main and Center Sts. (US 163). It's always handy to be located in a motel with a cafe and coin laundry nearby. The cafe is open from 6 a.m. to 10 p.m. and the laundry is only a 6-block roundtrip. 259-5547

MONTICELLO

Canyonlands Motor Lodge. *Moderate.* 389 N. Main St. (US 163). Here's a marvelous setting for a quiet game of croquet or an old-fashioned barbecue. Children will delight in the playground, pool, and color TV. 587-2266

Navajo Trail. *Moderate.* 440 N. Main (US 163). A family of 6 may have a room for $16 and there's a playground for the kids. The cafe, a block away, is closed on Sunday. 587-2251

Wayside. *Inexpensive.* 195 E. 2 North (US 666). There aren't many "extras" here, but you'll be comfortable and get a good night's sleep. The cafe ½ block away opens at 6 a.m. The ever-important coin laundry is 3½ blocks from the Wayside. 587-2261

NEPHI

El Tonya. *Moderate.* 420 S. Main St. (US 91). This is a small motel that allows pets, has a playground, free coffee in the rooms, a cafe nearby and is 2 blocks from a coin laundry. 623-1500

Safari. *Moderate.* 413 S. Main St. (US 91). Besides the playground there's a wading pool for small children. Adults may swim in the heated pool, play ping-pong or watch others from under a shade tree. A convenient feature of the rooms is that they have both front and rear doors. 623-1071

Starlite. *Moderate.* 675 S. Main St. (US 91). If you've been hiking hear the Anasazi Indian ruins you may want to hike 4 more blocks to the coin laundry. If not, head for a relaxing swim in the heated pool. 623-1937

OGDEN

Holiday Inn. *Expensive.* 3306 Washington Blvd. (US 89, 91). Not only is there a heated pool, but poolside service of food and, after 4 p.m., setups and 3.2 beer. Another out-of-the-ordinary service is the kennel. Also at

141

your disposal are a sitter list, color TV, cafe, room service, and free airport bus. 399-5671

Circle R. *Moderate.* 5223 S. 1900 West (State 84). Anyone who has driven late into the night can really appreciate a 24-hour cafe—there's one just 2 blocks from the Circle R. If you have time for relaxation, turn on the color TV and let the kids discover the playground. 825-1644

Weston's Desert Inn. *Moderate.* 1825 Washington Blvd. (US 89, 91 7 blks. N of midtown). Beauty shop, sundries counter are among the features here along with heated pool and early-opening cafe. 394-5503

Ogden TraveLodge. *Moderate.* 2110 Washington Blvd. (US 89, 91 2 blks. N of midtown). The restaurant next door is open late and there's a recroom for indoor fun. Heated pool, launderette nearby. 394-4563

Ben Lamond Hotel. *Moderate.* 2510 Washington Blvd. (US 89, 91). The rooms vary in size; some suites are available. The cafe is up and cooking at 5 a.m. and there are barber and beauty shops plus a movie theatre. Opposite a city park, this attractive facility has also some two dozen motel units. 394-5761

Millstream. *Inexpensive.* 1540 Washington Blvd. (US 89, 91). An unexpected delight is the stream running across the well-cared-for lawn in back and the picnic tables and playground. There is a cafe on the premises and space for truck and trailer parking. 394-9425

ORDERVILLE

Orderville. *Inexpensive.* US 89. Opens its seven attractively appointed rooms April through December. There are restaurant and launderette across the street. 648-2271

PANGUITCH

New Western. *Moderate.* E. 2nd at Center St. (US 89). Convenient to

Bryce Canyon, this little motel caters to travelers with swimming pool, some in-room refrigerators and thrifty family rates. Laundromat and restaurant are close. 676-8867

Bryce Way. *Moderate.* 429 N. Main St. (US 89). Their cafe, open Mon.–Sat., serves until 10 at night. The rooms are comfortable, most with large beds. There's also a heated swimming pool. 676-8881

Blue Pine. *Inexpensive.* 130 N. Main St. (US 89). Just the essentials: bed, sitter list, television. But the price is right and you don't have to check out 'til 2 p.m. Convenient to restaurant and laundromat. 676-2394

PARK CITY

Treasure Mountain Inn. *Deluxe.* 225 Main St. (State 224). Convenient to the slopes, this facility has kitchen apartments so, if you want to cook, there is an opportunity to economize. Some rooms have private terraces and the mountain views are a treat. Rec room and heated pool provide fun when you're not skiing. 649-9241

Silver King Lodge. *Deluxe.* 1505 Empire. This mid-sized inn is near the Ski Area and has pool, rec room where a roaring fire can be so welcome on frosty evenings. They have pool and sauna plus a private club selling drinks. 649-9581

PRICE

Green Well. *Expensive.* 655 E. Main St. (US 6, 50). Unlike most Utah accommodations, those in Price cost the most in summer. The explanation is the nearby Manti-La Sal National Forest. The nicely decorated rooms, swimming pool and on-premises lounge and cafe add up to a pleasant stay here. 637-3520

Crest. *Moderate.* 649 E. Main St. (US 6, 50). Their restaurant can give you breakfast at 5 a.m. The rooms are neat, the beds are large. It's two blks. to a launderette. 637-1532

El Rancho Siesta. *Inexpensive.* 394 W. Main St. (US 6, 50). You won't get much more than a siesta at this very basic motel, but it will be peaceful. Adjacent cafe cooks 6 a.m. to 10 p.m. 637-2424

PROVO

Holiday Inn. *Expensive.* 1460 S. University Ave. at I–15 1 mi. S of downtown. This typical chain motel is opposite a golf course and has pools for wading as well as swimming. They do their best with the liquor laws: set-ups at light beer. The rooms are spacious and there is one especially for handicapped guests. 374-9750

Columbian. *Moderate.* 70 E. 300 South (US 50A, 91, 89). There's a heated pool, coil for brewing the morning coffee and a sitter list. Laundromat is 5 blks. away, a restaurant awaits, 6 a.m.–10 p.m., across the street. 373-8973

Rodeway Inn. *Moderate.* 1292 S. University Ave. (US 189 at I–15). Thrifty family rates prevail but the only pets that do are small 'uns—leashed. Light beer and set-ups may be purchased and the cafe never closes. There's a golf course across the road and you can tee off early; inn check-out isn't til 2. 374-2500

Royal Inn. *Moderate.* 55 E. 1230 North (US 189). Probably the poshest place to stay in Provo, this handsome hostelry has a health spa with saunas and a whirlpool bath. There are lavish suites, two with their own refrigerators. Several rooms have private patios and all have free morning coffee, color TV. The inn houses a popular local restaurant and is near the Brigham Young campus. 373-0800

Uptown. *Inexpensive.* 469 W. Center St. (US 50A at State 114). Some kitchen units and agreeable family rates distinguish this small but serviceable motel. All pets are welcome. A block to a cafe, 5 to a launderette. 373-8248

RICHFIELD

Holiday Host. *Moderate.* 145 S. Main St. (US 89). Largest motel in town, so a good place to begin if you wheel into town *sans* reservations. There's a heated pool and a restaurant across the street. Pets are welcome. 896-5481

Rodeway Inn. *Moderate.* 69 S. Main St. (US 89). Children under 12 stay free, as is true in most motels in the eastern states but not too often around Utah. Heated pool, color TV are features. The inn's dining room is a locally popular steak house. 896-5491

ROOSEVELT

Bottle Hollow Resort. *Moderate.* US 40, 3 mi. E of town. This motel, actually in Fort Duchesne, is Ute Indian-owned and has water sports available and is one of the few lodgings in the state to offer entertainment. Very attractively designed. 722-2431

Frontier. *Inexpensive.* 73 S. 2 East. They've just added 20 new rooms here and charge only $1 per day extra for a kitchen unit. Pets are welcome; cafe operates 5 a.m.–10 p.m. 722-2201

SALT LAKE CITY

Utah. *Expensive.* South Temple at Main St. You can swim at a nearby pool and the hotel has a barber shop and beauty salon. Free bus to the airport is available. 328-9114

Royal Inn. *Expensive.* 206 S. West Temple St. Conveniently situated opposite the Salt Palace—one of its popular crowd-pullers is pro basketball—this inn tries to keep you happy: sauna, therapy pool, swimming pool . . . and a dance combo. Many of the sumptuous suites include a bar. Coffee shop never closes but the package store does. 521-9500

Desert Inn. *Moderate.* 50 W. 5 South St. There's a pool and adjacent sundeck for fresh-air relaxation. Suites are available and a third of the rooms have extra-large beds. You can get room service until 9 p.m. 322-2501

Imperial "400" Temple Square. *Moderate.* 476 S. State St. (US 89A, 91A). Again, you can be next door to the Salt Palace and opposite a park. The cafe next door stays open late and the motel itself offers you a swim. 328-9665

Country Club. *Moderate.* 2665 Parleys Way (US 40, 5 mi. SE from downtown). If you'd like to stay a little distance away from the central business district, here's your spot. Medium-sized inn offers free continental bkfst. and a heated pool with a sundeck. 486-1034

Covered Wagon. *Inexpensive.* 230 W. North Temple. It's close to I–80 and the rates are truly modest. Across the street is an all-night restaurant. 359-2091

Colonial Village. *Inexpensive.* 1530 S. Main St. They have a pool and are right next door to a popular German restaurant. A coin laundry is 3 blks. distant. 486-8171

Scenic. *Inexpensive.* 1345 Foothill Dr. (US 40, 3½ blks. SE of midtown). Opposite the shopping center, next door to a cafe, this motel is good for a quick overnight stop when you don't want to start off the day in mid-city. 582-1527

VERNAL

Dinosaur. *Moderate.* 251 E. Main St. Basketball is on top of the activities list here. The restaurant's one of the best in town and the rooms are clean and comfortable. 789-2660

Echo Park Lodge. *Moderate.* 511 W. Main St. (US 40). You can park at the door and there are picnic tables on the grounds. Restaurant and laundromat are just across the road. 789-1581

Ute. *Inexpensive.* 236 E. Main St. (US 40). The town park, with museum and sports opportunities, is across the way. Motel cafe opens 5 a.m. 789-0687

WENDOVER

Wend-over. *Moderate.* The heated pool beckons, but so do the gambling tables and machines, just over the state line in Nevada. 665-2211

ZION NATIONAL PARK

Pioneer Lodge. *Moderate.* State 15, 1 mi. S of park entrance. There's a heated pool, restaurant and the rooms are tastefully appointed. 772-3233

Bumbleberry Inn. *Moderate.* State 15, 1 mi. S of South Park Entrance. Plenty to do right here: sauna, therapy pool, swimming pool and various lawn games. There's a sundry counter and lots of nice rooms in quiet side halls. 772-3224

Zion Lodge. *Inexpensive.* In the park, it's 5 mi. N of the S. entrance. The Interior Dept. runds this thrifty *pied-à-terre* in the beautiful park. Some games and Saturday night dances complement the offerings of nature all around. Dozens of cabins have fireplaces. 772-3213

DINING OUT. There is nothing different or unique about Mormon cooking. Statewide restaurant quality has improved considerably since tourism developed into such a big, booming business. It's possible to discover an especially tasty cuisine in out-of-the-way locations, but don't count on it. Salt Lake City, however, is beginning to acquire a kitchen. The going is slow because liquor laws discourage heavy investment in grand cafes or exclusive type restaurants. But specialty places, offering French, Spanish and German dishes, are increasing. Seafood, believe it or not, is found fresh and well prepared in several Salt Lake City dining rooms. Some of the best menus will be found up nearby canyons or south of the city.

Restaurant price categories are as follows: *Expensive* $5.50–$9, *Moderate* $3.50–$5.50 and *Inexpensive* $2–$3.50. For a more detailed explanation of restaurant categories see THE ROCKIES & PLAINS *Facts at Your Fingertips* at the front of this volume.

ALTA

Alta Lodge. *Expensive.* State 210 at the Alta Lodge resort. Specialties are fondue and scampi. Lunch is a bargain. 742-3500

Rustler's Lodge. *Expensive.* At the Rustler Lodge Resort. A varied American-Continental menu in pleasant surroundings. Open Tues.–Sat. for lunch and dinner and Sunday for brunch. 742-3500

BRIGHAM CITY

Idle Isle. *Inexpensive.* 24 S. Main St. Prime rib and seafood here, but the kids will probably be most interested in their candy factory. 723-8072

CEDAR CITY

Sugar Loaf Cafe. *Moderate.* 301 S. Main St., 3 blks. S on US 91. Specialties include broasted chicken, steak. Open 6 a.m. to 10:30 p.m.; winter to 9 p.m. 586-6593

GREEN RIVER

Oasis Cafe. *Moderate.* On US 50 and 6, E of the bank. Seafood, chicken, steaks and a variety of short orders. 564-3475

HEBER CITY

The Hub. *Inexpensive.* On US 40 (Main St.). Open 24 hours for the weary traveler. Children's portions. 654-0171

KANAB

Chef's Palace. *Expensive.* 150 W. Center St., 1½ blks. W on US 89. Specialties are chicken and char-broiled steak. Open daily 6 a.m. to 10:30 p.m.; winter to 10:30 p.m. 644-5052

LOGAN

The Bluebird. *Moderate.* 19 N. Main St., across from the Tabernacle. A locally popular restaurant that makes its own candy and ice cream. Open 7:30 a.m. to 9 p.m.; Sun. noon to 8 p.m. 752-3155

Country Kitchen. *Moderate.* 636 S. Main St. Good food family style. 752-9913

The Loft House. *Moderate.* 1039 N. Main St. Steaks, chicken and shrimp are featured on the menu. There is also a coffee shop. The coffee shop opens daily at 5 a.m., the restaurant at 9 a.m. Both are open until 11 p.m. 752-9969

MOAB

Bob & Olive's Sundowner. *Moderate.* 1 mi. N on US 163. Steak and chicken here, liquor also available. 259-5201

Golden Spike Restaurant. *Moderate.* 550 S. Main. Steaks, sandwiches and salads are specialties of the house. 259-6652

OGDEN

Ye Lions Den. *Expensive.* 3607 Washington Blvd. on US 89–91. Prime rib and broiled steaks in Old English surroundings. Open for lunch and dinner Mon.–Sat. Open until midnight Fri. and Sat. 399-5804

Bratten's Grotto. *Moderate.* 3376 Harrison Blvd. near the Weber State campus. Seafood in a nautical atmosphere. Open 11:30 to 10 p.m., Sat. to 11 p.m. Sun. to 9 p.m. Closed Mon. 394-0567

Rigo's. *Moderate.* 2788 Washington Blvd. A large restaurant serving Italian cuisine. 394-0102

PARK CITY

Car 19. *Expensive.* 438 Main St. Mostly steaks served in an old railroad car. 649-9338

Treasure Mountain Inn. *Moderate.* 255 Main St. Moderate. Fine family dining at this resort hotel. They have a hunt breakfast on Sunday. Open 7 a.m. to 11 p.m. 649-9241

PRICE

Husky Highway House. *Moderate.* Rte. 1 W of town. The best in home cooking. 637-1862

Jean Selmes' Fine Foods. *Inexpensive.* 318 E. Main. Steak and seafood at good prices. Open daily 6 a.m. to 10 p.m. 637-3074

PROVO

Golden Spike Restaurant. *Moderate.* 150 S. University, ½ mi. S of Brigham Young University. Steaks, sandwiches and salad for the entire family. Open daily 6 a.m. to 11 p.m. 373-3900

Royal Inn. *Moderate.* 55 E. 1230 North St. Good steaks and home baking at this large restaurant near Brigham Young Univ. Open late on Fri. and Sat. 373-1671

RICHFIELD

The Wood Platter. *Moderate.* Main St. Steaks, chicken and—if you're tired of those—pizza. 896-9906

BJ's Family Restaurant. *Inexpensive.* 92 S. Main St. Special children's menu featuring steak, chicken and trout. 896-4951

Slice-em Thins Restaurant. *Inexpensive.* 69 S. Main St. An Old West setting for their speciality of prime rib. Open 5:30 a.m. to 11 p.m. 896-4444

ROOSEVELT

Frontier Grill. *Moderate.* 65 S. 2nd E. A variety of home-style cooking. Open 6 a.m. to 10 p.m. 722-9606

ST. GEORGE

Atkin's Sugar Loaf Cafe. *Moderate.* 309 E. 100 North St. The specialties here are broasted chicken and steak. Open 6 a.m. to 11 p.m.; winter to 9:30 p.m. 673-3471

Dick's Cafe. *Moderate.* 114 E. 100 North St. Western-style cooking with seafood, steaks and chicken the feature. Open 5 a.m. to 11 p.m. 673-3841

Trafalga Restaurant. *Moderate.* 70 W. 100 North St. The finest char-broiled steaks in St. George. 673-2933

SALT LAKE CITY

Editor's Choices

Rating restaurants is, at best, a subjective business, and obviously a matter of personal taste. It is, therefore, difficult to call a restaurant "the best" and hope to get unanimous agreement. The restaurants listed below are our choices of the best eating places in Salt Lake City, and the places we would choose if we were visiting the city.

TRI ARC 13TH FLOOR   Western American
Soup is served in individual tureens, and loaves of hot bread accompany every meal. There's also a great view of the entire Salt Lake Valley. Steaks and prime ribs are the staples of the menu. Average price for dinner (per person): $9.00. West Temple at 6th South, tel. 359-0751.

LA FLEUR DE LYS   French Cuisine
Serious diners choose this establishment. Sweetbreads, roast pheasant, and live lobsters cooked to order are part of the appeal. The rest is the posh atmosphere

and fine service. Average price for dinner (per person): $10.00. 338 South State St., tel. 359-5753.

RISTORANTE DELLA FONTANA — Italian Cuisine
Actually, there are representative dishes from many Mediterranean countries, and the normal dinner runs to a full seven courses. The dining room is in an old church, complete with fountain and ornate carved interior. A real local favorite. Average price for dinner (per person): $5.00. 336 South 4th East, tel. 328-4243.

QUAIL RUN — American Cuisine
The kind of country atmosphere that only the wealthy can produce, with fires often burning brightly in the huge fireplaces. Local residents regularly make the drive out of the city to enjoy the home baking, fresh flowers, and candlelit atmosphere. Open on Friday and Saturday evenings only. Average price for dinner (per person): $8.00. 9564 Wasatch Blvd., tel. 571-1331.

RESTAURANT MINOA — Greek/American
Though the atmosphere tries to project a feeling of Greece, it is the beef Wellington that is the main attraction on the menu. Other choices are uniformly well-prepared, and the service is very competent. Average price for dinner (per person): $5.00. 1140 East 3900 South, tel. 266-3513.

SKY ROOM — American Cuisine
You look down on the Mormon Tabernacle from the top of the Hotel Utah, with a decor that suggests an outdoor cafe somewhere in France. The food is among the best in the state, and there is dancing Friday and Saturday nights. Average price for dinner (per person): $7.00. South Temple & Main St., tel. 328-9114.

Other recommended restaurants:

Balsam Embers. *Expensive.* 2350 Foothill Dr. (US Alt. 40). Specialties include stuffed breast of chicken and medallions of veal. Open 6 a.m. to 10 p.m. Closed Sun. 466-4496

Log Haven. *Expensive.* Millcreek Canyon. Variety menu with a mountain setting overlooking a lake. They bake their own breads. Reservations required. Open Tues.–Sat. 6 p.m. to 10 p.m. On Sunday it's open early and closes late. 277-3005

Paprika. *Expensive.* 2302 Parleys Way (US Alt. 40). German and American cooking. Specialties are beef Strogonoff and sauerbraten. Open for dinner Mon.–Sat. 484-0901

Athenian. *Moderate.* 247 E. 2nd St. Authentic Greek food and the whole family is welcome. Open for dinner Mon.–Sat. 363-1387

Hawaiian. *Inexpensive.* 2928 Highland Dr., 4 mi. SE on State 152. Chinese and Polynesian food is accompanied by the sound of a Hawaiian thunderstorm. 277-2134

La Morena. *Inexpensive.* 346 W. 1st Ave. Good, authentic Mexican food. 355-1541

Spaghetti Factory. *Inexpensive.* 189 Trolley Sq. Great family dining in a fun setting. 521-0424

VERNAL
The Skillet. *Expensive.* 251 E. Main St. (US 40). Steaks, chicken, lobster and shish kebab. They do their own baking. Open daily 5 a.m. to 11 p.m. 789-3641

Diamond Lils Cafe. *Moderate.* 248 Main St. They are justly proud of their steak and prime rib. Open for lunch and dinner except Sun. Open late Fri. and Sat. 355-5680

WYOMING

WYOMING

The Cowboys Still Ride

by

BRUCE HAMBY, ROY PECK

and

LEAVITT F. MORRIS

Bruce Hamby has worked for the Denver Post *for many years, and is now its travel editor.*

Roy Peck is co-publisher of the Riverton Wyoming Ranger.

Leavitt F. Morris, former travel editor of the Christian Science Monitor *and still a frequent contributor to the publication, contributed most of the Exploring section on Wyoming.*

Wyoming is a vast, majestic land of contrasts—rolling plains, high plateaus, rivers, lakes, and snowcapped mountains; rich farmlands, grass- and sagebrush-covered prairies, sudden red- and purple-striped badlands; fiery, steam-belching geysers and hot springs; cowboys and Indians, oilmen and miners, ranchers and farmers, professors and artists; and buffalo, wild horses, elk, deer, antelope, moose, bear, mountain sheep, trout, sage chickens, wild turkeys, pheasant, and an abundance of cattle and sheep.

Wyoming is the last frontier of the forty-eight states; a land inhabited by real cowboys and Indians and rich in natural resources and exceptional mountain scenery; a progressive 20th-century state still living its 19th-century history.

For while today modern highways crisscross the state and rail, air and tourist facilities dot Wyoming's 97,9144 square miles (it is our ninth largest state), the forested mountain ranges, the lush high mountain valleys and the grass-covered prairies which first drew fur trappers, cattlemen and miners remain much as they were one hundred years ago.

Crumbling remains of isolated forts offer visual evidence of the bitter battles between U.S. Troopers and marauding Indians. Still visible ruts make it possible to follow the tortuous paths of wagon trains that inched their way west across the rugged terrain.

Today's traveler can still see, alongside modern four-lane highways, herds of antelope gracefully bounding across the plains. Majestic elk graze peacefully in protected mountain valleys.

Highway signposts and historical markers recall places and people still very real to Wyoming residents, not to mention millions of Americans whose sole relationship with the pioneer West is in the roll call of televison "westerns"—places like Fort Laramie, Medicine Bow, Cheyenne, Fort Bridger and names such as Buffalo Bill Cody, Jim Bridger, and William Sublette.

Descendants of Indians, who less than a century ago fiercely resisted the coming of the white man and his inroads on their hunting grounds, are still to be seen on Wyoming's Shoshone and Arapahoe Indian Reservation.

The oil fields, mining operations, even missile bases, are unmistakably 20th century but they are swallowed up in Wyoming's expanse. The state remains today a proud outdoor land of huge cattle and sheep ranches, some of which, measured in thousands of acres, are large enough to contain many an Eastern metropolis.

Much of Wyoming's scenic grandeur remains untouched and unspoiled in national parks and forests. Yellowstone and Grand Teton National Parks, joined together by the new John D. Rockefeller Parkway in the northwest corner of the state, annually attract more than two million visitors.

Colter's Hell

Wyoming is a young state. It celebrated its 75th anniversary in 1965 and oldtimers noted that the observance differed but little from that of July 10, 1890, when fireworks left over from a pioneer Fourth of July fete were used to celebrate the advent of statehood.

The first white men to visit Wyoming were probably French-Canadian fur trappers, who ventured south from Canada in the 1730's. Records show that the Lewis and Clark expedition, going up the Missouri on its historic trek west, met fur traders coming down the river with loads of pelts.

Modern Wyoming history, however, dates back to 1807, the year John Colter, an enlisted man with the Lewis and Clark party, left the group to head south into what we now know as Yellowstone Park. He became the first U.S. citizen to lay eyes on the marvels of the area, but when he returned east his tales of steam-heated pools and spouting geysers drew scoffs from unbelieving listeners. They called it Colter's Hell.

But even though Colter's tales drew laughs, his accounts of the rich, primitive areas abundant in game proved irresistible and many headed west to seek valuable fur-bearing animals.

For twenty years mountain men and trappers roamed the northern part of Wyoming. Tales of these courageous and foolhardy men, of their exploits and daring survive in legend.

There were David Jackson, the Sublette brothers, William and Milton, Jedediah Smith, Kit Carson, Jacques LaRamie and Jim "Old Gabe" Bridger. The wily old scout's fort and trading post was an important stop on the Oregon Trail, a place where the weary pioneers in the wagon trains could rest and obtain supplies for the final push to their destination, whether it be the Mormon capital at Salt Lake City, the wilderness lands of the Pacific Northwest or the gold fields of California. At one point altercations between Bridger and the Mormons led to violence and the Mormons burned Fort Bridger; it was rebuilt by the U.S. Army. Married three times to Indian girls, Bridger was the most colorful of the characters who wrote their names big on the pages of Wyoming history.

David Jackson, pioneer trapper, was one of the first men to explore what is now Jackson Hole in Grand Teton National Park, but no one perhaps is better remembered today than LaRamie whose name, with a slight change in spelling, now tags the Laramie River, Laramie County, Laramie Peak and the city of Laramie, home of the University of Wyoming.

Then there were the bad guys, the rustlers who hustled other men's cattle off the range, rebranded them and sold them as their own. Most colorful was Cattle Kate and her bartender boy friend. Kate, it is said, used her feminine wiles to convince friendly cowboys to present her with gifts, a steer or two, and in due time amassed a respectable herd. Her career as a cattle queen was pulled up short when the ranchers dangled her from the end of a rope.

While these and other equally resourceful and colorful men played a major role in early Wyoming history, it was a different breed that laid the foundation for settlement and eventual statehood.

For Wyoming was on the direct route of the mass migration west which followed the Depression of 1837. By the 1840's word of fabled lands west of the Rocky Mountains—the Oregon Country stretching to the shores of the Pacific—had trickled east, and thousands of fortune-hunting individuals and families began to trek West. Wagon trains rolled across southern Wyoming heading for the only access route through the formidable Rockies, the South Pass near the headwaters of the Sweetwater River.

Beset by Indians and sickness, the wagons struggled West, stopping for supplies and rest at the trading posts first established in trapping days. And forts the mountain men had built became headquarters for U.S. troops sent out to guard the long and lonesome trail.

Shortly after the Civil War two more developments helped move Wyoming toward statehood; the coming, almost simultaneously, of the railroad and the cattle drives.

The Coming of the Railroad

The railroad, following to a large extent the trail blazed by wagon trains and the Pony Express, came in the 1860's after Congress granted a subsidy to the Union and Central Pacific lines to establish a transcontinental route west to the Pacific. Within five years of the Congressional action, wood-burning locomotives appeared on the southern Wyoming prairies. Soon new communities began to sprout up along the line—Cheyenne, Laramie, Rawlins, Green River and Rock Springs. Today's traveler, speeding across country in air conditioned luxury, will find that today's rail route of the Union Pacific varies little if any from that original roadbed.

While the rails were pushed west, cattlemen from Texas began to push north through Wyoming, driving huge herds of cattle to summer pasture lands in Montana and Canada.

The rails and cattle were a natural combination. Cattlemen found in Wyoming plenty of free land covered with nutritious prairie grass. The railroad furnished a convenient way to send the cattle to market.

While a TV or movie western would have one believe that a real cowboy had one trusty gun, one trusty steed—and sometimes just one girl—the facts were otherwise. Riding herd on steers was hard work, harder on the horses than on the men, so the Texas cowboy who came up to Wyoming invariably had anywhere from two to six extra horses with him to change off during days of hard riding. Many of these horses eventually became strays, and later formed the foundation for extensive wild horse herds.

Still another animal entered the scene—and much blood was shed before the cattlemen of Wyoming reconciled themselves to the fact that sheep were there to stay. At first, the intrusion of the sheepherders was bitterly resisted, principally because the cattlemen claimed sheep cropped grass so close to the ground that nothing was left for the cattle. Homesteaders also fought with the cattlemen over the right to fence open ranges. The homsteaders won the last battle, in court, and the big cattle spreads were reduced and fenced off.

Wyoming is still the cowboy state, however, and cattle is still a mainstay of the economy, along with sheep, sugar beets, and the raising of hay. But all these agricultural products, as important as they are, are engulfed by a vast and growing minerals industry, for Wyoming is truly the energy capital of the nation with extensive reserves of oil and gas, coal, uranium, and oil shale. The world's largest open pit uranim mine is located in the Gas Hills of Fremont County. There is enough coal in the state, over five hundred billion tons, to meet the total energy needs of the world for more than one hundred years.

Coming up fast in the economic picture right behind agriculture and minerals is tourism and recreation. All the wonders of nature are on display to the visitor, the legendary way of life of cowboys and Indians still survives, and year-round recreation abounds—fishing, hunting, hiking, mountain climbing, trail riding, snowmobiling, camping, skiing, river floating, historical sightseeing, and camping.

Wyoming has become a blending of the people who explored, trapped, fought and died here—Irish and Chinese rail workers, Texas and British families who founded the first large cattle ranches, miners who dug for gold and iron, homesteaders. They form what must be the most independent roster of citizens to be found on the continent.

For example, in its territorial constitution, Wyoming pioneered in giving women the vote, an action preserved in the state constitution. Wyoming is called the Equality State. It had the first woman justice of the peace, Esther Hobart Morris, and elected the first woman governor in America, Nellie Tayloe Ross. It was one of the states to ratify the Equal Rights Amendment in 1973. Very early Wyoming granted women rights to own property. Wyoming has been progressive with the working man, a leader in legislating the eight-hour working day and workman's compensation. Wyoming people are fiercely independent and rugged individualism and free enterprise are prominent in the state's political philosophy.

In one national election the state will go overwhelmingly for the Republican candidate, yet four years later the Democrats might swamp the GOP. In Wyoming it is not uncommon for the state to have a Republican governor and a Democratic legislature, or vice versa.

This "independent" approach to life can sometimes take a puckish turn. Recently one house of the state legislature passed a law requiring all California cars to carry cowbells attached to their radiator caps; the other house tabled the measure.

While few storeowners observe an old law requiring them to provide hitching posts for horses, today's visitor to Wyoming can still get an authentic picture of Western living. Pass any ranch, you'll see the cattlemen and working cowboys in action; or in the summer months you can rub shoulders with the cowpokes at county fairs and rodeos.

Many of the big working ranches also accept guests; here the Western dude can play-act at cowpunching amidst some of the most magnificent scenery in the world, shouting, "Powder River, let 'er buck." Which is another story for another time.

GENERAL AND PRACTICAL INFORMATION FOR WYOMING

 WYOMING FACTS AND FIGURES. The state gets its name from the Delaware Indian *mecheweami-ing*, which means "at the big plains." Its nicknames are *Cowboy State* and *Equality State*. The Indian paintbrush is the state flower, the cottonwood the state tree, the meadow lark the state bird. "Equal Rights" is the state motto. "Wyoming" is the state song. Cheyenne is the state capital. State population is about 340,000.

Vast plains and rugged mountains are the natural features of this scarcely populated western state. The Great Plains of the east are covered with the hayfields and cattle ranches which, next to oil, are the chief source of income. Wyoming has an abundance of spectacular mountain scenery to counter the rhythm of its plains. In the northwest of the state, the 500 square miles of the Grand Teton National Park and Yellowstone National Park are an outdoorsman's paradise. Dramatic mountain ranges run through the center of the state, marking the Continental Divide. Wyoming's winters are relatively mild. Snowfall is light except in higher mountains. Summers are warm. There is little rainfall.

HOW TO GET THERE. *By air:* Frontier and Western fly into Cheyenne, Laramie and Casper.

By train: Amtrak passenger service is available to Cheyenne.

By car: I–80 crosses southern Wyoming entering from Nebraska in the east and leaving into Utah in the west. I–25 passes into the state from Colorado in the south. I–90, from Montana in the north and South Dakota in the east, serves the northern part of Wyoming.

By bus: Continental Trailways and Greyhound offer transportation to and within Wyoming.

 HOW TO GET AROUND. *By air:* Frontier Airlines serves Jackson, Cody, Worland, Rock Springs, Riverton-Lander, Casper, Sheridan, Laramie and Cheyenne.

By car: I–80 crosses the state in the south. I–90 and US 14 and 16 serve the north. I–25, US 26 and 287 run from Cheyenne in the southeast to Yellowstone in the northwest.

By bus: Greyhound, Continental Trailways, Pioneer Transit, and Jackson-Rock Springs Stages provide transportation within the state.

TOURIST INFORMATION. For all Wyoming travel, vacation, resort, and camping information write for brochures from Wyoming Travel Commission, 2320 Capitol Ave., Cheyenne, Wyoming 82001.

 SEASONAL EVENTS. *Cheyenne Frontier Days:* this is the world's number one rodeo. During the third week in *July*, over one thousand professional cowboys descend on Cheyenne to compete for $170,000 in prize money. And in addition to the rodeos, there are parades, nationally known entertainment (particularly country and western), carnival, dancing, Indians, band concerts, free chuck wagon breakfasts, and chuck wagon races. With good reason, this has been called the "Daddy of 'em All."

Other famous Wyoming rodeos include *Lander Pioneer Days* and *Cody Stampede* over the 4th of July, the *Fremont County Fair* during the third week of August at Riverton, the *Wyoming State Fair,* the last week of August at Douglas, *Central Wyoming Fair and Rodeo,* late July to early August in Casper, and Laramie *Jubilee Days,* with world championship roping, in mid-July.

The *Green River Rendezvous,* on the second Sunday of July at Pinedale, is a pageant that relives the era of Jim Bridger, Marcus Whitman, and Father DeSmet during the days when "mountain men" and the fur trade were king.

All-American Indian Days: in late July and early *August* at Sheridan. Nearly five thousand Indians from over forty plains tribes arrive for the pageant of the plains. A Miss Indian America is selected each year.

Almost every Wyoming community holds a pageant, rodeo, or western event during the summer. The *Wyoming Travel Commission* can tell you what events will coincide with your vacation.

NATIONAL PARKS. *Yellowstone National Park:* Yellowstone is the nation's first and largest national park. Located in the northwestern corner of Wyoming it is a scenic wonderland of spouting geysers, steaming hot springs, magnificent waterfalls, beautiful lakes, towering mountains, big game, wildlife, birds, fishing, and of course, the inevitable bear (don't pet him, he's not tame). Yellowstone has accommodations for nearly 10,000 persons. And it's large enough that even with the big crowds you can "get lost" if you wish. Yellowstone is open in the winter, too. Take a "Snow Bus" trip through the south entrance to Old Faithful Lodge. Winter scenery and Old Faithful geyser spouting on a frosty day are sights unsurpassed.

Grand Teton National Park: Just south of Yellowstone lies this great national park, now attracting more visitors than Yellowstone. Huge Jackson Lake reflects the spectacular beauty of the Teton Mountains. Unspoiled wilderness areas start at the roadside. Even the untrained can climb mountains, and gasp at undreamed-of views. Lakes and rivers, fabulous fishing, hiking, boating, square dancing and real western, mountain pleasures abound. Facilities will handle 3,000 visitors. The quaint western town of Jackson is nearby. In winter, ski at Snow King Mountain, Teton Village, or Targhee in the Tetons. Fish through the ice on Jackson Lake. Float the Snake River in summer. Snowmobile into the winter wonderland.

John D. Rockefeller, Jr. Parkway. A new national park dedicated in 1973. It fills the gap between Yellowstone and Teton National Parks. Beautiful forested land, camping, hot springs, wilderness horseback riding.

Wyoming has six National Forests. They are the Black Hills in northeastern Wyoming, Medicine Bow in southeastern, Bridger, Shoshone, and Teton in northwestern Wyoming, and the Big Horn National Forest in north central Wyoming.

Each forest has wilderness and primitive areas, thousands of campsites, all the wonders of the mountain West. Fishing streams abound, snowcapped mountains, wildlife. If you plan to utilize the national forest be sure and obtain a recreation sticker. Write to Shoshone National Forest, Cody, Wyoming; Bridger-Teton National Forest, Jackson, Wyoming; Big Horn National Forest, Sheridan; Medicine Bow National Forest, Laramie.

Fossil Butte National Monument, located near Kemmerer in southwest Wyoming, contains a rich concentration of fossils which illustrates the evolution of freshwater fishes—reminders of the great oceans that once covered this portion of the state. The Butte amounts to a living classroom for studies of ancient life and its evolution.

STATE PARKS. *Buffalo Bill State Park* is an hour's drive from the east gate of Yellowstone National Park on the north shore of Buffalo Bill Reservoir. It offers complete picnicking and day-use facilities plus minimum camping facilities. The adjacent reservoir features excellent trout fishing during most of the season, as do the north and south forks of the Shoshone River that feed it. A commercial concession, campground, trailer park and marina are also available.

Boysen State Park is located in central Wyoming and can be reached by driving either north or west of Shoshoni on US 20 or 26. The park is surrounded by the Wind River Indian Reservation, home grounds for the Shoshone and Arapahoe tribes. Day-use and overnight camping facilities are offered and the reservoir and the river provide trout and walleye fishing opportunities.

Sinks Canyon State Park. In a spectacular mountain canyon ten miles southwest of Lander, this park is one of the newest additions to the Wyoming park system. Here amid the unspoiled beauty of the Rocky Mountain West are hiking trails, nature walks, scenic overlooks, and countless glacier-fed pools and swirling eddys. Fishing is excellent. As an added attraction the river disappears into a gaping canyon wall cave and reappears in a crystal-clear trout-filled spring pool. Camping facilities are limited.

Seminoe State Park is surrounded by giant dunes of white sand, miles of sagebrush, thousands of pronghorn antelope and sage grouse. Located near Seminoe Reservoir twenty-eight miles from Sinclair, this is primarily a day-use facility, although some overnight camping is permitted. The closeby "Miracle Mile" of the North Platte River got the name for its reputation for trout fishing.

Keyhole State Park is eight miles from I-90 between Sundance and Moorcroft, along the southeastern shore of Keyhole Reservoir and within sight of Devil's Tower. Antelope, deer and wild turkeys are common in this area and the reservoir offers excellent fishing for trout, walleye, catfish and perch. The water is warm and camping and picnic sites are readily available.

Glendo State Park, four miles out of the town of Glendo, is the best developed area in Wyoming's park system. There are excellent day-use facilities, a complete commercial concession, cabin, trailer court, and marina operation, and some of the finest boating and trout fishing in the state. Arrive early on weekends to be assured of getting picnic and campsites.

Guernsey State Park, a few miles outside of Guernsey on US 26, is located on the shores of one of Wyoming's most attractive reservoirs. High bluffs surround the park and block the wind so the water is always warm for the swimmer and water-skier. Historically, this is the country of the Oregon Trail, and the State Park Museum has full information. Complete day-use facilities are available but camping space is limited.

Curt Gowdy State Park is located in the foothills of a mountain range separating Cheyenne and Laramie amid massive granite towers, rocky soils, and timbered slopes. Granite Reservoir and Crystal Lake offer fishing opportunities but no swimming beaches or facilities are provided. The hills around the lakes invite the hiker, rockhound, and, in winter, the snowmobiler. Still under development, this park offers very limited facilities.

 HOT SPRINGS. *Hot Springs State Park* is at Thermopolis. This is the world's largest, single hot springs and the site of the world-famous Gottsche Rehabilitation Center. Mineral waters and baths, hotel and motel accommodations, and large indoor and outdoor swimming pools are available. *Fort Washakie:* south of Fort Washakie on the road to Ethete, on the Wind River Indian Reservation, is the Washakie Plunge hot springs. This area too has facilities. *Saratoga Hot Springs,* near Saratoga on State 130, is another.

CAMPING OUT. Wyoming has literally hundreds of campgrounds offering everything from minimal to complete facilities. Yellowstone Park and adjacent Teton and Shoshone counties have many campsites available but only on a first-come, first-served basis. Reservations are taken only for large organized group parties such as the Boy Scouts.

Special regulations governing food storage apply at most Wyoming campsites due to the prevalence of bears. All food or similar organic material must be kept completely sealed in a vehicle or camping unit that is constructed of solid, non-pliable material, or it must be suspended at least ten feet above the ground and four feet horizontally from any post or tree trunk. The cleaner a camp is kept the less chance there is of being bothered by bears.

For complete information about the location and facilities of campgrounds in Wyoming contact the Wyoming Travel Commission, 2320 Capitol Ave., Cheyenne, Wyo. 82001.

FARM VACATIONS AND GUEST RANCHES. Wyoming is famous for its great variety of guest (dude) ranches. A selection of those available is included here; complete information is available from the Wyoming Travel Commission, 2320 Capitol Ave., Cheyenne, Wyo. 82001.

CM Ranch, near Dubois. Located in the Wind River Mountains amid beautiful scenery and rushing streams where the atmosphere is completely remote. Separate cabins with private baths. Family groups and teenagers are especially welcome. There are weekly rodeos, riding, fishing, hunting (in season), and pack trips. Les and Alice Shoemaker are wonderful hosts. Open June 15 to Sept. 30 to guests and Oct. 1 to Nov. 15 for hunters. CM Ranch, Dubois, Wyo. 82513.

Ranger Creek Ranch, located five miles from US 14 on a Forest Service road, thirty-two miles from Greybull. Facilities include a main lodge among double log cabins. Activities include horseback riding, fishing trips, pack trips, fossil collection, trout fishing, mountain climbing, hiking, moonlight rides, jeep trips and all kinds of games for children. Season runs from June 15 to Oct. 14 with hunting season from Oct. 15 to Nov. 15. Maurice Carney and James Moore are your hosts. Ranger Creek Ranch, Greybull, Wyo. 82426.

Seven D Ranch, located fifty miles northwest of Cody in Sunlight Valley. Activities include horseback riding, all-day rides, fishing, hunting, backpacking, pack trips, square dances, moving cows, haying, and gymkhanas. There are also special counselors for young children. Open from June 15 to Oct. 1. Contact Dewey Dominick, M.D., Seven D Ranch, Cody, Wyo. 82414.

Triangle X Ranch, north of Jackson in Teton National Park, just a mile off US 26. Fall hunting and outfitting. Summer float trips, horseback riding, packing. Winter cross-country skiing, snowmobiling, touring. A family ranch, children are welcome. Triangle X Ranch, Moose, Wyo. 83012.

Outfitters: Big game hunting for elk, moose, deer, pronghorn antelope, bighorn sheep, and bear abound in Wyoming. Many are found in remote wilderness areas where hiring of an outfitter is a must. Wyoming has more than two hundred outfitters, all must be licensed. It would be impossible to list them all here, but a few from each section of the state are: Pat Self, *Centennial,* Wyoming; James L. Bluejacket, *Shell;* Joe Detimore, *Dubois;* Les Shoemaker, *Dubois:* Jim Dale, *Riverton;* L. D. Fromte, *Afton;* Ted Hale, *Afton;* Stan Siggins, *Cody;* Harold Turner, *Moose;* Bert Turner, *Moran;* William S. Wood, *Ten Sleep;* and Charles B. Nichols, *Dubois.*

 MUSEUMS AND GALLERIES. *Buffalo Bill Historical Center* at Cody features two of the finest museums of western lore in America. They are the *Buffalo Bill Museum* and the *Whitney Gallery of Western Art.* The Buffalo Bill Museum contains the guns, saddles, painting, furniture, letters, personal effects, and a valuable trophy collection of the famed William F. Cody, "Buffalo Bill." The new Whitney Gallery features original art of such figures as Frederic Remington, George Gatlin, Alfred Jacob Miller and Charles M. Russell.

Bradford Brinton Memorial Ranch: This working ranch near Big Horn has a fine collection of pioneer western art, Indian relics, and sculpture. Guided tours begin in the main ranch house and nearby buildings, the horse and carriage barns, and a "trophy" lodge near the main entrance. Western artists Frank Tenney Johnson and Charles M. Russell, among others, are featured.

The *University of Wyoming:* Geological Museum has many exhibits which include restored dinosaurs made up of the actual fossil bones, fossil fish, prehistoric mammoth. Coe Library contains western lore museum, an oriental art exhibit, many valuable archives. Both are open to the public.

Other Western and pioneer museums can be found at Afton, Buffalo, Casper, Fort Bridger, Fort Laramie, Glendo, Green River, Greybull (rock collection), Jackson Hole, Kemmerer, Lander, Newcastle, Rawlins, Thermopolis.

The *Wyoming State Museum* in Cheyenne has minerals and gems, Indian and early-day western relics. Famous military button collection.

The *Wyoming State Pioneer Memorial Museum* at the State Fair Grounds in Douglas contains many pioneer, Indian, cowboy, and military relics.

At Riverton, a new museum in an old church, offers a real western experience in life-size dioramas.

HISTORIC SITES. Wyoming has many historic sites, some less than a generation removed from the Wild West Frontier.

Fort Laramie: One of Wyoming's most famous historical sites is Fort Laramie on US 26 in southeastern Wyoming, which makes it an interesting "first stop" in the state when entering from the east. Trappers built the original fort in 1834 and named it after Jacques LaRamie, a French fur trapper killed by the Indians in 1820. Later they sold it to the American Fur Company who then sold it in 1849 to the U.S. Government. For many years it was headquarters for U.S. Cavalry units and protected the pioneer from marauding Indians. A number of peace treaties with the Indians were signed at Fort Laramie. Abandoned in 1890, it was declared a National Monument by President Roosevelt in 1938. Much of Fort Laramie has been restored, and there are more than twenty historical structures. "Old Bedlam," which served as the bachelor officers quarters, is now completely restored and open to the public.

South Pass City: Gold discoveries were first reported in 1842 in the South Pass area some thirty miles southeast of Lander. Of course, Lander wasn't there at the time. Nobody came to the district, except a few trappers, until 1867 and 1868 mainly because the Indians of that region fought fiercely against encroachment on their lands. For several years mining boomed, but gradually died out after 1870. An authentic western gold ghost town remains, much as it was nearly one hundred years ago. The Carissa and Duncan mines may be seen. There is a museum and restaurant. Neighboring Atlantic City also contains many historical sites including old Carpenter Hotel.

The Oregon Trail, the Mormon Trail, and the original Pony Express Route pass near South Pass City.

Wind River Indian Reservation: The Shoshone and Arapahoe tribes live on this reservation in one of the garden spots of the West. Chief Washakie made peace with the white man early in order to choose this great hunting and fishing country for the Shoshones. The Shoshone Indian maiden Sacajawea who guided the Lewis and Clark expedition is buried near Fort Washakie just off US 287 within easy reach of either Riverton or Lander. Indians in their traditional dress are around the Reservation especially near St. Stephens Jesuit Mission, St. Michaels Mission (Episcopalian), and Fort Washakie.

Forts: Fort Bridger, built in 1842–43 by the trapper and guide Jim Bridger, is located in Fort Bridger State Park in southwestern Wyoming and has been largely restored. Fort Casper (on the outskirts of the city of Casper) has many pioneer and Indian relics preserved in a museum and part of the old fort has been restored. Fort Fetterman is near Douglas; Fort Sanders, near Laramie; Jenny's Stockade near Newcastle; Fort Bonneville near Pinedale; Fort Mackenzie near Sheridan; Fort Phil Kearney near Story in the Sheridan area; Fort Stanbaugh near Atlantic City; Fort McKinney near Buffalo; Fort D. A. Russell near Cheyenne; Fort Steele near Sinclair. Travelers should inquire for directions at the chamber of commerce in cities located nearest these famous forts of the West.

Pioneer Sites: St. Mary's Stage Station and the historical marker where ninety Mormons perished in a blizzard and were ravaged by wolves may be reached from South Pass City (inquire there). The first cabin built by a white man in Wyoming at Bessemer Bend (inquire at Casper Chamber of Commerce). Buffalo Bill Statue (inquire at Cody). Charcoal kilns (inquire at Evanston). Big Sandy Stage Station (inquire at Farson). Register Cliff with names of early pioneers and early graves (inquire at Guernsey). Hole-in-the-wall Gang (inquire at Kaycee). Crowheart Battle, where Chief Washakie cut out the heart of the Crow chief and saved his people (inquire at Riverton). First oil well in Wyoming at Dallas (inquire at Lander). Spanish Diggings, prehistoric quarries (inquire at Lusk). Ghost town Cambria (inquire at Newcastle). Father DeSmet's first Catholic Mass in Wyoming (inquire at Pinedale). Independence Rock (Father DeSmet called it the "Register of the desert"). First Masonic Lodge meeting in 1862 at Independence Rock. Site of Sweetwater Stage Station (inquire at Casper). Site of first county church in Wyoming. Methodist (inquire at Sundance). Trapper's Rendezvous point (inquire at Riverton). Early ghost coal mine camps (inquire at Kemmerer and Rock Springs). Tie hacks (inquire at Dubois). Teapot Dome (inquire at Casper). The Big Teepee ranch home (inquire at Shoshoni).

FAMOUS LIBRARIES. *William Robertson Coe Library* in Laramie on the University of Wyoming campus is the state's finest. It is famous for its many rooms of specialized archives. Western lore is featured in one room, another features valuable Chinese and oriental art. The petroleum library is one of the nation's finest. Wyoming library archives preserve many western literary treasures.

TOURS. Package tours in the park areas can be arranged through the Jackson Lake Lodge at Moran, Wyoming; or Yellowstone Park Company at Mammoth, Wyoming. Frontier Airlines, Stapleton Field, Denver, can be of assistance for tours both summer and winter. Union Pacific Railroad, Omaha, Nebraska, or Cheyenne, Wyo., are helpful on tours. Or address Wyoming Travel Commission. Travel tours, summer and winter sports can be arranged through the Snow King Inn, 733-5200.

INDUSTRIAL TOURS. Wyoming is one of America's great natural resource states. At Riverton, tours of the Gas Hills uranium mines and mills may be arranged. The world's largest open pit uranium mine is found in the Gas Hills. From Lander you may visit the U. S. Steel taconite iron mine. Located in Atlantic City at an elevation of over 8,300 feet, it is the highest iron mine in Wyoming.

The Green River or Rock Springs chambers of commerce will arrange visits to the trona mines near there. FMC Corporation has the world's largest natural soda ash mine west of Rock Springs.

The Casper Chamber of Commerce will arrange tours of the famous Teapot Dome oil field.

In Kemmerer, call the Kemmerer Coal Company to arrange a tour of one of the world's great coal mines.

Call the Gillette Chamber of Commerce to see oil fields and coal mines.

In Newcastle, visit the Accidental Oil Company, a historic tour of the oil industry, a gift shop in an oil tank.

SPECIAL INTEREST TOURS. Geological, historical, scenic tours available in both Yellowstone and Grand Teton National Parks. Wyoming's national monuments are worth seeing. They are *Old Fort Laramie* on US 26, and *Devil's Tower,* a spectacular volcanic neck, near Hulett off US 14.

Wagons West, a program of outdoor vacations with transportation in horse- or mule-drawn replicas of Conestoga wagons, is being operated from spring to fall by L.D. Frome, of Afton, Wyoming. This 5-day tour features chuck-wagon-style meals and accommodations in tents or in the wagons, and travels to the red rock country of Utah and the prairie historic trails and Wyoming Rockies around Escalante, Wyo.

GARDENS. The University of Wyoming campus: Beginning about May 15 and extending until about October 1 the campus is a blaze of flowers. Landscaping is spectacular. Many varieties of trees. Botanical gardens. Visitors are welcome. No charge. Laramie, Wyo.

MUSIC. Each summer Teton Village in Jackson Hole hosts the *Grand Teton Music Festival.* In past years Dr. Ling Tung, music director of the Philharmonia Orchestra and the Hong Kong Music Festival, has directed the Park's festival. Concerts have included symphonic and chamber pieces. The Watermelon Concerts, so-called because after the performance the audience and musicians sit down to discuss the performance over large slices of watermelon, have been very popular.

The *Concert Hall* in the new Fine Arts Center of the University of Wyoming at Laramie hosts numerous concerts and music festivals throughout the year. Their Walcker pipe organ, designed in Germany especially for the University, is one of the largest tracker organs in the United States.

In Casper, The *Civic Symphony Orchestra* performances are worth a combined symphony-skiing trip during the winter months.

Cheyenne and Lander also have outstanding musical events.

 STAGE AND REVUES. Wyoming, once considered culturally deprived, boasts an ever-increasing variety of theatrical entertainment. The University of Wyoming at Laramie has a new *Fine Arts Center* whose theatrical center functions not only to provide space where legitimate theater can be performed, but also as a teaching center. In Jackson, the *Jackson Hole Opera House, Pink Garter,* and *Dirty Jack's* offer outstanding theatrical and melodramatic productions throughout the summer. And Cheyenne, Casper, Cody, Sheridan, and Lander all have *Little Theaters.*

 NIGHTCLUBS. While Wyoming does have night spots which offer entertainment, many of her bars still retain the decor and atmosphere of the Old West of turn-of-the-century. Cheyenne has the Plains Hotel, with its old western "stand-up" bar, as does the Connor Hotel in Laramie. During the annual celebrations, Cheyenne Frontier Days and Laramie Jubilee Days, these two bars are the hub of activity.

The Gay '90's Lounge at Laramie's Holiday Inn has gone somewhat overboard on red, but the lounge, while small, is attractive.

The Triangle Bar in Kemmerer has the down-to-earth atmosphere of an old mining town.

Casper has the Reef, a South Seas nightclub with lively entertainment, and wild music at the Virginian Hotel bar.

Sheridan has the Mint Bar with a large collection of western cattle brands, and Rosie's Bar in Diamondville near Kemmerer still offers a miner's bucket of beer. The Hole-in-the-Wall in Kaycee finds cowboys, oil patch roughnecks and traveling men meeting for chatter.

In the New Wonder Bar in Casper millionaires and bums meet and wager on any event, sporting, elections, or whatever.

Jackson's world-famous Silver Dollar Bar in the Wort Hotel offers live entertainment year round.

 DRINKING LAWS. Wyoming bars open at 6 a.m. and close at 2 a.m. except Sunday from noon to 8 p.m. Minimum drinking age is nineteen. Liquor may be sold over bars either by the drink or the bottle, in cocktail lounges and in dining rooms by the drink, and in liquor stores by the bottle. No state permit is required.

SUMMER SPORTS. *Boating:* the numerous lakes and reservoirs in Wyoming provide ample opportunity for boating recreation. The Bridger National Forest, Flaming Gorge National Recreation Area, Grand Teton National Park, and all the Wyoming State Parks, offer particularly good boating waters. Raft and canoe trips down the rivers are also possible but care should be taken to explore the waters thoroughly before heading out.

Fishing: Wyoming's 20,000 miles of streams and over 264,000 acres of lakes provide unlimited fishing possibilities. Trout are particularly prevalent, but there are many other species of game fish.

Hunting: There are seasons for pronghorn antelope, moose, elk, black bear, whitetail and mule deer, and bighorn sheep. For complete hunting and fishing information contact the Wyoming Game and Fish Commission, Box 1589, Cheyenne, Wyo. 82001.

Horseback riding and pack trips: available throughout the state, particularly at dude ranches and in the Bighorn National Forest, Grand Teton and Yellowstone National Parks.

WINTER SPORTS. Skiing is a favorite winter sport, and Wyoming has some great ski areas, including the Teton Village and SnoKing at Jackson, Antelope Butte between Sheridan and Greybull on US 14, Medicine Bow west of Laramie, Happy Jack east of Laramie, Teton Pass west of Jackson, Snowy Range near Saratoga, Hogadon Basin near Casper, Pinedale, Meadowlark east of Worland between Ten Sleep and Buffalo, and Sleeping Giant west of Cody.

Grand Targhee is Wyoming's newest ski resort in the Tetons. Snowmobiling and ski touring are popular especially out of Dubois and Jackson Hole. Or tour Yellowstone National Park in the winter on a snowmobile.

SPECTATOR SPORTS. By far the most popular and prevalent spectator sport in Wyoming is the rodeo; nearly every community sponsors at least one. The major events, however, are these: *Cody Night Rodeo,* Jun. to Aug., nightly except Sun; *Cheyenne Frontier Days,* during the third week in July; *Central Wyoming Fair and Rodeo* at Casper, late July to early Aug.; *Lander Pioneer Days* and *Cody Stampede* over the 4th of July weekend; the *Fremont County Fair,* third week in Aug. at Riverton; and the *Wyoming State Fair,* the last week of Aug. at Douglas.

Stock car and motorcycle races are frequent and the state championships stock car races are held early in Sept. at Gillette.

Registered *quarter horse racing* takes place at Meadowlark Downs at Riverton.

SHOPPING. Welty's Store at Dubois. This is probably one of the West's finest and largest trading posts. You'll find almost everything that you could want from chic styles to buckskin jackets, hunting equipment, camping.

Also: Stuart Shop, in Casper, has fine women's wear. Jackson Lake Lodge at Moran and Gift Box at Riverton are outstanding gift shops. Paddy Rhoad's Rocky Mountain Jade Shop in Lander sells fine, authentic jade. Merritt's in Cheyenne supplies western wear. Pink Garter Plaza in Jackson has several specialty shops.

WHAT TO DO WITH THE CHILDREN. Both Yellowstone and Grand Teton National Parks are a paradise for children. At Yellowstone along with the geysers, hot springs, bubbling paint pots, there are game preserves where children can see thousands of elk, hundreds of bear, buffalo, moose, deer, mountain sheep and antelope in a near natural habitat. Beware the Yellowstone bear for though he appears cute and cuddly, he is a dangerous wild animal who has lost his fear of man. Under no circumstances should the bears be fed.

On the waters of these parks are swans, wild geese, pelicans, ducks, gulls and terns.

But mostly the parks afford children the chance to frolic uninhibitedly in the waters and along the nature trails and to enjoy the clean, fresh mountain air.

Rodeos, including Little Britches Rodeos where younger cowboys compete, take place in nearly every Wyoming community of any size and offer thrills and excitement to young and old alike.

Indian dances such as those performed at Jackson and Jackson Lake Lodge are performed in full ceremonial dress by the Indians native to Wyoming.

Stagecoaches, pulled by 4–horse teams, leave Roosevelt Lodge in Yellowstone and bounce over forest and sagebrush trails. Or a stagecoach ride is available around the town, leaving Town Square in Jackson.

 INDIANS. Arapahoe and Shoshone Indians preserve many of their native customs on one of the nation's largest reservations, the Wind River Agency in Fremont County. Two Indian missions still operate on the reservation—St. Stephens Jesuit Mission near Riverton and St. Michael's Mission near Ethete in the heart of the reservation. Chief Washakie, the famous Shoshone, is buried here and so is Sacajawea, the Shoshone girl Indian scout for the Lewis and Clark Expedition. Many of the old buildings remain from the days when Fort Washakie was an Indian trading post and government fort. It is now the Indian Agency headquarters. Tours of the reservation can be arranged there, or at the Chambers of Commerce in Riverton or Lander. More than 5,000 Indians live on the reservation. A favorite spot to start a tour is at Paul Hines General Store on US 287, fifteen miles northwest of Lander.

During summer many Indian celebrations, traditional Sun Dances and Powwows are held. Inquire for the dates. The Guide Book put out by the Riverton Chamber of Commerce lists the dates and is available by mail or in person.

The Arapahoe, fierce and fearless warriors, were among the last Indians to submit to a reservation. The Shoshone is famed for his horsemanship. Many are cattle ranchers. Both tribes provide sterling bronc busters and race horses for rodeos in Wyoming. A visit to the reservation is a must for Wyoming tourists.

Shoshone and Arapahoe Indian craft work may be found at Fort Washakie on the Reservation, at Riverton and Lander, and at the Wind River Native Crafts shop near Crowheart Butte. Museums in Lander and Riverton offer exhibits on Indian history and folk lore. And Indian pictographs and petroglyphs survive on sandstone cliffs.

RECOMMENDED READING. T. A. Larson's *History of Wyoming* is an interesting and informative look at the state's past.

EXPLORING WYOMING

Any avid watcher of TV westerns can tell you that Buffalo Bill, Jim Bridger, and Laramie are synonymous with the State of Wyoming, part of the roaring Wild West of nearly a century ago, and the exploits of these daring and brave men are a constant source of inspiration for TV script writers.

Today Wyoming is a peaceful state; its citizens gracious hosts to the thousands of visitors who come from all over the country to see its varied attractions and to participate in its many recreational opportunities.

Motorists glide smoothly and swiftly over the Lincoln Highway, US 30, I–80, modern-day counterpart of the Overland Trail where the cumbersome prairie schooners headed for the California gold fields once rumbled and swayed.

Wyoming sits in the lap of the broadest part of the Rocky Mountains. Rectangular in shape, its boundaries follow the

165

meridians of longitude and parallels of latitude. To the north lies Montana; to the east, South Dakota and Nebraska; to the south, Colorado and Utah; and to the west, Idaho and Utah.

The state occupies a lofty plateau, four to seven thousand feet above sea level. The mountain ranges average 11,500 feet, and many exceed 13,000, thus Wyoming is at a higher average altitude than any other state.

While the two national parks, Yellowstone and the Grand Teton, are the principal attractions for most visitors to Wyoming, many other worthwhile spots of interest can easily be taken in by making "loop" tours with off-the-beaten-path side trips.

The big loop tour can start at Newcastle, where US 16 runs into Wyoming from South Dakota's Black Hills. Newcastle is a trading center for the surrounding ranches and thus provides an early sense of the Old West. Cowboys in their high-heel boots, some with guns on their hips, clomp along the streets, battered Stetsons shading their eyes from the sun.

Follow US 16, northwest out of Newcastle, passing through the small communities of Osage, and Upton, an important oil producing center, then pick up US 14 at Moorcroft for the 33-mile side trip to Devils Tower National Monument, a stump-shaped cluster of volcanic rock columns 1,000 feet across at the bottom and 275 feet at the top. Looming over the Belle Fourche River some 1,280 feet and 865 feet above its wooded base, Devils Tower is the core of an extinct volcano. In 1906 it was proclaimed the first National Monument in the United States.

Exhibits in the visitor's center (about three miles from the monument's east entrance) explain the geology, history, and natural environment of the tower.

The best views of the tower are from the self-guiding nature trail. A nature trail leaflet is available either at the visitors' center or from a box at the beginning of the trail. The trip around the tower is about a mile or an hour's walk. Campsites with fireplace and table facilities and adaptable to both trailer and tents are provided on a first-come, first-served basis. The monument is open the year around.

Retrace US 14 to Moorcroft to US 16 and join I–90 for the trip through Gillette, a modern oil boom town, and on to Buffalo, a historic town near the Red Fork of the Powder River, where the power of the Indians in Wyoming was broken. The embattled Indians, under Chief Dull Knife, fell before the onslaught of a blue-coated U.S. Cavalry troop. Buffalo stands at the entrance to the 9,000-foot-high Powder River Pass, which, despite its height, is open the year around.

At Buffalo take a "detour" to the Bradford Brinton Memorial

Ranch, about twelve miles south on State 1703 leading southwest through Big Horn. The memorial is open daily to visitors without charge. Interesting things to see include the spacious 20-room main ranch house; an outstanding collection of western paintings; an extensive display of Indian arts and crafts; a collection of trophies from hunting trips; and the buildings which comprise a "working ranch"—stables, carriage barns, blacksmith shop, saddle houses, bunkhouse and servant quarters, and a large horse barn.

Returning to Buffalo, take US 87 to Sheridan, the largest city in northern Wyoming.

Indian Days at Sheridan

When the All-American Indian Days celebration is held in Sheridan—usually the last of July and the first two days of August—the frontier spirit of the Old West comes to life. Of special interest are the Indians. In addition to exhibiting their arts and crafts, they compete with each other in athletics, and delight the visitors with their native dances. Tribes from forty states gather here for the fun.

During the third week each July the Sheridan-Wyo. Rodeo, one of the oldest in the country, takes place. Sheridan is the headquarters for the Bighorn National Forest, covering 1,113,597 acres. There are sixty campsites and many picnic spots in the forest. Fishing and hunting expeditions can be arranged as can saddle and pack pleasure trips deep into the wilderness area.

In order not to retrace your route, drive on to Dayton, via I–90 and US 14, and take a look at one of the finest cattle and horse regions of the West. Genuine western hospitality reigns in Dayton where the locals like to use first names as soon as you're introduced and want you to reciprocate. Here in Dayton is America's oldest dude ranch and the Fourth of July celebration features a Bar BQ, with all visitors welcome.

Buffalo Bill Land

From Dayton drive over the summit of the Big Horn Mountains along US 14 to Greybull where US 20 and 16 join for the journey to Yellowstone National Park, the first and the largest in the U.S. park system. En route the town of Cody, at nearly 5,000-foot elevation, can be visited. Check in at a working or dude ranch for a few days of rest and unhurried sightseeing amid breathtaking scenery. An equestrian statue of the great scout, "Buffalo Bill" Cody, looks down the main street of the town that has taken his name. Mementoes of the famed Westerner are on exhibit in the

Buffalo Bill Historic Center, which includes Cody's boyhood home, and a replica of the old Cody ranch. Cody was born in LeClaire, Iowa, and his house was knocked down and re-erected here. During summer months, visitors line the main street to watch the cowboys in parade, then flock to the area for an exciting rodeo. The Whitney Gallery and Buffalo Bill Museum contain one of America's greatest collections of western art.

From Cody to Yellowstone National Park is fifty-three miles via US 14, 16, and 20, known collectively as the "Buffalo Bill Scenic Hiway to Yellowstone." Open from May 1 until Nov. 1, this hard-paved road snakes west through the Shoshone Canyon, tunnels its way beneath Rattlesnake Mountain, and affords sweeping panoramic views of the Buffalo Bill dam and canyon. There are spacious parking places where stops can safely be made to better appreciate the view and to take pictures.

The highway passes lush western ranch country through the Shoshone Valley, plunges into the Shoshone National Forest, then twists through the Absaroka mountains where such strange and colorful rock formations as the Chinese Wall, Laughing Pig Rock, the Devil's Elbow, the Camel, the Palisades, Chimney Rock, and Holy City are found in the area known as the Playgrounds of the Gods. Finally you enter Yellowstone Park, past Lake Eleanor, Sylvan Lake, to reach Yellowstone Lake, the largest high-altitude lake in the United States.

So vast is Yellowstone National Park—3,472 square miles—that weeks on end are needed to explore all of its scenic and varied attractions. No other national park embraces so many of nature's masterpieces. Most outstanding among the park's many natural wonders are the world's largest geyser basins and the thundering falls and canyon of the Yellowstone River.

Nowhere else in the world is there so large a wildlife sanctuary. Powerful binoculars are useful for looking closely at bear, elk, buffalo, moose, deer, and antelope. It's also the safest way, for although the black bear may appear amiable, they are extremely dangerous and it is strictly against park regulations to feed or walk near the bears.

An excellent highway system swings close to many of the prominent sights but accommodations within the park, including campgrounds, are far from adequate during the height of the summer season. Early reservations at the hotels, lodges, and inns are advised.

There are five entrances to Yellowstone National Park. From the north, by way of Livingston and Gardiner, Montana, I–90, US 10 and 89; from the northeast, by way of Billings and Silver Gate, Montana, I–90, US 10 and 212; from the east by way of Cody,

Wyoming, US 14, 16 and 20; from the south by way of Jackson, Wyoming, and Grand Teton National Park, US 26, 89, 187, 189, and 287; and from the west by way of West Yellowstone, Montana, US 20 and 191.

From the east entrance the highway passes Yellowstone Lake whose sparkling blue waters invite a tour of its 110-mile shoreline. Scenic cruisers operate daily during the summer and from their decks the wildlife and waterfowl can be observed in a truly natural setting virtually unchanged since fur trappers discovered the lake more than a hundred years ago.

On past the lake, the road leads to the Fishing Bridge where anglers attempt to lure the large trout that abound there. Rustic cabin accommodations are available at Fishing Bridge Village.

Scenic Treasures of Yellowstone

Starting out from Fishing Bridge, swing right onto the road leading to Canyon Village at Canyon Junction. This loop tour offers a close look at some of the park's outstanding scenery and passes near several areas offering good accommodations.

At Canyon Junction is one of the park's most spectacular sights, the magnificent Grand Canyon of the Yellowstone. This 24-mile-long, 1,200-foot-deep gorge is a visual delight. The countless shades of red and yellow within the canyon are enhanced by the emerald green of the surrounding forest. There are also two waterfalls, of splendid beauty and size, that will thrill you. While the canyon and the falls may be viewed and photographed from several angles, Inspiration Point on the north rim and Artist Point across the gorge are perhaps the best vantage points.

Mt. Washburn, rising 10,317 feet, is on your right as you drive the nineteen miles from Canyon Village to Tower Junction. The road slips through Dunraven Pass at an elevation of 8,859 feet before dropping a couple of thousand feet to Tower Fall where the Roosevelt Lodge provides excellent rustic accommodations. Pause here to enjoy steak cookouts and to allow the children the fun of riding on a stagecoach.

Mammoth Hot Springs, at the North entrance, is just about eighteen miles from Tower Junction and is but one more scenic spectacular in a region literally filled with them. The impressive travertine terraces of these fabled springs are sometimes vividly colored, sometimes snow white. If you want to spend some time here, there are accommodations at the Mammoth Hot Springs Hotel Motor Inn and Cabins.

Having reached the top of the loop at Mammoth Hot Springs

the route swings down twenty-one miles to Norris Junction, then fourteen miles to Madison Junction, and finally sixteen miles to Old Faithful.

Old Faithful

Nowhere in the world can match Yellowstone for the variety of geysers. Some erupt in rage and fury spewing thousands of gallons of water over one hundred feet in the air, others merely splash up a few inches.

And, most beloved of them all, is Old Faithful.

Old Faithful is one of the gathering points for all visitors to the park and no one leaves until he has seen this geyser shoot its thousands of gallons of steaming water high into the air. It "blows" about every hour on the hour and has not missed a performance in over eighty years. In the Old Faithful Visitor Center is a geyser diagram which explains in detail just what goes on beneath the ground to cause this phenomenon. Old Faithful Inn is hard pressed to take care of the demands for accommodations and reservations must be made far in advance.

If you have an appetite for still more geysers you can take a short side trip to Shoshone Geyser Basin or Heart Lake Geyser Basin. To reach the latter take the 17-mile drive from Old Faithful to West Thumb Junction where the Grant Village Campground offers camping facilities.

From West Thumb to Fishing Bridge and the start of this loop is a distance of twenty-one miles. In Fishing Bridge there are two worthwhile points of interest: the Bridge Bay Marina, capable of handling two hundred boats, and the Lake Hotel with every facility including a hospital.

Visitors to the park interested in seeing its remotest areas can do so by either hiking or on horseback. The Howard Eaton Trail, if you have the time, covers the park most thoroughly, but there are numerous shorter trails. You will need a pair of sturdy, comfortable hiking boots and it's best to break them in before arriving at the park.

For the experienced horseback rider there are more than nine hundred miles of trails. Horses may be rented but all trips into the wilderness areas must be accompanied by a guide.

You can visit Yellowstone all year round, and there are always accommodations open (though not always available) including Old Faithful Inn. In winter highways are open through the Gardiner Gate into Park headquarters, but most other roads are closed. From the south entrance access is possible by snow bus or snowmobile and this winter trip into the Park is spectacular.

Grand Teton National Park, 485 square miles packed with some of this country's best mountain, valley, and lake scenery, can be easily reached over a 22–mile stretch of smooth highway, US 89 & 287. Even though the area is compact the traveler here can spend several weeks, with each day revealing something new in scenic views and recreational offerings.

Scattered throughout Teton National Park are a variety of facilities and campgrounds. You can roll your bedroll on the ground, pitch your tent, find a simple tent village with the tents already pitched for you, utilize the marina on Jackson Lake, or enjoy the more comfortable motel surroundings at one of the lodges.

Rustic Luxury at Colter Bay and Signal Mountain

Set in the natural, wooded area on the shores of Jackson Lake are the Colter Bay Cabins and Signal Mountain Lodge. Many cabins are equipped with cooking facilities, heated with electricity, and have bathrooms and showers.

The Colter Bay and Signal Mountain Marinas are fully equipped including boat launching ramps and boat rentals. There is great fishing in Jackson Lake and a cruise that brings the mountain grandeur of the Tetons into your lap.

In the evenings there are programs about the area offered in an amphitheater, and a museum and information center are close by.

The magnificent scenery of the Grand Teton National Park extends continuously from the lakes and valleys skyward to 13,000-foot mountain peaks. Snowcapped and glacier covered, the towering mountains are a backdrop to the placid, emerald lakes, to craggy canyons and pristine forests.

Blinding Glaciers

By the way, be sure to pack sunglasses, for the brilliance of the sun on the snowfields and glaciers can be blinding. Perhaps nowhere else is there a greater variety of glaciated canyons than in the Tetons.

One of the most interesting and varied ways of touring the park is to hedge-hop from one accommodation to another. After Colter Bay Village it is a short move on to Jackson Lake Lodge. Here you have a choice of 375 luxurious rooms spread in the lodge itself and in adjacent cottages. In the Lodge's main lounge a ceiling-to-floor picture window frames the lake and the Grand Teton Range. Dining facilities are in a Coffee Shop Dining Room which seats 500 people. A few steps from the main lodge and cabins is the Olympic-sized pool. There is a teepee snackbar at poolside.

Moving on from Jackson Lake Lodge be sure and take the Teton Park Road to Jenny Lake Lodge, one of the most luxurious accommodations in the park. There are campgrounds here, too, excellent fishing sites, and most of the trails through the mountains start at this location.

At Colter Bay or Jackson Lake Lodge, saddle up and jog along astride a gentle mare through the piney woods and breathe in the sweet, clean air of early morning. The long ride (over three hours) ends with a bountiful breakfast of bacon and eggs to sate the big appetite you've worked up.

A beautiful new lodge, dining room, and lounge, and new rustic motel units have been built at Signal Mountain Lodge. The Lodge is famous for its western menu. Grocery store, gift shop, and filling station serve the visitor. Fishing guides for Jackson Lake are available from the marina. Signal Mountain Lodge operates its own river float trips.

You should also remember that one of the most important items you should pack for a visit to Grand Teton National Park is a pair of sturdy, comfortable hiking boots. Be sure to break them in before leaving on your trip.

Motor through the park first to familiarize yourself with the various areas so you can revisit and spend more time at those you find especially appealing. Then park your car and take to the trails, either on foot or on horseback, for intimate and uninterrupted views of the natural beauty of the region.

Each of the six major routes traversing the park offers an entirely different set of attractions. You might find that some trails are too long and arduous to be followed on foot, so rent one of the docile, sure-footed horses and settle back on the creaky leather for a relaxing ride through the dramatic scenery that characterizes Grand Teton. Other trails, shorter and less rugged, can be appreciated on foot. And, for the truly adventurous, there are combination horseback-and-foot-trails that end at the dizzying height of 11,000 feet on the Static Peak Divide. Many a mountain climber has been lured to the summit.

If the lowlands are your ticket, try the Lakes Trail which hugs the lakes at the bottom of Teton range. Branching out from this point, three other routes cut deeply into the canyon territory. Slicing into the mountains, Death Canyon, Cascade Canyon and Indian Paintbrush Canyon, with incredibly steep walls and myriads of wildflowers, are thrilling to behold. If you are lucky, you may catch a glimpse of one of the large and small wild animals that inhabit the region.

Skyline Trail and Teton Glacier Trail into the highlands are unforgettable visual experiences, but you should not attempt them alone or before mid-June or after mid-September. Before starting out, check in with officials. If you have had no experience but would like to give it a try, you can pick up the fundamentals right at the park.

If water is your element, float trips down the Snake River are available at the Lake or from Jackson. These exciting trips take either a half or a full day. Along the route the majestic Bald Eagle may be seen high in the trees in one of his few remaining natural habitats. You travel past the historic Menor's Ferry at Moose.

You may visit the Grand Teton National Park all year long with facilities open at Signal Mountain Lodge.

Gateway to the Tetons and the National Parks is Jackson, just eight miles from Moose on a straight new highway through the majestic Teton Mountains. Located at the southern entrance to the parks, Jackson is headquarters for the Teton National Forest, an area of 1,701,000 acres of wilderness land bordering on both Grand Teton and Yellowstone National Parks. This resort community offers year-round recreational opportunities. The town and nearby countryside abound with dude ranches, motels and entertainment centers, good fishing and hunting, and three exceptional ski slopes, Snow King, Teton, and Targhee. A Robert Trent Jones championship 18-hole golf course is also available. There is a modern airport with transportation service to the hotels and motels in Jackson, Teton Village, and Jackson Lake Lodge.

For those whose interests are culture and history Jackson offers both. On the one hand it remains entirely Western, and on the other boasts fifteen art galleries, a summer Fine Arts Festival, summer symphony, and summer stock theater. The Silver Dollar Bar in the Wort Hotel is world famous and the Pink Garter Theatre is home for the performing arts.

Arts Festival in the Mountains

With camera in tow, summer or winter, board the chair lift at Jackson and ride to the crest of Snow King Mountain some two thousand feet above. Or look out the 50-foot-high lobby windows of the new Snow King Inn and watch the skiers slaloming down Kelley's Alley.

Another scenic aerial tramway ride leaves from Teton Village, part of the Jackson Hole Ski area just twelve miles west of Jackson on the Wilson-Moose road. Teton Village is a "new town" of chalets and condominiums. The Ski Tram here rises 4,100 feet in an almost vertical ascent to Rendezvous Peak. The ride takes only fifteen minutes and offers a panoramic view of the Teton Range.

Or travel over scenic Teton Pass west of Jackson to the newest ski area in Wyoming, Grand Targhee Village. Targhee has some of the finest, earliest, and latest snow in the West. It takes forty-five minutes to get there from Jackson.

For the non-skier, Jackson Hole Country has weekend recreational opportunities which include cutter racing down the main street. These races usually are held during January and February with the All-American Cutter Race finals held on the weekend of George Washington's birthday.

Don't miss seeing the huge elk herd which winters right on the edge of the town of Jackson. Beginning in November, as many as 10,000 elk come into the refuge and remain into early May. You can ride horse-drawn feed sleds into the heart of the herd, take pictures of the feeding and even help distribute the feed to the animals.

From Jackson you may choose to complete this loop tour back to Cheyenne via Rock Springs. If so, take US 187 south and stop off at Pinedale.

This community is really "off beat" and after the crowds in Yellowstone and Grand Teton you'll find the tempo slow. It is the gateway to the Bridger Wilderness and the farthest incorporated town from a railroad. Pinedale is a true western cowtown and is surrounded by working cattle ranches. To the east are Wyoming's highest and most massive mountains, the Wind Rivers. If you like fishing and big game hunting settle in here for a while and it won't be long before you'll have your limit. There are more than one thousand lakes and streams. Six large lakes are accessible by road. In the quiet retreats of the Bridger National Forest there are many choice campsites. In Pinedale itself are modern motels, dude ranch accommodations, and restaurants.

If you're in town at noon on the second Sunday in July, don't miss Pinedale's lively celebration of her frontier heritage. The Sublette County Historical Society sponsors the event in which hundreds of local people, horses, mules, wagons, pack strings, and teepees parade as a living memorial to the Mountain Men and the fur trade of yesteryear.

One hundred miles farther south is Rock Springs, a thriving sheep-raising community. Beneath the surface of this town of 10,000 is a bituminous coal deposit of tremendous proportions. From Rock Springs take I–80 east back to Cheyenne.

Another route from Jackson to Cheyenne lies through Caspar. Take US 26 and 187 to Moran, then US 26 and 287 south, with a stopover in Dubois, the Rock Capital of the Nation.

The Dubois area, located on the upper Big Wind River and surrounded on three sides by Shoshone National Forest, is one of the richest places in the nation to prospect and search for rocks. Found in the region are gem quality agatized opalized wood, cast material, pine and fir cone replacements, amethyst lined trees and limb casts, and all types of agate equal or superior to any found elsewhere.

Two Tribes With One Reservation

Bordering the Dubois area is the big Shoshone and Arapahoe Indian Reservation. In July, first the Shoshone and then the Arapahoe Indians hold their sun dances. Dressed in full sun dance costumes, they dance continuously for three days and nights without taking food or water. US 287 and 26 passes through the reservation where the Indians tend to their horses and cattle or irrigate their haylands. On your way to Dubois note Crowheart Butte, a State Monument, commemorating the scene of the great battle between the Shoshone and Crow Indians.

Continuing on US 26 and 287 from Dubois the town of Lander, one of Wyoming's oldest communities, is worth a stopover for those of you making a leisurely exploration of the state. Sometimes called the place where the rails end and the trails begin, Lander is a great place to fish, hunt, and mountain climb.

Or follow US 26 into Riverton. Located in the center of the Reservation, the Riverton Museum has Indian displays. There are three Indian Missions in this vicinity: St. Stephens on State 789, St. Michael's Mission at Ethete, and Fort Washakie, the Indian headquarters in Fort Washakie.

Ghost Towns

From Lander a side tour of historic interest and scenic beauty can be made to the ghost mining towns of Atlantic City and South Pass City on State 28. At the latter town the Whitman Monument commemorates the stop on July 7, 1836, of Marcus Whitman's party on their trip to Oregon. Narcissa Whitman and Eliza Hart, members of the party, were the first white women to cross South Pass.

Drive to the Wind River Indian Reservation just outside Lander and bathe in the Reservation Mineral Hot Springs. Also visit Sacajawea's grave in the Indian cemetery at Wind River. She was the guide of the Lewis and Clark expedition from the Missouri River to the Pacific Coast and return during the period of 1805 to 1806. She died here in 1884. And Chief Washakie is buried in the government cemetery.

The Glacier Primitive Area high atop the Wind River Range is an isolated mountain region accessible only by foot or saddle horse. Within an hour astride a smart-stepping horse you become completely cut off from the outside world in a country of mountain grandeur. The region abounds in streams and lakes filled with game fish. These pack trips are under the supervision of competent guides. Rates are kept to a minimum and include everything necessary for the trip except personal items.

If you are in the mood for some meandering off the direct route to Rawlins, swing on to State 789 on up to Riverton, Shoshoni, Thermopolis, and Worland.

At Riverton you are invited to tour one of the four uranium mills. Tours can be arranged by appointment through the Chamber of Commerce. The world's largest uranium mine is near Riverton.

Shoshoni, home of the famous Boysen Lake Pike Derby, is a small town with fewer than six hundred people, but with one of the West's finest antique barbed-wire stores.

Thermopolis, on the Big Horn River, is a health resort famous for its hot springs. If you're an early riser, wander down at 8 a.m. for a dip in the thermal waters of one of the many swimming pools. Otherwise, you'll find them open until 10 p.m.

The Thermopolis Indian Pageant, Gift of the Waters, is a colorful festival that takes place on the first Sunday in august. And, on Labor Day, excitement runs high when cowboys try their luck at riding wild horses at the weekend rodeo.

US 20 from Shoshoni to Thermopolis goes right through the spectacular Wind River canyon. At the entrance to the canyon is Boysen Lake with 220 miles of shore line. It's a state park worth a fishing or sightseeing trip. Marinas are located at both ends of Boysen.

Travel north on State 789 to Worland, and if you've notified the Holly Sugar Corporation of your arrival, they'll reward you with an informative tour through the sugar plant, or visit the National Girl Scout Center West, out of Worland toward Ten Sleep. Close to Rawlins is the Medicine Bow National Forest, with a plentiful supply of coal, placid lakes, rushing, fish-filled streams, and thousands upon thousands of acres of shady forests. Bring a picnic basket and spend some quiet hours—or days, if you prefer—in this lovely region. Skiing is popular at three areas.

Laramie, at the altitude of more than 7,000 feet, offers an invigorating climate and clean, clear air. Nearly a century old, the town has flourished since its inception as a station on the Union Pacific Railroad line. Its name, immortalized in Wild West literature, movies, and television, was taken from one of its first settlers, Jacques LaRamie.

A short jaunt from Laramie proper is historic Old Fort Sanders, a stopping place for Western pioneers and Mormons. Forging west, they used the Overland Trail, now commemorated in the Laramie vicinity with stone markers. Traveling the smooth, well-developed highways of today, it is difficult to appreciate the hardship of crossing this rugged terrain in a prairie schooner.

Touring the University

Visitors are invited to tour this sprawling, landscaped campus and a brochure entitled "Roaming the University of Wyoming" includes a map and is most helpful in finding your way around. The points of interest include:

Geological Museum. This building contains the skeleton of a huge dinosaur that is more than 100 million years old. One of only five brontosaurus skeletons in the United States, it stands fifteen feet high and is seventy-five feet long. Also on exhibit are fossils, rocks and minerals, diagrams of geological processes, and Indian artifacts. The museum is open 8 a.m. to 5 p.m. on weekdays; 2 p.m. to 5 p.m. on Sundays and holidays.

Library. The spacious Coe Library Building contains more than 300,000 volumes and 1,500 periodicals, and is a despository for more than 500,000 government documents. The Western History Research Center, containing rare volumes, artifacts, and items of general historical interest is a continuing attraction.

Rocky Mountain Herbarium. Located on the third floor of the Aven Nelson Building, this collection contains more than 270,000 plant specimens. The Herbarium has the largest and most representative collection of plants of the Central Rocky Mountains and is one of the best-known herbaria in the United States.

In addition, the University offers an almost continual selection of cultural events, most of which are open to the general public.

Abraham Lincoln is honored with a Memorial Monument about ten miles east of Laramie on US 30. The bust by Robert Russin commemorates the sesquicentennial of Lincoln's birth and stands approximately 9,000 feet above sea level at the highest point on the Lincoln Highway, US 30. This enormous bronze head weighs almost four tons. Stop at Lusk and ramble around the free museum. Steep yourself in the atmosphere of the "woolly" West. The fascinating memorabilia on display recall the days when Indians roamed and stages rattled through the West.

Two and one-half miles south of Laramie is Monolith Portland Midwest Co., which produces varieties of cement. Tourists are welcomed.

From Laramie to Cheyenne, the state capital, I–80 swings past the highest point along the entire Lincoln Highway (8,835 feet, in the Sherman Hills). A good photo stop nearby is the Ames Monument, located about two miles off US 30 on a marked road. This 65-foot pyramid was erected in honor of the Ames Brothers, who helped finance the Union Pacific.

Cheyenne, now a peaceful, prosperous community, was known as "Hell on Wheels" in the days of the Old West. This spirit is revived once a year, usually during the last full week of July, at Cheyenne Frontier Days. At Frontier Park, the nation's top cowboys call on all their skill, strength and sheer nerve, to try to stay astride backs of bucking steers and horses. Parades, too, are a feature of these Frontier Days.

While in Cheyenne, visit the Capitol Building. Guided tours of the Gold Dome are available during June to August, but the panoramic view is worth a visit anytime. The State Museum, located on Central Avenue at 23rd Street, exhibits archeological and historical treasures of Wyoming and the Old West.

For six weeks starting in July, you can "do-si-do" under the stars on Wednesday evenings. Bring your partner down to Central Avenue and 17th Street for summertime square dance fun.

From Cheyenne there are three tours recommended by the Wyoming Travel Commission, two of which can be made in a day. These tours take in some fascinating points of interest as well as varied scenery. The tour which takes in "Old Bedlam," Fort Laramie and the Oregon Trail National Historic Site is 219 miles and is a perfect one-day auto outing. Beginning at Frontier Park, drive north on I–25, from the Randall Avenue Interchange past Warren Air Force Base, then swing northeast on US 85 for eighty-four miles to Torrington in the valley of the North Platte, once a corridor of human migration. Here you'll be following in the footsteps of the Sioux, Cheyenne, and Arapahoe as they hunted the vast herds of buffalo. Torrington was a way station for the Pony Express, as well as a stop on the Oregon and Texas Trails.

A few miles northwest on US 26 is Lingle where, just across the North Platte River, the bloody Grattan Massacre of 1854 took place and started thirty-five years of warfare between the Plains Indians and the U.S. Army.

A little farther along US 26 is Fort Laramie National Historical Site where eleven of the original buildings still stand. The National Park Service hopes to preserve and restore them.

Between the lectures of the park historian and the explanatory signs, you'll learn that the fort was first built privately as a place for traders and trappers to meet. Later it became a military outpost protecting the travelers going on to Utah, Oregon, and California. Kit Carson, Jim Bridger, John C. Fremont, John "Portugee" Phillips, and "Buffalo Bill" Cody at one time or another visited the fort. "Old Bedlam," the two-story officers' club known as the gayest spot on the Oregon and California trails, has been restored and refurnished. The fort became a station on the Cheyenne-Deadwood Stage Route after 1876, but was abandoned in 1890.

Oregon Trail ruts can still be seen in Guernsey at the mouth of the Platte River Canyon. If you'll look closely on Register Cliff you see the names of pioneers carved on rock walls. Because of the Warm Springs here travelers dubbed them the "natural bathtub of the plains." A side road leads six miles north to Sunrise, site of the largest iron mine in the Rockies.

From Guernsey stick to US 26 across the top of the Guernsey Reservoir and start your return trip south on US 87 to Wheatland at the foot of the rocky Laramie Mountains, a part of Medicine Bow National Forest. Twenty-five miles deeper south lies Chugwater where you begin to follow the route of the old Cheyenne-Black Hills Stage Line. From here State 87 and I-25 take you quickly back to Cheyenne.

Cowboys and Cavalry

If you want to extend this loop, follow US 26 west from the junction with I-25 where, instead of turning south to Wheatland, turn right to Douglas. On your left you'll pass the site of the old Horseshoe Stage Station and a little farther on the site of the Historic Burnt Wagon Train. US 87 and 26 pick up where I-25 leaves off and continue into Douglas, known as Tent Town when it was founded in 1886. Once a town jammed with soldiers, railroaders and cowpokes—rough, tough and ready to fight at the slightest provocation—Douglas saw its saloons filled nightly. Now only a hint of these rough-and-tumble days survives when, during the last full week in August, Douglas is the site of Wyoming's State Fair which includes a rodeo, horse show, and exhibits.

While in the Douglas area take some time off to swim in Jackalope Warm Springs, about seven miles away. The natural artesian spring furnishes 163,000 gallons every hour at 84-degree temperature. The water is changed completely four times daily. There is a shady picnic area with tables.

Jackalope is the imaginative name of one of the most implausible animals in North America. Were it not for the strange horns, it might be a large rabbit; where it not for its shape and coloring, it might be a species of antelope.

The first white man to fancy he saw this singular animal was a trapper named Ron Black, in 1851. An odd trait of the Jackalope is its ability to imitate the human voice of cowboys singing to their herds at night. Many wranglers have been startled to hear their lonesome melodies repeated faithfully from a nearby hillside. The phantom echo comes from the throat of some Jackalope. They sing only on dark nights just before a thunderstorm.

From Douglas take I-25, then US 20 and 26 into Casper, Wyoming's leading industrial city. Casper, a pleasant, scenic community, sits at the foot of Casper Mountain. Oil, uranium, and coal industries contribute a major portion of the city's income but not far behind are cattle and sheep ranching.

The Old Fort Casper Museum displays Indian and historic Western objects.

If you have time, drive west forty-three miles from Casper on US 20 and 26 to Hell's Half Acre. Here nature has carved some freakish formations in the shapes of towers, spires, and other unusual architectural effects. The locals refer to the area as "Devil's Kitchen."

From Casper you can return to Laramie and Cheyenne by following State 220, then State 487 into Rock River where US 30 joins I-80.

Another loop tour from Cheyenne covers 274 miles and takes in the scenic splendor of the forest of the Medicine Bow. This trip can be made easily in a day by getting an early start, and take along a picnic lunch for the area's hills and dells invite eating out in the open.

Take Happy Jack Road (Secondary Route 0107) at the junction with Dey Avenue. Drive west on Happy Jack across I-25, south of Francis Warren Air Force Base, then into the cool of the hills. It is a quick thirty-three miles to Medicine Bow National Forest in the Pole Mountain District where on either side you'll pass quaking aspen, slender lodgepole pine, douglas fir, and the stately ponderosa pine. A side trip on Forest Road Route 1175 takes you to Blair Campground, site of an old Indian camping spot and a place full of unusual rock formations.

Once back on Happy Jack (Forest Road 1166, which has a good gravel surface) you'll travel along Pole Creek, a stream stocked with trout and occasionally interrupted by beaver dams.

The new Curt Gowdy State Park, named after the famous sports announcer, is just west of Cheyenne not far from the Happy Jack area.

At the junction with US 30 (I-80) you drop down into Laramie where you pick up State 130 west to Centennial, gateway to the Snowy Range or Medicine Bow. Open late May to early October, the Snowy Range Highway passes through mountain and forest scenery that few regions can match for beauty and variety.

At an elevation of 8,400 feet you'll pass the home base of the University of Wyoming ski team, then descend through the deep scenic canyons of Libby Creek, Silver Run, and North Fork.

If you have time take the side trip north on state 130 to Saratoga, the center of deer and antelope country. There is excellent fishing in the North Platte River and the medicinal waters in Saratoga Hot Springs State Park are clear, odorless, and piping hot.

This loop tour then turns south to Riverside, through sprawling ranch country. State 230 runs parallel to the Continental Divide and dips briefly into Colorado. Keep on Colorado's State 125 until you reach the junction with Wyoming State 127 above Cowdrey. Turn northeast, and, with the massive Colorado Rockies at you back, continue to Woods Landing where State 230 runs beside the Laramie River into Laramie. From here, US 30 and I–80 will take you back to Cheyenne.

Looping into Nebraska

A third, and this time 365-mile, tour begins on US 30, at its intersection with US 85, and heads east across the rolling plain. It is about thirty-nine miles to Pine Bluffs on the state line, the highest point in Nebraska (5,424 feet). Continue east to Kimball then turn north on Nebraska State 71 for Wildcat Hills. The Game Refuge here is a good place to photograph wild life.

Viewed from the town of Gering, the landmark of Scotts Bluff rises sharply above the plains. Scotts Bluff National Monument marks the place where thousands of settlers stopped to replenish supplies and refresh themselves for their journey west to Oregon and California. Pony Express riders changed their mounts here for the dash across the country.

From the observation point of the monument (actually in the township of Gering) the landmarks on the trail route are visible for one hundred miles, all the way to Laramie Peak. By picking up Nebraska State 92 east you can visit Chimney Rock National Historic Site, an odd-looking spire of solitary grandeur that served as a beacon to mountain men and emigrants across the planes.

US 26 swings out of Scotts Bluff along the Platte to Torrington and Lingle, Wyoming, whose attractions have already been described. The community of Lusk, north on US 85, hosts the

181

popular Rawhide Pageant in August. Manville, ten miles distant on US 20, is the gateway to the "Spanish diggings," stone quarries of prehistoric man. These represent one of the earliest signs of life in the Platte Valley.

The loop route continues west through Keeline and Shawnee to Orin where historic "Bridger's Crossing" lies 1½ miles south of the Orin River. Follow US 87 south and as you travel the snowy Laramie Peak can be seen towering above the land in Medicine Bow National Forest.

Ten miles south of Orin is the Glendo Recreation Area, an excellent place to set up camping headquarters. Here you can boat, swim, or water-ski on the broad reservoir. The good fishing in the lake and on the streams promises excellent opportunities to catch your limit.

After Glendo you pick up I–25 to Wheatland, Chugwater, and over US 87 to Cheyenne.

AROUND THE STATE

HOTELS AND MOTELS. The larger towns in Wyoming have excellent hotel and motel accommodations; most have parking facilities, restaurants and bars. Rates are usually higher in summer, though some have special family rates. Cost figures generally are for the minimum or moderate priced rooms, unless a range is indicated. Listings are in order of price category.

The price categories in this section, for double occupancy, will average as follows: *Deluxe* $25, *Expensive* $19, *Moderate* $14, and *Inexpensive* $10. For a more complete explanation of these categories see the *Hotels & Motels* part of THE ROCKIES & PLAINS *Facts at Your Fingertips* at the front of this volume.

AFTON

The Corral. *Inexpensive.* 161 Washington St. Charming group of rustic cabins in the heart of the Star Valley cheese country. Children's playground. 886-5424

Lazy B Motel. *Inexpensive.* 219 Washington. Very nice. Television. Some cooking. On the road from Salt Lake to Jackson Hole. Pets allowed. 886-3362

ALTA

Grand Targhee Resort. *Deluxe.* In the Teton Mountains, out of Driggs, Idaho. Wyoming's newest ski resort. Early and late snow. Open summers. Swimming pool. One-, one-and-a-half- and two-level condominiums. 353-2308

BUFFALO

Cross Roads Inn. *Expensive.* At junction of Hwy. 16, I–25, I–90. A new motel just off the interstate. Dining room, cocktail lounge, swimming pool. Meeting rooms. Some pets accepted. 684-2256

Keahey's Motel. *Moderate.* 350 N. Main. Very nice, Some cooking units. Old-time hospitality. Television. In the historic downtown. 684-2225

Mountain View Motel. *Inexpensive.* 588 Fort St. Small, rustic group of units with Western decor. Picnic, area, charcoal broilers and playground. 684-2881

CASPER

Holiday Inn. *Moderate.* 300 West F St.

Large, with restaurant, cocktail lounge and swimming pool. 235-2531

Imperial "400." *Moderate.* 440 East A St. Small motel with large, well-appointed rooms and heated pool. 234-3501

Ramada Inn. *Moderate.* 200 West E and Center Sts. Beautiful Colonial lobby. Old West rustic charm. Beauty and barber shops. Pool, cocktails. 235-5713

Townhouse Motor Hotel. *Moderate.* 110 N. Center St. at 1st Ave. Casper's only new downtown hotel, on the site of the famous Gladstone. Skyline dining room. Cocktail lounge. Plenty of parking. 237-8325

Travelier. *Inexpensive.* 500 E. 1st St. Small but entirely adequate motel, TV, pets, cafe nearby. 237-9343

CHEYENNE

Hitching Post. *Expensive.* 1600 W. Lincolnway on US 30W. Long a Wyoming landmark near the downtown area. Large attractive rooms, indoor and outdoor pools, sauna, beautiful dining room, coffee shop, cocktail lounge, beauty salon, and gift shop. 638-3301

Holiday Inn. *Expensive.* 5401 Woodson Avenue. Short distance from airport. Large. 632-8901

Holding's Little America. *Expensive.* 1½ mi. west at jct. I-80 and I-25. Just west of the city limits, this new installation is a smaller version of the operation at Little America, Wyoming. Heated pool, coffee shop, dining room and cocktail lounge. Antiques and curios. 634-2771

Ramada Inn. *Moderate.* 3929 Lincoln Way. Medium-sized motel with comfortable rooms, dining room, cocktail lounge, heated swimming pool. 634-2171

Home Ranch. *Inexpensive.* 2414 E. Lincolnway. Medium-sized motel with

TV, playground, cafe nearby. Continental breakfast available. 634-3575

CODY

Holiday Inn. *Expensive.* 1603 Sheridan. Buffalo Bill Village. A new motel combined with one of the Cody-country's most famous historic attractions. Dining room, cocktail lounge, swimming pool, meeting rooms. Gift shop. Some cooking. 587-3654

Sunset Motor Inn. *Expensive.* 1601 8th St. Medium-sized motel with large, well-furnished rooms, heated pool and putting green. 587-4265

Absaroka Lodge. *Moderate.* 1514 11th St. This small, rustic motel is located on a rushing mountain stream. Dining room and large Western lobby with stone fireplace. Ask the owner about his grandfather, "Buffalo Bill" Cody. 587-3963

Buffalo Bill Village. *Moderate.* 1701 Sheridan. Large group of Western cabins, a trailer parking area, playground, heated pool and western entertainment. 587-3654

Irma Hotel. *Moderate.* US 20, 14 and 16. This Old West landmark, in the heart of downtown Cody, was built by "Buffalo Bill" Cody. 587-4221

Uptown. *Inexpensive.* 1562 Sheridan Ave. Comfortable rooms, TV, playground, pets. Cafe nearby. 587-4245

DUBOIS

Branding Iron. *Moderate.* 1½ blks. west on US 26, 287. In the heart of a real western town. Nearby cafe and cocktail lounge. Western charm. 455-2446

Stagecoach Motor Inn. *Moderate.* West side on main highway. In the best tourist tradition. TV, pets. A family atmosphere. 455-2303

EVANSTON

Ramada Inn. *Expensive.* 1 mi. west on US 30 at jct. I-80. Color TV, heated pool, spa, restaurant, bar. 9-hole golf course adjacent. 789-2810

Dunmar Motel. *Moderate.* 1019 Lombard St. A small motel with spacious grounds and rooms. Heated pool. 789-3770

Vagabond. *Moderate.* 212 Hwy. 30E, 1 mi. east on US 30, 189. Color TV, playground, pets. Cafe nearby. 789-2902

New. *Inexpensive.* 85 Park Rd. Comfortable rooms, some color TV, pets, free coffee. Cafe nearby. 789-2662

GILLETTE

Sands Motor Lodge. *Expensive.* 608 E. 2nd St. Spacious, well-appointed rooms with balconies, dining room, cocktail lounge, coffee shop, heated pool. 682-9341

Thunder Basin Inn. *Inexpensive.* East side on US 14–16. Newest. Geared for everyone. Dining room, coffee shop, cocktail lounge, swimming pool, meeting rooms. 682-5111

Western. *Moderate.* 306 W. 2nd St. Heated pool, some color TV, limited pets, free coffee. Cafe nearby. 682-4744

GREEN RIVER

Mustang Inn. *Moderate.* 550 E. Flaming Gorge Way, E on US 30 off I–80. Newly remodeled. Dining room, coffee shop, cocktail lounge, meeting room. 875-2468

Tomahawk Hotel. *Expensive.* 98 N. 1st St. A quiet, well-kept hotel in the heart of town. 875-2211

JACKSON HOLE

Ramada Snow King Inn. *Deluxe.* 400 Snow King Dr. Wyoming's newest resort hotel. Dining room, coffee shop, cocktail lounge, gift shop, boutique, art gallery, 1,000-person convention center. Spacious lobby with 50-foot-high window. Tennis courts, sauna, health club. Horseback riding. A complete summer and winter vacation center. At the foot of Snow King ski area on the edge of Jackson. 733-5200 1974. 733-5200

Teton Village-Jackson Hole. *Deluxe.* 12 mi. northwest on county 2001. This is Wyoming's newest year-round resort area. Opened in the fall of 1965 as a major new ski area, year-round facilities are being developed. Among the newly completed establishments are **Rendezvous,** with restaurant, cocktail lounge and sports shop, 733-3155; **Alpenhof Chalet,** with continental restaurant, cocktail lounge, bunk rooms, beauty salon and heated swimming pool, 733-3462; **Sheraton Jackson Hole Inn,** featuring exceptional lodging and dining, 733-3657; and the new **Hilton Inn,** 733-2311.

Antler Motel. *Expensive.* 43 W. Pearl. Famous for hospitality. Large fireplaces. Coffee shop across the street. Pets allowed. Worldwide reputation. 733-2535

Executive Inn. *Expensive.* 55 S. Jackson. Dining room and coffee shop. Meeting room. Famous for food. 733-4340

Jackson Hole Lodge and Motel. *Expensive.* US 26, 89 & 187. A mountain lodge with well-landscaped grounds and activities for families. 733-2992

Pony Express. *Expensive.* US 26, 89 and 187. Small motel with large, well-appointed rooms, children's playground and heated pool. 733-2658

Virginian Motel. *Expensive.* 1 mi. west on US 26, 89, 187. New and expanding. Dining room, cocktail lounge, gift shop, convention center. 733-2792

Wort Hotel. *Expensive.* Glenwood and Broadway Sts. Small Western hotel, long a favorite with skiers, tourists and the public. The bar is covered with silver dollars. Atmosphere is truly Old West. Dining room, cocktail lounge and art shows. 733-2190

Alphorn Lodge. *Moderate.* 652 S. Cache. A chalet-type motel. Step out of your room onto Snow King Mountain. Chair lift summer and winter with view of the Grand Tetons. Apres ski parties. Family bunkbeds. 733-3202

Woods. *Moderate.* 122 N. Glenwood St. Small motel, TV, cafe nearby. 733-2953

LANDER

Holiday Lodge. *Moderate.* At intersection US 26, 287 on south edge of Lander. Golf privileges. TV. 332-2511

Maverick Motel. *Moderate.* 808 Main St. A small, well-appointed motel with coffee shop and heated pool. 332-2821

LARAMIE

Holiday Inn. *Expensive.* US 287 and I-80. Large motel with a charming cocktail lounge in the Gay 90's decor, dining room, coffee shop, heated pool and spacious rooms. 742-6611

Ramada Inn. *Expensive.* 1 mi. south on US 287 at I-80. New dining room, cocktail lounge, meeting and banquet room. 742-3721

Circle S Motel. *Moderate.* 2440 Grand Ave. On the east edge of town, with attractively landscaped ground and pleasant rooms. Heated pool. 745-4811

Wyo. Motel. *Moderate.* 1720 Grand Ave. Small, friendly motel directly across the street from the new University dormitories. Well-appointed rooms and heated pool. Some of the units have garages available. 742-6633

Connor Hotel. *Inexpensive.* 3rd and Grand Ave. An older hotel in the heart of the downtown area. Attractive cocktail lounge and dining rooms, coffee shop. Free parking. 742-2123

LITTLE AMERICA

Little America Motel. *Expensive.* on US 30. A large oasis in the middle of the desert, there are probably more gasoline pumps here than anyone will see anywhere else. This motel has large, warm rooms, dining room. Coffee shop and cocktail lounge. 875-2400

LUSK

Pioneer Court. *Moderate.* 777 S. Main St. Small, charming motel with heated pool. 334-2640

Ranger Hotel. *Inexpensive.* Large hotel, long a favorite of the traveling public. Good restaurant and cocktail lounge. 334-2120

MEDICINE BOW

Virginian Hotel. *Inexpensive.* US 287. A Wyoming landmark. Dining room, coffee shop and cocktail lounge. 379-2377

MORAN
(Grand Teton National Park)

Jackson Lake Lodge. *Deluxe.* A large, new hotel with many resort features. Excellent Old West mural in restaurant, with gourmet menu. Giant picture windows overlook Jackson Lake and the Tetons. Horseback riding and pool, cocktail lounge, shops. 543-2855

Jenny Lake Lodge. *Deluxe.* On Teton Park Rd., 11 mi. southwest of Moran. A delightful group of mountain cabins, operated on a modified American Plan. Informal, with warm, spacious rooms in individual units. Lounge has delightful stone fireplace. 733-4647

Signal Mountain Lodge. *Moderate.* New lodge on the edge of Jackson Lake in full view of the Grand Teton. Dining room, cooking, cocktail lounge, gift shop, grocery store, filling station, boating. Fishing. Meeting rooms. Float trips. 543-2831

Togwotee Lodge. *Moderate.* US 26-287. A new, beautifully designed motel with sixty large, well-appointed units. Dining room. 543-2841

NEWCASTLE

Graham's. *Inexpensive.* 451 W. Main St. Small, well-furnished motel with coffee in the rooms, heated pool. 746-2796

Stet. *Inexpensive.* US 187. Charming, western motel with comfortable rooms. 367-4336

Fountain Motor Inn. *Moderate.* 1½ mi. east at jct. US 16, 85. Heated pool, color TV, pets. Free Continental breakfast. Cafe nearby. 746-4426

RAWLINS

Bel Air Inn. *Expensive.* 23rd and Spruce Sts. A new, well–appointed motel. Coffee shop, cocktail lounge, heated pool. 324-2737

Quality Motel. *Moderate.* 1617 Spruce St. on I–80 Business. Dining and coffee shop, lounge. 324-2271

Ferris Hotel. *Inexpensive.* 4th and Buffalo. An older hotel in the center of the downtown area. Coffee shop and cocktail lounge. 324-2216

RIVERTON

Thunderbird Motel. *Moderate.* 302 E. Fremont. A medium-sized motel with well-furnished rooms. 856-9201

Tomahawk Motel. *Moderate.* 208 E. Main. Downtown motel on Main St. TV. A new facility. 856-9206

Teton Hotel. *Inexpensive.* In the heart of downtown, this medium-sized hotel has a dining room, coffee shop, cocktail lounge, shopping arcade and parking. 856-2271

ROCK SPRINGS

Holiday Inn. *Expensive.* 2 mi. west on US 30 at I–80 Dewar Dr. exit. Color TV, indoor-outdoor heated pool, cafe, bar. Free airport bus. 382-9200

Nomad Inn. *Expensive.* 1545 Elk St., just off I–80. Color TV, heated pool, playground, pets limited, free coffee. 362-5646

Outlaw Inn. *Expensive.* 1630 Elk St., just off I–80. Old West motif, spacious rooms, large interior arcade, indoor heated pool, color TV, Cocktails, dining. 362-6623

El Rancho Motor Lodge. *Moderate.* 1430 9th St. A large, modern motel. Heated pools. 362-3763

Park Hotel. *Inexpensive.* 19 Elk St. A large hotel recently remodeled and redecorated. Good dining room and cocktail lounge. 362-3701

SARATOGA

Saratoga Inn. *Expensive.* Just across the river in Saratoga. Located on the North Platte River, golf course, tennis. Dining room, cocktail lounge. 326-5261

SHERIDAN

Sheridan Center Inn. *Expensive.* 609 N. Main. Dining room, cocktail lounge. Banquet, meeting rooms. Swimming pool. 674-7421

Trail's End Motel. *Moderate.* 2125 N. Main St. Small, attractive motel with an indoor pool. 672-2477

Wyoming Lodge. *Moderate.* 1744 N. Main St. New, modern motel with large rooms and heated pool. 674-6444

THERMOPOLIS

Holiday Inn. *Expensive.* In Hot Springs State Park. Pool, dining room, coffee shop, cocktail lounge, banquets and convention center. Mineral baths. 864-3131

Moonlighter Motel. *Expensive.* 600 Broadway. In the heart of town on US 20. New, excellent. Cocktails. 864-2321

Californian. *Inexpensive.* 501 S. 6th St. A small, quiet motel with pleasant, cool lawns and picnic tables. 864-2325

TORRINGTON

Oregon Trail Lodge. *Inexpensive.* On US 25. A small motel with large, attractive rooms and heated pool. 532-2101

Trail Hotel. *Inexpensive.* 20th & Main Sts. A small hotel with comfortable rooms. 532-2151 .

WORLAND

Townhouse Motor Inn. *Moderate.* 119 N. 10th. Pool, dining room, TV. 347-2426

Sun Valley Motel. *Inexpensive.* 500 N. 10th St. A small motel with attractive, well-planned rooms. 347-4251

Washakie Hotel. *Inexpensive.* 544 Big Horn Ave. One of the most charming of Wyoming's hotels. Coffee shop and dining room excellent and the cocktail lounge one of the state's best. 347-4244

WHEATLAND

Wyoming Motel. *Moderate.* 1101 9th St. Pool, a family motel. 322-2574

YELLOWSTONE NATIONAL PARK

Note: these accomodations are operated by Yellowstone Park Co.

Canyon Village. *Moderate.* A huge hotel operated by the Yellowstone Park Company under license of the Park Service. Dining rooms, cocktail lounge, coffee shop, cafeteria, barber and beauty shops. Horses. 344-7311

Mammoth Motor Inn & Cabins. *Inexpensive.* North end of Park. Open year round. Snowmobile trips. 344-7311

Old Faithful Inn. *Inexpensive.* Another lodge operated by the Yellowstone Park Company, this one across the road from Old Faithful. Dining rooms, coffee shop, cocktail lounge, beauty and barber shops. 344-7311

DINING OUT. Wyoming is not particularly interested in exotic cuisine, and as a result, steak-and-potatoes are often the best fare. Beef is somewhat cheaper here than in some other states, and the cuts are quite good. Native trout is excellent and usually well prepared. For other worthwhile restaurants, check hotel listings. Restaurants are listed in order of price category.

Restaurant price categories are as follows: *Deluxe* $8 and up, *Expensive* $5–$7, *Moderate* $3–$5, and *Inexpensive* $1.50–$3. These prices are for *hors d'oeuvres* or soup, *entrée*, and dessert. Not included are drinks, tax and tips. For a more complete explanation of restaurant categories refer to THE ROCKIES & PLAINS *Facts at Your Fingertips* at the front of this volume.

BUFFALO

American Legion Club. *Moderate.* 1 mi. east on US 16, I–90 Business. Open to the general public in the evenings, long a favorite with area people. Smorgasbord served during the summer on Sunday evenings. Open 5 to 10 p.m.; Sat. to 11 p.m.; Sun. 3 to 10 p.m. Closed Mon. 684-7711

Cross Road Inn. *Moderate.* On the edge of town just off I–90. A fine dining room and coffee shop for family and friends. Open 6 a.m. to 9 p.m.; Sat. to 11 p.m. 684-2256

Idlewild. *Inexpensive.* 36 N. Main St. A pleasant place supported by local service organizations. Specializes in steak and trout. Open 6 a.m. to 9 p.m. 684-7341

CASPER

Benham's Supper Club. *Expensive.* Just off I–25 at Center St. exit. A fine businessman's lunch and charcoal-broiled steaks are served in an attractive dinner club atmosphere. Open 11 a.m. to 11 p.m. Closed Sun. 234-4531

Branding Iron Inn. *Moderate.* 129 W. 2nd St. This friendly Western restaurant is a good place to take the family for steaks and sandwiches. Open 11 a.m. to 9 p.m. Closed Sun. 237-3557

187

CODY

Bronze Boot. *Moderate.* 4 mi. west on US 14, 16, 20. This charming Western restaurant offers prime steak and well-prepared accompanying items. Open 5 p.m. to midnight. Closed Sun. 587-3668

Irma Grill. *Moderate.* 1192 Sheridan Ave. This restaurant, located in the hotel "Buffalo Bill" Cody built, has long been known for good food. Specialties are steak, prime ribs, and trout, Open 6:30 a.m. to 10 p.m. Closed Sun. in winter. 587-2121

DUBOIS

The Westerner. *Moderate.* Ramshorn St. at 1st St. In the center of town, the Longhorn Room of this motel offers traditional meals in a relaxed setting. Open 5 a.m. to 10 p.m. 455-2400

JACKSON

Open Range. *Expensive.* 99 N. Cache St. French and International menu. One of Wyoming's finest restaurants. Unsurpassed service. Open 5 to 10:30 p.m.; Sun. 11 a.m. to 3 p.m. Closed Nov. 15 to Dec. 15. 733-3544

Pink Garter. *Expensive.* In Pink Garter Plaza. A new luxurious restaurant and lounge. Many specialties, cosmopolitan menu, exotic. Luxurious, intimate decor. Open 5 to midnight. 733-3334

Chateau. *Moderate.* 14 W. Broadway. A restaurant with good family-style food. Specialties are spaghetti, lasagne, frittatas, chicken. Open 8 a.m. to 8 p.m.; 24 hours a day in summer. 733-3780

Silver Spur. *Moderate.* 65 N. Cache St. Coffee shop and dining room. A favorite local hangout. Good for families. Open 7 a.m. to 10 p.m. Closed Sept. 15 to May 24. 733-3279

LANDER

Miner's Delight. *Deluxe.* In Atlantic City (ghost town), out of Lander off US 28. Pal and Gina have the finest restaurant in the old Carpenter Hotel in a gold ghost town. Continental cuisine includes crepes, escargots, coq au vin. An absolutely delightful eating experience in the atmosphere of the Old West. By reservation only. Open 7 to 10 p.m.; Sun. 6:30 to 9 p.m. 332-3513

Maverik Restaurant. *Moderate.* 10 Main St. A favorite stopping off place for the traveler. Family food. Daily specials. Open 6 a.m. to 11 p.m. 332-4868

LARAMIE

Cavalryman. *Expensive.* 1 mi. south of town on US 287. Steak, prime rib, and lobster served up in an Old West setting. Open 5 to 10 p.m.; Sat. to 11. 745-5551

Diamond Horseshoe. *Moderate.* 2 mi. north of US 30, 287. The menu includes Chinese and American food and children's portions are available. Open 24 hours. 742-2107

MORAN

Signal Mountain Lodge. *Moderate.* 32 mi. north of Jackson on the shore of Jackson Lake in Teton National Park. A lakeside lodge in full view of the Grand Tetons offers excellent food in the lodge dining room. Open 7 to 10 a.m., 6:15 to 10 p.m. 543-2831

RAWLINS

Venice Cafe. *Inexpensive.* 1300 Spruce. A typical small-town restaurant with a good Italian menu. Daily specials. Open 5 a.m. to 10:45 p.m. 324-9928

RIVERTON

Teton Room. *Moderate.* 3rd and Main Sts. Located in the Teton Hotel, this is a beautifully decorated room. Steaks in the Wyoming tradition and plump Wyoming lamb chops. Smorgasbord on

Wednesday evenings. Open 5:30 to 10 p.m. 856-2271

ROCK SPRINGS

Outlaw Inn. *Moderate.* On Elk St. just off I–80. Hearty food is served in the dining room of this motel. Open 6 a.m. to 10 p.m.; Fri. and Sat. to midnight. 362-6623

WORLAND

Washakie Grill. *Moderate.* 544 Big Horn Ave. A Western hotel from times gone by, but the lounge and dining room are modern. The steak, prime ribs, and lamb chops served here are excellent and the service is fast. Open 6 a.m. to 10 p.m.; Sat. to 11 p.m. 347-4244

MONTANA

Riches in the Hills

by

BILL OWEN

Bill Owen is a graduate of the University of Montana where he was editor of the Montana Kaimi, *the student daily newspaper.*

Nature's unmistakable supremacy over man is evident from your first glimpse of Montana. If you come from the East, as did explorers Meriwether Lewis and William Clark, early fur trappers, prospectors, mountainmen and, later, the railroad builder, you are awed by the intrinsic beauty and tranquil solitude found nowhere else. This is what the last frontier must have looked like when Lewis and Clark brought their boats up the Missouri River into what is now known as Montana. Against the background of "badland" rock formations, Hereford, Angus, and Charolois cattle and sheep graze where once there were great buffalo herds. Alternate plowed and planted, brown and gold, strips of wheatland turn the countryside, where wild prairie grasses once grew, into a checkerboard. Along today's flat, super-speed highway, only a grove of cottonwood or an occasional farmhouse breaks the regularity of the countryside, while the glint of a distant grain elevator signals the location of a town. The emptiness of Montana, however, will impress you even more. Do not think it surprising if you drive for thirty miles without seeing another soul.

Then, as you move westward, the thin blue line of the horizon turns jagged, serrated by the jagged crests of the Rocky Mountains—home of early-day miners, trappers, and lumbermen and modern-day sportsmen. Here are ghost towns and mining gulches, thick stands of fir, larch (tamarack), and pine, wilderness areas ideal for the outdoor enthusiast, national forests and parks for family camping, mountain lakes, and, most importantly, the majestic snow-capped peaks of Glacier National Park.

This is "Big Sky Country." The people here are a tough, independent breed, raised to accept others for what they are, not who they are. A close-knit society, they take an almost nationalistic pride in their state. But it is a pride that visitors find justified. John Steinbeck once wrote "for other states I have admiration, respect, recognition, but with Montana it's love, and it's difficult to analyze love when you're in it." Ernest Hemingway too seemed to feel this love and spent long periods of time here.

The beauty of this region is inextricably bound up with its history. The Blackfeet, Crow and Sioux fought many bloody battles trying to preserve the land they loved. In the 17th and 18th centuries the Indians believed that this great buffalo ground was the promised land. Indeed it was until the white man began pushing westward. The Blackfeet saw the beauty of what is now Glacier National Park and made it sacred ground. Montana's battlefields and reservations attest to that tragic struggle.

At the turn of the 19th century (1804) Lewis and Clark poled and hauled a fifty-five-foot keelboat and two pirogues westward to the headwaters of the Missouri near Three Forks, Montana, keeping one eye open for Indians and wild animals and the other in search of the mountains. It is well they were alert, because in 1806, on a separate expedition, Lewis had his first encounter with "the great white bear (Grizzly)" three miles southwest of what is now called Great Falls, Montana. Lewis, favoring discretion over valor, ended up in the Missouri River, and later logged the incident in his journal as a "curious experience." Lewis and Clark's initials can still be seen carved in Pompey's Pillar near Billings, but the extent of their feelings for Montana have been left to later writers. Bernard De Voto's *Journals of Lewis and Clark* and *Across the Wide Missouri* and Don Barry's *A Majority of Scoundrels* recapture the flavor of those days.

After this initial exploration, the fur trade began in earnest and changed the course of Montana history. Eastern money was used to sponsor expeditions into the Northwest, and the profit from the sale of fur went back to the East. Little remained in the territory. Men like Jim Bridger, Jedediah Smith and "Liver Eatin' " Johnson trapped beaver, mink and otter for the fur hats of eastern moneymen. They also mapped and charted the area for the miners and settlers who were to follow later.

They were a rugged breed, these early Montanans, and tales of their courage, daring, and hardship make fascinating reading. Montana novelists A. B. Guthrie in *The Big Sky* and Frank Linderman in *Lige Mounts, Free Trappers* have successfully re-created the scene, while K. Ross Toole, the leading authority on Montana history, gives an accurate account of the early days in *Montana: An Uncommon Land.*

The era of the mountainman and fur trapper lasted only three decades, and had ended by 1840. By this time the westward expansion along the Oregon Trail had begun. Guthrie's *The Way West* describes the struggles of the early-day pioneers. For twenty years travelers along the Oregon Trail, which crossed to the south of Montana, left Montana relatively untouched. Occasionally a steamboat made a brief excursion up the Missouri River to replenish supplies of the few remaining fur trappers. By 1932 riverboats had reached Fort Union and by 1859 the boats had reached Fort Benton, Montana, head of navigable waters.

Gold and Every Man's Last Chance

Then came the Civil War, with its stream of refugees headed west for a new life. The discovery of gold in the Montana hills in 1862 helped to spur on that migration into the Montana territory. Mining camps such as Bannack and Virginia City mushroomed overnight. Sweating miners and snorting burros traveled up the craggy gulches of Western Montana in search of the precious ore. A hundred ghost towns commemorate this period of Montana history, and Helena, the capital city, still has the main street named "Last Chance Gulch."

These early settlers were courageous people with strong beliefs, and the ability to set up communities overnight. Slow, steady growth is not typical of Montana. Merchants shipped their goods by steamboat up the Missouri, or overland by wagon from Utah and Wyoming. Cattlemen from Texas brought huge herds of longhorns to graze on the lush prairie grasslands. They all came—the reverends, womenfolk, lawyers, doctors, merchants, miners, trappers, horse thieves, murderers and scoundrels.

Man lived by the law of the land. Each community set up its own brand of justice. Vigilantes dispensed "hemp" justice in the

Virginia City area to some of the more undesirable elements of the community such as Henry Plummer and his gang, called "The Innocents." Henry and his twenty-four followers incurred vigilante wrath because they were road agents, killing a recorded 102 victims between the winters of 1862 and 1864. Henry was the sheriff of Bannack, Montana, when he assembled his unholy crew. All of the Innocents were caught and hanged by the vigilantes between December 21, 1863, and January 11, 1864.

Meanwhile, the U.S. Army was having a tougher time in its role as judge and jury trying to keep the now thoroughly alarmed Indians and the pushy settlers apart. The Indians saw their buffalo and game driven off, their lands taken and their treaties broken. Finally, in 1876, they made their views known to General George Custer on the Little Bighorn River, just south of what is now Billings. But it was too late. The white man was here, and there was no driving him out.

Other kinds of people begin to enter the Montana story in the decades following the Civil War. The trapper and miner is now joined by the steamboat captain, the wagon master, the frontier storekeeper. Up until a few years ago, all the streams that flowed from the mountains were named after famous ladies of the day.

The frontier was being conquered. The kid in the army blanket, lying on the prairie, wonders if that rustle beyond the firelight is just a breeze. The cowboy up from Texas rides herd on the longhorns and doubts if anything can be as cold as this Montana blizzard. And the settlers continue to eke out a living on the land. A sense of this period is reflected in the work of Charley Russell, Montana's cowboy artist, who has gained a reputation as one of the foremost western artists. Two museums, one in Great Falls and the other in Helena, display his paintings, bronzes, and wax models. They are for anyone interested in western art. And in Miles City is a display of early photographs taken by L. A. Huffman, an early pioneer.

Then came the railroad. As it pushed westward across the "Hi Line" (Highway 2), farming and ranching communities began to appear. The railroad named these new towns. According to legend a group of railroad men sat around a world globe one night, each taking turns spinning it. Wherever they put their finger when the globe stopped became the name of the next town. That is how Glasgow, Havre, Malta, Inverness, Harlem, and Hinsdale got their names. Others retained their Indian names, such as Cut Bank and Wolf Point, or were named after early residents.

The coming of the railroad meant huge profits for eastern financiers and, once again, little was returned to the state. The railroads were given choice land by the government for their right of ways, and the railroads, in turn, made fantastic promises to lure people into the new "Garden of Eden." Butte became a capital of labor and political strife as verbal and physical wars waged between the mining factions. The disillusioned immigrant farmer began to discover that things don't grow so fast in the "Garden of Eden" as the railroad promotional brochures said they would. Buffalo hunters left huge piles of rotting carcasses, the only evidence of the once-great herds of plains buffalo. The Crow, Blackfeet and Sioux were pushed onto governmental reservations and forgotten.

The 20th-Century Montanan, A New Breed

And now we reach the 20th century and new types of Montanans begin to appear: forest rangers, environmentalists, grazing and agricultural experts; oilmen finding new mines under the prairie; dam builders harnessing the rivers at Fort Peck, Hungry Horse and Libby; men piloting jet planes from Great Falls; small-time farmers forced, because of scientific advances and high economic factors, into conglomerate farming; and politicians who have developed a feeling for the aesthetic beauty of Montana and are willing to say no to a rapidly advancing industrial complex. Bolstered by a knowledge of the history of Montana, each holds a new awareness of what Montana is and can be.

K. Ross Toole, in *Montana: An Uncommon Land,* says "Politically Montana did not evolve by trial and error. Politics sprang forth the handmaiden of men battling both the wilderness and each other. And the combat was ruthless. These men, too, were literally wresting wealth from the earth. There were no theorists among them. And so, almost before it had begun, Montana's political story was characterized by violent feuds, open corruption, and personal schisms among the "copper kings" which shook the very foundations of the new land and set the course of political events for many years to come." And set the course they did. Montana was controlled by industry until the mid-1950's and industry still holds a strong grip on the workings of the state. However, many people are becoming active in state issues and are opposing the vested business interests—thinking instead of what is best for the state rather than who will profit most by the transaction.

Problems brought on by an increasingly mobile society have forced Montanans to take a closer look at their state. Because of the shortage of fuel in the country, tremendous pressure has been brought to bear on eastern Montana for part of the 1.5 trillion tons of coal buried under the prairie of the Powder River and Williston Basins. Probably no issue is closer to the energy debates than the conflict between consumption and conservation. It is a problem that has plagued Montana for many years. Only thirty percent of the land in Montana is owned by private individuals while the other seventy percent is controlled by the Federal government or private corporations. As of this writing, twenty-five major corporations have leased land or mineral rights in eastern Montana. The private individual stands no chance of preventing a corporation from coming on his land and strip mining because the mineral rights are not sold with the land. They are retained by the state. Condemnation procedures are quickly brought forth against those that try to oppose a mining process.

Another great problem that faces Montana is an ever-increasing flow of people who once traveled through on the way to the West Coast but who now are beginning to return to the state as residents. This influx has created a tremendous market in land speculation, causing land prices to soar, and many people have come to realize that the slowness that once characterized Montana's growth was really a blessing in disguise. Caught unprepared for the vast amount of subdividing, especially in the recreational areas around Flathead Lake, the state has had to scramble to stay on top of the situation. This is one of the most crucial problems Montana has to face, for on it hinges the preservation of the state's unspoiled beauty and of her citizens' well-being.

Still a Land of Wide-Open Spaces

In this largest of the Rocky Mountain states—a little over 575 miles east to west and 275 miles north to south—there are fewer than 700,000 people spread over 147,138 square miles. The largest cities are Billings and Great Falls—each with approximately 100,000 people. But although the Montanan seems isolated, he enjoys his wide-open spaces. He knows about economic development and recognizes that Montana cannot remain forever as it is today. He may have come to enjoy the elbow room or he may be descended from the stock that came to Montana over a hundred years ago. Whether his ancestors found gold or not, that breed tended to think that too many people could mess things up. A lot of Montanans, despite the exhortations of their Chamber of Commerces, still think the same way.

If such a generalization is worth anything, so is the one about the friendliness of Montanans. The mining camp tended to judge a man by what he was, not what he was worth. Money meant very little. It couldn't improve your aim, or tell you where to sink your pick. Personal characteristics were more important than show, and even today affluent Montanans of the old school step softly.

Don't be deceived by Montana's wide-open spaces or the apparent simplicity of her people. Space means very little out here—a hundred miles for a high school ball game or an evening of bridge is nothing. And a few of these homespun types in their Stetsons and jeans are equally at home in Tiffany's—when they choose to be.

We are proud of our state, and, although history has taught us to be protective of its wealth and beauty, we can promise one thing: if you come to enjoy Montana, Montana and its citizens will enjoy you.

GENERAL AND PRACTICAL INFORMATION FOR MONTANA

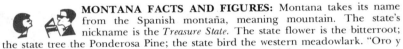

MONTANA FACTS AND FIGURES: Montana takes its name from the Spanish montaña, meaning mountain. The state's nickname is the *Treasure State*. The state flower is the bitterroot; the state tree the Ponderosa Pine; the state bird the western meadowlark. "Oro y Plata" ("Gold and Silver") is the state motto; "Montana," the state song.

Helena is the state capital. The state has a population of 682,133 (1970 census) and encompasses 147,138 square miles. It is the fourth largest state in the union, following Alaska, Texas, and California.

The climate on the east side of the Divide is harsh during the winter months; milder on the west side which is protected by the mountains. There is usually heavy snowfall on the higher elevations and on the unprotected plains. The summers are generally cool. If traveling in the mountains, it is advisable to bring along some warmer clothing.

HOW TO GET THERE. *By air:* Western, Eastern, Northwest, Frontier, and Hughes Airwest serve Montana flying principally into Billings and Great Falls.

By train: Amtrak provides service to Billings, Butte, Helena, Missoula, Glacier Park, and Havre from Chicago and Seattle.

By bus: Continental Trailways, Greyhound, Mid-Continent, and Intermountain Transportation have buses running to major cities in Montana.

By car: I–94 enters Montana from North Dakota in the east, I–90 from Wyoming in the south and from Idaho in the west, and I–15 from Alberta, Canada, in the north and Idaho in the south.

HOW TO GET AROUND, *By air:* Frontier flies to Missoula, Kalispell, Bozeman, Billings, Miles City, Glendive, Sidney, Wolf Point, Glasgow, Havre, Lewiston, Helena and Great Falls. Northwest lands in Billings, Bozeman, Butte, Missoula, Great Falls, and Lewiston. Western has service to Butte, Great Falls, West Yellowstone, and Billings. Eastern flies between Helena and Billings. Hughes Airwest has flights between Kalispell and Great Falls.

By train: Two trunkline rail systems carry passengers year round. The "Hi-Line" (which parallels US 2) serves Havre and Glacier Park. The "Low-Line" (running near I–90 and 94) stops at Billings, Butte, Helena, and Missoula.

By bus: Greyhound, Continental Trailways, and Intermountain Transportation are the principal carriers serving the major cities. Glacier Transportation serves Great Falls, Choteau, Glacier Park, and Kalispell; Clark Fork Valley Express, Bozeman, Helena, Missoula; Brown Bus Lines, Kalispell, Libby, Troy.

By car: I–94 runs east-west from Glendive through Miles City to Billings where I–90 continues to Bozeman, Butte, and Missoula. The northern east-west route, US 2, is the principal access to Glasgow, Havre, Shelby, Glacier National Park, and Kalispell. I–15 and US 91 run north–south through Butte, Helena, and Great Falls to Shelby.

 TOURIST INFORMATION. For information and brochures about points of interest, travel, and campgrounds in Montana, write the Advertising Unit, Montana Dept. of Highways, Dept. OW–45, 1315 Eighth Avenue, Helena 59601.

An Information Center is open from 8 a.m. to 5 p.m. during the summer months at Highway Building, 6th and Roberts Sts., in Helena.

 SEASONAL EVENTS. The State Advertising Department in Helena furnishes on request a *Montana Vacation Events* folder which gives the exact dates and location of the current year's activities.

Principal annual events are:

January: Montana Winter Fair, Bozeman.

February: Winter Carnival, Whitefish.

March: Montana State University Rodeo, Bozeman; *Winter Snowmobile Rally,* West Yellowstone.

April: Figure Skating Club Annual Ice Show, Great Falls; *Billings Symphony Folk Festival,* Billings.

May: Figure Skating Annual Ice Show, Butte; *Vigilante Parade,* Helena; *Mon-Dak Wagon Train,* a twenty-mile trip, Sidney; *fishing season* opens the third weekend; *Gates of the Mountains launch trips* open mid-month, Helena; *Cherry Blossom Festival* on the east shore of Flathead Lake; *rodeo season* begins last week.

June: Glacier National Park and main roads into *Yellowstone* open, and park accommodations are available beginning mid-month; *Missouri River Cruise* from Fort Peck to Fort Benton (participants supply their own boats) takes place mid-month from boat docks in Glasgow; *Last Chance jeep tour* of Helena, mid-month; *Midland Empire Horse Show* at Billings; *Cherry Blossom Festival* including regatta, blossom viewing, Polson; *National Intercollegiate Rodeo Finals,* Bozeman, third week; late June or early July, *reenactment of Custer's Last Stand* at Crow Agency.

July: Fair season begins: *Whitefish Lake Regatta,* Whitefish; *Diamond Jaycee Rodeo,* Polson; *Wild Horse Stampede* at Wolf Point attracts riders from throughout the nation; *Home of Champions Rodeo,* Red Lodge; *Western Montana Quarter Horse Show,* Missoula, mid-month; *Indian Powwows* throughout the month; *North American Indian Days* at Browning, the Blackfeet invite other Indians to join a four-day encampment featuring dances, games, races and a rodeo; *Logger Days,* Libby; *Gallatin Saddle Club Horse Show,* Bozeman; *Yellowstone River Raft Race,* Terry; *Boat Float,* Livingston; *Montana State Fiddlers Contest,* Polson; late July or early August, *North Montana State Fair and Rodeo,* Great Falls.

August: Copper Cup Regatta, Polson; *Festival of Nations,* Red Lodge; *Midland Empire Fair and Rodeo,* Billings; *Last Chance Stampede,* Helena; *National Freshwater Trout Derby* at Livingston offers $1,000 for the largest trout caught; *Northwest*

197

Montana Fair, Kalispell; *Crow Indian Fair and Rodeo,* Crow Agency; *Bozeman Roundup Rodeo,* Bozeman; *Western Montana Fair,* Missoula; *Tri-County Fair and Rodeo,* Deer Lodge.

September: Milk River Wagon Train from Landusky to Malta.

October: Buffalo Roundup on the National Bison Range near Moiese; *hunting season* begins; *Northern International Livestock Exposition,* Billings.

November: Ski season begins.

December: Snowmobile Roundup at West Yellowstone, through Mar.

NATIONAL PARKS AND FORESTS. *Glacier National Park,* crowning the continent across the Rocky Mountains of northwestern Montana, contains one of the most spectacularly scenic portions of the entire range. Although today there are still some forty glaciers, the park is named for the Ice Age glaciers which carved out the rugged scenery. Covering over 1,600 square miles, it is the U.S. section of the Waterton-Glacier International Peace Park (the rest lies across the Canadian border in Alberta).

The Going-to-the-Sun Road, which links the east and west sides of the park by crossing the Continental Divide at Logan Pass, is one of the most beautiful drives in the world but the over nine hundred miles of well-kept trails throughout the park are the only access to many isolated and magnificent areas.

For detailed information write Superintendent, Glacier National Park, West Glacier 59936.

Yellowstone National Park. Three of the five entrances are in Montana: at Gardiner on US 89, the Beartooth Highway (US 212), and US 191 and 287. (See section on Wyoming for detailed information about the park.)

Bighorn Canyon National Recreation Area. Focal point of this 63,000-acre area in northern Wyoming and southern Montana is the 71-mile-long Bighorn Lake. Boating, camping and picnic facilities are available. (See also section on Wyoming.)

Beaverhead National Forest, in southwestern Montana east of Divide, is a great hunting and fishing area and one of the few places in the nation where grayling can be caught. In addition to scenic rugged mountains and alpine lakes there are hot springs and winter sports here. Park headquarters are at Dillon.

Bitterroot National Forest, west of the Divide in southwestern Montana, contains the Selway-Bitterroot Wilderness, largest in the U.S. Mountain lakes, hot springs, scenic drives, fishing, hunting and winter sports are also available. Headquarters are in Hamilton.

Custer National Forest, located in the southeast, partly in Montana, partly in South Dakota, offers winter sports, trout fishing and big-game hunting. Granite Peak, at 12,799 feet, is the highest point in Montana. There are also primitive areas, alpine plateaus, glaciers and hundreds of lakes. Grasshopper Glacier has millions of grasshoppers imbedded within its depths. Headquarters are at Billings.

Deerlodge National Forest headquartered at Butte has wilderness areas, alpine lakes, fishing, hunting, and winter sports.

Flathead National Forest, south and west of Glacier National Park, is a heavily timbered area of rugged, glaciated mountains. There are wilderness and primitive areas here and fishing, hunting, boating, swimming, winter sports, and scenic drives. Headquarters are in Kalispell.

Gallatin National Park in south central Montana includes dramatic quake area camps and the beautiful Beartooth Scenic Highway. One of the gateways to Yellowstone. Headquarters are in Bozeman.

Helena National Forest, straddling the Continental Divide in west central Montana, offers fishing, hunting and wilderness areas. The Gates of the Mountains Wilderness, where the Missouri River pushes through the Big Belt Range, contains a deep gorge lined with 2,000–foot limestone walls. Headquarters are in Helena.

198

Kaniksu National Forest. See Idaho.

Kootenai National Forest, in the northwest corner of the state, offers wilderness, beautiful timber (including Giant Cedars), hunting, fishing, and winter sports. Headquarters are in Libby.

Lewis and Clark National Forest in north central Montana contains nearly two million acres of canyons, mountains, meadows and wilderness. The 1,000-ft.-high, 15-mi.-long Chinese wall is here. Headquarters are in Great Falls.

Lolo National Forest, mostly west of the Divide in west central Montana, includes the famed Lewis and Clark Highway over the Bitterroot Mountains and fishing, hunting, scenic drives and winter sports. Headquarters are in Missoula.

STATE PARKS. The *Lewis and Clark Caverns State Park,* just off I–90 forty–seven miles east of Butte, contains the largest limestone caverns in the northwest. Delicate, varicolored stalactites and stalagmites make this one of the most beautiful caverns in the country. Guide service through the caverns is available.

Giant Springs State Park, four miles northeast of Great Falls on Missouri River Dr. Here, one of the world's largest freshwater springs flows at a rate of 388 million gallons of water per day.

James Kipp State Park, northeast of Lewistown off US 191, is the area said to have provided a hiding place for Kid Curry. Drinking water, stoves, tables, sanitary facilities, fishing, boating and boat ramp are available.

Long Pine State Park is located west of Kalispell off US 2.

Lost Creek State Park, northwest of Anaconda off I–90, offers fishing, sanitary facilities, stoves and tables in the ghost town country near big mining centers.

Medicine Rocks State Park, north of Ekalaka off State 7, provides drinking water, stoves, tables and sanitary facilities amidst 220 acres of weird sandrock formations.

Makoshika State Park, out of Glendive off I–90, is set in colorful badlands created by wind and water erosion. Stoves, tables and sanitary facilities are available.

West Shore State Park is located south of Kalispell on Flathead Lake off US 93.

HOT SPRINGS. *Sleeping Child Hot Springs,* 3 mi. S of Hamilton on US 83, then E on State 38, then 11 mi. SE on County 501, offers swimming in natural hot springs and pool. Open daily 10 a.m. to 11 p.m. Adults, $1.50, children under 10, $1.

In addition there are hot springs in the Bitterroot National Forest near Hamilton and in the Beaverhead National Forest near Dillon. And locally around such towns as White Sulphur Springs, Hot Springs, and Camas.

CAMPING OUT. State Parks and Recreation areas are open from May to Sept. Camping is limited to fourteen consecutive days. Fees in some areas range from $1 to $2 per night per car, or $10 per season. Complete information and brochures are available from the Montana Fish and Game Dept., State Parks Division, Helena 59601.

Montana has far too many recreation areas to list all of them here conveniently, so only information on the principal areas will be given (see also section on State Parks). "Complete facilities" as used here will mean that drinking water, stoves, tables, sanitary facilities, fishing, boating, swimming, and boat ramps are all available at the area.

Ashley Lake, fifteen miles southwest of Kalispell on US 2, then thirteen miles north on an unnumbered road. Complete facilities.

Big Arm, fifteen miles north of Polson on US 93 along the west shore of Flathead Lake. Complete facilities except no boat ramp.

Bitterroot Lake, twenty-three miles west of Kalispell off US 2. Complete facilities.

Canyon Ferry, ten miles east of Helena on US 12 then nine miles north on State 284. Complete facilities.

Clark Canyon Reservoir, twenty miles south of Dillon on US 91, I–15. Complete facilities.

Cooney Lake, twenty-two miles south of Laurel on US 212 to Boyd then nine miles west. Complete facilities except boat ramp.

Deadman's Basin, twenty-three miles east of Harlowton off US 12. Complete facilities except drinking water.

Elmo, sixteen miles north of Polson of US 93 on the shore of Flathead Reservoir. Complete facilities.

Finley Point, twelve miles north of Polson off State 35. Complete facilities including golf course.

Fort Peck Dam and Reservoir, twenty miles southeast of Glasgow on State 24, is the world's second largest earth fill dam. Complete facilities.

Hell Creek, twenty-six miles north of Jordan off State 200. Complete facilities including rockhound areas.

Hooper, seventy-three miles east of Missoula off State 200. Drinking water, stoves, tables, sanitary facilities and rockhound areas.

Lake Mary Ronan, twenty-three miles north of Polson on US 93, then seven miles northwest on unnumbered road. Complete facilities.

Logan, forty-five miles west of Kalispell off US 2. Complete facilities.

Nelson Reservoir, seventeen miles northeast of Malta on US 2, then north. Complete facilities.

Painted Rocks, twenty miles south of Hamilton on US 93, then twenty-three miles southwest of State 483. Complete facilities.

Rock Creek, fifty miles south of Glasgow off State 54. Complete facilities.

Rosebud, at Forsyth on the Yellowstone River. No swimming or drinking water.

Thompson Falls, two miles northwest of Thompson Falls on US 10A. No swimming.

Tiber Dam Reservoir, thirty-eight miles east of Shelby on US 2 to Tiber then south on unnumbered road. Complete facilities.

Wayfarer, south of Bigfork off State 35. Complete facilities.

Whitefish Lake, out of Whitefish on west shore of lake off US 93. Complete facilities.

Woods Bay, one mile west of Bigfork off State 35. Complete facilities.

Yellow Bay, fifteen miles south of Bigfork on State 35 along east shore. Complete facilities.

TRAILER TIPS. For information about trailer and campground sties, contact Montana Fish and Game Dept., State Parks Division, Helena 59601.

West Yellowstone: Beaver Creek National Forest, 8 mi. N on US 191, has 65 sites with flush toilets and boating. Open June 1 to Oct. 1.

Kalispell: Bitterroot Lake State Park, 20 mi. W on US 2, then 5 mi. N on Marion Rd., has 15 sites and swimming boating and fishing. Open May 1 to Oct.

East Glacier Park: Two Medicine National Park, 8 mi. NW on State 49 then 4 mi. W on County Rd., has 125 sites, store, snack bar, swimming, boating, fishing. Open June 1 to Oct. 15.

Fort Peck: Rock Creek, 31 mi. S on State 24 then 5 mi. W on dirt road, has 25 sites and swimming, boating, and fishing. Open May 1 to Oct. 1.

West Glacier Park: Fish Creek National Park, 4 mi. NW on Park Rd., has 180 sites, flush toilets, swimming and fishing. Open June 1 to Oct. 15.

FARM VACATIONS AND GUEST RANCHES. Montana has hundreds of guest or "dude" ranches which are either working ranches with crops and livestock where guests are another source of income, or mountain ranches primarily for guests which run only horses for that purpose. Either type of ranch is an excellent way to get the best of Montana, for you meet congenial and characteristic local types, have available the necessary guides for pack trips, fishing, hunting, etc., and can make sidetrips to points of interest. Yet, you have thoroughly modern accommodations on the whole.

Most "dude" ranches require advance reservations. The best sources of information are the railroads or airlines serving the state or the *Montana Dude Ranchers Assn.,* Billings, Montana, which will be glad to furnish an up-to-date list of ranches. Most ranches open for June–Sept. season only, and most will meet you at train or plane.

For those of you on the road, what follows is a list to which you can write or call.

Yellowstone Park Area. *Aller's Boulder River Ranch,* McLeod, Montana, in the Absaroka Mountains, thirty miles south of Big Timber on I–90. Working ranch.

Beartooth Ranch, Nye, Montana, off I–90, southwest of Columbus. Working ranch. Fall hunting.

Covered Wagon Ranch, Gallatin Gateway, Montana, four miles from northwest corner of Yellowstone on Gallatin River.

Diamond J Ranch, Ennis, Montana, on Madison River for fishing and near Virginia City for history. Pool. Write for reservations.

Elkhorn Ranch, Bozeman, Montana, near Yellowstone.

Four K Ranch, Fishtail, Montana. Working ranch (you can help brand!). Thirty-two miles south of Columbus, off I–90.

Flying Cloud Guest Ranch, Wise River, Montana, forty-five miles southwest of Butte in Beaverhead National Forest.

G Bar M Ranch, Clyde Park, Montana, operating stock ranch some thirty miles off I–90 northwest of Livington. Horses and fishing.

LaMarche Creek Guest Ranch, Wiser River, Montana, southwest of Butte. Astride the divide in the Big Hole River Country.

Lazy K Bar Ranch, Big Timber, Montana. In the Crazy Mountains north of Big Timber.

Lone Mountain Guest Ranch, forty miles south of Bozeman. Part of the Big Sky complex, this resort provides summer and winter recreation in an atmosphere typical of a western ranch.

Madison Fork Ranch, West Yellowstone, Montana. Six miles west of the west entrance to Yellowstone. Private dry fly stream and lake on Madison River.

Ox Yoke Ranch, Emigrant, Montana. North of Livingston off I–90. Working ranch, not resort. Fishing, riding.

Parade Rest Ranch, West Yellowstone, Montana; nine miles out of the park.

Rockin' Horse Ranch, Gallatin Gateway, Montana, forty-two miles south of Bozeman.

Sixty Three Ranch, Livingston, Montana. Specialize in pack trips and big game hunting.

S/R Ranch, Big Timber, Montana. Cattle ranch, with 13,000 acres. Guests can help on normal ranch operations if they choose.

320 Ranch, Gallatin Gateway, Montana, fifty-five miles south of Bozeman.

Tee Bar O Ranch, Roscoe, Montana, southwest of Billings on Route 307.

Watkins Creek Ranch, Hebegen Lake near West Yellowstone. Lake sports.

Willow Ranch, Jackson, Montana. Western vacation ranch for *boys and girls.* In Big Hole Basin southwest of Butte on Route 278.

X Bar A Ranch, Big Timber, Montana, operating ranch north of the park.

Glacier Park Area. *Bear Creek Ranch,* East Glacier Park, Montana, five miles west of the Divide off US 2 to the south. Open all season and for fall hunting. Trail rides into the park and Flathead National Forest.

Chief Mountain Ranch, near Babb, Montana, on US 89 north of Browning. Park pack trips a specialty.

Western Montana Area. *Flathead Lake Lodge,* one mile south of Bigfork on the east shore of Flathead Lake. This dude ranch on a lake has pools, lake sports and rides, horseback riding, barbecues, square dancing.

Rocky Bar O Ranch, Bigfork, Montana, special for girls 13–17 and for boys and girls 8–12. Special children's pack trips.

Diamond L Bar Ranch, near Lake Lindbergh on edge of Mission Range Wilderness Area, northeast of Missoula on Route 209. P.O. address, Seeley Lake, Montana. All facilities except you prepare own meals in cabin kitchen to cut costs. Food available at ranch store.

Whitetail Ranch, near Ovando south of Lincoln, specializes in pack trips and big game hunting.

Double Arrow Ranch, Seeley Lake, Montana. Northeast of Missoula. Pack trips into Bob Marshall Wilderness Area.

Bar A Ranch, Seeley Lake, Montanta. Operating ranch in Swan Valley.

Other Areas. *Circle 8 Ranch,* Choteau, Montana. Horse ranch roughly twenty-six miles from Choteau on eastern face of Rockies. Nearest area to Great Falls. Licensed guide into wilderness areas; fall hunting.

Korell's Guest Ranch, Utica Montana. 50-plus miles west of Lewiston on the Judith River. Pool. Hunting and fishing.

 MUSEUMS AND GALLERIES. The *Montana Historical Museum & C. M. Russell Art Gallery* at 225 N. Roberts St. in Helena presents a capsule history of Montana in dramatic dioramas and a notable collection of Charles M. Russell's art. Open from 8 a.m. to 8 p.m., Memorial Day to Labor Day; off season, Mon. to Fri. 8 to 5, weekends from noon.

Charles M. Russell Museum & Original Studio at 1201 4th Ave. N. in Great Falls exhibits Russell paintings, bronzes, and wax models including the Trigg collection. There are also Russell's own collection of Indian costumes and gear, and changing exhibits, lectures, films and children's theatre. Open 10 to 5, Mon. to Sat. and Sun. from 1 p.m., mid-May to mid-Sept. Closed Mon. off season.

Museum of the Plains Indians & Crafts Center, one-half mile west of Browning at the junction of US 2, 89, exhibits the art of the Northern Plains Indians and sells authentic Indian crafts. Dioramas, maps, costumes, and archeological exhibits explain Indian life. Open 8 to 8, June to Sept. 14; to 5 p.m. Sept. 15 to 30. Oct. to May, Mon. to Fri. by appointment.

Range Riders Museum and *Pioneer Memorial Hall,* on US 10, 12 in the west end of Miles City, presents exhibits and memorabilia from the era of the open range. Open 8 to 8, June to Aug.; to 6 p.m. Apr. to May, Sept. to Oct.; closed Nov. to Mar.

J. K. Ralston Museum & Art Center, 221 5th St. S.W. in Sidney, exhibits historical artifacts from the region and original Ralston paintings. Open 1 to 5, 7 to 8:30 p.m. daily except Mon., June to Aug.; to 5 p.m., Sun. and Tues. to Fri., Sept. to May.

Ketterer Art Center, in a restored pioneer home at 35 N. Grand in Bozeman, has permanent and changing exhibits by Montana artists and craftsmen. Open daily, except Mon. 1 to 5:30 p.m.

World Museum of Mining, W. Park St., one mile west of Butte at Golden Girl Mine, has indoor and outdoor displays of mining tools, equipment, relics and an old-time mining town. Open daily 9 to 9, June to Sept.; daily except Mon., 10 to 5 p.m., Oct. to May.

Big Sky Historical Museum, south of Red Lodge on US 212, has a large collection of western frontier guns, Indian artifacts and antiques. Open 8 a.m. to 9 p.m. June to Sept. 15. Closed rest of year.

Fort Benton Museum, 1800 Front St. in Fort Benton, has dioramas and displays on steamboats, Indians and agriculture. Open 10 to 6, June to Aug.; May 19 to 31 and Sept. 1 to 15, 1 to 5 p.m. Closed rest of year.

Beaverhead County Museum, 15 S. Montana St. in Dillon, offers Indian artifacts, geological displays, and memorabilia of frontier and mining days. Open daily 9 to 5, 7 to 9 p.m. June 16 to Aug.; rest of year, weekdays only to 5 p.m.

H. Earl Clack Memorial Museum, one-half mile west of Havre on US 2 on the Hill County Fairgrounds, presents exhibits on the history, development, geology and archeology of the area. Open daily 9 a.m. to 10 p.m., Memorial to Labor Day. Rest of year by appointment.

The L. A. Huffman Photographic Museum, in Coffrin's Old West Gallery at 1600 Main St. in Miles city, offers an excellent collection of photographs depicting early-day Montana. Open 9 a.m. to noon, and 1 to 5, Mon. to Sat.

Gallery '85, on Emerald Dr. two miles northeast of Billings in Billings Heights, has permanent and changing exhibits of works by contemporary Montana artists and craftsmen as well as art of the pioneer west. Open daily except Sun.: Apr. to Dec., 10 to 5; June to Aug., also 7 to 9 p.m.

HISTORIC SITES. *Fort Union Trading Post National Historic Site,* twenty-three miles north of Sidney via State 200 on an unnumbered road at the fork of the Missouri and Yellowstone Rivers. The American Fur Company built this fort in 1828 and for a long time it served as one of the most important frontier outposts. Now being restored.

Custer National Monument. Located in southeastern Montana, this scene of the famous Last Stand memorializes one of the last armed efforts of the Northern Plains Indians to resist the westward march of the white man's civilization. On June 25–26, 1876, in the valley of the Little Bighorn River, several thousand Sioux and Cheyenne warriors did battle with the U.S. Army troops under the command of Lt. Col. George A. Custer. Although the Indians won this battle, killing Custer and all his men, they lost the war against the white man who brought an end to their independent, nomadic way of life. Dioramas, exhibits, and background and history programs are offered.

Big Hole Battlefield National Monument. In August 1877, a force of U.S. Army troops staged a surprise attack against a band of Nez Percé Indians led by Chief Joseph. Having refused reservation life, this nomadic tribe made a courageous though futile attempt to reach Canadian sanctuary. Audio-visual programs and displays of firearms and frontier relics are available at the visitors center.

Bannack Monument, off US 91 near Dillon, was Montana's first territorial capital and site of the first big gold strike, on Grasshopper Creek (1862). Now a well-maintained ghost town.

Chief Joseph Battlefield, sixteen miles south of Chinook on a country road. The site of the final battle and surrender of Chief Joseph of the Nez Percé thus bringing an end, in 1877, to Montana's Indian wars.

Chief Plenty Coups Memorial, thirty-five miles south of Billings at Pryor. This small museum features Indian relics of the former Crow Indian chieftain.

Indian Caves Monument, five miles southeast of Billings off US 87, 212. Indian pictographs can still be seen on the cave walls where Indians lived 4,500 years ago.

Fort Benton, on the riverfront near Main St. in Fort Benton. The Ruins of an old trading post and blockhouse still remain from the frontier days when the town was an important commercial center.

Fort Owen Monument, off US 93 at Stevensville south of Missoula, is a restoration of Montana's first white settlement. Also here is *St. Mary's Mission,* the oldest church in the Pacific Northwest.

Madison Buffalo Jump Monument, west of Bozeman off I–90, seven miles west of Logan. This buffalo jump demonstrates a hunting technique used by prehistoric man in Montana as long as two thousand years ago.

Missouri River Headwaters Monument, thirty-one miles northwest of Bozeman on I–90, near Three Forks. Here Lewis and Clark discovered the Jefferson, Madison

and Gallatin Rivers joining to form the Missouri.
Pompey's Pillar, off I–94 east of Billings, where Clark carved his initials.
Prehistoric fossil field, south of Fort Peck Dam in the northeastern corner of the state.
Prehistoric Indian site (Hagen), near Glendive off I–94.
Virginia City, southwest of Bozeman on Route 287–289. Restored early-day mining boom town and political capital.

FAMOUS LIBRARIES. *City-County Library of Missoula* at Pine and Pattee Sts. has an outstanding collection of historical works on Montana and the Northwest.

TOURS. *Glacier Park, Inc.*, offers two- to five-day tours of Glacier National Park and Waterton Lakes National Park, Canada. Tours include lodging, meals, launch cruises and transportation via scenic coaches. Bus service is also available between hotels, and to and from depots and lakes. This is essentially a scenic tour on the park's lakes and highways. For complete information and rates write Glacier Park, Inc., East Glacier, Montana 59434 (off season, Sept. 15 to May 15, write to P.O. Box 4340, Tucson, Arizona 85717).

The *Crow Indian Tribe* of Montana sponsors tours which include an overnight stop on the Crow Indian Reservation just one-half mile from the historic Custer National Battlefield on the Little Big Horn. These tours also include an overnight stop at one or more Montana or Wyoming guest ranches, actual operating ranches whose accommodations are rustic-modern and which offer horseback riding, fishing and evening campfires. Some tours include a comprehensive look at Yellowstone and Glacier National Parks. For complete information write American Plains Indian Tours, Box 2185, Great Falls 59401.

INDUSTRIAL TOURS. *Copper.* In Anaconda you can see the smelter, Mon. through Fri., at 9:30 a.m. and 1:15 p.m. In Butte, inquire at Chamber of Commerce about one-mile-deep underground mine tour (9:30 a.m. and 1:30 p.m. Mon.–Fri.) and the view of Berkeley Pit, open mining. At Great Falls, refinery and wire mill have tours 10 a.m., 2 p.m. Mon.–Fri. (10 a.m. Sat. only).

Lumber. At Bonner, east of Missoula on US 10, the US Plywood Company conducts tours explaining every phase of modern wood processing. The tours take two hours and can be taken Monday through Friday. Also, at Libby, inquire about tour times of the St. Regis Paper Company, one of the largest in the Northwest. The mill is just off US 2. Wear low shoes.

Aluminum, Anaconda Aluminum Co., Columbia Falls, Mon.–Fri., 10 a.m. and 2 p.m. May–Labor Day.

Electricity. The Montana-Dakota Utilities Co., Lewis and Clark Station, two and one-half miles southeast of Sidney on State 23, generates electric power using lignite for fuel. One-hour guided tours are given Mon. to Fri. 8 a.m. to 4 p.m. Children thirteen years and under must be accompanied by an adult. Make arrangements a day in advance by calling the Plant Superintendent, 482-1614, or write Box 808.

Mining. A self-guided tour around the old frontier mining town and early-day mining museum in Butte can give you a better understanding of the way life was in the early days of Montana. Further information is available by writing the Butte Chamber of Commerce.

SPECIAL INTEREST TOURS. Buffalo, at the *National Bison Range*, at Moiese (south of Charlo and the Nine Pipe National Migratory Waterfowl Refuge), may be seen from June through Labor Day on self-guided automobile tours. There is also the possibility of seeing the majestic elk, deer, antelope, mountain goat and bighorn sheep.

Wilderness walks into many of the remote areas of Montana designed especially for the visitor who may not have the equipment or stamina of a local goat are arranged by the Montana Wilderness Assn., Box 548, Bozeman, Montana. If you can, write ahead; if you're passing through and get the urge, call them; they may be able to work you in. These walks have informed guides and are unique.

Forest fire fighting is explained in full at the Aerial Fire Depot west of Missoula, Montana, on US 10. Special tours are held from mid-June until Labor Day. Call for times.

Ranching may be analyzed on a self-guided range tour in the Beaverhead National Forest near Dillon on Interstate 15 in southwestern Montana. The drive takes about five hours and signs explain modern cattle and sheep grazing techniques. Contact Supervisor of Forests, Dillon, for instructions.

Earthquake damage explained in self-guiding tour around Hebegen Lake on US 287 between Ennis and West Yellowstone.

Missouri River boat cruises, à la Lewis and Clark, are held in June each summer depending on when water is best. They usually take three or more days and everything's furnished. Contact State Advertising Department in Helena, or Chamber of Commerce, Fort Benton, for current information.

Gates of Mountains launch near Helena, every day, 10 a.m.–2 p.m., May 15–Labor Day.

Big Mountain summer chair lift operates June 15–Labor Day for a high view of the Western Rockies.

Snowmobile rides in Yellowstone from West Yellowstone in winter are a thrill. Contact Harold Young, West Yellowstone.

Figure Eight Drive scenic tour of mountains and ghost towns every summer day from Helena.

Last Chance Gulch Tour around Helena on an automotive train explores the city's past and present history including Pioneer Cabin. Built in 1865, this building has been renovated and furnished with pioneer artifacts. Tours take one and one-half hours and leave from the Montana State Historical Museum at 8:30 a.m. 10:30 a.m., 1:30 p.m., and 3:30 p.m. daily June 15 to Labor Day.

 STAGE AND REVUES. The University of Montana (Missoula) and Montana State University (Bozeman) are worth checking out if you are in the areas during the fall, winter, and spring. Many student and professional events take place during this time and the prices are usually very reasonable. The hotels in major cities will be aware of any professional shows and local scheduling—such as Community Concert Series.

Summer theater is as follows: Big Fork, *Big Fork Summer Playhouse,* weekly shows beginning in June and running through August. Shows usually start around 8 p.m. and there is a $2.50 admission charge. Fort Peck, *Fort Peck Summer Theater* presents shows throughout the summer. Admission is charged. Virginia City, *Playhouse,* 19th-century drama every night June through Labor Day. Helena, the *Old Brewery Theatre* offers nightly summer productions from early July to September.

Kalispell, *Fort Kalispell Summer Memodrama Theater and Saloon* provides theater during the summer months. Plays range from musicals, drama, comedy, to melodrama. West Yellowstone, *Golden Garter-Old Gray Mare Theatre* gives nightly musical comedy and melodrama performances June 15 to Labor Day. Adults, $2.50, children 6 to 16, $1.25, five years and under, free. *Playmill Theatre* also offers comedy and melodrama Mon. to Fri. at 8:30 p.m., Sat. at 7 and 9:15 p.m. Adults $2.50-$3, children under twelve, half price.

205

MUSIC. The *Symphony Association* at Great Falls sponsors concerts during the late spring and summer. Billings and Helena both have their own symphonies and during the summer months Helena has *municipal band concerts.*

 DRINKING LAWS. The legal drinking age in Montana is 18 years. Bars are open until 2 a.m. Monday through Saturday nights. No liquor or beer can be sold until 1 p.m. on Sundays. You can buy liquor by the bottle at state liquor stores in each town. No special license is required. You may order liquor by the drink in Montana bars, and some sell bottles over the counter.

SUMMER SPORTS. *Fishing.* Licenses are required: non-resident seasonal is $10, but you can purchase a $1 daily permit after purchasing a 25¢ conservation license. The fishing season usually starts in May and ends around Nov. 30. Local inquiry to the State Fish and Game Department will give you further information about laws and locations of the types of fish you want.

Some of the good fishing spots are:

Madison River Drainage. One-half mile south of Ennis on Route 287 (seventy acres); four miles south of Ennis on west side of river (27 acres); six miles south of Ennis on west shore of river (30 acres); twelve miles south of Ennis at Varney Bridges (five acres); twelve miles south of Three Forks and three miles north of Norris cutoff road (604 acres); seven miles north of Ennis on northwest side of Meadow Lake (5.5 acres); Sun Ranch Road, forty miles south of Route 287 (inquire locally).

Stillwater River Drainage. Six miles south of Columbus on Stillwater River, Route 307 (four acres); at Johnson Bridge three miles south of Absarokee (two acres); Nye Bridge, three miles south of Nye (six acres); Rosebud Isle at town of Fishtail (nine acres).

Flathead River Drainage. Six miles east of Somers at New Holt Bridge (five acres).

Smith River Drainage. Eighteen miles north of White Sulphur Springs (three thousand acres).

Clark Fork Drainage. Rock Creek, south of Missoula turnoff on I–90 just east of Clinton (107 acres); *Yellowstone Drainage.* On Rock Creek along State 212 southwest from Billings, there are numerous areas between Red Lodge and Roberts.

For *lake* fishermen, the state provides public access at these lakes: *Aared,* ten miles west of Brady; *Upsata,* ten miles northwest of Ovando; *Sophie,* near Eureka; *Broadview Pond,* near Broadview; *Park Lake,* south of Helena; *Savage Lake,* near Troy; *Dailey Lake,* 22 miles south of Livingston; *Boot Jack Lake,* near Kalispell; *Skyles Lake,* near Whitefish; *Sweet Grass Canyon Lake,* twenty miles northwest of Melville; *Flathead,* at Woods Bay south of Big Fork; *Loon,* six miles east of Big Fork; *Carpenter,* near Eureka; *Crystal,* south of Libby.

A quick rundown on respected fishing locations by type of fish: *Blackfoot River,* western Montana near Bonner, rainbow and cutthroat trout, sockeye salmon in headwaters.

Big Hole River, southwestern Montana, rainbow, brown, grayling, and cutthroat trout.

Bitterroot River, near Hamilton, rainbow, brook, and brown trout with some cutthroat in lakes at headwaters.

Clark Fork River, drains west of Missoula, various trout species, with boat fishing on Cabinet Gorge Reservoir for salmon as well.

Flathead Lake. Cutthroat, rainbow, Dolly Varden, and sockeye salmon, with some bass in protected bays; salmon plentiful in fall.

Fort Peck Lake: pike, catfish, and other warm-water species.

Gallatin River, near Bozeman, good trout stream heading in Yellowstone Park.

Georgetown Lake, near Anaconda. Black, spotted, rainbow, and eastern brook trout, silver salmon.

Jefferson River, above Twin Bridges, and the *Madison River* near Ennis, very good for rainbow and brown trout.

Judith River, near Lewistown, various trout species.

Kootenai River, near Libby and Troy, cutthroat and Dolly Varden.

East Montana lakes: stocked with warm-water species.

Marias River near Shelby and Tiber Reservoir; trout fishing both in stream and reservoir.

Milk River, Glasgow to Havre, trout near headwaters, tending to crappie and walleye pike out on plains and in Fresno Reservoir.

Missouri River, trout in the headwaters; boat fishing at Holter, Hauser and Canyon Ferry Dams, for brown trout, rainbow, and salmon. Downstream harbors sturgeon, walleye pike, northern pike, sunfish, crappies, catfish and perch.

Musselshell River, eastern central Montana, good for brown trout.

Sun River, west of Great Falls on east slope of Rockies, good for eastern brook, rainbow, and grayling.

Yellowstone River, good from Yellowstone Park headwaters through southeastern Montana. Cutthroat high in headwaters region, then rainbow, brown and whitefish in Livingston to Columbus area, parallel to I–90. Pike, catfish, drum and Ling take over east of Billings on the hot, dry plains where the river meanders.

Hunting. Hunting licenses cost $150 for non-residents. This entitles you to a variety of game, but the non-resident must put in for drawings, by regions, in order to get the appropriate tags. Applying in time does not insure you of your first-choice region. Most areas also require that you hunt with a resident, who can double as a guide. Fines can be very expensive if a warden catches you out alone in a guide area.

For full hunting details contact the Montana Fish and Game Dept. Because of increased hunting pressures, the seasons tend to vary from year to year depending on the amount of kill in the previous year. There is usually an early elk and deer season in the wilder hunting areas (around the wildernesses) in September. The regular deer and elk season begins in October and generally runs until the end of November. Antelope hunting, on a drawing-quota basis only, begins one week earlier than deer and elk season and ends around the middle of November. Goat, sheep and moose, also on the quota system, begin in mid-September and run until November. Black and brown bear season opens around March 15 and runs until mid-November. Bird hunting begins in early September and runs till the end of the year for ducks and geese, November 30 for grouse and pheasant. Special quotas pertain to ducks and geese on the Central Fly Way.

Montana has twenty-three game preserves, where many special rules apply to each species. Write for full instructions before coming to hunt.

Golfing. There are thirty-five courses in Montana at most principal cities. Some are public, many private, but easy to get on if you go through your hotel or local tourist center. Your attention is especially called to three courses in beautiful vacation settings at Polson, Kalispell, and Whitefish, all public. There is a course at East Glacier; the nearest to Yellowstone is Bozeman. Greens fees are moderate and many of the clubs have the normal pro shop services.

Riding. See list of *Guest Ranches.* The bigger towns all have saddle clubs who can help you find riding facilities in a pinch.

Rock Hunting. Montana is a rockhound's paradise. Sapphires, rubies, garnets, and moss agates are common types. The State Advertising Department has a special pamphlet for rockhounds, and agate shops are frequent on the highways.

Boating. Water-skiing and power-boating are common on the larger lakes and reservoirs. Montana boating laws, fairly standard, are available from the State Fish and Game Commission in Helena.

 WINTER SPORTS. *Skiing.* Write for a complete guide on skiing from the U.S. Forest Service, 200 E. Broadway, Missoula 59801. Major ski areas in Montana are as follows: *Big Sky.* The late Chet Huntley's dream features what looks to be some of the finest skiing in the nation. At the time of this writing four runs have been opened with ten more to be completed. Fully modern lifts assure no waiting. Condominium rates, excellent restaurant. Located forty-five miles from Bozeman in the heart of the Gallatin Canyon, the resort also offers a dude ranch.

Big Mountain Ski Area. Whitefish, Montana, alt. 4,774–7,000 feet. Opens around Thanksgiving, closes around May 1; lodge at area and hotels and motels are in Whitefish; double chair lift, vertical T-bar, Pomalift, and rope tow; excellent runs for all classes; ski patrol, ski school, shops, rental equipment, a cafeteria and restaurant. Accessible by car, Amtrak, Air West.

Red Lodge-Grizzly Peak, sixty-five miles southwest of Billings and six miles west of Red Lodge; alt. 7,400–9,400 ft.; season Nov. to May; hotels and motels at Red Lodge; two double chair lifts, one Pomalift; seven miles of trails and slopes from beginner to high intermediate and expert; access by Northern Pacific or Northwest, Frontier or Western Airlines to Billings and from there by bus; ski patrol, ski school, rental, and chalet for meals.

Other Montana areas: All have some kind of lift and generate considerable local activity. *Bear Paw,* thirty miles south of Havre; *Beef Trail,* eight miles southwest of Butte; *Belmont,* twenty-five miles northwest of Helena; *Bridger Bowl,* sixteen miles northeast of Bozeman; *Deep Creek* on Wise River, forty-five miles southwest of Butte; *Grass Mountain,* twenty-three miles east of Townsend; *Kendall,* at ghost town twenty-three miles north of Lewistown; *Lionhead,* nine miles southwest of West Yellowstone; *Kings Hill,* sixty-five miles south of Great Falls, near Neihart; *Lookout Pass,* eleven miles west of Saltese; *Lost Trail,* forty-five miles south of Hamilton; *Marshall Mountain,* four miles east of Missoula; *Mission Valley,* two and one-half miles south of Polson; *Rainy Mountain,* thirty-eight miles west of Dillon; *Termatts,* twelve miles east of Kalispell; *Turner Mountain,* twenty-one miles northwest of Libby; *Wraith Hill,* twelve miles west of Anaconda; *Z-T,* sixteen miles south of Butte.

 WHAT TO DO WITH THE CHILDREN. The extensive parks and recreation areas in Montana give children a chance to run free and untethered and to work off their excess energy in the clean air of the mountains, lakes and valleys.

The opportunities to see animals in their natural habitats are unlimited, but near Ronan the *Ninepipe* and *Pablo National Wildlife Refuges* are particularly good spots to see waterfowl. Over 185 species have been observed here including ducks, geese, grebes, bitterns and cormorants. And at the *National Bison Range,* 300–500 head of buffalo roam over an 18,000-acre range.

Fish, and trout in particular, of all sizes can be seen at the *Fish Hatcheries* in Great Falls and in Lewiston. And there are picnic facilities nearby.

Ghost towns and restored *frontier towns* give a sense of the frontier and mining past. Maiden, Kendall, and Gilt Edge, all near Lewiston, are ghost towns left over from the mining days of the 19th century. Helena's *Frontier Town* is a replica of a pioneer village, hewn out of solid rock and cut from giant trees. *Virginia City* is a restored gold boom town with newspaper office, livery stable, general store, blacksmith shop and others. There is a train ride to *Nevada City* where there are authentic replicas of early mining stores, homes, and schools. The Nevada City Depot has a *railroad museum* with antique engines and cars.

At the end of a jeep railway and tram ride from Butte are *Lewis and Clark Caverns* where children can go underground into a wonderland of colorful rock formations.

 INDIANS. There are seven Indian tribes living in Montana: Blackfeet Reservation, Browning; Flathead Reservation, Confederated Salish and Kootenai Tribes, Dixon; Crow Reservation, Crow Agency; Fort Belknap Reservation, Harlem; Fort Peck Reservation, Assiniboine and Sioux Tribes, Poplar; Northern Cheyenne Reservation, Northern Cheyenne Tribe, Lame Deer; Rocky Boy Reservation, Chippewa-Cree Tribe, Box Elder. At various times during the year these reservations hold powwows, dances, celebrations, fairs, rodeos, parades, and craft and art displays. For information and schedules write to the appropriate agency headquarters.

The Crow Indian Tribe offers a special tour which includes a night on the reservation. (See section on *Tours).*

 RECOMMENDED READING. A. B. Guthrie, Jr.'s novel, *The Big Sky,* is an excellent re-creation of the life of the early mountain men, trappers, and miners in Montana. Frank Linderman's *Lige Mounts, Free Trappers,* a novel, is also set in this period. For Montana history, read K. Ross Toole's *Montana: An Uncommon Land.*

An Official Travel Guide and Highway Map, listing points of interest, museums, campgrounds, and fishing areas, is available free from Montana Department of Highways, Helena 59601.

EXPLORING MONTANA

A good starting point for visitors coming from the east is Wibaux on I–94. Throughout the state, highway signs tell you about historical happenings in the area. For example, four miles east of Wibaux a sign indicates that less than a century ago this was buffalo and Indian country. From here to Billings you drive your car through the area where the U.S. Cavalry fought the Cheyenne and Sioux tribes in the late 1870's. The trail was opened by the white buffalo hunters, and after 1866 was used by the Army and cattlemen driving their herds up from Texas to new grazing lands. From Glendive on, the route parallels the Yellowstone River and the Northern Pacific Railroad that brought sod-busters and gave life after 1880 to most of the towns you will pass.

T.R. Got Vigor

Wibaux (pop. 766) was once the preserve of a dreamer. Pierre Wibaux left a textile fortune in Napoleon II's France to become one of the biggest cattle barons of the late 1880's. His statue is just west of town. To the south Teddy Roosevelt's cattle used to drift over from their North Dakota base. T.R. accumulated some of his well-known vigor in these badlands. Today, however, a stray

209

drilling rig is as common as a drifting cow, for this is in the Montana portion of the famous Williston Basin, and the oil boom after World War II hasn't abated. The old fortunes were made in cattle; now new men dreaming of money are jeeping around, hunting for leases and geological strata.

Glendive, where the highway crosses the Yellowstone River, was named by one of Montana's first "dudes." Sir George Gore was guided into the area by Jim Bridger in 1855. He had with him several six-mile wagons, three-yoke ox wagons, twenty-one French carts painted red, forty employees, 112 horses, seventy rifles, fifteen shotguns, a linen tent, bottles of French wine and a heavy volume of Shakespeare. After killing 105 bear and two thousand buffalo, elk and deer, Sir George withdrew to St. Louis. He named Glendive Creek after a stream in his native Ireland, and left Montana a tradition of trigger-happy hunters that eventually led to an active Fish and Game Commission. This area is still fine hunting ground for antelope and deer, but the bear and most of the fine dude ranches are in higher country now.

Glendive is a division point on the Northern Pacific Railroad, a county-seat shipping center for grain, beef and oil. It has a fine museum of prehistoric reptile fossils. Makoshika State Park, three miles south of town, will give you a good idea of what the badland rock formations of the region look like. Try to see these twisted remains of geologic change near sunrise or sunset, when the Sioux thought they looked like Makoshika—"hell cooled over."

Yellowstone Country

The Yellowstone River, called the *Roche Jaune* by the Indians because of its occasional yellowish boulders, has been the dominant highway of the region for years. Captain William Clark followed it on his way back from the Pacific, and generations of Montanans have looked to it for protection, direction, and a sometimes reliable drink for man, cow, or crop.

From Glendive down I–94 to Miles City you pass a number of streams flowing northward into the Yellowstone. There's the town of Fallon near O'Fallon Creek, named for Clark's nephew, and Terry, named for General Alfred H. Terry who was Custer's commander. Then comes the Powder River, so named because it often is dried up and dusty. The 91st Division in World War I immortalized the cry, "Powder River, Let 'er Buck." Along the Powder and through all this country were the really big cattle spreads like the LO, Niobarra, Rafter Circle, Diamond Bar and XIT. Their successors are still there, and water is still their lifeblood.

The Tongue River forks into the Yellowstone at Miles City. Clark camped on its banks in 1806, and Fort Keogh was established here in 1877, the year after Custer's fall. Keogh was a captain who fell with him. From Fort Keogh, General Nelson Miles ranged out after the Custer debacle eventually to defeat the Indians.

In Miles' honor, the civilian shacks near the fort took his name and the settlement grew into a great cowtown and after the Indian wars, it became a northern terminus for longhorn drives up from Texas, and beneath these cottonwoods that Western tradition is still alive. At the stock sales yard or on Main Street, Stetsons and sharp-toed boots are part of a Montanan's everyday wardrobe.

Miles City was the home of frontier photographer L. A. Huffman. Coffrin Photo Studio, Red Rocks Inn, and Range Riders Museum (west of the city) have good collections of his work as well as range and Indian memorabilia. The U.S. Livestock Experiment Station is at the western city limits, and nearby is a seismic station where the U.S. monitors nuclear blasts around the world.

Fort Peck and the Missouri

Either Miles City or Glendive offers you the most convenient takeoff for a roundtrip to the north to see Fort Peck Dam and the Missouri River where Lewis and Clark first entered Montana.

Fort Union, one of the three or four important forts of the trapper's West, stood where the Missouri and Yellowstone Rivers join northeast of Sidney, a center of irrigated sugarbeet farming and of an extensive coal field. Fort Union is being restored as a national historic landmark.

On US 2, "The Hi-Line" westward to Fort Peck Dam, you pass Culbertson, named for an old fur trapper. Its economy now is based on wheat, some cattle—although beef ranching is not extensive north of the Missouri—and a new plant to crush oil from safflower seeds. If you have time, drive north of Culbertson to the area of Froid and Medicine Lake where you will see the best examples of the extensive, highly mechanized wheat farming which characterizes this section of Montana. Note the strips of alternately plowed and planted land, widely adopted after the dust storms of the Depression 30's. Alternate planting conserves moisture in the non-planted strip, while the planted strip forms a break to slow wind erosion. The zebra-striped land pattern extends across northern Montana to the mountains.

On US 2, west of Culbertson, you will pass Poplar, headquarters of the Fort Peck Indian Reservation. The agency, as Indian reservation headquarters are called, was set up here in 1876, and it was here that Sitting Bull finally surrendered. The Indians are remnants of the Assiniboine tribes who lived in the vicinity when Lewis and Clark first arrived. The reservation is one of seven in the state.

Past Poplar you come to Wolf Point, a former fueling station for steamboats. Now a county seat, Wolf Point gets its name from its early reputation as a hunting spot for wolves. Its Wild Horse Stampede in July is one of the toughest.

Fort Peck Reservoir, seventeen miles southeast of Glasgow, off the main highway, is formed by the waters of the Missouri River retained by the world's second largest earthfill dam, 250 feet above the river surface. The lake is 180 miles long with 16,000 miles of shoreline, most of which is surrounded by a wildlife refuge. Rock Creek State Park on the eastern shore and Hell Creek State Park on the south offer good camping and picnicking facilities, but make local inquiry about road conditions. Drive south to join I–94 either at Glendive or Miles City.

Custer Stood Here

Continuing westward from Miles City, detour to Custer Battlefield National Monument. From I–94, turn south about forty-seven miles west of Forsyth onto Route 47. This highway turns off near the mouth of Big Horn River where Manuel Lisa founded the first Montana fur post in 1807. The battlefield is thirteen miles southeast of Hardin. As an alternate, you may want to continue on I–94 to see the initials Clark left on Pompeys Pillar, a 200-foot towering landmark on the Yellowstone from which the Indians used to send smoke signals. A gravel road straight south from the Pillar will also take you to Hardin and the battlefield area.

Custer's Last Stand is the Montana incident most familiar to Americans. The government's museum tells the story of the ill-fated Yellow Hair, as the general was called. The battlefield is two miles southeast of Crow Agency, headquarters for the Crow Indian reservation. Inquire at the battlefield about the opportunities to visit the Crows. They have a rodeo, dances and tours in August, and the battle is reenacted.

On June 25, 1876, George Armstrong Custer, flamboyant Civil War hero and—his detractors claim—a headstrong glory-seeker, led 225 cavalry troopers into an attack on some four thousand Sioux and Cheyenne warriors, one of the largest Indian armies ever assembled. His defeat affected the whole area. The Indians won that battle but lost the war when a shocked nation demanded that the Army, based mostly at Miles City, end the Indian threat once and for all. In 1915, Chief Yellow Hand of the Cheyenne, a participant in the Little Big Horn Battle, described seeing Custer just before he fell. Custer's eyes, he said, showed insanity and hatred, but no fear. The guns, maps, and dioramas of the museum, and the many white headstones on the skyline marking the areas of battle will help you understand what happened on that fateful day.

From Hardin you may wish to take a side trip southwest on Route 513 forty-five miles to Yellowtail Dam. The $94-million dam underscores the importance of reclamation in this barren area. For many years, reclamation of land by storage of water has been a major theme in Western politics. The dam provides irrigation for 43,500 acres, while the power plant generates nine hundred million kilowatts.

Near the dam is old Fort C. F. Smith. Ten years before Custer put the area on the map, this was one of a string of important posts that were built to protect the Bozeman Trail which led up from the Oregon Trail near Casper, Wyoming. The Bozeman Trail later was avoided because of the continued hostility of the Indians.

The Range Rider Rides Again

Billings, northwest of the Custer Battlefield, is the largest city of Montana. Named for the president of the railroad that gave it life, Billings has sugarbeet and oil refineries, livestock yards, and two small colleges. They say of its Northern Hotel that if you sit still long enough in the lobby, you'll meet everyone in the state you know.

Among the Billings' sights is the statue of the Range Rider of the Yellowstone, which William S. Hart, cowboy hero of silent movies posed for. This is along Black Otter Trail which follows the rim above the city to the north. Five miles from Billings there's a Pictograph Cave with the most important scratchings of prehistoric man on the Great Plains.

Billings is a modern shopping center and the banking hub for the eastern region. Its Midland Empire Fair in August is one of the state's largest. See the Brown Barn for Western art.

From Billings turn south on US 212 for a breathtaking ride along the Beartooth Scenic Highway which cuts through the western portion of Custer National Forest. If you have the time, call at forest headquarters in Billings to get information on a hundred hiking, horseback and camping possibilities. You will begin to climb sharply after passing the town of Red Lodge. You get to Beartooth Pass (elev. 10,940 ft.) passing alpine meadows and mountain lakes and viewing, off to the west, Granite Peak, Montana's highest at 12,799 feet. The road dips into Wyoming and into Yellowstone Park. This is your natural opportunity to include Yellowstone Park in your tour of Montana. The mountains you spiral around on this trip are the Absaroka, from the Indian word other tribes gave to the Crows: Up-sa-rah-qu, or sharp people. Southeast of Red Lodge, you will pass one of Montana's top winter sports areas. And in Red Lodge there's an outstanding August International Festival of Nations.

Return to Montana from Yellowstone

You may return to our route swiftly from the Gardiner entrance toward Livingston on I–90. (Or cross the park to the West Yellowstone entrance where, incidentally, an airport receives scheduled service.) If you take the Gardiner route (US 89), the area around Emigrant was the site of Yellowstone City, where gold was discovered in 1862. You're getting into ghost town country; the State Advertising Department has a fine list.

Back to Livingston, named for a Northern Pacific official. This is a great fishing center. Drive west over Bozeman Pass into the Gallatin Valley which the Indians called Valley of the Flowers. They weren't far wrong; this is one of the richest agricultural valleys in Montana. Bozeman Pass was the divide between mountain and plains Montana in the old days. East of the pass was Indian country, where white settlement proceeded with great risk; west was mountain country where mining boomed and brought in trade and towns. Dan Bailey's fly-tying factory is worth a visit in Livingston.

Bozeman, settled in 1864, was named for a frontiersman who founded that short-lived trail north from Wyoming. Today it's the home of Montana State University (with an enrollment of eight thousand students), headquarters for the 1,700,000–acre Gallatin National Forest, and the center of purebred livestock, small grain, and dairying. The college fieldhouse and the museum on the southwest corner of the campus are worth a side trip. If you are interested in grain or cattle farming, the Montana Agricultural Experiment Station is one of the best in the country.

Bozeman is also headquarters for the Montana Wilderness Association which every summer conducts numerous walking and riding trips for visitors into the remote wilds of the state.

Follow I–90 west from Bozeman to Three Forks. Just north of the town you'll find the Missouri River Headquarters State

Monument, where three rivers meet: the Jefferson, the Madison, and the Gallatin. The rivers where named by Lewis and Clark for their bosses, the President and Secretaries of State and Treasury, when they reached the forks in late July 1805 after their long struggle upriver. This juncture is the beginning of the Missouri River proper, which then flows east 2,500 miles to the Mississippi at St. Louis.

The Three Forks of the Missouri was a bloody battleground in the early days. Blackfoot Indians from the north, Crows from the east, Snakes from the south, and the Nez Percés and Flatheads from over the divide to the west, all converged on the forks at various times to fight over game or to discourage trappers. Manuel Lisa, aided by John Colter of the Lewis and Clark party, tried to build a post as early as 1810 but this was only one of many attempts that failed because of the Blackfeet.

One of Montana's leading natural attractions, Lewis and Clark ' Caverns, is thirteen miles further west on your interstate route. This is a safe, underground limestone cavern where guided tours operate daily from May 1 to September 30. The 90-minute walk through this fantasia of stalactites and stalagmites takes steam out of the kids and is a refreshing change from Indians, cows, and complicated history.

Turn south from the caverns on US 287. You are following the famous Madison River trout stream. The most important turnoff is at Ennis west to Virginia City. But if you haven't already visited it on your trip up from Yellowstone, first go on south to the site of the 1959 earthquake on the shores of Hebegen Lake. The U.S. Forest Service has excellent displays and campgrounds here. An 80-million-ton rockslide blocked the river, created Quake Lake, and killed at least twenty-eight people in one of the West's most dramatic natural disasters.

Williamsburg of the West

Now back to Virginia City, a boom town that has been carefully restored. Here you can recapture the feel of those post-Civil War gold rushes which first drew large numbers of people upriver and overland to the mountain West.

Six prospectors fleeing from the Indians tried to change their luck in Alder Gulch on the Stinkingwater, now more decorously called the Ruby River. It was May 26, 1863. They discovered gold. Within a month, ten thousand people were sweating and snorting in the area. Within a year thirty-five thousand people were working within a ten-mile radius. In the months and years to come, $300 million in gold dust came out of this provincial gravel.

Last mining operations didn't end until 1937.

Virginia City was the territorial capital for ten years. Here the vigilantes took the law into their own hands after outlaws had murdered two hundred residents. More important, this was the first home for many of the families, businesses, churches and lodges that later spread over Montana.

At Virginia City, the visitor will see more authentic details of the mining frontier than anywhere else in the West, thanks to a dedicated couple, State Senator and Mrs. Charles Bovey. They have spent a fortune in restoring both Virginia City and neighboring Nevada City. A narrow-gauge railroad operates in the summer months to ferry tourists between the two cities and provide the chance to see some beautiful, untamed country. You can enjoy wooden sidewalks, authentic saloons, good museums, an old assay office, a Wells Fargo office and Boot Hill Cemetery where six of the vigilantes' guests rest. Nearby is the original Robbers Roost where the gang of Henry Plummer, the sheriff who turned outlaw, lay in wait.

From Virginia City, rejoin the interstate route for a visit to Butte. Follow Route 287 west from Virginia City to Twin Bridges, drive south on Route 41 to Dillon. This is the site of Western Montana College and headquarters for the Beaverhead National Forest, one of the great hunting and fishing areas of the West. Join I–15 at Dillon and proceed north to Butte.

Bannack, a ghost town twenty miles to the west of Dillon on Route 278, is now a Registered Historic Landmark. The very first capital, it was also the first camp of any note: gold was first struck here in 1862. Lewis and Clark pushed southward into this area from the Three Forks and it was here that they decided to turn west to cross the Continental Divide. This is less developed than Virginia City, but quaint and quiet.

Butte—the Richest Hill on Earth

Butte was settled in 1864 and is the historic homebase for the mighty Anaconda Copper Mining Co., ACM or "The Company," as it is known to Montanans. It was named Anaconda after the snake capable of great, but constricting, embrace.

First gold and then silver were discovered around Butte, but the big fortunes were made after 1870 in copper. The "war of the copper kings" dominated Montana politics for the next three decades.

From beneath these five square miles of bleak hilltop have come more than $5 billion in ores. More than nine thousands miles of mine shafts run below Butte. The huge Berkeley Pit gives an excellent view of modern open-pit mining methods, where scrapers and earth movers replace the sweating worker, the burro, and the rickety hoist.

Today Butte is an industrial and distributing center, and an international Port of Entry. While you are there, be sure and see the Old Town and the Mining Museum. The early-day displays will take you back to the frontier days of Montana.

Three big names in Montana history were the copper kings: Marcus Daly, William Andrews Clark, and F. Augustus Heinze. Clark eventually made the U.S. Senate in 1900 after a corrupt election that put Montana on the national political map. Daly, a founder of ACM, lost to Clark in his battle to have nearby Anaconda named capital over Helena, but nonetheless his company was the power in Montana for a half century. Heinze gave the other giants fits with his court cases. He eventually pulled out with $10.5 million, which he later lost in the Wall Street panic of 1907.

The ACM has produced the biggest share of the state's wealth in the form of copper, zinc, and chrome, as well as playing a dominant role in its lumber industry. Today it has diversified with an aluminum plant at Columbia Falls near the west entrance to Glacier Park.

Anaconda, the smelter town which is practically a western suburb of Butte, is the site of the Washoe Smelter with its 585-foot smokestack, highest in the world. The smelter tour offered in the summer is an excellent companion tour to underground mine and open-pit excursions in Butte. Marcus Daly was determined that Anaconda should be the queen city. One of the monuments of that dream was the Hotel Marcus Daly, opened in 1889, the year Montana became a state. The splendid Victorian bar is a mahogany and gilt showpiece and the floor features an inlaid mosaic head of Tammany, Daly's favorite racehorse. No patron was allowed to step on that head.

Ghost Towns Galore

From Anaconda, drive north on I–90 through Warm Springs, where the state mental hospital is situated, to Deer Lodge, one of the earliest mining camps, but now the home of the state prison. Here is W. A. Clark's old mansion at 311 Clark Street. Follow the interstate to Garrison where you turn eastward on US 12 to climb over McDonald Pass to Helena, the state capital. (You slipped over to the west side of the Continental Divide north of Dillon; now you go back over it.) Just over the Divide you might enjoy Frontier Town, Old West museum, restaurant, stockade, jail, store, chapel. and bar.

If you are enthusiastic about ghost towns, swing west from Anaconda on Route 10A to Philipsburg, a famous silver mining center. East of Philipsburg is Granite, one of the best-preserved of the old silver towns. Between 1865 and 1913 it produced $32 million. Drive north from Philipsburg between the Flint Creek Range and the John Long Mountains to Drummond. You'll be back on the interstate and can turn east to pick up the route at Garrison, passing Gold Creek, scene of the very first Montana gold strike in 1850. It was developed by the Stuart brothers. Granville Stuart became a leader in mining and cattle and was later appointed Minister to Uruguay. If you should choose the direct route north from Butte to Helena, don't miss the Elkhorn ghost town, just south of Boulder on I-15 and one of the best preserved.

Helena got its start when some discouraged miners took their "last chance" in 1864 on what is now the main street of the city—and made a strike. The area subsequently produced $20 million in gold. It is said that by 1888 Helena had fifty millionaires and was the richest city per capita in the country.

The American Smelting and Refining Co. has a plant in East Helena and the city is a prosperous distributing center for the surrounding Prickly Pear Valley. But the main business of Helena is government, and the trappings of politics are the real attraction. The state capitol is faced with Montana granite, topped by a copper dome, and adorned by Western artists, most notably the Russell masterpiece, *Lewis and Clark Meeting the Flatheads*, on the third floor. In front of the capitol is a statue of Thomas Francis Meagher, an Irish revolutionary of note who somehow harangued his way West to become an "acting" territorial governor of Montana. He eventually fell, amid great mystery, into the Missouri River at Fort Benton and presumably drowned. Some say the vigilantes pushed him.

Some Montanans from time to time bemoan what they consider a cultural lag. But the State Historical Museum, east of the capitol, takes second place to none. It has good dioramas covering the complete story of Montana, the largest collection of Charlie Russell's art in the state, and a comprehensive gun collection. If you get Montana fever, ask to see a copy of the *Montana Magazine of Western History*. The museum has an excellent research library, too. The Cathedral of St. Helena, replica of the Votive Church of Vienna, is worth seeing.

Politics is a great sport in Montana. When the legislature is in session, the town fills up with performers and spectators. There are company lobbyists, cattlemen from the plains, grain growers—both the conservatives and the more liberal Farmers Union agents—timbermen, the Butte and Great Falls labor leaders, conservationists and recreationists from the mountain West, educators and students plus the ever-watchful eyes of the railroads, oil, mining and trucking interests. The political fates of the state in the past have often matched a conservative, Republican plains group against the more urban, labor-conscious mountain men who are often Democratic. Political generalizations are difficult, but for the past few decades the Democrats have had the two U.S. Senators and the one western Congressman, while the Republicans have held the governorship and the one plains congressional seat to the east. But victory margins often are narrow and tempers can wear thin in a state which takes its politics and individualism seriously.

Helena has been the stomping ground for several great Senators, including Thomas Walsh, the prosecutor of the Teapot Dome scandals; Burton K. Wheeler, FDR's isolationist opponent of the '30's; Mike Mansfield, present Senate majority leader who came up from the Butte mines; and Jannette Rankin, the country's first congresswoman. If that seems too political, reflect that Gary Cooper and Myrna Loy were born in the area.

Gates of the Mountains

Sixteen miles north of Helena, on I-15, you come to the Gates of the Mountains, a 2,000-ft. gorge in the Missouri River named by Lewis. Nervous about what he would find in the Rockies (remember he had been trudging upriver and hadn't been in the mountains, yet), he thought the gorge "the most spectacular" he had seen, but of "dark and gloomy aspect." A two-hour summer river cruise lets you check his opinion in almost the same setting.

You should also explore Canyon Ferry Dam and Reservoir. The best route is to go southeast out of Helena on Route 287, then turn northeast on Route 284. This road will take you across the 210-foot-high dam, which has created a 24-mile-long lake. As you drive on its east shore, the lake will be on your right hand. To the left you will come to the turnoff for Diamond City which will take you to yet another ghost town and, if you persist, to the old site of Fort Logan, where some buildings still stand. Return to Helena by way of White Sulphur Springs and Townsend.

North from Helena, keeping to I-15, we approach Montana's biggest city. Great Falls, with 58,761 residents, is actually the largest city in a four-state area of Montana, Wyoming, North Dakota and Idaho. It was named for the falls in the Missouri to the northeast. It is the site of Malstrom Air Force Base, one of the important links in the SAC and Air Defense Command system protecting North America. Minutemen missiles abound hereabouts. Hydroelectric plants near the falls, an Anaconda Company smelter and plant which produces copper and aluminum rods and wire, and a fertile winter wheat and livestock area have made Great Falls a boom town.

Great Falls was home base for cowboy artist Charlie Russell. A fine gallery of Russell's work may be seen in his old studio at 1201 4th Avenue North. From this town his fame spread even to Hollywood, but he preferred the Mint Saloon and the leathery cronies of the open-range days. The Rainbow Hotel is a Great Falls landmark similar to other Montana hotels such as the Northern in Billings, the Placer in Helena, or Butte's Finlen. See the great falls themselves and the nearby springs which flow at a rate of 388 million gallons daily.

If you want to make a side trip to Russell's country, take US 87 southeast of Great Falls to US 191, then drive northward across the Missouri River to join US 2 at Malta. From Great Falls, you will be traveling through the heart of the Judith Basin cattle country, the Russell National Wildlife Refuge, and, in the Little Rocky Mountains, the outlaw camps of Landusky and Zortman. Until recently this area was not accessible by good roads. When you get to US 2, the Chief Joseph Battleground, south of Chinook, recalls the last of the Montana Indian Wars. The Nez Percé chief, Joseph, led the U.S. Army on a chase across the breadth of Montana but was finally caught by General Miles coming up from the Yellowstone. Chief Joseph lost the last round here in the Bearpaw Mountains in 1877, and said, "Where the sun now stands I will fight no more forever."

Return by US 87 from Havre to Fort Benton or proceed northeast from Great Falls if you skipped the side trip.

Fort Benton, now a sleepy and usually bypassed county seat, was once the economic capital of the Rocky Mountain West. For two decades, it was the center of steamboat travel on the Missouri River—a direct link with St. Louis and the "States."

After Lewis and Clark passed by, Fort Benton slumbered until an American Fur Company post was established in 1846 by Alexander Culbertson, a great trader. The steamboat on the Missouri had reached this point by 1860. So when the mining camps sprouted in the mountains to the southeast, Fort Benton merchants were ready with goods to be wagon-hauled to the camps. Hundreds of boats puffed up the Missouri River to serve the gold camps and to link up with the Mullan Road wagon trail over the Rockies to Walla Walla, Washington. In its peak year (1879) Fort Benton docked forty-nine steamboats.

Today Fort Benton has an excellent museum and you can visualize from its old levees the days when it was a bustling port. Not until the Northern Pacific Railroad pushed through to reach the Pacific Coast in 1883 did Benton and the steamboat era begin to decline. Guthrie's *Three Thousand Hills* or Paul Sharp's *Whoop-Up Trail* are good reading on Benton.

From Fort Benton, the Missouri moves eastward 180 miles through the untouched Missouri River Breaks to the beginning of Fort Peck Reservoir. A national battle is shaping over whether this relatively wild waterway is to be preserved as a scenic and recreation refuge or dammed for waterpower and irrigation. For the canoeing enthusiast, this stretch of river provides a rare opportunity.

Blackfoot Country

From Fort Benton, turn north and west for the Blackfoot Indian country around Browning, which also is the gateway to Glacier National Park, the Alps of America. You take Route 223 north from Fort Benton to Chester, and then go west on US 2. Near Shelby, where Dempsey fought Gibbons in 1923, and Cut Bank, you pass through one of Montana's prolific oil areas. More than 1,100 oil wells and one hundred gas wells dot the dryland wheat farms of the area.

Browning is the headquarters for the 2,400-acre Blackfoot Indian Reservation. In the summer months, the town is alive with the colorful tribesmen, and each first week of July they celebrate North American Indian Days with traditional dances. It's the Montana event the U.S. State Department feels is of most interest to foreign tourists.

The Museum of the Plains Indians, a half mile west of town, was opened in 1941 and has been continuously improved. It is now under the wing of the Smithsonian Institution in Washington. The carvings and costumes, murals and dioramas are first class; so, too, is the crafts shop. Operated by the Bureau of Indian Affairs, the museum is only open from June 1 to September 15.

Glacier National Park is Montana's great natural "spectacular." Since 1910, the more than 1,500 square miles of jagged mountain scenery have drawn travelers, lured by its many glaciers and alpine lakes, well-developed campgrounds, and motel and hotel accommodations of all types. A quick drive through can touch the highlights, but there are endless opportunities for hiking, camping, and fishing to meet each vacationer's tastes and time. The park season runs from June 15 to September 10, when most

221

hotels and cabin camps are open. The main roads, however, may stay clear until mid-October depending on the weather.

Most of Glacier Park is accessible only by its one thousand miles of foot and horse trails; on-the-spot inquiry and attention to park regulations is essential—this is rugged country. When the park itself is closed, US 2 may be used to the south from Browning to West Glacier. Local inquiry is advisable if the weather looks bad. And, don't feed the bears.

Starting from Browning, you'll visit the Glacier Park Lodge at East Glacier on US 2. This is typical of the huge log hotels developed by the Great Northern Railway in the early days of the century to handle what was primarily a time-to-burn railroad trade. This hotel, like its sisters, Many Glacier Hotel and Lake McDonald Lodge, offers a variety of riding, hiking, golf, and fishing (no license needed in the park). Be sure to inquire about guided tours and lectures offered by the National Park Service naturalists. They will increase your enjoyment of this alpine beauty spot.

From St. Mary you can also swing north to Waterton-Glacier International Peace Park in Canada, an extension of the same kind of mountain terrain as you find on the American side, but perhaps less crowded in the peak months. Also note on the north route the access road to Many Glacier Hotel on Swiftcurrent Lake; you leave the highway at Babb and drive a few miles west to what many consider the park's most varied center of activity. All of the recreation activities are developed here, with trails to Grinnell Lake and Glacier. George Bird Grinnell, the naturalist, was instrumental in the establishment of the park.

On a quick tour, you'll want to see Two Medicine Valley and Lake. Turn west about four miles north of East Glacier on State 49. A seven–mile road leads to a lake (launch trips during the season) ringed by high peaks. There is a self-guiding, well-marked nature trail at Trick Falls, a safe, quick introduction to Glacier.

There's a good campground at St. Mary Lake and another at Rising Sun on the north shore highway. Four miles west of the latter at Sun Point there are an information station and self-guiding trails. The frontal range of the Rockies at this point is known as Lewis Range.

The most spectacular drive through Glacier is over the Continental Divide via the Going-to-the-Sun highway. From Browning and East Glacier, drive north on State 49 and 287 to St. Mary, and then turn westward for the 50-mile drive over Logan Pass to the west end of the park. If you are hauling a camper, and your rig is over thirty feet in length—including your car—you had better make arrangements to leave your camper and pick it up later. Park rules forbid vehicles over thirty feet long on this highway and you will realize why when you begin your climb.

From St. Mary Lake in the east to Lake McDonald in the west the highway crosses 6,664-ft. Logan Pass. It is the great spot to stop and view the park for from here you have 100-mile vistas. Ask about the trail to Granite Park Chalet.

After Logan Pass, descend west along the Garden Wall, one of America's greatest mountain highways. Below at Avalanche Campground, there is an easy two-mile trail to Avalanche Basin, a natural amphitheater with walls two thousand feet high and waterfalls for a backdrop. The red cedars and the rushing streams give you a sense of what the park must be like deep in the interior if you haven't the time for longer hikes or rides.

Lake McDonald is ten miles long and a mile wide. Lake McDonald Lodge near the head of the lake on our highway is the center. There are public campgrounds here and at the foot of the lake at Apgar, as well as several classes of accommodations at both spots. The hike to Sperry Glacier and Chalet is popular.

Flathead Country

Coming over Logan Pass you cross to the west side of the Continental Divide again. Both the North and South forks of the Flathead River flow southwestward through Flathead Lake to join eventually the Columbia River and drain into the Pacific Ocean.

At this point in your exploration, you can see one of the biggest of the hydroelectric power projects which have played an important role in the recent history of the area. Eight miles west of the exit from Glacier Park on US 2 is the turnoff for Hungry Horse Dam. Leave the main highway at Martin City for a quick glance at this huge concrete dam which backs up the South Fork of the Flathead River. The dam is 564 feet high, the reservoir is thirty-four miles long. The road around the reservoir passes through beautiful wilderness. You may meet some logging trucks, for this is big timber country; most of it is cut in the Flathead National Forest administered in nearby Kalispell.

Back on US 2, you can reach Kalispell via Columbia Falls, where the Anaconda Company has built a huge aluminum plant powered by electricity from Hungry Horse Dam. Visitors may tour the plant. Kalispell is a lumber and vacation center. Each year 1,500,000 Christmas trees are shipped from here. The region is also noted for potatoes, sweet cherries, and lovely Flathead Lake, on US 93 to the south. Many people from the eastern plains have come here to retire where nature is bountiful and there's always enough water. You can't help notice lumbering in the area. The big logging trucks bring loads of Ponderosa pine, Douglas fir, larch (tamarack) and spruce from the hills to the mills. It's all power-tool work now—chain saws, big tractors, and steel helmets. Plywood mills and paper plants are moving in.

If you want to see more beautiful scenery and get a feel for the lumber industry, take a circular side trip from Kalispell west along US 2 to Libby where the St. Regis Paper Company has one of the largest lumber mills in the state. Tours of the operations are possible. Then swing north along 37 to Eureka, but make local inquiry first for this Kootenai River Valley will shortly be flooded by the new Libby Dam, another major part of the Columbia Basin development which will back water into Canada.

From Eureka drive back south to Kalispell along Route 93, passing Whitefish, site of well-known vacation lake. On the mountainside above is Big Mountain Ski Area, one of the best developed in the West. It's served by the Great Northern Railway and well-thought-of by skiing sophisticates because of its relative lack of crowds and its reliable snow. If you come in early spring be sure and catch the Whitefish Winter Carnival. It will provide entertainment for the whole family.

Flathead Lake and the Mission Valley

South from Kalispell, go around Flathead Lake by either the west shore, US 93, or east shore, Route 35; both give excellent views of this largest freshwater lake west of the Mississippi, twenty-eight miles long and from five to fifteen miles wide. On the east shore the lake nestles up to the white-topped Mission Range. On the west it blends into the foothills of the Cabinet Mountains. On the east shore you'll find at Yellow Bay a state park and the Montana State University Biological Station (good museums open in summer). On the west shore, there are two good state parks and numerous commercial accommodations. The east shore is also the home of the annual Cherry Blossom Festival in May. Cherries from this area reach the entire United States.

South from the lake by US 93 brings you into the heart of the Mission Valley, site of the Flathead Indian Reservation. There's an especially interesting stop at St. Ignatius, where one of the early Jesuit missions to the Indians is still preserved. This was a headquarters for Father DeSmet, the "blackrobe" who influenced the early West in both Wyoming and Montana.

Southwest of St. Ignatius near Ravalli, you may see from the highway some of the herd kept at the National Bison Range. Drive from Ravalli along Route 10A to Dixon and then turn off on the gravel road to range headquarters at Moiese. During the summer months there are daily self-guided auto tours to search out the herd of between three and five hundred bison, with their accompanying bands of deer, antelope, elk and bighorn sheep. The range covers 19,000 acres, and is one of the oldest wildlife preserves in the country.

In the year 1800, an estimated sixty million buffalo roamed the prairies of the continent in both the United States and Canada. A century later that number had been cut to fewer than three hundred. Today because of conservation, there are again about 20,000 in both countries. May and June are good wildflower months on the range; in October there is a horseback roundup of the bison herd which draws many visitors.

US 93 returns us to the I-90 system near Missoula, the prosperous home of the University of Montana (beneath the "M" on the mountain). The University has 8,000-plus students and leading forestry, law, and journalism schools. This is headquarters for Region I of the U.S. Forest Service, as well as a lumber and distributing center. From Hell Gate Canyon on the Clark's Fork River to the east of town, the Blackfeet raided the more peaceful Flatheads, hence the canyon's name. Missoula is now the home base for novelists A. B. Guthrie, Jr., and Dorothy Johnson, author of *The Hanging Tree*, which was made into a movie starring Gary Cooper, and *The Bedside Book of Bastards*, which takes a humorous look at our world's less than glamorous personalities.

Seven miles west of Missoula, on the main highway, is the center of forest fire-fighting activities for the northern Rocky Mountains. Here parachutists are trained to "smoke jump" into the bad fires. Research on how to prevent and fight these disasters is carried on. During the summer season the center is open daily for tours.

At Bonner, seven miles east of Missoula on I-90, U.S. Plywood maintains a major lumber mill (tours), and to the south on US 93 the visitor can make a one-day swing of the Bitterroot Valley. Just east of Stevensville is the St. Mary's Mission at Fort Owens State Monument, oldest mission in the Northwest. This is well preserved and a lovely reminder of the early-day missionary efforts of the Jesuits among the mountain tribes. Here was the first permanent white settlement in the state in 1841.

Indian history fans may wish to push out of the valley southeastward along US 93 and Route 43 to the Big Hole Battlefield National Monument. Chief Joseph and his Nez Percé fought one of their great delaying actions at this point.

Also stemming off the Bitterroot Valley is highway US 12, west off US 93 from Lolo. This follows closely the final westward swing of Lewis and Clark down into the Columbia Basin. The terrain is wilderness forest at its best, with good camping and picnic spots. A grove along the way is named for Bernard De Voto, Harvard historian of the Lewis and Clark journeys. Travellers Rest near Lolo was a stopping place for the explorers on both westward and eastward journeys.

This Lewis and Clark Highway is the most interesting summer exit from Montana if you have time. However, I–90 also leads directly west from Missoula into the Idaho panhandle and on to Spokane, major economic center for the entire region west of the Divide.

AROUND THE STATE

HOTELS AND MOTELS. Many new representatives of the national hotel and motel chains are now in Montana, but during the prime tourist season reservations are still advisable. In fact, if you want to stay in or around Glacier or West Yellowstone parks you may well have to book reservations as much as a year in advance. Rates are lower during the off-season.

The price categories in this section, for double occupancy, will average as follows: *Deluxe* $24, *Expensive* $20, *Moderate* $15, and *Inexpensive* $11. For a more complete description of these categories, see the *Hotels & Motels* portion of THE ROCKIES & PLAINS *Facts at Your Fingertips* at the front of this volume.

ANACONDA

Vagabond Lodge Motel. *Moderate.* 1421 E. Park. TV, cafe nearby, park adjacent. 563-5251

ASHLAND

Lazy FZ Motel. *Inexpensive.* ½ mi. W on US 212. Cafe nearby. 784-2400

BAKER

Roy's Motel. *Inexpensive.* 327 W. Montana Ave. TV, playground, free coffee, cafe one–half mile, public pool nearby. 778-3321

BIGFORK

Holiday Resort. *Moderate.* E. Lake Shore. TV, cafe, sundeck, all facilities and water sports on Flathead Lake. Open Apr. to Oct. 982-3482

BIG SKY

Big Sky Resort. *Moderate* to *Expensive.* 40 mi. S. of Bozeman on US 191. The late Chet Huntley's ski resort in the heart of the Gallatin Canyon. Rooms, hostel, condominiums. Nursery for children. Open year round. 995-4269

BILLINGS

Ramada Inn. *Expensive.* Mullowney Lane and I–90. Heated pool, color TV, excellent bar and restaurant, dancing, entertainment. Free airport bus. 248-7151

War Bonnet Inn. *Expensive.* On I–90, 27th St. S. Exit. Color TV, pool, lounge, dancing, entertainment, restaurant, conference rooms. Free airport bus. 248-7761

Cherry Tree Inn. *Moderate.* 823 N. Broadway. Near downtown, color TV, suites and apartments, Pool and playground nearby. 252-5603

Dude Rancher Lodge. *Moderate.* 415 N. 29th St. Downtown motor hotel with distinctive Western atmosphere. Good restaurant, color TV. 259-5561

Holiday Inn. *Moderate.* NE on US 10,

87, 212. Heated pool, color TV, restaurant, conference rooms. 245-6611

Imperial "400" Motel. *Moderate.* 2601 4th Ave. Heated pool, color TV, restaurant nearby. Friendship Inns chain. 245-6646

Hotel Northern. *Moderate.* 28th St. and 1st Ave. Downtown near the railroad station, this is a leading hotel in southeastern Montana. Restaurant, coffee shop, bar, barber and beauty shops, garage, TV, free airport bus. Member Best Western. 245-5121

Ponderosa Inn. *Moderate.* 2511 1st Ave. Two heated pools, color TV, sauna, 24-hour cafe, bar, dancing, entertainment. 259-5511

Rimrock Lodge. *Moderate.* 1203 N. 27th St. Heated pool, TV, cafe, bar, barber and beauty shops, free airport bus. 252-7107

Westward Ho. *Moderate.* 1315 N. 27th St. Color TV, sundeck, free coffee. 245-4128

Overpass. *Inexpensive.* 615 Central Ave. TV, free coffee, cafe one-half mile. 252-5157

BOZEMAN

Holiday Inn. *Expensive.* 5 Baxter Lane. Color TV, indoor heated pool, saunas, cafe, bar. 587-4561

City Center Motel. *Moderate.* 507 W. Main. Color TV, indoor heated pool, sauna, free coffee. 24–hour cafe adjacent. 587-3158

Imperial "400" Motel. *Moderate.* 122 W. Main St. Color TV, heated pool, free coffee, cafe nearby. 587-4481

Sunset. *Inexpensive.* 810 N. 7th Ave. TV, 24–hour cafe nearby. 587-5536

BROWNING

War Bonnet Lodge. *Moderate.* ½ mi. S on US 2, 89. Color TV, cafe, bar, beauty shop. 338-5061

BUTTE

Finlen Hotel and Motor Lodge. *Expensive.* Broadway and Wyoming Sts. Restaurant, TV, bar, beauty shop, meeting rooms, free garage. 723-5461

War Bonnet Inn. *Expensive.* 2100 Cornell. Color TV, heated pool, cafe, meeting rooms. 792-9121

Capri Motel. *Moderate.* 220 N. Wyoming. Color TV, free Continental breakfast, 24-hour cafe nearby. 723-4391

City Center. *Moderate.* 541 W. Park St. Color TV, pool, free coffee, 24-hour cafe four blocks. 792-0401

Ramada Inn. *Moderate.* 2900 Harrison Ave. Color TV, heated pool, 24-hour cafe, bar, entertainment, meeting rooms, free airport bus. 494-3500

Mile Hi Motel. *Inexpensive.* 3499 Harrison Ave. Color TV, heated pool, restaurant adjacent, free coffee. 494-2250

CHINOOK

Rear Paw Court. *Inexpensive.* 775 Montana at W. 2nd St. TV, free coffee, cafe nearby, some kitchenettes. 357-2150

COOKE CITY

Watuck Motor Lodge. *Moderate.* NE on US 212. Heated pool, cafe, riding, fishing, jeep tours, pack trips, snowmobiling available. 838-2251

DILLON

Royal Inn. *Moderate.* 7 blks. N on US 41. Color TV, heated pool, cafe. 683-4214

Creston. *Inexpensive.* 335 S. Atlantic St. TV, free coffee, 24-hour cafe one-half mile. 683-2341

ENNIS

El Western Motel. *Moderate.* ¾ mi. S on US 287. Color TV, cafe nearby. On the Madison River. Hunting, fishing, float trips, guides available. Near Virginia City. Closed Dec. to Mar. 682-4217

Rainbow Valley Motel. *Moderate.* 1 mi. S on US 287. TV, playground, cafe nearby. Float trips, hunting trips arranged. 682-4264

Sportsman's Lodge. *Inexpensive.* ¼ mi. N on US 287. Heated pool, cafe, bar. Fishing and hunting guides and trips. Air-strip nearby. 682-4242

GARDINER

Westernaire. *Moderate.* 1 mi. N on US 89. TV, cafe ¾ mile. Open Apr. to Oct. 848-7397

Mountain View. *Inexpensive.* ½ mi. N on US 89. TV, free coffee, cafe nearby. Patio overlooks Yellowstone River. 848-7331

GLACIER NATIONAL PARK

Glacier Park Lodge. *Expensive.* On State 49. Heated pool, playground, restaurant, bar, beauty shop, 9–hole golf course, pitch 'n putt, putting green, shuffleboard, volleyball, ping-pong, riding, fishing. Reservations advised. Open June to Labor Day. 226-4841

Lake McDonald Lodge. *Expensive.* 12 mi. NE on Going-to-the-Sun Rd. Restaurant, riding, fishing, boating. Set among Giant Cedars. Reservations advised. Open June 15 to Sept. 10. 888-5431

Many Glacier Lodge. *Expensive.* 12 mi. W of Babb off US 89. Restaurant, bar, barber and beauty shops, fishing, boating, riding, pack trips, volleyball. Near Swiftcurrent Lake. Reservations advised. Open June 15 to Sept. 2.

Village Inn. *Expensive.* 2 mi. N at Apgar Village. Cafe nearby, beach, fishing, boats available. Near Lake McDonald. Open late May to early Sept. 888-5632

Rising Sun Motor Inn. *Moderate.* 6 mi. W of St. Mary Park entrance on Going-to-the-Sun Rd. Restaurant, playground, on lake. Open June 15 to Labor Day. 732-4102

St. Mary's Motel and Lodge. *Moderate.* In St. Mary, at the east gateway to Glacier. Restaurant, lounge, coffee shop, store and garage. 732-4431

Swiftcurrent Motor Inn. *Moderate.* 13 mi. W of Babb on Swiftcurrent Lake. Cafe, camp store, resort activities. Open June 15 to Aug. 732-4311

Tamarack Lodge. *Inexpensive.* 8 mi. W of West Glacier on US 2. 24-hour cafe, one mile. Flathead River float trips, free RR, airport pickup. 387-5568

GLASGOW

Campbell Lodge. *Moderate.* 3rd Ave. S. at 6th St. Color TV, free Continental breakfast, cafe nearby, sundeck. 228-9328

Rustic Lodge. *Moderate.* 125 7th St. N. Color TV, playground, free Continental breakfast, 24–hour cafe nearby, playground. 228-2451

Roosevelt. *Inexpensive.* 422 3rd Ave. S. Some TV, free coffee, cafe nearby. 228-4341

GLENDIVE

Holiday Lodge. *Expensive.* 222 N. Kendrick Ave. Color TV, heated pool, sauna, cafe nearby, putting green, recreation room. 365-5656

Jordan. *Inexpensive.* 223 N. Merrill Ave. Some TV, pool privileges, free coffee, cafe and restaurant, beauty shop. 365-3371

GREAT FALLS

Heritage Inn. *Expensive.* 1700 Fox Farm Rd. Color TV, indoor heated pool, cafe, bar, dancing, entertainment. Free airport bus. 761-1900

Holiday Inn. *Expensive.* 1411 10th Ave. S. Color TV, heated pool, cafe, bar, dancing, entertainment. Free airport bus. 761-4600

O'Haire Manor. *Expensive.* 17 7th St. Color TV, indoor heated pool, free coffee, restaurant, bar, entertainment, dancing, beauty shop. 454-2141

Ponderosa Inn. *Expensive.* 220 Central Ave. Color TV, rooftop heated pool, free coffee, 24-hour cafe, bar, entertainment, dancing. 761-3410

Country Club. *Moderate.* 2 mi. S on US 91 at junction of US 87, 89 Bypass. Color TV, heated pool, cafe, bar, 452-9523

Imperial "400" Motel. *Moderate.* 601 2nd Ave. N. Color TV, heated pool, free coffee, cafe nearby. 452-9581

New Villa Motel. *Moderate.* 726 10th Ave. S. Color TV, free coffee, cafe nearby, 453-6596

Royal Motel. *Inexpensive.* 1300 Central Ave. TV, cafe nearby, city pool nearby. Some kitchenettes. 452-9548

Starlit. *Inexpensive.* 1521 1st Ave. N.W. TV, heated pool, playground, free coffee, 24-hour cafe nearby. 452-9597

HAMILTON

Sportsman Motel. *Moderate.* 410 N. 1st St. Color TV, free coffee, cafe nearby. 363-2411

HARDIN

Lariat Motel. *Inexpensive.* 709 N. Center Ave. TV, cafe nearby. 665-2683

HELENA

Colonial Hilton. *Expensive.* 2301 Colonial Dr. Color TV, heated pool, sauna, cafe, bar, dancing, entertainment, barber and beauty shops. Free airport bus. 443-2100

Coach House Motor Inn. *Moderate.* 910 N. Last Chance Gulch. TV, heated pool, 24-hour cafe, bar. Free airport bus. 442-6080

Helena TraveLodge. *Moderate.* 22 N. Last Chance Gulch. Sauna, color TV, *Golden Spike* restaurant and coffee shop, *Four Georgians* lounge, dancing, entertainment. Free airport bus. 443-2200

Holiday Motel. *Moderate.* 1714 11th Ave. Color TV, cafe nearby, clean, comfortable accommodations. Member Best Western. 442-1770

Imperial "400" Motel. *Moderate.* 524 N. Last Chance Gulch. Color TV, pool. 442-0600

Sleeping Giant Lodge. *Moderate.* 2101 11th Ave. Color TV, free coffee, health spa with sauna and exercise equipment, heated pool, *Hare and Hound* lounge, cafe. Free airport bus. 443-2300

KALISPELL

Devonshire Motor Inn. *Moderate.* Main and 5th Sts. Color TV, free coffee, cafe. 756-7136

Four Seasons Motor Inn. *Moderate.* 350 N. Main St. TV, cafe. 756-7104

Blue and White. *Inexpensive.* 640 E. Idaho St. Color TV, free coffee, cafe adjacent. 756-4311

LEWISTON

Yogo Inn Motel. *Moderate.* Main St., east on US 87. Color TV, heated pool, cafe, bar, picnic tables, grill. 538-8721

B & B. *Inexpensive.* 520 E. Main St. Color TV, free coffee, cafe nearby. 538-5497

LIVINGSTON

Del Mar. *Moderate.* ½ mi. W on US 10 Business. Color TV, heated pool, playground, free coffee, 24-hour cafe in area. 222-3120

229

MALTA

Maltana Motel. *Moderate.* 138 1st Ave. W. Color TV, playground, free coffee, 24-hour cafe nearby. 654-2610

MILES CITY

Red Rock Village. *Moderate.* 1½ mi. E on US 10, 12, TV, indoor heated pool, cafe, bar, dancing, entertainment. Free airport bus. 232-4030

War Bonnet Inn. *Moderate.* 1015 S. Haynes Ave. Color TV, heated pool, free Continental breakfast. 232-4560

Miles Howard Hotel. *Inexpensive.* 606 Main St. Bar, barber and beauty shops. Some TV. Restaurant nearby. 232-4220

MISSOULA

Village Motor Inn. *Deluxe.* 100 Madison St. just off Van Buren St. exit of I-90. Color TV, heated pool, therapy pool, sauna, steam baths, restaurant and lounge, beauty shop. 728-3100

Executive Motor Inn. *Expensive.* 201 E. Main St. Color TV, heated pool, cafe. 543-7221

Holiday Inn. *Expensive.* 630 E. Broadway. Color TV, heated pool, cafe. 549-2387

Red Lion Motor Inn. *Expensive.* 700 W. Broadway. Color TV, heated pool, 24-hour cafe. 728-3300

Florence Hotel. *Moderate.* 111 N. Higgins. Color TV, Empire dining room, barber and beauty shops. 543-6631

Forest Inn Motel. *Moderate.* On De Smet Rd. US 10W. TV, restaurants nearby. 728-5110

Hubbard's Ponderosa Lodge. *Moderate.* 800 E. Broadway. TV, cafe nearby, close to town and university. 543-3102

Stewart Motor Inn. *Moderate.* 3530 Brook. Color TV, heated pool, sauna, 24-hour cafe nearby. 728-5050

Ninety Three Motel. *Inexpensive.* 2205 Brooks. Caters to families, some kitchenettes, near shopping center. 549-8742

Sweet Rest Motel. *Inexpensive.* 1135 W. Broadway. TV, kitchenettes, 549-2358

POLSON

Queen's Court. *Moderate.* E on US 93. TV, free Continental breakfast, cafe nearby, boats, fishing, water-skiing available. On Flathead Lake. 883-5385

RED LODGE

Alpine Village. *Moderate.* ¼ mi. N on US 212. TV, large rooms. 446-2213

Bunk House Motor Lodge. *Moderate.* 320 S. Broadway. Color TV, free coffee, cafe nearby. 446-1414

Yodeler Motel. *Moderate.* 601 S. Broadway. TV, free coffee, cafe nearby, playground adjacent. 446-1435

SIDNEY

Park Plaza Motel. *Inexpensive.* 115 6th St. S.W. Color TV, free coffee, cafe nearby, park opposite. 482-1520

VIRGINIA CITY

Fairweather Inn. *Inexpensive.* On State 287. Coffee house opposite, Old West decor. Open June 22 to Labor Day. 843-5377

Nevada City. *Inexpensive.* 1½ mi. W on State 287. Cafe and music hall nearby, gold-mining camp decor. Open May 20 to Sept. 15. 843-5382

WEST YELLOWSTONE

Big Western Pine Motel. *Moderate.* 234 Firehole Ave. on US 191. Color TV, heated pool, cafe nearby, tennis, outdoor fireplaces. Snowmobile available. Open year round. 646-7622.

Roundup Motel. *Moderate.* 3 Madison Ave. Color TV, heated pool, kitchenettes, near restaurant and cocktail lounge. 646-7301

Travel Inn. *Inexpensive.* 103 Gibbon Ave. Heated pool, TV, some kitchenettes, snowmobiles available. 646-7652

Travelers Motor Lodge. *Inexpensive.* 227 Yellowstone Ave. TV, heated pool, restaurant nearby. 646-7313

WHITEFISH

Viking Lodge. *Expensive.* 1¼ mi. N on E. Lake Dr. at Whitefish Lake. TV, heated pool, sauna, cafe, bar, entertainment, recreation room. 862-3547

Downtowner. *Moderate.* 224 Spokane Ave. TV, free coffee, cafe nearby. 862-2535

Mountain Holiday Motel. *Moderate.* 1 mi. S on US 93. Color TV, free coffee, cafe one mile. 862-2548

WEST POINT

Big Sky Motel. *Inexpensive.* ½ mi. E on US 2. TV, cafe nearby, garage. 653-2300

 DINING OUT. Steak, prime ribs and lobster are big favorites in the area and many restaurants cater to this taste. Local game, too, finds its way onto many menus and is worth eating whether it's trout, elk, deer, or buffalo. Prices are for medium-priced items on the menu.

Restaurant price categories are as follows: *Deluxe* will average $9 and up, *Expensive* $6-$8, *Moderate* $3.50–$5.50, and *Inexpensive* $2–$3.50. These prices are for *hors d'oeuvres* or soup, *entrée* and dessert. Not included are drinks, tax and tips. For a more complete explanation of restaurant categories refer to THE ROCKIES & PLAINS *Facts at Your Fingertips* at the front of this volume.

BILLINGS

Golden Belle. *Expensive.* Broadway at 1st Ave. N. in the Northern Hotel. Winner of a Holiday Award for dining distinction. A Gay 90's restaurant specializing in steak and seafood. Open 7 a.m. to 11 p.m., Sun. from 8 a.m. 245-5121

House of Prime Rib. *Expensive.* 1200 N. 27th St. in the Rimrock Lodge. Specialty is prime rib, also serves steak, lobster. Own baking. Open 7 a.m. to 10 p.m. 259-2880

Dude Rancher Lodge. *Moderate.* 415 N. 29th St. Specializing in steak and clam chowder. Good family restaurant. Open 6 a.m. to 10 p.m. 259-5561

BOZEMAN

Topper. *Moderate.* 1235 N. 7th Ave. In the Rambler Hotel. Prime rib is the specialty and children's plates are available. Open 11 a.m. to 1:30 a.m.; Sun. 4 p.m. to midnight. 587-3176

4 B's. *Inexpensive.* 421 W. Main St. A restaurant popular locally that serves chicken, roast beef and steak. Open 24 hours. 587-4661

BUTTE

Lydia's. *Expensive.* 5 mi. S on US 10S. Excellent steak and Italian cuisine, or lobster, chicken. Soft candle lighting. Open 5:30 p.m. to midnight; Sun. and hols. 3:30 to 11 p.m. 494-2000

4 B's Restaurant. *Inexpensive.* 1201 S. Montana at Front St. A locally popular restaurant specializing in chicken and their own desserts. Children's plates are available. Open 6 a.m. to 10 p.m. 792-5311

COOKE CITY

Watuck Lodge Dining Room. *Moderate.* On US 212. Aged steaks and quiet atmosphere set this restaurant off. Open 6 a.m. to 10 p.m. 838-2251

GLACIER NATIONAL PARK

Glacier Park Lodge. *Expensive.* On State 49. Complete dinners of prime rib, trout, steak served with their own baked goods. Open 7 to 9 a.m., noon to

1:30 p.m., 6 to 8:45 p.m. Closed day after Labor Day to June 15. 226-4411

Many Glacier. *Expensive.* Twelve miles west of Babb off US 89. Complete dinners of prime rib, trout, steak served with their own baked goods. Open 7 to 9 a.m., noon to 1:30 p.m., 6 to 8:30 p.m. Closed day after Labor Day to June 15. 732-4311

Lake McDonald Lodge. *Moderate.* Twelve miles northeast of Going-to-the-Sun Rd. Complete dinners of trout, prime rib, steak. Open 7 to 9 a.m., noon to 1:30 p.m., 6 to 8:30 p.m. Closed Sept. 4 to June 14. 888-5431

GLASGOW

Sams Supper Club. *Expensive.* 307 1st Ave. N. An old establishment in Glasgow. Features great steaks, many cooked by Sam himself, and great service. Open 5 to 11:30 p.m. Closed Sun. 228-4614

Clansman. *Moderate.* 101 4th St. N. Excellent sandwiches for lunch and a wide variety of dinners. Open 24 hours. 228-2561

GREAT FALLS

4 B's Red Lion Supper Club. *Expensive.* 3800 10th Ave. S. The motif is Bavarian and the food prime rib, lobster, and steak: Open 5 to 11 p.m.; Fri. and Sat. to midnight; Sun. 4 to 10 p.m. 761-4550

Freight House Restaurant and Bar. *Expensive.* In the old Milwaukee Railroad Depot. Features sandwiches and steak and lobster. The prime rib is excellent. Open 9 a.m. to 11 p.m. 761-8865

Jack Club. *Moderate.* 1512 Vaughn Rd. Steak, lobster, prawns, chicken. Excellent food, particularly the ravioli. Open 5 p.m. to midnight; Sun. from 3 p.m. 452-2207

HAVRE

Red Lion Supper Club. *Expensive.* 604 W. 1st St. One of a chain serving delicious steak, lobster, seafood. Open noon to 3 p.m., 5 to 11 p.m.; Fri. and Sat. to midnight; Sun. to 10 p.m. 265-9930

HELENA

Black Sands Supper Club. *Expensive.* 1200 Euclid Ave. Exquisite food served in a Continental atmosphere. Music for your dining pleasure. A good steak house, also lobster, prime rib, Oriental cuisine. Open 10 a.m. to 2 p.m., 6 to 10 p.m. 442-3600

Colonial Supper Club. *Expensive.* 2301 Colonial Dr. Excellent steaks and prime rib. Also features chicken and seafood. Open 5 to 11 p.m.; Sun. 8 a.m. to 10 p.m.

Golden Spike. *Expensive.* 22 N. Last Chance Gulch. Food with a distinctive old-time goodness. Open noon to 3 p.m., 5 to 10:45 p.m. Closed Sun. 443-2355

Jorgenson's. *Moderate.* 1720 11th Ave. Located in the Holiday Inn, this restaurant serves a wide assortment of good food family style. Open 6:30 a.m. to 10 p.m.; Sun. to 8 p.m. 442-6380

KALISPELL

Hennessy's. *Moderate.* ¼ mi. S just off US 93. Chicken and steak are the specialties of this locally popular restaurant. Open 11:30 a.m. to 2 a.m. 756-3119

MILES CITY

Crossroads Inn. *Moderate.* E on US 10. Seafood. Steak. Chuck-wagon dinners, Tues. to Fri. during the Summer. Sun. buffet. Open 5 to midnight. 232-9999

MISSOULA

Frontier Lounge. *Expensive.* 2 mi. NW on US 10A. An intimately lit restaurant specializing in steaks and baked potatoes. Dancing Wed., Fri., and Sat.

Open 5 p.m. to midnight; Fri. and Sat. from 5:30. Closed Sun. 549-9984

Red Lion Supper Club. *Expensive.* 1210 W. Broadway. A solid restaurant featuring good beef. Wine list. Relaxing atmosphere. Open 5 p.m. to 1 a.m.; Fri. and Sat. to 2 a.m.; Sun. 4 to 10 p.m. 543-6192

Ming's. *Moderate.* 1049 W. Central. Chinese-style dinners in an Oriental atmosphere. Boneless chicken and snow peas is the specialty. Open noon to 10 p.m.; Fri. and Sat. to midnight. 728-9000

POLSON

The Ranch. *Moderate.* On 6th St. W. Good steaks and chicken and information for the Flathead area. Widely known in this region. Entertainment Fri. and Sat. Open 5:30 to 11 p.m.; Fri. and Sat., 5 p.m. to midnight; Sun., 1 p.m. to midnight. 883-2300

WEST YELLOWSTONE

Dude. *Expensive.* Boundary St. at Madison Ave. A locally popular restaurant that serves steak, prime rib, and lobster. Open 5 to 11 p.m. Closed Apr. and Nov. 646-7573

Three Bear. *Moderate.* W of West Gate on US 20, 191. Complete dinners. Specialties are steak and prime rib. Open 7 to 10 a.m., 5 to 10 p.m. Closed Oct. to Dec., Mar. to Apr. 646-7353

WHITEFISH

Big Mountain Chalet. *Expensive.* On top of Big Mountain. A beautiful view awaits you when you come here for food after a hard day of skiing or boating. Dining in the sky. A diverse menu including steak, lobster, crab, ham; salad bar, Open 5:30 to 10:30 p.m. 862-3511

Frenchy's Chinese Gardens. *Expensive.* S on US 93. Chinese food at its best. Open 5 to 11 p.m.; Fri. and Sat. 4 to midnight; Sun. 4 to 11 p.m. 862-2852

NORTH DAKOTA

The Polychromed Prairies

by

JOHN R. MILTON

John R. Milton teaches creative writing at the University of South Dakota and has recently published books on Oscar Howe and Crazy Horse. He has lived in both North and South Dakota.

Because of its position just south of the Lake Winnipeg, Canada, fur country, North Dakota was first explored by the French and British. Between 1738 and 1800 this area was visited by Pierre de la Verendrye, Jonathan Carver, David Thompson, Charles Chaboillez, and Alexander Henry, all noted explorers or fur traders. The first non-Indian child to be born in the state, however, was the daughter of Pierre Bonza and his wife, Negroes, at Henry's Pembina trading post in 1802. Two years later, Lewis and Clark, accompanied by Sacajawea (spelled "Sakakawea" in North Dakota), crossed the state, spending the winter with Mandan Indians, fighting the cold but also commenting on the delightful sunshine. Extensive fur-trapping operations followed immediately. The way was opened for early tourists when, in 1832, "The Yellowstone" made the first steamboat trip up the

Missouri River to Fort Union. Among the passengers during the first years were George Catlin, Prince Maximilian, and John James Audubon. With them came Protestant and Catholic missionaries, but the first permanent settlement was at Pembina in 1851.

Just after the organization of Dakota Territory in 1861, refugees from the Sioux massacre in Minnesota fled to North Dakota for safety. Ironically, they were shortly followed by the Sioux themselves as the army chased Little Crow and his band out of Minnesota. Scattered battles were fought west of the Red River, but they were not serious enough to deter the homesteaders. Greatly increased migration to the northern plains coincided with the building of the Northern Pacific Railroad. Because the railroad went temporarily bankrupt before it spanned the state, impetus was given to migration by the sale of eleven-million acres of the railroad's land grant. Speculators came from Minnesota, Iowa, Illinois, Ohio and elsewhere to buy pieces of land ranging up to 75,000 acres. Not pioneers, they came to get rich quickly. The soil was excellent, and although the growing season was short it featured long and sunny days.

The railroad then advertised widely, using the success of the bonanza farms to lure people from Norway, Germany, Poland, Iceland, and Russia in addition to states east of North Dakota. Most of the advertisements emphasized the "choice prairie, the hard wood timbered lands, the natural meadows, the healthful climate," and of course the convenience of the railroad. The timber was actually in neighboring Minnesota; otherwise the advertising was fairly accurate. Wheat quickly became the major crop, especially spring wheat and the hardy durum used to make macaroni. But the bonanza farmer did not diversify his crops, nor did he always live on his property and take part in community affairs. As a result, he lasted only twenty years, with a few exceptions. As the population grew and the number of smaller farms increased, the land dried out. In their haste to make a profit from the rich soil, the farmers had overworked it. By the time of the big winds in the 1930's, the land was ready to be blown away.

Meanwhile, Custer and his troops had been annihilated by the Sioux, the Indians had been punished and put on reservations, higher education was inaugurated in Jamestown College and the University of North Dakota, and Theodore Roosevelt had come to the state for his health. After all this, in 1889, North Dakota was admitted to statehood. President Harrison signed the proclamation for North and South Dakota at the same time, covering the names so that he would not know which of the two states had been admitted first. Today North Dakota is given alphabetical precedence.

Dakota for Dakotans

At the time North Dakota became a state, the Republican Party was in control. It has retained control ever since, more or less, although state politics have been stormy. Behind many of the controversies of the past seventy-five years has been a feeling of resentment by North Dakotans over their dependence on St. Paul, Minneapolis, and the East. In the early days the railroad, with headquarters in St. Paul, wielded both economic and political influence. Today, Minneapolis is the financial center of the northern prairie region. But North Dakotans are extremely independent, when they can be, and are reluctant to admit competition from outside the state. With the help of A. C. Townley and the Nonpartisan League formed in 1915, they established a state mill and elevator association, a state bank, and a state hail insurance program. These come under occasional criticism, but they still operate and testify to the state's fear of exploitation by outside corporations. For many years most official communications within the state bore the legend, "Buy Dakota Maid Flour" (made at state mills). Later the imprint was changed to "Buy North Dakota Products."

The tension between outstate big business and instate socialism has made North Dakota unique in local politics. Lynn Frazier, the state's first Nonpartisan governor, was removed from office after a recall measure had been passed by the legislature in 1920; however, two years later he was elected to the U.S. Senate. William Langer, the third Nonpartisan governor, was disqualified from office in 1932 and then elected again in 1936. Thomas Moodie, a Democrat, was elected in 1935 and immediately declared ineligible.

The general image of the state is just as confused. Strangers from afar view North Dakota as a Siberian wasteland or a hot dust bowl. It is true that this state holds the western hemisphere record for absolute range in temperature—from 121 degrees above zero to 60 below in the same year. It is true that writers have emphasized the drought in the 1930's because the dust storms were North Dakota's major crisis in modern times. But those days are gone. Crop rotation, irrigation, and conservation methods have stabilized the land, and each year seems to bring a bumper crop. Although industry has not really penetrated the state as yet, the building of the Garrison Dam on the Missouri River has at least made available a vast potential of power for new development. Upstream from the dam lies the largest man-made lake, 609 square miles, and boats now speed back and forth where dust once blew.

North Dakota is a state of contrasts: monotony and beauty, freedom and loneliness, courage and defeat, heat and cold (although dry air moderates both). One can be frightened by the immensity of the land and sky even while experiencing a tremendous exhilaration. It is the tension between these extremes that is exciting and stimulating, if you watch the people closely enough to notice it. Yet, Theodore Roosevelt once said that he could not have become president except for what he learned in North Dakota. One can indeed learn a great deal. A man out in the open is on his own, and he is likely to be independent and self-sufficient in whatever he does.

North Dakota is raw material when compared to many states. Its people are that way too. Highly intelligent, innately bright, they need only be trained (as they are) in order to lead successful lives in a wide variety of vocations and professions. They are eager to learn, and they are now in the midst of a limited but promising growth in schools, art, bookshops, and musical concerts which were denied their parents. Towns are far apart, but highways are straight and fast. Fargo, Jamestown, and Bismarck stand at intervals of one hundred miles; yet, residents drive back and forth as easily as they would go downtown in a large city. From the fertile Red River Valley bordering Minnesota to the western buttes and Badlands, there are no large cities. But there are attractive modern towns resting upon a past which is very close and reaching toward a future which is symbolized by the huge sky of a space-age future.

GENERAL AND PRACTICAL INFORMATION FOR NORTH DAKOTA

 FACTS AND FIGURES. *Dakota* means "allies" in the Sioux language. The state's nicknames are *Flickertail State* and *Sioux State.* The state flower is the wild prairie rose; the state tree, the American elm; the state bird, the western meadow lark. "Liberty and Union, Now and Forever, One and Inseparable" is the state motto. "North Dakota Hymn" is the state song.

Bismarck is the state capital. The state population was 617,761 at the last census.

Lake Sakakawea, formed when the Garrison Dam was erected across the Missouri River, is the largest man-made fresh-water lake in the United States; 609 sq. mi. with 1,340 miles of shoreline.

The world's largest buffalo, a steel and concrete replica of those that once roamed freely across the prairies, stands on a hill overlooking Jamestown.

The geographical center of the U.S., as determined by the Geological Survey, lies ½ mi. S of Rugby, N.D.

North Dakota is the only state that operates a state bank, Bismarck; and mill elevator, Grand Forks.

HOW TO GET THERE. *By air:* Northwest, North Central, and Frontier airlines fly into North Dakota principally from Minneapolis–St. Paul, Rapid City, and Billings.

By train: Amtrak passenger service is available from Minneapolis in the east and from Billings and Havre in the west stopping at Fargo, Bismarck, Williston and Grand Forks.

By bus: Greyhound, Continental and Interstate Transportation Co. are the major interstate carriers in North Dakota.

By car: I–94 and US 2 provide access to the state from Minnesota in the east and from Montana in the west. US 85, 83, 281, and 81 reach the state from South Dakota in the south and run through to Canada in the north.

 HOW TO GET AROUND. *By air:* Frontier flies to Williston, Minot, and Bismarck. Northwest provides service among Bismarck, Fargo, and Jamestown and between Fargo and Grand Forks. North Central lands in Devils Lake, Grand Forks, Fargo, Bismarck, and Minot.

By train: Amtrak has two branch lines, one through Fargo, Grand Forks, Devils Lake, Minot and Williston, the other through Fargo, Jamestown, Bismarck and Dickinson.

By bus: in addition to the service provided by Greyhound, Continental, and Interstate Transportation Co., Star Bus Lines serves Grand Forks, Devils Lake and Minot and other local carriers connect the smaller cities.

By car: I–94 is the major east–west route across the southern portion of the state and US 2 across the northern. US 81, 281, 83 and 85 run north–south. US 52 extends in a rough diagonal from Fargo and Jamestown in the southeast to Minot, Kenmare, and Portal in the northwest.

 TOURIST INFORMATION. The *Roughrider Guide to North Dakota* is a particularly useful summary of the principal attractions, parks, campgrounds, museums, and events in North Dakota. This brochure and other information are available from North Dakota Highway Dept., State Capitol Grounds, Bismarck 58501.

The Greater North Dakota Assn., Box 1781, Fargo 58102 also provides useful information.

 SEASONAL EVENTS. *February:* The *Winterfest* in Minot at mid-month features curling and hockey competition, Festival of Ethnic Foods, snowmobile races, which include the Regina Minot Itasca International 250 Race, a beard-growing contest, and other exciting events.

March: At Valley City, early in the month, is the *North Dakota Winter Show*, the largest agricultural exposition in the northwest, which includes a livestock show and three-day rodeo. At the Winter Show Building. The *National Curling Finals* are held at Grand Forks.

May: Fishing Derby, Fort Totten: competitive fishing on Devils Lake. *Stock car racing* begins mid-month at Grand Forks Speedway. Beginning in late-month, the Fort Totten Reservation holds *powwow, horse and chariot races* Sun. afternoons through Sept. at Fort Totten.

June: Beginning in June for 8 wks., the *International Festival of the Arts* takes place in the International Peace Garden. A cultural festival, this features special activities in each area of the arts including dance, drama, music, fine art, sculpture, and crafts and performances by the International Music Camp participants. The *State Championship Horse Show* takes place mid-month at Rugby. On the Turtle Mountain Reservation at Belcourt there are *Sun Dance* and *Grass Dance* in early June. Late in the month there are the *Upper Missouri Valley Fair* at Williston and the *Centennial*

Celebration at Grand Forks. The *Lewis and Clark Pageant*, at the Ft. Mandan Historic Site in Washburn, depicts the early explorers' era.

July: Dickinson hosts the *Roughriders Festival.* The *North Dakota State Fair* at Minot highlights fair activities with a midway, rodeo and entertainment. At mid-month, Bottineau hosts a *Water-Ski Carnival* at Lake Metigoshe. *Buffalo Days* at Jamestown offers several attractions including the Stutsman County Fair and State Dairy Show, historic trail rides between Ft. Ranson and Ft. Lincoln, and parades and rodeos. The *Red River Valley Fair* and the *State Machinery Show* are at Fargo.

August: Champions Ride Rodeo, at Home on the Range for Boys in Sentinel Butte, features the top rodeo riders and calf ropers in the world of rodeo. The *All-Indian Rodeo and Powwow* on the Fort Berthold Reservation at New Town.

September: The World Championship, All-American Indian Activities Association, Powwow and Rodeo Finals is a major Indian event in North Dakota. Held in early September on the Standing Rock Reservation at Fort Yates, it attracts Indians from all over the nation. The *Badlands Trail Ride* draws horseback riders from across the state for a six-day ride through the badlands area around Kildeer and Medora. *Annual Threshing Bee* at Edgeley consists of threshing on grounds with steam and gas engines, large display of pioneer tools, rope making demonstrations, parades, and antique cars and trucks. In Fargo, the *Imagination Art Festival* focuses on the multiple arts available in the area including workshops, displays, demonstrations, and performances in the visual, performing and popular arts. *Pioneer Days*, held in Bonanzaville, U.S.A., in West Fargo, demonstrate pioneer methods in action.

October: New Leipzig hosts the *Annual Sauerkraut Day*, Wishek, and the *October Fest* in community celebrations tied closely to the German population of the region.

December: Ski season begins.

NATIONAL PARKS. The *Theodore Roosevelt National Memorial Park* in western North Dakota is the nation's only national memorial park and a memorial to the 26th President who, in addition to his other vigorous pursuits, was a champion of conservation and natural resources.

Set in the area the Indians called *mako sica*—bad lands to cross—the Park displays the harsh natural beauty of canyons and valleys, of buttes and cliffs, shaped and molded by centuries of wind, water, and fire.

There are two major units to the Park: the South unit whose attractions include prairie dog towns, nature trails, burning coal veins, columnar junipers and a variety of wildlife; and the North Unit, 65 mi. N on US 85, which offers a majestic view of a more rugged section of the badlands. A third unit, Teddy Roosevelt's Elkhorn Ranch site on the Little Missouri River north of Medora, is accessible only over rough dirt roads. Consult Park Headquarters in Medora before setting out.

The rebuilt *Old West cowtown of Medora* is located at the entrance to the South Unit. Theodore Roosevelt and the Marquis de Mores made history here. The park headquarters has a visitor center and museum, open 8 to 8 in the summer and 8 to 5 in winter. Theodore Roosevelt's original Maltese Cross cabin stands nearby.

STATE PARKS. *Beaver Lake State Park,* 2 mi. N & 1 mi. E of Burnstad, offers swimming, fishing, picnicking, camping, and trailer space. *Fort Lincoln State Park,* 4 mi. S of Mandan on Rte. 1806, is on the Missouri River. It was from here that Custer set out on the disastrous Little Bighorn Expedition. Besides camping and picnicking, visitors can see the original fort site, restored blockhouses, Indian mounds and a museum. *Icelandic State Park* is 5 mi. W. at Cavalier, Rte. 5. Swimming, fishing and boating are available. Camping and trailers are permitted. *Lake Metigoshe State Park* is 13 mi. NE of Bottineau and is near the *International Peace Garden.* A variety of wildlife is found here, and deciduous forests, rolling glacial moraine and beautiful lakes make this one of the most attractive areas in the state where visitors can enjoy fishing, water sports, picnicking and camping. *Turtle River State Park*, 22 mi. W on Rte. 2, Grand Forks, in the forests of the fertile Red River Valley, has water sports, fishing, cabins, ski chalet, camping and trailer facilities for summer and winter fun. *Lake Sakakawea State Park*, 1 mi. N of Pick City, has facilities for camping, boating, fishing, and swimming, picnicking and water-skiing on Lake Sakakawea. *Little Missouri Bay State Park* is 18 mi. N of Killdeer on Rte. 22. Located in some of the state's most rugged badlands terrain, this park offers camping, picnicking, canoeing, hiking, and horseback riding. There are no roads in the interior of the park. *Doyle Memorial State Park*, 7 mi. SE of Wishek, has primitive camping, picnicking, swimming and fishing. *Sully Creek State Park*, 2½ mi. S of Medora on the East River Rd., is an ideal area for horseback riders and offers primitive campground, horse corral, and picnic area.

Entry fees at state parks are $1 per vehicle per day or $4 per vehicle for an annual permit. A fee of 50¢ per vehicle is charged for groups of ten or more traveling together. In addition, a $2 per night, $10 per week, or $15 annual camping fee is charged. North Dakota has approximately 200 camping areas. For a complete list and map write to the North Dakota State Travel Division, Bismarck.

 FARM VACATIONS AND GUEST RANCHES. *Bel-Brothers Ranch.* A Turtle Mountains setting with a trailer house for guests (outside toilet). Also for campers. Riding, pack trips, Wild West shows Sundays. Seven children in family. Box 204, Dunseith 58329.

Joe J. Hansel Farm. A working farm with cattle, ponies, pigs, chickens, geese. Riding and fishing. Serve one meal a day. Seven children. Meets all nearby transit. Rte. 1, Box 80, Langdon 58249.

Kauk Creek Farm. A beef and dairy operation where you can pitch in or relax. Three small children, German cooking. Room for one small family. Rte. 1, Box 163, Wishek 58495.

Lakeshore Fun Farm. Work is producing grain, while fun is ponies, horses, boating and swimming. Complete farmhouse for 10. Penn 58362.

T-Bone Ranch. Grain and livestock here. Cottage has wood-burning range, Franklin fireplace, bunkbeds. And, of course, T-bone steaks fattened before your eyes. Rte. 1, Stanley 58784.

CAMPING OUT. For a complete list of campgrounds and their facilities contact the North Dakota State Travel Division in Bismarck. Given below is a brief list of campgrounds at or near the major cities or tourist attractions.

Theodore Roosevelt National Memorial Park: in the South Unit, Cottonwood Campground has fishing, fireplaces, picnic tables, drinking water and flush toilets; North Unit, Squaw Creek Campground has playground, fireplaces, picnic tables, drinking water and flush toilets. There is no charge for use of the picnic or camp grounds and there are evening campfire programs in summer. Normally, the South Unit is more crowded than the North Unit.

Lake Sakakawea: Totten Trail Park, E of US 83 and S of Garrison jct., has swimming, fishing, boating, fireplaces, picnic tables, drinking water and pit toilets.

Devils Lake: Lakewood Park, 5 mi. SW of city, has swimming, fishing, boating, playground, fireplaces, picnic tables, drinking water and flush toilets.

Bismarck: General Sibley Campground, 4 mi. S on Washington St., has fishing, boating, playground, fireplaces, picnic tables, showers, drinking water, and flush toilets.

Fargo: Lindenwood Park, 5th St. and 7th Ave. S., has fishing, boating, playground, fireplaces, picnic tables, showers, drinking water and flush toilets.

Jamestown: Jamestown Reservoir-George's Landing, 7 mi. N on US 281 then 2 mi. E, has swimming, fishing, boating, playground, fireplaces, picnic tables, showers, drinking water and flush toilets.

Williston: Lewis and Clark Recreation Area, 18 mi. E on Rte. 1804 then 3 mi. S at Lake Sakakawea, has swimming, fishing, boating, drinking water, and flush toilets.

 TRAILER TIPS. Mobile home and camper trailer regulations are: length not more than 70 feet, width not over 8 feet, height not over 12½ feet. Wider mobile homes and trailers require special permits and are not allowed to travel at night, or on Saturday p.m., Sunday and holidays. Speed limit for all mobile homes is 50 mph.

In addition to the facilities already listed under *Camping Out,* the following areas also have trailer facilities:

Theodore Roosevelt National Memorial Park: in the South Unit, Cottonwood Campground has 53 trailer sites; Squaw Creek has 18 sites.

Lake Sakakawea: Totten Trail Park has large areas devoted to trailer sites; Fort Stevenson Recreation Area, 3 mi. S and ½ mi. W of Garrison, has a large area devoted to trailer sites, sewage disposal and hookup, and 10 electrical connections in addition to complete campground facilities.

Devil's Lake: Lakewood Park has 30 trailer sites with electrical hookups.

Bismarck: General Sibley Campground has 120 trailer sites, 95 electrical hookups, and sewage disposal.

Fargo: Lindenwood Park has 40 trailer sites with 30 electrical hookups.

Jamestown: Jamestown Reservoir has 50 sites with 39 electrical hookups.

Williston: Lewis and Clark has 50 sites with electrical hookups and sewage disposal.

 MUSEUMS AND GALLERIES. Historical: *Bismarck: Historical Society Museum,* on the Capitol Grounds. The State collection of 19th-century Indian and pioneer artifacts can be seen Mon. through Fri., 9 to 5; Sat. 9 to 4: Sun. in summer, 1 to 5. Free. Another collection is at the *Camp Hancock Museum,* Main and 1st Sts. Open mid-May to mid-Sept. 9 to noon and 1 to 5, Mon. through Fri., and from 9 to noon and 1 to 4 on Sat. Free. *Devils Lake: Pioneer Museum,* at Fort Totten, 14 mi. S on Rte. 57. Open daily 1 to 5, June to Labor Day.

Art: *Grand Forks: University Art Gallery,* U of North Dakota. Features work of artists in and around North Dakota; regional grass roots art. Mon. to Fri., noon to 9:30; Sat. & Sun. 1 to 5. Free. Closed University holidays. *Medora: Western Gallery.* Pioneer quiltwork displays and sculpture and paintings by western artists. Daily May to Oct., 8 to 8. Free.

Special Interest: *Abercrombie: Fort Abercrombie State Park Museum* features a rare Red River ox cart from the early fur trade, Indian artifacts, pioneer and military exhibits. May to Oct., Mon. to Sat. 9 to 9, Sun. 10 to 9. Adults 25¢, children 10¢. *Fargo: Herbarium & County Museum,* in Minard Hall on University campus. Open from 1 to 5, Tues. through Fri. *Grand Forks: University of North Dakota Zoology Museum.* Mon. to Fri., 9 to 6; Sat. 9 to 5. Free. *Jamestown: Fort Seward Historical Society, Inc.,* 321 3rd Ave., SE. General collection. June to Sept., Wed., Sun. 2 to 5 & 7 to 9. Free. *Stutsman County Memorial Museum,* 321 3rd Ave. SE. Indian artifacts, medical, military and musical exhibits. June to Oct., Wed., Sun. 2 to 9. Free. *Mandan: Fort Abraham Lincoln State Park Museum.* Mandan Indian artifacts; 7th Cavalry and Custer. May, Sept. to Oct. daily 9 to 5; June to Aug. 9 to 9. Adults 25¢; children 5 to 12, 10¢; under 6 free. *Medora: Doll House Museum,* 18th-, 19th- & 20th-century dolls and toys. 8 to 8, May to Oct. Adults 50¢; children 25¢. *Fur Trade, Wild Life, and Indian Museum,* May to Oct., 8 to 8. Adults $1; children 6 to 15, 25¢; under 6 free *Wahpeton: Richland County Historical Museum,* housed in an

241

old schoolhouse. June to Oct. 20. Tues. to Sun. 2 to 5; Oct. 20 to May. Fri. to Sun. 2 to 5. Free. Closed holidays. *West Fargo: Bonanzaville, USA,* museum furnished with many artifacts telling the story of the early settlement days in North Dakota, located in the Cass County Fair Grounds. June through Oct. Mon. through Fri. 9:30 to 5, Sat. & Sun. 1 to 5; rest of yr. Tues., Thurs. & Fri. 9:30 to 4. Adults $1, children 6 to 16, 50¢, under 6 free. *Williston: Frontier Museum,* 3 mi. N on US 2, 85. May to Labor Day, Mon. to Sat. 7 to 9; Sun., hols. 2 to 8. Adults $1; students 50¢; under 9 free.

HISTORIC SITES. Many sites and remnants of forts remain from the Indian wars. Perhaps the ones remembered best were associated with those two archfoes, Lt. Col. George A. Custer and Sitting Bull. Custer is often referred to as a "general," but he lost his brevet commission because of a number of "mistakes." Sitting Bull is known as the chief of the Sioux, but, in reality, he was the peace chief, or civil chief.

Custer commanded the 7th Cavalry at *Fort Lincoln:* from here he took his men to Montana where he and approximately 200 of his unit were killed. The fort is gone, but many of the foundations of the original building may be seen around the parade ground, about 5 mi. S of Mandan. The site of Custer's home is marked in Officers Row across the road. Up on the hill, in 1875, stood an infantry post, Fort McKeen. Three blockhouses have been rebuilt there. An excellent museum tells the story of Custer's fame and misfortune. The museum is open May through October, 9 a.m. to 5 p.m. on weekdays, and 1–5 p.m. on Sundays and holidays. Near the museum stand reconstructed Indian earth lodges at a spot visited by Lewis and Clark in 1804.

Sitting Bull fled to Canada after Custer's death, but returned in 1881 to surrender at *Fort Buford,* 5 mi. W of Williston on US 2 and then 17 mi. SW following the signs. On the Missouri, the stone powder magazine and the officers' headquarters still stand. A military cemetery is nearby. Museum, open June 15 to September 15, 9 to 6. Free.

Medora, west end of the state on US 10, was the scene of many fascinating events involving Theodore Roosevelt and the Marquis de Mores. The Rough Riders Hotel gave its name to Roosevelt's regiment in the Spanish-American War. The Joe Ferris Store was visited often by Roosevelt. St. Mary's Catholic Church was built by the Marquis. All of these buildings date back to about 1885.

Just west of Medora, and ½ mile S of US 10, are the ruins of the De Mores packing plant and the intact 26-room chateau in which he lived. Admission charged, 8 a.m. to 5 p.m. Guided tours only. Closed when weather is bad.

The *Fort Mandan Historic Site,* 4 mi. W of Washburn, overlooks the site of the Lewis and Clark winter camp near the Mandan Indians. A pageant depicting the Lewis and Clark era is held annually in June.

Pembina Historic Site and Museum, 50 mi. NE of Grafton via US 81, I–29 in Pembina. This is the site of the first settlement in North Dakota established in 1812. The museum is open 9 to 5 daily, May 15 to Sept. 15; closed rest of year.

Twenty-eight mi. NW of Ellendale is the *Whitestone Battlefield Historic Site.* This is the site of the largest major battle between whites and Sioux Indians east of the Missouri River.

The best preserved military post of the Indian Wars period in the Trans-Mississippi West is located at the *Fort Totten Historic Site* at Fort Totten. Fifteen original buildings remain with a museum and summer theater located on the site.

Fort Union National Historic Site, 5 mi. W of Williston on US 2, then SW on an unnumbered road. Fort Union was constructed as a fur trading post in 1828 at the confluence of the Yellowstone and Missouri Rivers. It was built and operated by the American Fur Company. The first steamboat, the "Yellowstone," owned by the

Fur Company, navigated the Missouri to Fort Union in 1832. Guided tours of the site are provided by National Park Service during summer months. (This Historic Site is shared with Montana.)

FAMOUS LIBRARIES. The *Chester Fritz Library* on the campus of the University of North Dakota in Grand Forks has a display of Oriental tapestries and other art works. Open Mon. to Fri. 8 a.m. to 4:30 p.m.

GARDENS. The *International Peace Garden*, with over 2,300 acres on both sides of the Canadian border, is 13 mi. N of Dunseith. Dedicated as a monument to the peaceful coexistence the United States and Canada have enjoyed for 200 years, the Garden forms a tranquil setting with flowers, trees, pools and walks. An all-faiths Peace Chapel with quotations from men of peace throughout history is an impressive sight. Camping, picnicking, and cabins are available. The Garden is open year-round, but the best time to visit is from May through September.

MUSIC. The *International Music Camp*, held each summer at the International Peace Garden, has become recognized as one of the leading summer schools of fine arts in both the US and Canada. This unique cultural center includes instruction, performances and exhibits in all areas of the fine arts. On alternative years, a select group of 140 music students serve as "musical ambassadors" from the U.S. and Canada and present a series of good-will concerts throughout England, Western Europe, and North America. These tour bands and choirs have won top honors at three international youth music contests and festivals in Europe.

Through June and July, the International Music Camp gives Sun. afternoon concerts in the International Peace Garden led by internationally known guest conductors.

STAGE AND REVUES. *Fort Totten Little Theatre*, in Old Cavalry Sq. of the Fort Totten Historic Site, offers summer musicals produced by the Devils Lake Community Theatre. Performances take place from July to mid-Aug. on Thurs., Sat., and Sun. at 8 p.m. Adults $2.50, children under 12, $1.50.

Sosondawah Amphitheatre, on the Dickinson State College campus, has summer melodrama productions from late June to July, Wed. to Sun. at 8:30 p.m. Adults $1.50–$2, children, 75¢–$1.

Medora Musical, in the Gold Seal Amphitheatre 1 mi. SW of Medora. This stage production in an open-air theatre that overlooks the Medora countryside presents early Dakota territory history in a blend of comedy, music and special acts as a tribute to Theodore Roosevelt, the 26th Pres., who ranched in Medora as a young man. Performances nightly July 1 to Labor Day. Adults $2.50, children 6–16, $1.25.

DRINKING LAWS. Liquor can be purchased by the drink at bars and by the bottle at stores from 8 a.m. to 1 a.m. No liquor is sold on Sunday, after 6 p.m. on Christmas Eve and all Christmas Day, election day, and Memorial Day. Legal drinking age is 21.

TOURS. *Theodore Roosevelt National Park*, located in the western North Dakota badlands, has a 28-mile circle scenic drive through the badlands. Wild animals abound. The earth formations are multicolored, and flowers bloom in odd places in the summer. For an unusual

243

night scene, see the burning coal vein in the South Unit. For further ideas, talk to the rangers inside the Medora entrance to the park.

The *Lewis and Clark Trail,* which follows the scenic Missouri River through the heart of North Dakota, also parallels Lewis and Clark's famous Missouri River Expedition. Boat launching facilities, historic sites and recreation areas are located at several locations on the trail. The *Garrison Dam,* one of the largest rolled earth dams in the nation, and the 200-mile-long man-made lake, Lake Sakakawea, are part of the immense river system.

INDUSTRIAL TOURS. The *William Langer Jewel Bearing Plant* in Rolla offers tours to those who make appointments. Operated by the Bulova Watch Company for the federal government, this plant produces tiny jewels from synthetic sapphires for defense weapons and time-pieces. It is the largest jewel bearing factory in the U.S. 477-3193

Westgo Industries in West Fargo is a manufacturer of truck bodies, rock pickers and auger elevators as well as the installation of truck equipment and related items. Tours of their plant at 405 W. Main Ave. take place Mon. to Fri., 1–1:30 p.m. 282-3264

Rugby Creamery Company offers tours of their installation at 209 W. Dewey St. in Rugby which include a look at the making of cheese, butter, ice cream and at milk bottling. Tours Mon. to Fri., 10 a.m. to 2 p.m. 776-5288

SPECIAL INTEREST TOURS. *Sully Hill National Game Preserve,* 12 mi. SW of Devils Lake on State 57, has a self-guided auto tour through this scenic acreage where bison, elk, and deer can be observed in a near natural habitat. There are also flocks of ducks, geese and swans. Open May to Oct., daily 8 a.m. to sunset. The *Audubon National Wildlife Refuge* at Garrison Dam has a short auto tour for wildlife observation. Open daily during daylight hours.

The *Old Danish Mill* in Kenmare is one of six such mills in the nation. Built over 70 years ago, it could grind 200 bushels of grain a day. The millstones weigh 1,800 lbs., the wooden gears are hand hewn, and its mechanism still operates. Open daily 7 a.m. to 9 p.m.

Bonanzaville, USA, restored in the tradition of the bonanza farm days, is located in West Fargo. A vintage church, school, barbershop, general store, theater and other historic buildings have been restored and furnished as they were in the early days of North Dakota statehood. A museum in the village helps tell the historic tale.

Frontier Village, on I–94 in SE Jamestown, is a reconstructed authentic frontier village with railroad depot, land office, fire hall, newspaper-print shop, jail, knick-knack shops, restaurant, drug store, barbershop, church, school, and log cabin. Towering above the village is the world's largest buffalo. This landmark, 46 ft. long and 26 ft. high, made of 60 tons of steel reinforced concrete, is a memorial to the vast herds of buffalo that once thundered across these prairies. Open Memorial Day to Labor Day, 9 to 9.

SPORTS. *Fishing.* Major sport, particularly since completion of Missouri River dam. Small lakes included in 128 areas. All-year angling fine for perch, crappies, blue gills, catfish, and bullheads. Best winter fishing in well-stocked Garrison Reservoir. Game fishing great except March 27 to May 7, northern pike, muskellunge, walleyes, sauger, trout, and bass. Non-resident license: week, $2; season, $6. "Whopper Club" membership (Game and Fish Department) for large catfish and pike. *Hunting.* Extremely popular. Whitetail deer throughout state; mule deer in west; antelope in southwest. Birds galore. One of the best duck areas in the United States. Pheasants in southern

244

third of the state, geese coming down flyway from Canada enticing. Partridge; three kinds of grouse. Write Game and Fish Department, 2121 Lovett Avenue, Bismarck, North Dakota 58501 for further information. *Golf.* Eastern section best. Fargo boasts four courses. One of Grand Forks' two links, Lincoln Park, borders Red River. Wahpeton's Bois de Sioux course has elaborate 1966 clubhouse; Chahinkapa Park, next door, offers excellent swimming pool. Sand greens found west of Valley City. The Travel Division has a complete list. *Swimming.* In state parks and reservoirs. Along Missouri, water sports at Garrison, Riverdale, New Town, Williston. Jamestown Reservoir and Ashtabula Reservoir (20 mi. N of Valley City) have complete aquatic facilities. Most towns over 10,000 population have pools. *Horseback riding.* Horse rentals and guided trail rides available at Rhame, Turtle River State Park at Arvilla, Medora, Peaceful Valley Ranch in Theodore Roosevelt National Park and the Little Missouri Bay State Recreation Area north of Killdeer. *Canoeing.* The water level is best in late May and early June but in some cases canoeing on the rivers is possible into late fall. Some parts of the Missouri River are recommended for experienced canoers only. For those unfamiliar with the territory, county maps are available from the Maps Sales Division of the State Highway Dept.

Skiing. There are six ski areas located at Devils Lake, Bottineau, Rolla, Edinburg, Arvilla and Fort Ranson. Cross-country skiing is becoming increasingly popular and the North Dakota countryside lends itself well to this sport. *Snowmobiling.* Theodore Roosevelt National Park and all the state parks have snowmobiling trails.

SPECTATOR SPORTS. *Rodeo* is a big event in North Dakota and nearly every town of any size sponsors one or more throughout the year. Among the major events are North Dakota State Fair at Minot and Roughrider Festival at Dickinson. *Hockey:* the University of North Dakota Fighting Sioux in Grand Forks competes in the Western Collegiate Hockey Association. The Canadian Estevan Bruins, a semi-pro hockey team, thrills fans in Bismarck. *Curling.* The National Curling Finals are held annually in Grand Forks and several other competitions take place locally, particularly in the eastern and northern portions of the state. The colleges offer *basketball* and *football* action. *Auto racing.* Stock car racing takes place at the Grand Forks Speedway from mid-May to mid-Sept. on Fri. and hols., 8 to 10:30 p.m. Adults $2; children to 14, $1.

WHAT TO DO WITH THE CHILDREN. Playground facilities and parks are available at many towns in North Dakota. A few areas have amusement centers and zoos. In *Bismarck*, the Riverside Sertoma Park is located near the Missouri River. It includes a playground. Next to the Park is the Dakota Zoo with over 100 species of native animals. The zoo is open every day from 10 a.m. to 8 p.m. mid-May through September. A miniature train ride takes visitors through the zoo. The playground at *Devils Lake* is in the Sullys Hill Game Preserve 14 mi. S of town. *Jamestown* features the world's largest buffalo and Frontier Fort for the children. In *Minot*, the Roosevelt Park and Zoo includes not only many animals but also a children's amusement park with a swimming and wading pool.

In *Wahpeton*, children enjoy the zoo and birds at Chahinkapa Park on the Red River while mom strolls through the gardens and dad plays golf (half in North Dakota and half in Minnesota). An Old West adventure can be enjoyed at the restored cowtown, *Medora*. Special features include: feeding of the elk and buffalo, the Medora Zoo, Dollhouse Museum, art gallery, Medora Museum, and the Medora Musical.

Williston's Spring Lake Park has wild animal collections, swimming, playgrounds and hiking trails. Open all year from 8 to 5.

The *Fish Hatchery* at Garrison Dam produces northern pike, walleye, smallmouth bass and rainbow trout for waters in the area. There is an aquarium where children can get a close look at these different types of fish.

INDIANS. North Dakota has four American Indian Reservation locations across the state which are inhabited by the Sioux, Mandan, Hidatsa, Arickara and Chippewa Tribes. A South Dakota reservation known as the Lake Traverse Indian Reservation extends a little into the southeastern corner of North Dakota.

The *Turtle Mountain Indian Reservation,* located about ten miles east of the International Peace Gardens and ten miles south of the Canadian border, is the home of the Turtle Mountain Band of Chippewa. Although the smallest in area (only two townships), this reservation has the largest population of the four. The tribal headquarters is located in the community of Belcourt. Area powwows are usually held in July.

The *Fort Totten Indian Reservation,* located just south of the city of Devils Lake, is the home of the Sisseton-Wahpeton Sioux Tribe, better known as the Devils Lake Sioux. A well-preserved Cavalry Post stands on this reservation land. The tribal headquarters is located in the community of Fort Totten. A number of rodeos and powwows are conducted from spring to early fall.

The *Fort Berthold Indian Reservation,* located near the center of the western half of North Dakota, is the home of the Three Affiliated Tribes (Mandan, Hidatsa, Arickara). This reservation is divided into five segments which surround beautiful Lake Sakakawea. A forty–unit motel is owned and operated by the tribes on the Four Bears Recreation Complex. The tribal council office is located in the community of New Town. Rodeos and powwows are held throughout the summer months.

The *Standing Rock Indian Reservation,* located on the west bank of Oahe Reservoir (Missouri River), also extends into South Dakota. The North Dakota portion includes all of Sioux County. The tribal council headquarters is located in the community of *Fort Yates.* Chief Sitting Bull was buried at Fort Yates. Also at Fort Yates is a statue of the Indian woman who turned to stone when she looked around, this incident giving its name "Standing Rock" to the area. Powwows and rodeos are held at various communities throughout the summer months.

All of the above reservation locations offer an abundance of recreational activity. Your visit will be quite welcomed at any one of these areas.

RECOMMENDED READING. *The History of North Dakota* by Elwyn B. Robinson is a good general history of the state. Two other excellent books deal with specific periods: *Nothing but Prairie and Sky: Life on the Dakota Range in the Early Days* by Walker D. Wyman and *The Day of the Bonanza* by Hiram Drache.

EXPLORING NORTH DAKOTA

Except for the northern fur traders, Fargo has always been the main entry to North Dakota. It is the state's largest city, with a population of 50,000, and it wants to be Eastern and cultured. In this endeavor it has help from its Minnesota neighbor, Moorhead, just across the river, which has two colleges. The Fargo-Moorhead area has been designated a standard metropolitan area with a population of 123,000.

The Northern Pacific Railroad brought life to this area in 1871 as fortune seekers dashed up and down the Red River of the North trying to guess where the railroad would cross. Once the tracks reached Moorhead, a settlement called "Fargo in the Timber" sprang up on the west side of the river, with a post office called first Centralia then Fargo, after the head of the Wells-Fargo Express.

The rich soil of the Red River Valley is the result of glacial action which formed Lake Agassiz centuries ago. The people of the area recognize their reliance upon agriculture. More than three thousand farms are located within a 50-mile radius. Major crops are grains, potatoes, and sugar beets. In northwest Fargo, the North Dakota State University conducts agricultural research, maintains grain and animal experimentation farms, and through its Institute for Regional Studies stimulates research into the resources of the region. The interest in culture lags behind that in agriculture, but the arts are being encouraged. Poets and publishers of little magazines work back and forth between Fargo and Moorhead to give the area significant literary activity.

Fargo keeps its eye on Minneapolis but goes ahead with projects to modernize and beautify the city. Several years ago a slum area was replaced by a new Civic Center costing ten million dollars. For this, Fargo was designated an All-American city. A newer project is called "Main Avenue Urban Renewal" and involves six blocks along both sides of Main Avenue, parallel to the Northern Pacific tracks.

In contrast to the city's concern for the future is the Forsberg House collection of historical objects and paintings; but for a more serious look into the past, one must drive to Fort Abercrombie, about an hour to the south on US 81. Partially restored, this was the first federal fort in North Dakota, established in 1857. It was subjected to a long-term attack by the Sioux Indians during the 1862 uprising in nearby Minnesota. The grounds now contain a stockade, blockhouses, and museum.

Just a few miles south of Abercrombie, the North Dakota State School of Science and the Indian School are located in Wahpeton.

A recent teacher at this Indian School was Mrs. Robert Horne, a great-great granddaughter of Sacajawea, the Indian girl who helped guide the Lewis and Clark expedition as far as Idaho in 1805.

Side Trip to Grand Forks

The border between North Dakota and Minnesota is mainly comprised of the Red River of the North. This unusual river flows northward, emptying into Lake Winnipeg. To drive north from Fargo on US 81 is to cross some of the flattest land to be seen. Paradoxically, the tallest structure in the state rises from the prairie—the tower for Fargo's Station KTHI-TV (2,063 feet) south of Mayville on State 18. At the end of a 77-mile stretch lies Grand Forks, with a large, growing air force base, and the expanding University of North Dakota. Here, in the center of the nation, a new program in education is proceeding successfully while at the same time scholars are interpreting the past. The old and the new exist together, the union symbolized not long ago when a spacecraft flew high above an ox-cart train celebrating an anniversary. North of Grand Forks, in the northeast corner of the state lies Pembina, site of the first two settlements in North Dakota, now a state park. The first, in 1797, was for fur traders. These men later resented the Scottish immigrants brought by the Earl of Selkirk in 1812.

Westward Through Flatlands

Although the early fur traders came in from the North, and Lewis and Clark came in from the South, the main entry to modern North Dakota is Fargo. The 19th-century trail which ambled west from here is now a fast four-lane highway which gently winds its way across the flat and broad prairie. Where tall grass once grew, and buffalo bones were scattered over the earth, wheat now waves in the brisk winds. The land appears crude and monotonous, yet Holger Cahill found here a mystic quality which he wrote about in his novel, *The Shadow of My Hand*. The horizon seems too far away to reach, even in a speeding automobile. Sky is everywhere, and one must look down occasionally at the ducks swimming in sloughs and ditch-pools to realize that he is not in an airplane. The first real break in the flatness is the Sheyenne River Valley. Here in Valley City is the oldest of the state teachers colleges. North of the city, Lake Ashtabula is a 27-mile recreational area formed by the damming of the Sheyenne River. The entire valley is a refreshing oasis on the plains, with fishing, boating, swimming, and camping.

The landscape changes little as we proceed west, except that slightly rolling hills, low ridges, shallow coulees, and a few small lakes indicate the western end of glacial Lake Agassiz, the huge lake of ten thousand years ago that flattened eastern North Dakota. The glacier probably ended at the Missouri River, and at that time the Missouri probably flowed in what is now the James River Valley. Here the highway passes Jamestown, said to be the prettiest city in the state because of its two rivers, the valley which curves like a crescent, the parks and trees, and the wide streets. In 1872, Jamestown was the site of Fort Seward, built to protect the railroad workers and the travelers who crossed the river at this point. From where the fort stood, a little north of town and above the valley, one can look down at the river and a good portion of the valley in which Jamestown stands. Almost immediately below is the nationally famous Crippled Children's School, directed by Dr. Ann Carlson. Across the valley, on the opposite bluff, stands Jamestown College, one of North Dakota's two private liberal arts colleges (Presbyterian). On another hill nearby, a pioneer town and a large buffalo statue are new landmarks.

Up the river one mile, the Jamestown Dam Recreation Area is a 14-mile lake behind a large earthen dam. This is the most popular swimming, boating, fishing, and picnicking area for many miles around. Upstream thirty miles, the Arrowwood National Wildlife Refuge is a nesting and feeding ground for migratory birds and various kinds of wildlife. Twice a year the skies over Jamestown are almost blackened by millions of migrating ducks and geese. Because there is no longer an unlimited number of ducks for hunting, a one-million dollar Northern Prairie Wildlife Research Center has been built in Jamestown. At the Center's I. G. Bue Laboratory, research is carried on to try to maintain the kind of hunting conditions which have existed in the past. Adding to Jamestown's reputation as a wildlife center, Carl E. Strutz recently discovered an Aleutian Goose, long thought to be extinct. Strutz is a resident of Jamestown and is associated with the International Wild Waterfowl Association.

Art in Jamestown tends to be imitative, especially of the Western past, although a variety of paintings may often be seen on exhibit in local restaurants. J. A. Kirkpatrick maintains a studio at 412 Seventh Avenue Northwest, and a large mural and several paintings of his may be seen at the Hawkins Clinic Drugstore. Kirkpatrick reproduces scenes of the Old West, somewhat in the manner of Frederic Remington and Charles Russell. His details, though authentic, are given an aura of romanticism. A different kind of reproduction of the Old West stands high on the western bluff, visible from the town below and the highway beyond.

Hailed as the world's largest buffalo, it is a statue of an American bison, forty-six feet long by twenty-six feet high and weighing sixty tons. Its bones are eight-inch steel beams; its flesh is steel rods and wire mesh; and its skin is sprayed concrete. Some early accounts tell of buffalo herds ranging up to ten thousand animals, and a Great Plains total of one million. To the Indians, the buffalo was life itself. It provided them with food, clothing, and shelter. And so the statue is not merely a tourist gimmick but a serious memorial to a way of life now past. Near the statue, reminiscent of early days, is Frontier Village, with railroad depot, land office, fire hall, newspaper shop, jail, old-fashioned restaurant, drug store, barber shop, prairie school, and other facilities.

Whitestone Battlefield

One of the state's more interesting battlefields is an hour's drive south of Jamestown on US 281 and then west from either Monango or Ellendale. Whitestone Battlefield has a museum and picnic grounds. On this spot a battle was fought in 1863 between troops under General Sully and the Sioux Indians.

To continue south on 281 would take you into South Dakota; a longer tour follows US 281 north through Devils Lake and on to Canada. Devils Lake was named by the Indians "Bad Spirit Lake" for its turbulence during storms and for its undrinkable water, much like ocean water. For years, visitors to this area were bothered by the city's drinking water, but recently installed facilities have changed that situation and provide good water now. Yet, among the more than one thousand Sioux Indians living on Fort Totten Reservation, bordering the lake on the south, there are still tales and legends which give a mysterious atmosphere to the lake. One tells of an Indian brave sitting on the shore who stuck his knife into a log. The log slid into the lake and turned out to be a sea monster which is said to still live in a hole at the bottom of the lake. Another story concerns a party of Sioux returning from a successful battle against the Chippewa: As they crossed the lake they were swallowed up. During certain weather conditions the lake sends off a vapor which tends to magnify birds swimming on the water, and this has led to talk about phantom ships. Or were they really birds after all? In recent years the waters of Devils Lake have risen and sweetened and now are a center for fishing and water sports.

The Indians now living here are descendants of three separate Siouxan tribes—the Wahpeton, the Sisseton, and the Yanktonai. Their subagency is at Fort Totten, across the lake from the town of Devils Lake. At one time the fort was the last outpost for three hundred miles of unprotected prairie. Its Cavalry Square, the only one of its type remaining, has been preserved. Its original (1870) design and condition remain nearly intact. Some of the buildings are open to the public, and there is a display of frontier objects in the old hospital building. The surrounding countryside was once very bleak, and posed a survival problem for the early settlers. Wallace Stegner has described those problems in his fine novel, *The Big Rock Candy Mountain.* Summer turned to winter—without an intervening eastern autumn. The land turned brown and gray, and alternating rains and freezes made huge ruts in the roads, and the landscape more desolate. The wind blew all the time and made people tense. The land is not quite so desolate now, but wind still blows, and it affects the people in at least two ways: those who cannot endure it are made irritable; others learn to live with it and seem somehow more stable and calm for it. It can work either way.

In any case, the visitor will be less impressed by the wind than by the scenic drive along the shores of Devils Lake, the fort, and Sully's Hill National Game Preserve with heavy woods, numerous wild birds, elk, deer, bison, and picnic grounds with play areas. Here the wind does not matter as it does out on the open plains. Continuing north, US 281 shortly arrives at the second of North Dakota's four Indian reservations. The land area of the Turtle Mountain Reservation is the smallest of the four, but the enrollment is the largest. Over nine thousand Indians are registered here, mostly Chippewa, although only half of them live in the county. Only part of the group is socially recognized as Indians, the others are of mixed blood, or *Metis.* These people are descended from an earlier Minnesota Chippewa tribe which was pushed out of the eastern Great Lakes region by the Iroquois and in turn (because they had Eastern firearms) drove the Sioux from the Minnesota woods onto the plains of the Dakotas. Once the Sioux adapted themselves to their new environment, they became a proud people who looked down on the Chippewa. Today there is no real animosity, although the Chippewa are largely confined to this area near the Candaian border, while the Sioux have three reservations of considerable size.

Indians Bearing Jewels

Rolla, just east of the Turtle Mountain Reservation, is a small farming town which paradoxically boasts the largest jewel bearing factory in the United States. Operated by the Bulova Watch Company for the Federal Government, this plant produces tiny jewels from synthetic sapphires for defense weapons and time-pieces. At Belcourt, within the reservation but still on the main highway, is the reservation headquarters. A few miles west an Indian-owned company makes and sells Chippewa gift items.

At Dunseith, the highway turns north again for a short run to the Canadian border. This area is perhaps the only one in North Dakota which looks a little like Minnesota, or Wisconsin, or Ohio, for there are trees, lakes, and hills. In some respects the more attractive drives and campgrounds are on the Canadian side, but they are reached with no fuss and no formalities. The International Peace Garden is really a series of gardens on both sides of the border. These are laid out in a formal and classic arrangement and are surrounded by two thousand acres of landscaped park. The gardens serve as a reminder that Canada and the U.S. have always been at peace and that there is no need to guard the border. It is merely marked at intervals. Near the Peace Garden is another wooded lake area, Lake Metigoshe State Park, reached from Bottineau. Although this border area is possibly the most beautiful part of the state, and North Dakota license plates bear the name "Peace Garden State," few state residents spend much time there. The one local attraction is the International Music Camp held each summer, with concerts and an art exhibit, on the U.S. side of the gardens.

Quite by coincidence, the geographical center of North America is only a half–hour's drive to the south, at Rugby on State 3. A monument designates the exact spot determined by the 1931 U.S. Geological Survey.

Through Cleveland to the West

Since we began this northern tour at Jamestown, we might mention that whether you stay on the east-west Interstate 94 or go north to the Peace Garden, the next destination is Bismarck, the capital city. Between Jamestown and Bismarck is the major flyway to Canada for ducks and geese. Obviously, it is a favorite place for hunters and makes North Dakota one of the most rewarding duck-hunting areas in the United States. The land has many hillocks and sloughs. It is here that most of the German-Russians settled after the railroad advertising lured them from South Russia. They speak little English, and they were slow in adopting conservational methods of farming so that they lost most of their valuable topsoil during the dust bowls of the 1930's. Their story is included in Lois Phillips Hudson's excellent novel, *The Bones of Plenty*. Mrs. Hudson now lives in Washington, but she grew up near Cleveland, thirty miles west of Jamestown. To see the exact location of most of her story, drive only four or five miles south of Cleveland on a gravel road.

If you take the northern tour when you leave Rugby, drive west on US 2 to Minot. Once a railroad town made up mostly of tents, Minot is now one of the largest cities in North Dakota. It is just getting over its growing-pains, having been fairly successful in getting rid of those elements which once made it a rather wide-open town. It is a relatively rich town, the center of a large agricultural district and of a field of lignite coal that amounts to billions of tons. Oil was discovered in this area, from Minot past Williston, and will bring in a great royalty in the future. Adding to the economy is Minot Air Force Base, a dozen miles north of the city. Because North Dakota guards the northern circle route between Russia and the Midwest, it has become an important defense center.

Garrison Dam

South on US 83 about forty miles is Garrison, which gave its name to one of the largest earthen dams in the world. Part of the Missouri River Basin project, this dam is also one of the most important structures along the entire river. It is over two miles long, or wide, and also serves as the roadbed for State 200. Recreation areas have been constructed along the lake upriver from the dam, denying the fact that North Dakota is known as a water-less prairie. The dam's statistics are impressive, but its real importance is seen in flood control, recreation, and expanded possibilities for irrigation and cheaper electric power. For the water to back up some two hundred miles, three towns had to be eliminated. A new town was built for the displaced people and was called, appropriately, New Town. Most of the land covered by the lake is, or was, part of the Fort Berthold Indian Reservation, which lies on both sides of the river. About 2,500 Hidatsa (Gros Ventres), Arikara, and Mandan Indians are enrolled at the agency in New Town. However, in 1952, only 1,700 of these people were actually living on the reservation and there will be fewer each year because of the flooding of the Missouri Valley.

Bismarck and the West

Facing each other across the Missouri River, Bismarck and Mandan are still associated with cavalry and Indians. It is at this point, too, that the West begins. In some years the grass will be green on the east side of the river and brown on the west. Increasing aridity is one of the signs of going west. The peculiar mark of Bismarck is the state capitol, a white limestone and black granite skyscraper shooting up eighteen stories from the prairie. Many people have thought it ridiculous that in a land of wide expanses there should be a need for a skyscraper. However, it might be noted that North Dakota's flatland is dotted with grain elevators—white cylinders sticking up into the sky—and the capitol is at least a symbol of these important structures. Along with the ever-present hawks and geese, the capitol may also represent a "looking-up" which has become part of the character of North Dakotans. The "looking-back" in Bismarck may be accomplished at the fine State Historical Museum, or the Camp Hancock Museum, or even at the memorial statue of Sacajawea, the Shoshone girl who gave much help to Lewis and Clark. Bismarck was the nearest settlement when Lt. Col. Custer (he was no longer a general, having lost his brevet commission) was preparing to go after Sitting Bull and Crazy Horse. It was to Bismarck that Custer's troop flocked for their off-duty entertainment, and it was to Bismarck that news first came of Custer's death. The people here still talk about Custer and debate his decisions and actions.

But the past, vivid as it still is, does not keep the people of Bismarck from going forward. Their city is as crisp, clean, and modern as any in the state. Bismarck sponsors the largest state-wide art show, usually in November. Because the city is more isolated than those in the eastern part of the state, the people are more ready to do things for themselves. As a result, the visitor is likely to feel that curious and wonderful Western combination of energy and relaxation which carries a city forward even while it remains immensely proud of its frontier past.

Fort Abraham Lincoln

Across the river, Mandan has some of the appearances of a frontier town and western clothing becomes even more evident. About five miles to the south is the site of Fort Abraham Lincoln, perhaps the historical and spiritual center of the state. Standing in one of the reconstructed blockhouses of Fort McKeen at the top of the hill, one sees a vast panorama of river, bluffs, coulees, Indian lodges, and Custer's old campground. It is almost possible to hear the bugles over the wind, and to see the troops riding up the draw to the west on their way to battle. It is an easy walk around the ruins of the old cavalry post, where troops, far from their eastern homes, led a crude life before they went out to chase Sitting Bull, many of them never coming back. Grouped loosely around a parade ground now in grass, the stone foundations are marked, and it is not difficult to imagine the incidents of 1875. An excellent museum nearby has exhibits showing details of that year and inexpensive books which explain the post, the Indians, and the cavalry.

Behind the museum once stood a Slant Indian village. Although Lewis and Clark spent the winter of 1804–05 a little farther upriver, it is likely that they also stopped here to visit the Indians. Several of the earth-lodges have been authentically restored, and the largest one may be entered as the Indians themselves once entered it. Below the village is a park on the shore of the river with camping and picnicking. Downriver is the site of Fort Rice, also prominent during the Indian wars. Farther south, about seventy miles from Bismarck, is the Indian community of Fort Yates. The older Standing Rock Sioux frequently sit in front of the grocery store at Fort Yates, reminiscing and telling their legends to eager visitors. It was at Fort Yates that Sitting Bull, mighty chief of the Sioux, was buried. His grave was opened one night in 1953 by South Dakota Indians who felt that the chief did not belong in North Dakota. They claim to have found Sitting Bull's bones, which they then reburied near Mobridge, South Dakota, However, North Dakotans say that the chief was originally buried in lime, so that there could be no bones. In any case, both states now claim to have the well-known chief, while almost a century ago no one wanted him. Meanwhile, in a fine Indian school at Fort Yates, the children of the chief's grandchildren are taught to forget Sioux and speak English. And the town attracts tourists to the lake formed by damming the Missouri River in South Dakota.

Roosevelt National Park

From Mandan west the interstate highway follows for a while the route taken by Custer when he set out after Sitting Bull. One hundred miles to the west lies the most spectacular part of North Dakota. The Badlands are now a part of Custer National Forest and also include Theodore Roosevelt National Memorial Park, the only national memorial park in the nation. Here one can see wild horses, or perhaps the bighorn sheep, as well as buffalo, deer, and antelope. Amusing prairie dogs have built several large towns and sit straight and alert by their holes. Coyotes, porcupines, bobcats, rabbits, beaver, and other small animals live within the park, while overhead soar hawks and an occasional eagle. The landscape has a strange and wild beauty, both in topography and in color. Hillocks, buttes, domes, cones, pyramids, and ridges are piled up along the Little Missouri River valley. Stripes of brown, red, gray, and yellow run across the buttes. Lignite veins stand out in black. Old fires of underground coal have burned pinks and reds into the clay. The vegetation has its colors too: blue-gray and silver of sage, light green of the rather scarce grass, dark green of the cedars, and the various colors of fruit from small trees and bushes. In addition to common flowers, the white gumbo lily grows here, and the purple and white Mariposa, as well as the lemon-yellow prickly pear cactus. Altogether, the Badlands are an exciting place.

Famous men have lived here. Theodore Roosevelt came to hunt in 1883 and returned to take part in the open range cattle industry. His first ranch was established seven miles south of Medora, and the second about thirty-five miles north. Because he was an easterner and wore thick glasses, he was labeled a "four-eyed dude," a name which was softly changed to "Old Four-eyes" after he subdued a local bully. The Marquis de Mores, a young, rich, handsome Frenchman, came west on a hunting trip at about the same time and decided to build a packing plant in the Badlands so that cattlemen need not ship east. Although his 1883 venture failed, De Mores left behind him a number of buildings, an impression not yet forgotten, and the town of Medora, which he founded and named after his wife. More recently, but still in the image of the West, Tom Mix, the early cowboy star of the screen, lived in Medora for a short time.

There are two major units in the Roosevelt Memorial park. The South Unit borders I–94. The North Unit is a half–hour drive to the north on US 85. Both units are reached from Belfield. Visitors should probably go first to Park Headquarters inside the Medora entrance to the South Unit. Here information can be obtained concerning the roads in the Badlands, places to see, campgrounds, trails, evening entertainment, and trailer space. Remember that a large segment of the Badlands is still wild, and the "eastern dudes" are not encouraged to go off alone without full information or advice from the rangers.

The De Mores Historic Site is immediately southwest of Medora and features the 26–room chateau, with many of the original furnishings, and the ruins of the packing plant. Nearby is the Medora Zoo with birds and animals native to the region in their natural surroundings. The town itself has a museum of fur trade, Indian, and wildlife collections, and one may see restored historic buildings within Medora.

AROUND THE STATE

 HOTELS AND MOTELS in North Dakota are mostly geared to family travelers and, although the summers are short, the frequent heated swimming pools can be used for several marginal months of the year. Rates are lower here than most other states.

The price categories in this section, for double occupancy, will average as follow: *Deluxe* $24, *Expensive* $20, *Moderate* $16, and *Inexpensive* $12. For a more complete description of these categories, see the *Hotels & Motels* section of THE ROCKIES & PLAINS *Facts at Your Fingertips* at the front of this volume.

BISMARCK

Holiday Inn. *Expensive.* 1215 W. Memorial Hwy. A large member of this well-known chain. Family rates. In-room coffee, restaurant, cocktail lounge, room service. Spacious nicely furnished rooms. Indoor heated pool, recreation area, playground. Kennels for pets. Color TV. 223-9600

Seven Seas Inn. *Expensive.* At Exit 31 on I-94. Overlooking Bismarck and Mandan, this large motel is within minutes of the State Capitol. Children under twelve, free. Lounge and dining room with nautical atmosphere. Indoor pool, whirlpool, color TV, elevator and meeting facilities. 663-7401

Town House Motor Inn. *Expensive.* 1800 N. 12th St. Located just north of the State Capitol grounds. Offers indoor heated pool, sauna, putting green, color TV. Lounge and dining room. Family rates. 223-8001

Bismarck Motor Hotel. *Moderate.* 2301 E. Main St. Partly two-story, this medium-sized motel has family rates. Recreation area. Restaurant next door. 223-2474

Fleck House Motel. *Moderate.* 2nd St. and Thayer Ave. Two-story medium-size downtown motel with large attractive, air-conditioned rooms. Family rates. Pool, color TV. 24-hour restaurant nearby. 255-1450

Colonial. *Inexpensive.* Near I-94 Business Exit 34, two blocks west of Memorial Bridge. Two-story medium-size motel with color TV, heated pool, playground, free coffee. Cafe nearby. 663-9824

CARRINGTON

Chieftain Motor Lodge. *Inexpensive.* At junction US 52–281 and State 200. A medium-size motel. Family rates and connecting units. Restaurant, cocktail lounge, coffee shop. Tastefully decorated. Complete meeting facilities. Private collection of Indian artifacts and antique gems. 652-3131

Del Claire. *Inexpensive.* On US 281 just south of State 200. Large rooms and family rates. Color TV, pool privileges, air-conditioning. Restaurant adjacent. 652-3161

DEVILS LAKE

Artclare. *Moderate.* 1 mi. SE on US 2. Besides connecting units, there are two-room units and efficiencies. Recreation area. Lounge and restaurant. Indoor heated pool, color TV. 662-4001

Davis Motel. *Inexpensive.* On US 2W. Located in an area of good hunting and fishing, this small motel offers air-conditioned comfort. TV, some color. Several drive-ins and restaurant nearby. 662-4927

DICKINSON

Nodak. *Moderate.* 26 6th Ave. E. A small motel but with a variety of accommodations including connecting units, two-room units, four kitchenettes, and two housekeeping apartments. Heated pool, recreation area. Restaurant nearby. 224-5119

West Plains Motel. *Inexpensive.* W. Villard St. on west edge of town on US 10. Another small operation. Recreation area. Restaurant nearby. Heated pool. 225-5138

FARGO

Fargo-Biltmore. *Expensive.* 3700 W. Main Ave. An attractive and excellent large two-level motel with everything the modern traveler wants. Good restaurant, cocktail lounge. Spacious rooms. Heated pool, children's area, color TV. 282-2121

Kahler Motel. *Expensive.* South of town on I–94 and US 81. On nicely landscaped grounds with spacious, tastefully decorated rooms. In-room coffee, restaurant, cocktail lounge. Heated pool and playground. Color TV. Meeting facilities. 235-3141

Motel 6. *Inexpensive.* 2202 S. University Ave. Heated pool, TV, 24–hour cafe adjacent. 235-4411

GRAND FORKS

North Star Inn. *Moderate.* 2100 S. Washington, on Business loop I–29 South. A medium-size, very attractive motel with excellent restaurant. Lounge, indoor pool and recreation area. Family rates. Meeting facilities. 772-8151

Plainsman Motel. *Moderate.* 2201 Gateway Dr. Medium-size motel with air-conditioning, TV, gift shop. Weekly rates available. Babysitting service offered at small hourly cost. Restaurants and shopping areas nearby. 775-8134

Westward Ho. *Moderate.* West on US 2, west of I–29. There is a variety of things to do for the family at this medium–size motor hotel, including lawn games, miniature golf, a putting green, model Western village, and pool. Family rates. The motel has well-decorated rooms. Chuck House Ranch is an excellent restaurant with entertainment in lounge. Pets. A good place to stop. 775-5341

JAMESTOWN

Tumbleweed. *Moderate.* 824 20th St. S. W. at jct. of US 281 and I–94. Up the hill from Ranch House. Indoor heated pool. Restaurant and lounge. Family rates. Spacious paneled rooms have TV, phones, and air-conditioning. 252-5222

Jamestown. *Inexpensive.* 1018 4th Ave. S.W. This medium–size motel has TV, free coffee, 24–hour cafe nearby. Free airport bus. 252-0471

MEDORA

Bad Lands Motel. *Moderate.* On I–94 Business. All rooms in this large motel have two double beds and air-conditioning. Pool. Children under six, free. Pets welcome. Dining facilities in *Rough Riders Hotel.* 623-4422

Rough Riders Hotel. *Moderate.* 2 blks. N of I–94 Business. All rooms have one double bed and air-conditioning. Pool privileges. Children under six, free. Dining facilities in *East Room* and *Chuck Wagon Cafeteria.* 623-4433

MINOT

Ramada Inn. *Expensive.* 1505 2nd St. N.W. Restaurant, coffee shop, cocktail lounge with entertainment, room service. Indoor heated pool. Meeting and banquet facilities. Airport courtesy car. 838-6161

Sandman. *Moderate.* At US 2 and 52 Bypass. A medium-size motel with well-furnished rooms. Restaurant, room service, color TV, and recreation room. Heated pool. Meeting facilities. 838-4088

Thunderbird Motel. *Moderate.* 1900 4th Ave. S.E. Located across from State Fairgrounds. A small motel with restaurant adjacent. Color TV. 838-5488

WAHPETON

Valley Motel. *Inexpensive.* West on US 81, back from highway. On expansive grounds. Family rates and connecting units. TV, air-conditioning. Indoor pool, open year round. *Kelly's Restaurant, Bar and Lounge* next to motel. 642-5528

WILLISTON

El Rancho. *Moderate.* 1623 2nd Ave. W. This medium-size motor hotel offers varied accommodations, including larger new rooms, some with kitchens. Some air-conditioning. Restaurant, cocktail lounge. Heated pool, recreation area. 473-6321

Dandy Motel. *Inexpensive.* 1021 2nd Ave. W. Very clean, old and small motel. Nine units with kitchenettes. TV, Restaurant and stores nearby. Pets allowed. Weekly rates available. 572-2163

 DINING OUT. North Dakotans like good food, but they lean heavily to steaks and other staples. One does not often find exotic foods (even at high prices) in the state. When these people go out to have a special treat, they do not expect fancy trimmings, just good food. The listing below categorizes each restaurant according to the medium-priced items on its menu.

Restaurant price categories are as follow: *Deluxe* $8.50 and up, *Expensive* $6–$8, *Moderate* $3.50–$5.50, and *Inexpensive* $2–$3.50. These prices are for *hors d'oeuvres* or soup, *entrée*, and dessert. Not included are drinks, tax and tips. For a more complete explanation of restaurant categories refer to THE ROCKIES & PLAINS *Facts at Your Fingertips* at the beginning of this volume.

BISMARCK

Gourmet House. *Moderate.* On US 10 W of the Missouri River Bridge. A reliable, charming restaurant specializing in steak, lamb, and lobster at lunch and dinner. Cocktail lounge. Open noon to 12:30 a.m., Mon. from 5 p.m. Closed Sun. 663-9801

Jerry's Supper Club. *Moderate.* 3 mi. W on US 10, I-94 Business. A steak and seafood restaurant with a lot of local clientele. Children's plates. Open 5 p.m. to 12:45 a.m. Closed Sun. and hols. 633-9130

DEVILS LAKE

The Ranch. *Moderate.* On State 20, just S of jct. US 2. Rustic Western decor in a remodeled barn. Steak is the specialty. Cocktails, children's plates. Open 11:30 a.m. to 2 p.m., 5 to 11:30 p.m. Closed Sun. and hols. 662-3421

DICKINSON

Esquire Steak House. *Moderate.* 43 Sims St. Watch your steak or other specialty being broiled at this locally popular restaurant. Also serves seafood, chicken, and spaghetti. Cocktails. Open 11 a.m. to 1:30 p.m., 5 p.m. to 1 a.m. Closed Sun. 225-5264

FARGO

Black Angus. *Expensive.* Broadway and 2nd Ave. N. Offers daily luncheon buffet. Steaks and seafood served during the evening. Nightly entertainment in the *Red Ram Lounge.* Open 11 a.m. to 1 a.m.; Sun. to 10 p.m. 232-8931

Tale of the Whale. *Expensive.* West on US 10 and 52. Located in the Fargo-Biltmore Motor Hotel, this restaurant features steaks, seafood, and several gourmet dinners for two. Each dinner is complete with salad bar, homemade breads. Open 11:30 a.m. to 2 p.m., 5:30 to 11 p.m. Closed Sun. and hols. 282-2121

GRAND FORKS

Palace Dining Room. *Expensive.* 2¼ mi. W on US 2, ¼ mi. E of I-29. Located in the Westward Ho Motel, this restaurant offers such specialties as Chateaubriand and lobster thermidor. Open 5 to 10:30 p.m.; Fri. and Sat. to 11 p.m. Closed Sun. 775-5341

The Bronze Boot. *Moderate.* On US 81, N of jct. US 2. Features steaks broiled over an open charcoal pit, and chops, Chinese food. Lunch is chuck-wagon

259

style. Cocktails. Open 11 a.m. to 1:30 p.m., 5 to 11 p.m. Closed Sun. 772-9854

JAMESTOWN

Mac's. *Moderate.* Jct. I–94 and US 281, 52. A well-recommended family restaurant, not large, but very pleasant. Ham, beef, chops are served. Open 7 a.m. to 10:30 p.m. 252-4243

MINOT

Gordon's Holiday Spot. *Moderate.* 1901 S. Broadway, S on US 83. Fine beef and chicken specialties but with a general menu. Cocktails. Open 7 a.m.

to 10 p.m.; Sun. 7 a.m. to 2 p.m. 838-4840

RUGBY

Andrew's Steak House. *Moderate.* S on US 2 in the Hamilton Motel. Popular in the area, this restaurant serves seafood and chicken as well as steak. Children's plates. Bar and lounge. Open 5 p.m. to midnight. Closed Sun. 776-5255

VALLEY CITY

Howard's. *Moderate.* 2 mi. W off I–94. Next to Flickertail Inn. Popular in a rather wide area. Specialties are steak and ribs. Cocktails. Open 5 p.m. to midnight. Closed Sun. 845-9733

SOUTH DAKOTA

SOUTH DAKOTA

Black Hills and Badlands

by

JOHN R. MILTON

John R. Milton teaches creative writing at the University of South Dakota and has recently published books on Oscar Howe and Crazy Horse. He has lived in both North and South Dakota.

If the traveler could get high enough above the state and look down, he would see South Dakota has four major physical features: the eastern prairie, the Missouri River, the western plains, and the Badlands and Black Hills. Of these, the river is most important. It enters from the north, bisects the state as it flows south, and then turns to become the southeast boundary for 150 miles. The two parts of the state, separated by the river, are often known locally as East-river and West-river, leading to occasional rivalry in politics, economics, and sports. East of the river are the major colleges and universities, all but one of the population centers, gently rolling farm lands, and enough pheasants to attract hunters from all over the world. West of the river are the Black Hills, most of the state's Indian reservations, and millions of acres of wide-open cattle country. The climate at the eastern edge of the state is much like that in Minnesota and Iowa, while at the western end the air is drier and the wind blows more often.

Physically, then, South Dakota has all the variety of a transition region. From the climate and elevation (965 feet) of the Midwest, it climbs to high plains (3,500 feet) and Harney Peak (7,242 feet), and comes to resemble the West. Again, the Missouri River is the rough line which divides the two quite different regions.

It was up the Missouri that Lewis and Clark boated and portaged on their historic journey of exploration from St. Louis to the Pacific Ocean. They were not, however, the first white men to enter what is now South Dakota. Chevalier de la Verendrye, French explorer, reached the center of the state in 1743, near today's Pierre, the state capital. The first known "settler" was Pierre Dorion, who married a Sioux woman and lived on the lower James River in 1775. Dorion later served as a guide for Lewis and Clark; their trip out in 1804 and back in 1806 opened the immense northwest country to commerce, particularly fur trading. Their journals mark the beginning of the literature of South Dakota.

Not until half a century later did Dakota become much more than a wilderness which fur traders had to cross in going from St. Louis to the richer fur trapping regions of the Northwest. The establishment of Dakota Territory in 1861 and the Homestead Act of 1862 brought in the first long-term settlers, although half of them left the territory during the 1862 Sioux uprising in nearby Minnesota. A larger wave of homesteaders arrived with the railroads in the 1870's, and men of adventure were lured across the territory by the promise of gold in the Black Hills. Lt. Colonel George A. Custer's expedition discovered gold in 1874, perhaps the most important incident in South Dakota history. A year earlier, much of the nation had gone into backruptcy, and finding of gold helped both financially and psychologically to bring recovery from the panic. On the other side of the ledger, the discovery brought about a series of Indian wars with the Sioux who resented this invasion of their holy land. Custer's famous defeat at Little Bighorn brought a call for reprisal and led to even further bloodshed throughout the territory.

By the time South Dakota was admitted as a state in 1889, four groups inhabited the area within its borders—farmers in the eastern section, miners in the Black Hills, and cattlemen and Indians in between. Later, Hamlin Garland and Ole Rölvaag were to write about the stark life of the farmers, while a host of novelists exploited the romance and myth of the other groups. For a century, South Dakota has had this double image.

Today the cowboy still rides his horse, and there remain large herds of buffalo in the western part of the state, but jeeps and light airplanes are also used to round up both cows and buffalo. Despite disastrous blizzards in 1873, 1880–81, and 1888, the cattle industry which began shortly after the Civil War still flourishes. Ranches are a little smaller, however, and open lands are not quite so extensive. Some farming operations, moreover, have penetrated the range land. More gold is still produced in the Black Hills than anywhere else in the nation, and silver and twenty-seven other minerals are mined in commercial quantity. The Indian population has grown a little, with about 32,000 currently living in the state. More than 27,000 of them are on the nine reservations.

Men of the Soil

So although the marks of the Old West remain in South Dakota, the major industry is agriculture, including crops and livestock. The dust bowl of the 1930's was a major tragedy still vividly remembered, but South Dakotans come from hardy stock (including Swedish, Norwegian, German, Dutch, and German-Russian) and have recovered nicely. Even the absence of defense plants during World War II did not seriously injure the economy of the state. South Dakota is one of the few debt-free states in the nation. Its people have been accustomed to saving money. They do not launch out into building and expansion until there is an absolute need for it. The early residents were men of the soil—strong, enduring, and not inclined toward frivolity or luxury. Yet, the very first influx of settlers came not from Europe but from the neighboring states of Iowa, Wisconsin, Minnesota, and Illinois, and these were people who had come into contact with the cultures of the eastern United States. This has meant that South Dakotans have been basically conservative and religious, but there is an element which is cultured, well-educated, inclined toward liberalism, and often dissatisfied with the slowness and the "leave-things-as-they-are" attitude of its fellow citizens. Even this group, however, has been influenced by the land and the sky and generally chooses to remain in South Dakota in order to enjoy the freedom and open spaces of a region as yet relatively unpopulated.

The population of South Dakota has doubled in the last seventy years but remains low at around 665,000. The state is 55 per cent rural. Of its people who are engaged in manufacturing, 36 per cent live in one city—Sioux Falls. There is room to move around in, which the residents of the state appreciate. The population increases each year at a pace lower than the birth rate, which suggests that the young people often leave the state to find better opportunities for employment, more money, and a more diversified social and cultural life. Those who stay are a curious mixture of the pioneer-cowboy and the sophisticated modern. Close proximity to Minneapolis, Denver, and Omaha, and easy driving without the congestion found on eastern and coastal highways, means frequent participation in city life. The word "conservative" in South Dakota really means "independent." The people want to be individuals; they fear big government and large and lonely cities.

However, they are uneasy, because the old way of life does not buy the many things which modern life seems to require, such as bigger schools, wider highways, and increased luxury. Interstate highway construction has proceeded rapidly, but only because it need not deal with metropolitan difficulties. Books and paintings are not quite considered luxuries, but neither are they easily available. South Dakota, in effect, is still a pioneer state in many ways, just beginning to feel the pressures of complex society. Its people are friendly and easy-going, not taking well to formality and artificiality. They would like to remain that way, even while meeting the problems of the modern world.

GENERAL AND PRACTICAL INFORMATION FOR SOUTH DAKOTA

 FACTS AND FIGURES. In Sioux Indian, *Dakota* means "allies." The state's nicknames are *Coyote State* and *Sunshine State*. The pasqueflower is the state flower; the black hills spruce, the state tree; the ring-necked pheasant, the state bird. "Under God the People Rule" is the state motto. "Hail, South Dakota" is the state song.

Pierre is the state capital. The state population was 665,507 at the most recent census.

The broad Missouri River runs from north to south through the center of the state, separating the lake-dotted prairies of the east from the rolling uplands of the west. In the southwest are the strange eroded formations of the Badlands, the most spectacular bit of landscape of its kind in the world. In the west is the somber beauty of the forested Black Hills, site of Mt. Rushmore. South Dakota is a state of big, highly mechanized farms, and cattle and grain are the chief sources of income. Mining, centered in the Black Hills, is not so important, but South Dakota is the nation's leading producer of gold. There is little industry. The climate is variable, with hot summers and cold winters in the west, and high humidity in the east.

 HOW TO GET THERE. *By air:* North Central, Western, Frontier and Ozark Airlines provide service principally into Sioux Falls, Aberdeen and Rapid City.

By bus: Greyhound, Continental Trailways, Jack Rabbit Lines, and Midwest Coaches provide the bulk of the passenger service into the state serving Sioux Falls, Aberdeen, Rapid City and Pierre.

By car: I–90 enters South Dakota from Minnesota in the east and from Wyoming in the west. I–29 is the principal access from Nebraska in the south and US 281 from North Dakota in the north.

 HOW TO GET AROUND. *By air:* North Central and Western provide service between cities in South Dakota. One or both land at airports in Sioux Falls, Brookings, Watertown, Aberdeen, Huron, Mitchell, Pierre, and Rapid City.

By bus: Jack Rabbit Lines offers extensive service within the state serving all of the major cities and many smaller ones. Sedalia-Marshall-Boonville Stage Line provides transportation to Sioux City, Yankton, Mitchell, Rapid City, Huron, Pierre, and Aberdeen.

By car: the principal east-west routes are I–90 across the lower half of the state and US 212 across the upper half. The major cities served by I–90 are Spearfish, Sturgis, Rapid City, Wall, Kadoka, Murdo, Kennebeck, Chamberlain, Mitchell, and Sioux Falls. US 81, 281, and 83 run north–south, and I–29 runs north–south through Brookings, Sioux Falls, Beresford and Vermillion.

TOURIST INFORMATION. A free brochure, *South Dakota Vacation Guide,* as well as information and other leaflets are available from Travel Director, Dept. of Highways, Pierre 57501.

SEASONAL EVENTS. *January:* Pierre hosts a *Winter Carnival* early in the month.

February: The Black Hills Stock Show takes place in Rapid City during the first week. Deadwood is the site of *Annual Winter Wonderland* the third week.

March: Sioux Empire Arts Festival runs all month in Sioux Falls. The *Little International Livestock Show* in Brookings is South Dakota State University's agricultural and home economics show. Patterned after the Chicago International Exposition, it takes place during the third week. Among the ethnic festivals is Freeman's *Schmeckfest* during the last few days of the month.

April: Brookings opens the month with a *Fine Arts Festival* and Rapid City holds an *Arts and Crafts Fair* at mid-month. At Sioux Falls near the end of the month is the *Sioux Empire Gem & Mineral Show.*

May: The *Jackrabbit Stampede,* which includes a rodeo, takes place on the South Dakota State University north campus at Brookings early in the month. At mid-month is the *South Dakota Gem & Mineral Show* at Watertown.

June: The *Black Hills Passion Play* opens the month and is performed Sun., Tues., and Thurs. at Spearfish into Sept. Among this month's ethnic festivals are *Danish Days Celebration* at Viborg and *Annual Czech Days* at Tabor. DeSmet is the site of *Old Settlers' Days* during the second week and of *Pioneer Acres Gas and Steam Show* the third week. The *Crystal Springs Rodeo* at Clear Lake closes out the month.

July: The month opens with Mobridge's *Sitting Bull Stampede,* a parade and rodeo around the 4th of July. Other Independence Day celebrations include the *Annual Black Hills Roundup* at Belle Fourche, the century-and-a-half-old *4th of July Celebration and Rodeo* at Ft. Pierre, and *Sunfish Sailboat Regatta* at Lake Madison. At mid-month is the *Corn Palace Stampede* at Mitchell. During the last week is *Gold Discovery Days* at Custer which includes a Pageant of the Gold Rush, Custer's war with the Sioux, and Indian raids. A rodeo and carnival are also part of the festivities. Closing the month are the *Dakota Wagon Train* from Faith to Deadwood and the *Annual Black Hills Trail Ride* at Rapid City.

August: The *Annual Days of '76,* which includes a rodeo, begins early in Aug. at Deadwood. During the second week, the *Black Hills Motorcycle Classic* at Sturgis includes AMA sanctioned Gypsy Tour and motorcycle racing. *Oahe Days* at Pierre and *Sioux Empire Fair* at Sioux Falls both have rodeos as part of their events.

Country and western entertainment and livestock exhibits make up the *Day County Fair* at Webster and Lake Madison is the scene of the *South Dakota Sunfish Championship Regatta.* The third week Rapid City hosts the *Central States Fair* with a Wild West rodeo, carnival, and Indian dances. The *Antique Festival and Steam Threshing Jamboree* at Prairie Village outside Madison displays antique farm machinery and has parades, arts and crafts shows, rides, and steam railroad. The *Rosebud Sioux Rodeo and Pow Wow* in Rosebud includes dances, Indian arts and crafts displays, and a traditional buffalo dinner. Late in the month, the *South Dakota State Fair* takes place at Huron.

September: Late in the month are the *Black Hills Steam & Gas Threshing Bee* at Sturgis, the *Corn Palace Festival* at Mitchell, and the *Vanishing Trails Expedition* at Wall.

October: Pheasant hunting season opens about the third week.

November: Black Hills *deer hunting season* opens Nov. 1.

December: Deadwood hosts the *Annual Black Hills Snowmobile Classic* and *ski season* begins.

NATIONAL PARKS. *Wind Cave National Park,* is located in the Black Hills north of Hot Springs. Wind Cave, one of many in the Black Hills, was named for the wind currents that blow in or out depending on atmospheric pressure. The whistling sound of the air coming out led to its discovery in 1881. The 28,000 acres of park which surround the cave are covered with prairie grasslands and forests. On a wildlife preserve are bison, elk, deer, and prairie dogs. Tours, nature trails, and camping and picnicking facilities are available.

Jewel Cave National Monument, in the Black Hills west of Custer, is a nearly 1,300-acre area covered with ponderosa pine and wildflowers. It surrounds Jewel Cave, a series of subterranean chambers and limestone galleries whose jewel-like calcite crystals produce unusual effects. Guided tours and picnicking facilities are available.

Badlands National Monument, 62 mi. E of Rapid City via I-90, US 14, 16, 16A, is one of the most impressive pieces of natural sculpting in the world. Over millions of years, layer upon layer of mud, sand, and gravel along with skeletons of the animals of the period—dinosaurs, saber-tooth tigers, bison and tinier water and marsh creatures—were built up to a depth of over 600 feet. Probably during the great land upheaval which formed the Rocky Mountains, the earth's crust rose and the action of wind and water began to form the cones, spires and jagged peaks, the banded gullies and canyons which now make up this colorful region. This is a simple but striking demonstration of geologic processes. A Visitor Center is open year round, accommodations and meals are available during the summer, and there is camping nearby at Cedar Pass and Sage Creek.

The *Black Hills National Forest,* nearly 1¼ million acres, encompasses almost all of the Black Hills. Formed when wind and water eroded the softer limestone and sandstone surrounding the granite core (or, if you prefer, by the tears of Paul Bunyan upon the death of his blue ox, Babe), the area is now one of towering spires, magnificent forests and mountain scenery. Named by the Indians for the dark appearance given by the thick pine covering, these mountains were considered sacred ground. Harney Peak, at 7,242 feet, is the highest mountain in the Black Hills.

A variety of recreational activities are possible throughout the year including camping, picnicking, hiking, swimming, boating, fishing, hunting, and skiing. The visitor center at Pactola Lake has information and exhibits on the forest and wildlife.

Custer National Forest. Part of this 2½-million-acre forest lies in northwestern

South Dakota. Mostly rolling hills and grassland, it offers camping and picnicking facilities and hiking trails.

STATE PARKS. *Custer State Park,* 3 mi. E of Custer on US 16A, is one of the largest state parks in the U.S. Over 72,000 acres are given over to this park in the rugged Black Hills. On the park's wildlife refuge are herds of bison, deer, and bighorn sheep and other native animals. Four lakes and many streams offer excellent fishing and swimming. The park also has a zoo, museum, and theatre and facilities for camping, picnicking, boating, horseback riding, and hiking.

Fort Sisseton State Park, 12 mi. N of Webster on State 23, then 10 mi. N on an unnumbered road, was built in 1864 during the Sioux Indian uprising and is an excellent example of a stone frontier fort. The visitors center has historic exhibits and picnic facilities are available.

Bear Butte State Park, 6 mi. NE of Sturgis on State 79, is the site of a huge volcanic bubble which rises 1,400 feet above the level of the surrounding plains. Indians still regard it as a religious shrine. The Cheyenne Indian Shrine is at the visitor center. Camping, picnicking, boating, swimming, and fishing facilities are available.

Fisher Grove State Park, 7 mi. E of Redfield on US 212, covers 306 acres and offers camping, electrical hookups, picnicking, hiking, boating, fishing, and golf.

Hartford Beach State Park, 15 mi. NW of Milbank on State 15, offers camping, picnicking, boating, swimming, fishing, flush toilets, and electrical hookups.

Newton Hills State Park, 7 mi. S of Canton off US 18, offers complete camping, picnicking, boating, swimming and recreation facilities.

Union County State Park, 11 mi. S of Beresford off I–90, offers camping, picnicking, and hiking.

Palisades State Park, 10 mi. E of Sioux Falls on I–90, then 14 mi. N on State 11, has camping, picnicking, fishing, and hiking.

Oakwood Lake State Park, 10 mi. N of Volga off US 14, offers complete camping, picnicking, boating, swimming and recreation facilities.

Lake Herman State Park, 2 mi. W of Madison off State 34, offers camping, electrical hookups, picnicking, boating, swimming, and fishing.

Roy Lake State Park, 3 mi. W of Lake City off State 10, offers camping, electrical hookups, picnicking, boating, fishing, swimming, and hiking.

Lake Hiddenwood State Park, 4 mi. NE from Selby off US 212 and US 83, offers camping, electrical hookups, picnicking, boating, and swimming.

Sica Hollow State Park, 15 mi. NW of Sisseton off State 10, offers picnicking, horseback riding, and hiking.

CAMPING OUT. From May to Sept. a carload permit is required, good for use at all state parks and recreation areas. The fee is $2, and an additional $2/night camping fee is charged at many areas. A five-day camping limit applies in many areas.

In addition to the state parks, camping facilities are available at most recreation areas. The larger ones are listed below.

Agostura, 10 mi. SE of Hot Springs off US 18, offers sixty-four sites. Facilities include fishing, boating, swimming, and pit toilets.

Farm Island, 3 mi. E of Pierre off State 34, offers seventy-two sites. Facilities include boating, swimming, fishing, electrical hookups and flush toilets.

Gavins Point, 6 mi. W of Yankton on State 52, has sixty sites. Facilities include boating, swimming, fishing, electrical hookups and flush toilets.

Pickerel Lake, 10 mi. N of Waubay on US 212, has sixty-seven sites. Facilities include boating, fishing, swimming, electrical hookups and pit toilets.

269

Yankton, 5 mi. W of Yankton on State 52, has fifty-five sites. Facilities include boating, swimming, fishing, electrical hookups and flush toilets.

 TRAILER TIPS. In addition to the state parks and recreation areas already covered, there are a number of city, county and civic campgrounds with trailer facilities.

Huron Memorial Park Campground, in Huron, 1 mi. E of State 37, has trailer sites with water, sewer, and electric hookups and air conditioning and sanitary dump. The season runs from Apr. to Sept. and there is a minimum $2.50 fee.

Burke City Park, 300 ft. off the side of US 18 and 47, is open all year and has water, sewer, and electric hookups and a sewage disposal station. There is no minimum fee but spaces are limited.

Groton City Park, on Main St. 2 blks. S of US 12 on the north side of Groton, has water and electric hookups and sewage disposal station. It is open from May to Oct. and there is no minimum fee.

Maxwell Park, on the north side of US 14 in Arlington, has water and electric hookups and a sewage disposal station is nearby. The season runs from Memorial Day to mid-Sept. The minimum fee is $1 and reservations are accepted.

FARM VACATIONS AND GUEST RANCHES. Dude ranches and vacation farms, a popular form of vacationing in other states, are becoming increasingly popular in South Dakota. The following is a sampling of what is available:

4T Guest Ranch, located approximately in the center of the Black Hills. Horseback riding, pack trips, fishing and many kinds of western ranch excitement. Contact 4T Guest Ranch, Nemo 57759.

Guy's Vacation Ranch, located in the LaCoteau Hills of northeastern S.D. Both children and adults enjoy the routine farm life. Horseback riding, hunting, fishing, and cookouts are available. Swimming, sunbathing and water-skiing during the summer. Winter season, sledding, skiing and skating. Write Hurshell Guy, RR 3, Veblen 57270.

Hutchinson Ranch, located in southcentral S.D. Ranch living for a day, week, or month. Can accommodate a family of six or fewer, or couples. Also camping facilities. Transportation facilities, horseback riding, swimming, rock hunting, fishing, hiking or just relaxation. Larry A. Hutchinson, White River 57579.

Medicine Creek Ranch, located 4 mi. from the Big Bend Reservoir, on the Lower Brule Sioux Indian Reservation. Live a real ranch life. An offer for young people 9 to 14 years of age to spend a vacation on one of Dakota's large ranches, under supervision. Berwyn Svoboda, Medicine Creek Grazing Assn. Inc., Reliance 57569.

Rafter J Bar Ranch, located in the shadow of Mt. Rushmore. Dude ranch, camping, tenting or trailers. Enack bar, picnicking and trail rides. Col. Bob Higgins, Box 128, Hill City 57745.

Terry Valley Dude Ranch, located at the base of Terry Peak. Dude ranch, hunting, fishing, trail rides, sightseeing, snowmobiling. Year-round activities. Terry Valley Development, Box 35, Trojan Route, Lead 57754.

Triangle I Ranch, located 12 mi. W of Rapid City. Bus tours and horseback riding. Trail rides, swimming, relaxation, good food and rest. Carl Sanders, Triangle I Ranch Lodge, Rte. 1, Box 125, Rapid City 57701.

The Webster Ranch, this ranch offers sessions of 2 weeks to girls only. Under supervision of a married lady and an expert horsewoman and counselor for young girls. The accepted ages are 11 to 15. Larry A. Vickers, The Webster Ranch, Frederick 57441.

MUSEUMS AND GALLERIES. The *Museum of Geology*, in O'Harra Memorial Building on the campus of the South Dakota School of Mines and Technology in Rapid City, has excellent exhibits of rocks and minerals from the Black Hills and fossils from the Badlands. Open June to Aug., Mon. to Sat., 8 a.m. to 6 p.m.; Sun., 2 to 8 p.m.; Sept. to May, Mon. to Fri. 8 to 5. Free.

Sioux Indian Museum and Crafts Center, at 1002 St. Joseph St. in Rapid City, exhibits historic and contemporary Sioux clothing, weapons, pictures, and arts and offers for sale authentic Sioux craft items. Open June to Aug., Mon. to Sat., 8 to 5; Sept. to May, Tues, to Sat., 10 to 5; Sun. from 1 p.m. all year. Free.

Horseless Carriage Museum, 10 mi. S of Rapid City on US 16, displays antique cars and 10,000 other artifacts of automotive and general history including firearms, musical instruments, clothing, drugstore items, and doctor and dentist equipment. Open May to Oct., 8 a.m. to 8 p.m. daily; closed rest of year. Adults $1.50, children 6 to 12, 40¢, under 6 free.

South Dakota State Historical Society, in the Soldiers' and Sailors' War Memorial opposite the State Capitol in Pierre, has pioneer, Indian and historic exhibits including a lead plate buried by the first known white men in South Dakota. Open Mon. to Fri., 8 to 5; Sat. from 10 a.m.; Sun. from 1 p.m. Free.

Pioneer Auto Museum and Antique Town, at the junction of I–90 and US 83 in Murdo, has a collection of over 200 antique cars, many still in running condition. There are also antique farm machinery, horse-drawn carriages and wagons, a blacksmith shop, other antiques and exhibits. Open daily: June to Aug., 7 a.m. to 10 p.m.; Apr. to May, Sept. to Nov., 8 a.m. to 6 p.m.; and on request during the rest of the year.

Way Park Museum, in Way City Park on Mt. Rushmore Rd. in Custer, is an 1875 log cabin which houses historical and mineral exhibits. Open June to Aug., daily 8 a.m. to 8 p.m.; closed rest of year. Donation.

How the West Was Won Memorial Museum, at 624 Crook St. Frontier in Custer, is another log building and houses guns, photographs, and other memorabilia from westward expansion. Also here is the *Black Hills Museum of Mining and Minerals* which displays early mining equipment and ores and minerals from the region. Both museums are open May to Oct., daily, 7 a.m. to 11 p.m.; closed rest of year. Adults $1.25, children and servicemen, 75¢.

Adams Memorial Museum, at Sherman and Deadwood Sts. in Deadwood, has exhibits of pioneer days in the Black Hills. Open mid-June to Labor day, daily 8 a.m. to 8 p.m.; rest of year, Mon. to Sat., 9 to 5; Sun. from 2 p.m. Donation.

Dakota Territorial Museum, on Summit Ave. in Yankton's Westside Park, is housed in the restored Dakota Territorial Legislative Assembly Building and offers historical exhibits from early pioneer days. Open Memorial Day to Aug., daily except Tues., 1 to 4 p.m.; rest of year by appointment only. Free.

Because this is Indian country, almost every museum in the state has a few Indian artifacts. Two special museums are only one hour apart. In Sioux Falls, the *Pettigrew Museum,* at 141 N. Duluth Ave., combines Indian exhibits with other historical subjects and natural history. In Vermillion, the *W. H. Over Museum* is on the University campus, on Clark Street. Some exhibits here change from time to time, but Indian materials are excellent because the University is a state center of Indian studies. There are also old guns, equipment, uniforms, bones of prehistoric animals, stuffed animals, an extensive rock and agate collection, and special collections of art and musical instruments. Pettigrew Museum is open Mon. to Sat., 9 a.m. to noon, 1:30 to 5 p.m.; Sun., 2 to 5 p.m. Free. The Over Museum is open Mon. to Fri., 10 a.m. to 4:45 p.m.; Sat., 10 a.m. to noon, 2 to 4:30 p.m., Sun., 2 to 4:30 p.m. Free.

HISTORIC SITES. *Mount Rushmore National Memorial.* Here the faces of four great American Presidents—Washington, Jefferson, Lincoln and Theodore Roosevelt—have been carved and blasted out of the granite of a 6,000-ft. mountain in the Black Hills. These 60-ft.-high heads are the dream of Gutzon Borglum who began the work in 1927. Fourteen years later, in March 1941, he died without having completed it; his son, Lincoln Borglum, took over, finishing in October of that year. Today, more than 2 million visitors each year come to marvel at this massive work.

The memorial is open all year, but snow in the hills can make driving difficult in winter. Located 22 mi. S of Rapid City off US 16A.

What will be the largest statue in the world is being carved out of solid granite atop Thunderhead Mountain, 5 mi. N of Custer off US 16, 385. Korczak Ziolkowski, who assisted Gutzon Borglum on Mt. Rushmore, has undertaken singlehandedly to depict Crazy Horse, the Sioux chief who defeated Lt. Col. Custer, astride an enormous horse. This *Crazy Horse Memorial* will be 641 feet long and 563 feet high, and is intended to honor not only the great Indian chief but also the unconquerable spirit of man. Ziolkowski's 57-room home displays a scale model of the statue. Open daily 6 a.m. to 9 p.m. Admission: $3/carload.

The *Sitting Bull Monument,* on a hill overlooking the Missouri River, marks the burial site of another famous Indian. The bust for this monument was also the work of Korczak Ziolkowski. Located 3 mi. W of Mobridge on US 12, then 4 mi. S on an unnumbered road.

The *Battleship U.S.S. South Dakota Memorial,* at W. 12th St. and Kiwanis Ave. in Sioux Falls, commemorates the famous World War II battleship. The outline of the memorial is the same dimension as the South Dakota. A museum exhibits relics and mementoes of the ship. Open Memorial Day to Labor Day, daily, 10 a.m. to 8 p.m.; closed rest of year. Free.

Nine mi. E of Pine Ridge on US 18 and then 7 mi. N on an unnumbered road is the *Wounded Knee Battlefield* where the last major confrontation between the Sioux and the U.S. Army took place. A monument marks the mass grave site of the many Indians, including women and children, who were shot during and following this battle.

Buried in *Mt. Moriah Cemetery* in Deadwood are such Wild West characters as Wild Bill Hickok, Calamity Jane, and Preacher Smith.

TOURS. *Gray Line* offers a varied program of tours of the Black Hills and Badlands which can include the Passion Play. Free pickup and return to hotels and motels. Write Gray Line of the Black Hills, P. O. Box 1106, Rapid City 57701.

Rushmore Coach Lines has the closest guided tours to Mt. Rushmore and the Southern Black Hills. Daytime tours to points of interest in the Black Hills and an evening schedule to the lighting program at Mt. Rushmore. Free pickup and delivery in the Keystone area. Write Box 253, Keystone, 57751.

The *Needles Highway Scenic Drive,* NE from Custer on State 87, passes tall, granite spires which give the highway its name. This is the most scenic route to many of the other Black Hills attractions.

INDUSTRIAL TOURS. The *Sioux Falls Stockyards Co.,* in the Livestock Exchange Building at Rice St. and Cliff Ave. in Sioux Falls, offers daily tours of the entire stockyard operation from receiving through selling and shipment. Tours are given 24 hours a day.

Homestake Forest Products Co., on W. Oliver St. in Spearfish, gives one-hour guided tours of its lumber production facilities at 10 a.m. and 2 p.m., Mon. to Fri. June to Sept. (Closed to tours Oct. to May.) Adults 50¢, children under 12, 25¢. 642-2731.

272

Black Hills Jewelry Manufacturing Co., at 700 Jackson Blvd. in Rapid City, shows how it produces gold jewelry. Contact Milt Shaver, 343-0157.

Homestake Mine, on Lead's Main St. between Mill St. and the city limits, offers 1½-hour tours of its surface workings and information about gold production. Given June to Aug., Mon. to Sat., 8 to 5; May, Sept. to Oct., Mon. to Fri. to 4 p.m.; closed Nov. to Apr. Free.

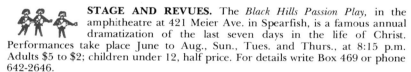 **SPECIAL INTEREST TOURS.** The *Black Hills Central Railroad* offers a 2½-hour, round-trip tour between Custer and Hill City in an 1880 steam train with open and closed cars. The train passes through the magnificent scenery of the Black Hills and near Crazy Horse Memorial. From mid-June to Aug. there are three trips daily (phone 574-2222 for schedule). Round trip fare: adults, $5; children 6 to 12, $2.50; under 6, free. Also, out of Hill City is a 96-mile trip to Deadwood over Nahant Pass. Excursions take place Sat. only, leaving 8 a.m. and returning 6:40 p.m. Fare is $15 which includes refreshments and lunch. Reservations required.

Tours of the *Missouri River Dams* are given regularly, seven days a week, from May 27 to Labor Day. Big Bend Dam at Fort Thompson has tours from 8 a.m. to 4:30 p.m.; Ft. Randall Dam at Pickstown, from 9 a.m. to noon and 1 to 5 p.m.; Oahe Dam at Pierre, 9:30 a.m. to 6 p.m.; and Gavins Point Dam at Yankton, from 10 a.m. to 6 p.m.

The *Corn Palace,* at 604 N. Main St. in Mitchell, while especially interesting for its unusual mixture of architectural styles and its exterior mosaic murals of colored corn, grain and sudan grass, is also open for inspection inside during the summer months. African Trophy Display, art exhibits, souvenirs, free tours and information booth are all accessible from 8 a.m. to 9 p.m. daily, June 1 to Labor Day.

STAGE AND REVUES. The *Black Hills Passion Play,* in the amphitheatre at 421 Meier Ave. in Spearfish, is a famous annual dramatization of the last seven days in the life of Christ. Performances take place June to Aug., Sun., Tues. and Thurs., at 8:15 p.m. Adults $5 to $2; children under 12, half price. For details write Box 469 or phone 642-2646.

The *Crazy Horse Pageant,* which portrays the life of the Sioux warrior, is given every summer, mid-June to late Aug. in the amphitheatre, 5 mi. SE of Hot Springs on US 18, 385. For details phone 745-4140.

Rockerville Meller Drammer Theatre, in the Rockerville Ghost Town near Keystone, offers melodrama and vaudeville from early-June to Labor Day, nightly at 8:30 p.m. Adults $2; students, $1.50; children 6 to 12, $1; children under 6, free. Phone 348-1991.

The *Black Hills Playhouse* in Custer State Park performs contemporary plays in conjunction with the University of South Dakota. On Mon. evenings is "The Legend of Devil's Gulch," the story of the gold rush and arrival of the white man in the Black Hills. Presented mid-June to late Aug., Mon., Wed. to Sun., 8:30 p.m. Tickets are $3.50 to $3. For detailed information phone 255-4141.

On 8th St. in Custer is the melodrama, *"The Hangin' of Flyspeck Billy,"* the tale of a Custer City lynching in 1881. Performances at mid-June to Aug., Mon. to Thurs., 8:30 p.m. Adults $1.50; children 6 to 12, 75¢.

DRINKING LAWS. Liquor may be purchased both by the bottle (in stores) and by the drink. Liquor may be sold in stores from Mon. to Sat., 7 a.m. to midnight; by the drink to 2 a.m.; Sun. 1 to 10 p.m.; subject to local option. Legal drinking age is 18 for 3.2 beer; 21 for all other alcoholic beverages.

SUMMER SPORTS. *Fishing.* The four huge lakes created by damming the Missouri River have made South Dakota one of the finest sportfishing areas for walleye and northern. The reservoirs and streams of the Black Hills offer excellent trout fishing and there are many largemouth bass in stockponds across the state. Nonresident license fees are $8 for a full year or $3 for a five-day permit. *Hunting.* Many consider South Dakota the Pheasant Capital of the World and grouse, prairie chicken, quail, and partridge are plentiful. There are also seasons for duck and geese. Nonresidents may hunt deer with rifles or deer and antelope with bow and arrow. Nonresident waterfowl licenses are $30, big game are $35, and small game $25. *Boating* and *water-skiing.* The same four reservoirs on the Missouri which offer exciting fishing provide ample space for boating and skiing. *Swimming.* In addition to the lakes and reservoirs, there is Evans Plunge, the largest, indoor warm-water pool in the world at Hot Springs. *Golf.* There are numerous courses, although most are 9-hole. Brookings, Canton, Chamberlain, Clark, Milbank, Mitchell, Pierre, Sioux Falls, Vermillion, Watertown, Webster, Pickstown, Yankton, Belle Fourche, Deadwood, Lead, Rapid City, Spearfish, and Sturgis all have one or more courses.

WINTER SPORTS. *Skiing.* There are five ski areas in operation in South Dakota. Best known is Terry Peak in the Black Hills whose 1,200-foot vertical drop from over 7,000 feet makes it the highest ski area east of the Rockies. Facilities include both chair and poma lifts and cross-country trails. The other areas are Great Bear Ski Valley near Sioux Falls, LaCoteau near Sisseton, Deer Mountain Ski Area near Lead, and Inkpa-du-ta near Big Stone City. Ski season generally runs from Thanksgiving to April. *Snowmobiling.* Miles of Forest Service trails in the Black Hills are open to snowmobiles, and shoreline trails in the Northeast Lakes region are cold but extensive. Some of the rolling ranch land of Central South Dakota is open with permission of the owners.

SPECTATOR SPORTS. *Horse racing.* Park Jefferson in Jefferson offers pari-mutuel racing from June to Sept. *Greyhound racing.* The Black Hills Track at Rapid City and Sodrac Park in N. Sioux City have races from June to Sept.

SHOPPING. Authentic Indian items are available throughout the state but the *Sioux Indian Museum and Crafts Center* in Rapid City and at the *Arts and Crafts Center* in Rosebud on the Rosebud Indian Reservation near Mission have particularly interesting displays.

WHAT TO DO WITH THE CHILDREN. Sioux Falls is a good place to bring children because the small but excellent *Great Plains Zoo* (at Kiwanis Ave. and 18th St.) is next to *Dennis the Menace Park.* In the zoo, the children may roam freely and safely. In the park, they may play on a jet plane, a fire engine, and an army tank. A short drive leads to *Terrace Park* (Menlo Ave. and W. Madison St.) where children may fish in a stocked lake. In Rapid City, *Dinosaur Park* on Skyline Dr. has life-size models of prehistoric dinosaurs; eons ago these beasts romped on this spot. Gift shop; soft drinks. See also *Bedrock City,* home of the Flintstones, on the west edge of Custer.

At *Reptile Gardens,* 6 mi. S of Rapid City on US 16, children may view an extensive reptile collection which includes an underground snake den. There are performing animals and children may ride giant tortoises. *Marine Life Aquarium,* 3 mi. S of Rapid City on US 16, has native and tropical fish and performing seals and porpoises. *Story Book Island* is a fairyland park in Rapid City where nursery rhymes come to life. Animals are erected in gigantic living color expecially for children's enjoyment. Open all year, the park is free.

 INDIANS. Approximately five percent of South Dakota's population is Sioux Indian. Once a woods people, the *Sioux* were driven from Minnesota by the Chippewa, who had obtained firearms from the white man to the east. The Sioux adapted themselves readily to life on the plains, becoming essentially nomadic in peace and adept horsemen in war. The horse provided transportation, and the buffalo gave them almost everything else. A proud and mighty people, they have not fared well on the reservation during the past century. Their name, "Sioux," is an abbreviated French corruption of a name given to them by their traditional enemies, the Chippewa, "Nadowe-siw-eg," meaning "enemies" or "the snake-like ones." But the Indians have always called themselves "Dakota," which means "allied" or "friends." Because the Dakota Nation is made up of many tribal groups, this name is fitting, and it has become in turn the name of two states.

South Dakota has eight reservations. Three of them are no longer marked on highway maps—*Sisseton* in the northeast corner, *Yankton* in the southeast, and *Standing Rock* on the Missouri River at the North Dakota border. In effect, these lands have been fully passed over in rental or sale. *Cheyenne River*, west of the Missouri between Pierre and Mobridge, is near the place where Sitting Bull was killed. *Crow Creek*, east of the Missouri between Chamberlain and Pierre, is the home of the Yanktonnais Tribe, and right across the river to the west are the Teton Sioux of *Lower Brule*. A few fort sites and Big Bend Dam are worth looking at here. Of major interest are the two southern reservations. *Rosebud* has the *Sioux Indian Museum* at St. Francis. *Pine Ridge* is the site of the *Battle of Wounded Knee*, west and north of Denby.

The two kinds of *dances* performed by the Indians may be seen at the town of Pine Ridge in the summer. Inquire at the Agency for times and places. Arts and crafts may be purchased here, and summer activities also include rodeos. See also the Indian church, decorated in Sioux symbols. *Our Lady of the Sioux Catholic Church* has Indian murals on the walls, a peace pipe above the altar, and a Christus which looks very much like an Indian.

The only rules for visitors to the reservations are those of common courtesy. No special permission is needed to bring cameras.

 RECOMMENDED READING. Herbert Schell's *History of South Dakota* is the most recent state history. *Black Elk Speaks* is the story of one of the state's most famous Indians, as told by Black Elk himself to John Neihardt. Doane Robinson's *History of the Sioux Indian* is the most comprehensive account of the state's earliest people.

EXPLORING SOUTH DAKOTA

Like its sister state to the north, South Dakota has been known throughout the rest of the country for its summer droughts and winter blizzards because writers such as Hamlin Garland and Ole Rölvaag gave this impression half a century ago. While the state's weather and terrain do vary markedly at times, the overall picture is not discouraging. An increasing number of visitors annually discover that South Dakota is both exciting and comfortable at almost any time of the year. Because it is big and has relatively few people (16th in size and 44th in population), points of interest are often far apart by Eastern standards; yet, it is possible to drive across the state in either direction in one day at moderate speeds. The two largest cities, Sioux Falls and Rapid City, are situated at opposite ends of the state along the same major highway, US 16 and I–90. A north–south highway (I–29) is complete from State 28 to the southern tip.

Where Iowa, Minnesota, and South Dakota come together, just a little east of Sioux Falls, is the center of a region called "Siouxland" by most of the people, by the newspapers, and by the television stations. The name was first applied by novelist Frederick Manfred, who is claimed by all three states.

Indians of Sioux Falls

Sioux Falls itself has been closely associated with the Sioux Indians. First established at the falls of the Big Sioux River, the town was abandoned in 1862 when the Indians went on a rampage in what is now referred to as the Sioux Uprising. The town remained deserted until May 1865, when a fort was built and the settlers returned to stay and found the present city. As for the Indians, the Pettigrew Museum, Eighth Street and Duluth Avenue, has an excellent collection of their arts and crafts, including a cowhide Blackfeet tipi and a large gun collection. In marked contrast to its stormy past, Sioux Falls now boasts the first nuclear equipment in a commercial plant to be used for super-heating steam. The Pathfinder Atomic Power Plant, seven miles northeast on Brandon Road (County 140), is open to visitors almost every day of the year. Add a third fact: the Sioux Falls Stock Yards currently tops the nation in sheep receipts. This, then, is a good picture of modern-day South Dakota: Indian lore, agriculture, and splitting atoms.

Animals—Alive and Kicking

Sioux Falls is a bustling city of 77,000 with fine stores, elegant residential areas, parks, and two colleges, Augustana and Sioux Falls. As the city expands and new highways are built, the residents fully expect that Sioux Falls will be the important crossroads of the northern region. Some of the more impressive commercial concerns are several first-class printing companies. In terms of volume, however, the leading industries are the stockyards and packing companies.

Sioux Falls has live animals, too. Its Great Plains Zoo near the west edge of town, just off US 16 in Sherman Park, is one of the finest small zoos in the country. In addition to those animals and birds which are found on the Plains, the zoo exhibits llamas and lions, and others. Adjoining the zoo is a children's park with a jet plane, army tank, fire engine, and other items which may be climbed on and played in. Four blocks away, in the same park, see a 1,600–year–old Indian burial mound.

Because, in a sense, the heart of the nation is its livestock industry, visitors may take a two-hour tour of the Morrell Meatpacking Plant at 1400 North Weber Avenue and the Sioux Falls Stock Yards. Approximately 100 beef, 200 sheep, and 750 hogs are processed at Morrell's every hour. Needless to say, it is not difficult to get an unusually good meal in Sioux Falls — featuring beef on the plate. Beef on the hoof is a common sight on every farm in the surrounding area, and you will see the herds as you leave Sioux Falls and drive north on US 77. At Dell Rapids the Sioux River has cut a gorge through the red quartzite, forming the Dells. For a close look, leave the car and walk on the top of the cliffs. Then, continue north on I–29 to Brookings, home of South Dakota State University. Coughlin Campanile is 165 feet high and has been named "The Singing Silo" by students. In the South Dakota Memorial Art Center there is a collection of paintings by Harvey Dunn, many of which were used as national magazine cover illustrations. Tours may be made of the 960-acre farm run by the Agricultural Experimental Station.

The northeast corner of the state, above Brookings, is lake country. Watertown, on US 81, has a large lake with recreation areas. The Mellette House, 421 Fifth Avenue Northwest, which has been restored and furnished in the style of the 1880's, was the home of the first governor of South Dakota. At Milbank, on US 77, a monument marks the birthplace of American Legion Junior Baseball. Here also are the world's largest mahogany granite quarry, the only granite bowling lanes, and a windmill (near railroad depot) built in 1885. The agency for the Sisseton-Wahpeton reservation is located in Sisseton, north again on US 81. Turn west twenty miles to Lake City for excellent fishing. This is where Inkpaduta, a renegade Indian, held white women as hostages during the Indian wars. One of the best-preserved forts of that time is seven miles west of Lake City and about the same distance south. Fort Sisseton was built in 1864 at a cost of two million dollars, with bricks being hauled in from St. Cloud, Minnesota, supplies from St. Paul, and many stones from as far away as Wahpeton, North Dakota. During the 1880's, the fort was the social center of the eastern half of Dakota Territory.

Webster, south on State 23, has one of the five salt-water conversion plants in the U.S. A guided tour is available. The plant is used to make fresh water from brackish water. At Aberdeen, west of Webster on US 12, the Fischer quintuplets live in a new house with almost as many electrical circuits and outlets as a hotel. They were born in 1963. Aberdeen is a railroad town and farm shipping center which was settled largely by German-Russian immigrants. Two authors lived here, L. Frank Baum who wrote the *Wizard of Oz* stories, and Hamlin Garland whose homestead is near Ordway.

US 281 runs straight and fast south from Aberdeen. For almost one hundred miles, to Huron, there is little to see except fields. But, this is the world-famous pheasant country. The problem is often not one of finding pheasants, but avoiding them. At certain times of the year they literally swarm across the highway at intervals, and the motorist must slow down and keep a careful watch. Several times each year, unwary drivers find unwary pheasants coming through the windshield. The bird has been memorialized in Huron, on US 14 near Memorial Park, with a steel and fiberglas statue, forty feet high, billed as the world's largest pheasant. Huron seems to like big things: the high school auditorium seats 8,000. The town itself, however, is small and pleasant. Huron College is on Illinois Avenue. Huron is the hometown of former Vice-President Hubert H. Humphrey. The pharmacy in which he worked his way through college is still owned by the family who employed him and still in business.

From Huron it is only an hour's drive south on State 37 to the Mitchell Corn Palace. This huge building looks more Oriental than Midwest with turrets and spired domes that soar into the South Dakota sky and flags and pennants that wave in the breeze. Each year the outside of the building is decorated in murals made of colored corn and cereal grasses. Two to three thousand bushels of corn are needed to make the designs. Late in September an elaborate festival is held here, at Main and Sixth streets. Near the campus of Dakota Wesleyan University, two blocks south of the junction of State 37 and US 16, is a museum sponsored by a unique organization, The Friends of the Middle Border. Among the people who began this venture were Hamlin Garland, John Dewey, and James Adams.

If you take time to talk with the small-town people in the eastern half of South Dakota, you will find them friendly, genuine, and perhaps a bit homey or unsophisticated. Some are reserved, but all are willing to help a stranger. They are Norwegian, German, Czech, Dutch, Swedish, and Danish in background, although in some towns (especially those with the colleges) there is a more diverse population. Withal, the most exciting place in this half of the state is Gavins Point, near

Yankton. From Mitchell take State 37 south to State 50, then east to Yankton. As you reach the edge of town, you will see the beautiful Gothic buildings of Mount Marty College and Sacred Heart Hospital. Turn right (west) on State 52 for approximately four miles. Stop first at the Federal Fish Hatchery and Aquarium, where you can see rainbow trout, catfish, bass, northern pike, and other fish. In the hatchery building there are hatching jars which hold up to forty million eggs. The aquarium has thirteen display tanks, each fitted realistically with rocks, tree trunks, and gravel. The huge catfish and sturgeon vie for attention, but the most fascinating fish is a prehistoric carryover, the paddle fish. He has a long flat paddle instead of a nose, and is found in only two places in the world: the Missouri River and the Yangtze River in China.

Fishing in Lewis and Clark Lake

Just above the hatchery turn left and drive across the mile–long earthen dam which backs up the Missouri to form Lewis and Clark Lake. The power plant, located on the Nebraska side of the river, is open to visitors. Besides taking a conducted tour, you will want to examine the exhibits in the lobby and perhaps plot your own personal tour of the area from the large map. Outside, the observation deck gives an awesome view of the river, one of the mightiest in the world until partially tamed by six dams in South Dakota, North Dakota, and Montana. The dams have altered the land, changed the psychology of the people, and provided immense potential in irrigation and electric power. The lakes created range from forty to more than two hundred miles long. They currently provide some of the best fishing in the nation. As you watch speedboats and fishermen, remember Lewis and Clark came up this fearsome river in keelboats propelled by hand. Nearby, up on the bluff, they made camp and held their first formal council with the Sioux Indian nation. This was the site of the main camp of the Yankton tribe of Sioux, and one occasionally finds arrowheads, beads and pieces of pottery along the lake shore, washed up by the river which swallowed the old Indian villages.

Back on the South Dakota side of the river many attractions await your pleasure. At the marina there are boats available for fishing or sightseeing. For almost forty miles up the river (take State 52 and be prepared to turn off on the side road of your choice) there are many areas for picnicking, camping, or exploring. Near the dam and marina is Fort Dakota, built recently to resemble an authentic frontier city inside stockade walls. Meals and refreshments are available here, and a small train takes passengers on a mile–long trip around the grounds. The stockade includes a schoolroom, a jail, a newspaper office, a chapel, a soda parlor, and a saloon, all done in frontier style.

It would be easy to spend several days on Lewis and Clark Lake, but for accommodations it is necessary to return to Yankton. This is a small, unassuming city, which was perhaps the scene of more historical events than any other place in the state. Its many 19th-century houses give it an air of dignity, and much of its tradition has been set by Yankton College, the first in Dakota Territory. Yankton was the territorial capital before South Dakota became a separate state, and the first legislature met in the home of William Tripp. The house has been restored as a museum in Waterworks Park overlooking the river. When the Indians rebelled in 1862, a stockade was erected at Third and Broadway to protect residents of both Yankton and Sioux Falls. The oldest daily newspaper in the state is still being published on Walnut Street. Its first issue appeared during the Black Hills gold rush of 1875, and a year later it carried the story of Custer's death under these angry and biased headlines: "Telegraphic: Death. Custer and His Entire Command Swept out of Existence by the Wards of the Nation and the Special Pets of Eastern Orators." To the settlers who lived in the midst of a. clear danger; to them the Indian was simply a menace. Modern South Dakotans have also been slow in changing that early opinion, so that its Indians must still fight hard for recognition. Nevertheless, the state has been represented by an Indian Congressman.

Wild Bill Hickok's Killer

As in most Western towns, the old and the new blend nicely. A marker shows where Jack McCall was hanged for the murder of Wild Bill Hickok, and a sign explains somewhat apologetically that his was the last hanging in South Dakota, 1877. At Second and Capital streets, the Gurney Seed and Nursery Company is one of the largest of its kind, doing mail order business throughout the United States. Do not leave Yankton without enjoying a steak at *The Black Steer*, 300 East Third, an outstanding steakhouse in a region which prides itself on good beef. Continue east on State 50 to Vermillion, the last stop on our tour of the eastern half of the state.

Because of the constant threat of flooding by the Missouri, Vermillion is a river town which had to be relocated on higher ground. Lewis and Clark stopped here, getting out of their keelboats and walking a few miles north to Spirit Mound (now on

State 19), held sacred by the Indians. Thirty years later the American Fur Company built a fort on the river, and in 1843 John James Audubon, the famous naturalist and wildlife painter, visited the fort and walked through the present city. Vermillion is a typical sleepy town except for the University of South Dakota which gives it a cosmopolitan atmosphere and keeps it growing. The story is told that when Yankton was being considered as the capital for the new state, Sioux Falls was given first choice of state institutions; Vermillion had second choice. Sioux Falls took what to them seemed a sure thing, the state penitentiary, and has regretted the decision ever since. Vermillion chose the state university. Its first president (and lone faculty member) was Dr. Ephriam Epstein, a Russian Jew who had become a Baptist clergyman only to organize a secular university.

Cultural Center

Vermillion is the cultural center of the state, because of the activities of the University. It has a collection of old documents and historic newspapers in the library, and it has the excellent but crowded W. H. Over Dakota Museum on East Clark Street. Here are Indian relics, firearms, stones, fossils, a Pioneer Room, an Indian panorama, and the Arne B. Larson collection of old musical instruments, one of the largest anywhere. The museum also has a widely known collection of pioneer and military photographs which are often used to illustrate books about the Old West. A number of Indian activities are associated with the museum and with specific Indian organizations on campus. Dr. James Gillihan is director of the museum.

Carrying the past into the present, Oscar Howe, a Sioux Indian who is artist-in-residence at the university, paints with the symbols of his ancestors but gives them contemporary designs and meaning. Winner of many national competitions, Mr. Howe finds his paintings in great demand. His studio and gallery are in the museum. Also working in contemporary techniques but basing his themes on regional history is Dr. Robert Marek, musical composer. The *South Dakota Review*, emphasizing Western American literature and regional writing, is published at the University. Frederick Manfred is writer-in-residence. The university radio and television stations, under the current direction of Martin Busch, are leaders in their field, producing programs of a regional emphasis which appear on educational channels throughout the Midwest. The university is active in many other areas which affect the state as a whole, including research centers in social work, psychology, speech and hearing, government, and geology.

Partly because of the university, the town of Vermillion is growing at a rate which confounds the city fathers. In 1965 the total building permits were exceeded only by those in Sioux Falls, the largest city in the state. The comfortable old homes on tree-lined streets now stand in contrast to new residential areas near the river bluff.

A fast, pleasant drive back to Sioux Falls (I–29) completes the tour of Eastern South Dakota.

The western half of South Dakota is in some ways a different country altogether, with greater aridity, fewer trees and people, wider and more open spaces, and drier air which is easier to breathe. There are more Indians, and, until you get to the Black Hills, everything is farther apart. This means that the traveler must decide whether to head straight for the Hills or to devote at least several days to seeing many fort sites or Indian reservations. The Missouri River flows southward across the state, and is the dividing line between the two halves of the state. It is crossed by five major highways, four of which go to the Black Hills, and by two state roads. US 12 crosses at Mobridge, in the north.

The municipal auditorium at Mobridge has several murals by Oscar Howe depicting the ceremonies and historical events of his Indian people. The Land of the Sioux Museum, at the north end of Main Street, has Indian relics. Again you are in the middle of Sioux country. Sitting Bull was born and was slain not far from Mobridge. A monument to his memory stands on a hill with an exceptional view of the Missouri and its valley, three miles west on US 12 and two miles south on an unnumbered road. Whether the old chief really rests beneath his monument is a matter of debate: South Dakotans say yes, he does, and North Dakotans say no, it is impossible. Wakpala, north about ten miles on US 12 and then east at Sherwood's Corners (saloon and filling station) on a dirt road, is the location of St. Elizabeth's School for Indians. The director of the school from 1958 to 1961 was William McK. Chapman, former editor for *Time, Sports Illustrated,* and *House and Garden.* In 1965 Chapman published a book devoted entirely to his experiences at Wakpala. *Remember the Wind: A Prairie Memoir,* destined to make Wakapala a good deal more famous than it had been, is both humorous and tragic in its presentation of the Sioux Indians.

To the south again, Highway 212 crosses the river west of Gettysburg and then goes through the center of the Cheyenne River Indian Reservation. This is lonely country. South once more, US 14 passes through Pierre at the river. Pronounced "peer" by the natives, this is the capital city of South Dakota. Rich in history, it has not yet become a modern or impressive city. Early fur trade centered around the fort which was across the river, and the current economy is based on government almost as much as on cattle and crops. The state legislature is highly conservative and boasts of keeping the state out of debt. In fact, the state has a surplus in its treasury, a condition almost unbelievable in this day of deficit spending. However, it has meant that the school system lags in building, in staffing, and in salaries. One source of new potential is the Oahe Dam with its power plants six miles north on State 514. This is the largest of the six Missouri dams and the largest rolled earth dam in the world.

At the south end of the state, US 18 crosses the river on top of Fort Randall Dam. Remains of the old fort may be seen on the south shore just below the dam. Abandoned in 1892, the parade ground is still visible, as well as excavations of several buildings, and the ruins of the chapel. If you like ruins, this is one of the best until you get to Fort Laramie, Wyoming. West is cattle country, and Winner was the scene of an old-style cross-country cattle drive only a few years ago. The cowboys are still rugged, even though they bunk in motels. At Mission you are well into the Rosebud Indian Reservation. Six miles west of town turn left on an unnumbered road and drive eleven miles to the reservation headquarters and seven miles more to the St. Francis Indian Museum. A few hours to the west, again on US 18, lies one of the most famous (or infamous) battlefields in the West. Nine miles past Denby, turn north for six miles on another of those unnumbered roads so common in the West. The spot is marked by a monument, a museum, and a library. A Nevada Paiute Indian who claimed to have seen a vision following an eclipse of the sun in 1889 convinced many Indians that they were invincible and that they should drive the white man off the face of the earth. The confusion and terror which followed have been referred to as the Messiah Craze. Ghost shirt rituals reached their height, and after Sitting Bull was killed his followers gathered near Wounded Knee Creek. The U.S. Seventh Cavalry searched the band for weapons. A shot, presumably accidental, set off a fight in which sixty-two women and children were among the Indian dead. The public was aroused by this slaughter. Some people suggested that cattlemen had encouraged a war-scare to keep homesteaders out of the newly opened range. The proud Sioux, after this last conflict with the U.S. Army, did not take well to farming so they remained poor for a long time. Today they engage successfully in arts and crafts, which may be seen at Pine Ridge.

Another route to the Rosebud and Pine Ridge Reservations

takes you across the new (1966) Francis Case Bridge on State 44 west of Platte. This is the longest bridge between the Mississippi and the Pacific, spanning a mile–wide channel.

The Badlands

The Missouri may be crossed at Chamberlain, on the main route (US 16 and I–90) from Sioux Falls to Rapid City; or, north on State 47 and back down on 47W takes you across Big Bend Dam and circles a small area where many forts and trading posts once stood. It will also take you through another Indian reservation. Crow Creek is on one side of the river and Lower Brule on the other side. On the way now to the Badlands and Black Hills, you may wish to see the Pioneer Auto Museum and the well-run Indian Museum in Murdo, an old cowtown which still lives largely off cows. At Kadoka, another cowtown, the Badlands Petrified Gardens have on display many of the petrified woods, fossils, and minerals to be found in the Badlands. The Badlands themselves are reached by turning south on Alternate US 16, just eighteen miles west of Kadoka. The headquarters are at Cedar Pass, another nine miles, where exhibits and audio-visual programs illustrate this fantastic area of wind- and water-eroded rocks. Millions of years ago this jagged and desolate area was a flat grassland and the home of prehistoric beasts such as the sabertoothed tiger and the titanosaur. Then the earth's crust rose and volcanic ash drifted down. Rivers carved gorges and the winds of thousands of centuries slowly wore away the softer rock and left sharp spires, rounded cones and grotesque designs. The Badlands are a rich fossil bed, but it is illegal to remove specimens. Picture-taking, however, will provide a thrill almost equal to the finding of a tiger bone. Subtle colors, especially striking in early morning and late afternoon, are difficult to capture but are worth many hours of trying. As for the fossils, see them under plexiglass along the fossil trail, exactly where they were found.

As you come back to the main highway again, at Wall, stop to see the wildest drugstore in the West. At Wasta, the Sioux Indians have built an authentic Indian camp where the Old West comes to life again.

The fabled Black Hills are entered from Rapid City, a fast-growing community which depends primarily upon ranching, farming, and tourism. Growth was stimulated during the war years by an air base. More recently missile sites have been erected nearby. But there is no doubt that its economy and its people are deeply affected by the Black Hills, which begin to rise on the edge of the city. There is probably more sightseeing to be done within ten miles of Rapid City than in hundreds of miles elsewhere in the state. The South Dakota School of Mines on St. Joseph Street has an outstanding geological museum. A federal Indian museum in Halley Park has dioramas and other displays of Sioux life. For the children, a fairy tale playground is located on Story Book Island, two miles southwest on State 40; and lifesize models of dinosaurs, who once romped around rather heavily in this very spot, stand on a hill by Skyline Drive. South on US 16 are the reptile gardens (five miles) where the children may ride a giant tortoise, a horseless carriage museum (ten miles) where Dad can reminisce, and Rockerville (twelve miles) where a placer mining town has been re-created.

The Black Hills are really green, of course, close up. From a distance they look black, as they did to the Indians who considered them to be a holy place. The white man invaded the Hills almost overnight, and most of the towns and villages which you see now are still mining for gold—the tourist's gold. Tourism is the big business, although the Homestake Mine in Lead (pronounced Leed), nearing its 100th year of profitable operation, produces more gold than any mine in the Western Hemisphere. Tours are conducted here, but only on the surface.

For an exciting underground tour, go to the Broken Boot gold mine in Deadwood, one mile west of town on US 14A. It no longer produces gold, but that hardly matters to the visitors who venture into the tunnels. Deadwood is also the place where Wild Bill Hickok and Calamity Jane are buried (in Mount Moriah Cemetery look for signs downtown). Deadwood is a one-street town; its main thoroughfare runs down the narrow Deadwood Gulch and the side streets are little more than alleys up the mountain. A highway is being built on top of Deadwood Creek, because there is no other level place for it. At Hill City (on US 16) you can go up the mountain in a small steam train. Or drive up the mountain from Hill City (south on US 16 and State 87) to Sylvan Lake, the prettiest spot in the Hills and a popular resort area. If you want to go still higher, take an exciting jeep ride up Harney Peak—way up.

Everything in the Hills seems dramatic, from the natural heights and curving roads to the elements which man has introduced. Mount Rushmore, about twenty-five miles southwest of Rapid City on US 16A, is impressive enough as a mountain, but man has added to nature here. Carved into the granite face of the mountain are the amazingly detailed likenesses of Washington, Jefferson, Lincoln, and Theodore Roosevelt. Blasted with dynamite and carved under the supervision of Gutzon Borglum, each face is almost seventy feet high. This is the one place no one misses on his first trip to the Hills. Signs will direct you to the best places for taking pictures of the faces on the mountain.

A thrill for children is Bedrock City, on the west edge of Custer, where the Flintstones stand in concrete amid a prehistoric atmosphere. Flintstone movies are shown in the theatre, and there is a playground and a camping area.

Five miles north of Custer on US 16 an even larger memorial is being slowly carved out of the mountains. When Crazy Horse and his horse are completed they will be over five hundred feet tall and over six hundred feet long. The sculptor, Korczak Ziolkowski, welcomes visitors to his home, studio and gallery. Drama in a different fashion is found in Custer State Park, where, from the Game Lodge, the visitor may take a jeep ride out to one of the largest buffalo herds in the country. The trip is a far cry from automobile travel on four-lane highways, for the jeeps cross rough terrain, go up small mountainsides, cross dry creek beds, and head out onto open prairie to take you inside a buffalo herd. Don't forget the camera this time, because you may be staring a ferocious-looking bull right in the eyes before the day is over. It's perfectly safe, but a thrill nevertheless.

Drama on stage is found at the Black Hills Playhouse, which celebrated its twenty-fifth season in 1970. Ten miles east of Custer, go north on State 87 and watch the signs. Directed by Dr. Warren Lee, the playhouse operates as part of the summer session of the University of South Dakota, but its actors come from all over the country. Plays are presented six nights a week during the summer, both legitimate theater and melodrama. One of the most popular performances is Dr. Lee's own historical fantasy, *The Legend of Devil's Gulch.* Farther north, at Spearfish, the *Black Hills Passion Play* entered its fortieth season in the U.S. in 1971, after originating in Germany. Incidents in the life of Christ are presented by a cast of hundreds in a natural mountain amphitheatre.

Spearfish is the logical place of departure from the Black Hills if you are going north or west. If you are going south from here, Hot Springs makes a good last stop. But first visit the caves about ten miles north of town. Wind Cave National Park takes its name from curious air currents which blow in and out of the cave. Park rangers conduct safe tours underground. Above ground there are herds of buffalo, deer, and antelope, and visitors should not get out of their cars in the presence of these wild animals. Before leaving the state, plunge into the largest indoor natural warm-water pool in the world, Evans Plunge, 1145 North River Street in Hot Springs. The relaxing mineral waters will give you a chance to think back on the many things you have seen and done in South Dakota, the friendly land of infinite variety.

AROUND THE STATE

 HOTELS AND MOTELS in South Dakota, because they are generally smaller than those in the east or west, offer the tourist a homelike atmosphere and friendly good will. Rates out of season may be lower than the in-season categories we quote.

The price categories in this section, for double occupancy, will average as follows: *Deluxe* $24, *Expensive* $20, *Moderate* $16, and *Inexpensive* $12. For a more complete description of these categories see the *Hotels & Motels* section of THE ROCKIES & PLAINS *Facts at Your Fingertips* at the front of this volume.

ABERDEEN

Holiday Inn. *Moderate.* 2727 6th Ave. S.E. Indoor heated pool, color TV, restaurant, lounge, playground, recreation room. 225-3600

BELLE FOURCHE

Kings Inn. *Moderate.* 518 National St. Color TV, heated pool, restaurant and lounge. Bowling alley, beauty salon and laundromat adjacent. 892-2691

Gay. *Inexpensive.* 109 6th Ave., 1 blk. E of US 85. At the northern entrance to the Black Hills, this small motel is pleasant and comfortable. Color TV, free coffee. 24-hour cafe nearby. Family rates. 892-2612

BROOKINGS.

Staurolite Inn. *Expensive.* 2515 6th St., ½ mi. from South Dakota State University. Heated pool, color TV, sauna, coffee shop and dining room, bar and lounge, meeting rooms. Dry-cleaning service and courtesy car service is available. 692-9421

Brookings Downtown. *Inexpensive.* On US 14, 2 blks. from Main St. An appealing motel with heated pool and color TV. Well-furnished rooms. Family rates and units. Restaurant nearby. 692-6345

CHAMBERLAIN

Lake Shore. *Inexpensive.* On River St. Nice view of Missouri River. Small

quiet motel with comfortable rooms. Color TV, free coffee. Restaurant nearby. 734-5566

CUSTER

Rocket Motel. *Moderate.* 211 Mt. Rushmore Rd. Newly remodeled, color TV. Restaurant nearby. Closed Dec. to Apr. 14. 673-4401

Sylvan Lake Resort. *Moderate.* 8 mi. N of State 87, 89 in Custer State Park. Has a variety of hotel rooms and cabins, with kitchens in some. Most have room phones, but the emphasis is on outdoor living. Restaurant area, boats, fishing, riding. In the Black Hills overlooking the lake. 574-2561

DEADWOOD

Western Motor Inn. *Moderate.* 137 Charles St. on US 85. Color TV, restaurant, attractive rooms. 578-1611

HURON

Plains. *Inexpensive.* 4th St. N.E. and Jersey Ave. Color TV, heated pool. Extra-large rooms tastefully furnished. Restaurant and cocktail lounge. Family rates. Bowling available nearby. 352-6755

Traveler. *Inexpensive.* 241 Lincoln N.W., W on US 14 Business. Small and comfortable. Nicely landscaped grounds with picnic area and playground. Color TV, free coffee. Cafe nearby. Family rates. 352-6703

KADOKA

H & H El Centro. *Moderate.* ¼ mi. NE on US 16, I–90 Business. Large, well-furnished rooms. On spacious grounds with heated pool, wading pool, recreation area. Color TV. Restaurant. Meeting facilities. 837-2287

MITCHELL

Anthony. *Inexpensive.* 1518 W. Havens, W on US 16. Has cheerful rooms with color TV, phones, and air-conditioning. Recreation and picnic area. Restaurant next door. 996-7518

MOBRIDGE

Wrangler. *Moderate.* ½ mi. W on US 12. A small, two-story motel overlooking Lake Oahe. Spacious and well-furnished rooms. Recreation area. Color TV. Restaurant 1 blk. Main thing here is the view and the convenience to the dam. 845-3641

MURDO

Graham Motor Lodge. *Moderate.* ¼ mi. SW on US 16. Inviting and attractive. This medium-size, nicely decorated motel offers TV, heated pool, free coffee, playground. Cafe nearby. Pioneer Auto Museum nearby. Family rates. 669-2441

PIERRE

Holiday Inn. *Expensive.* 125 W. Pleasant Dr. at St. Pierre St. on US 14 and 83. Color TV, heated pool, restaurant, bar, dancing, entertainment. Family plan. 224-5981

State. *Moderate.* 640 N. Euclid on US 14 and 83. While quite small, this motel has very pleasant rooms with air-conditioning and color TV. Restaurant nearby. 224-5896

RAPID CITY

Gill's Sun Inn. *Deluxe.* 1901 W. Main St. on I–90 Business Loop. This medium-size motel has a wide variety of well-maintained and attractive units, including studios and suites. TV, some

color; heated pool, restaurant, bar. Baby sitters, house physician and dentist. 343-6040

Holiday Inn. *Deluxe.* 1902 LaCross St., NE on I–90. A large, two-story chain member with nicely furnished rooms. Color TV, heated pool, playground, free coffee, restaurant and cocktail lounge. Meeting facilities. Airport courtesy car. Family rates. 348-1230

Town 'N Country. *Expensive.* 1215 Mt. Rushmore Rd., S on US 16. Handsome, medium-size motel of one and two stories set back from the highway. Very charming and spacious rooms, many newly built. Color TV, 2 heated pools, playground, rock and gem shop. Tour arrangements. 343-5383

Imperial "400" Motel. *Moderate.* 125 Main St. A two-story, downtown motel with colorful rooms. Color TV, heated pool, free coffee, sauna, restaurant, lounge, coffee shop. Meeting, banquet and convention facilities. 343-5435

Jensen's Motor Lodge. *Moderate.* 1916 Mt. Rushmore Rd. Heated pool, some color TV, free coffee. Restaurant nearby. 342-3270

Tip Top. *Moderate.* 405 St. Joseph St. A medium-size motel with well-furnished rooms plus a few kitchen units. Heated pool, sun deck, color TV. Coffee shop and cocktail lounge. Family rates. 343-3901

Dakota Motel. *Inexpensive.* 220 E. St. Joseph St. TV, some kitchenettes. Restaurant adjacent. Tours arranged. 342-2896

SIOUX FALLS

Holiday Inn Airport. *Expensive.* 1301 W. Russell St. at West Ave. Color TV, heated pool, whirlpool bath, sauna. Recreation room. Putting green. Restaurant, bar, dancing, entertainment. Free airport bus. 336-1020

Lindendale Motel. *Moderate.* 4201 S.

Minnesota Ave. A small motel, large rooms. Spacious grounds with shade trees, heated pool, children's play area. Some color TV. Restaurant and shopping area a few blocks away. 336-1970

Ramada Inn. *Moderate.* 2400 N. Louise at jct. I–29 and State 38. Color TV, heated pool, restaurant, lounge, dancing, entertainment. Close to airport, shopping, Great Plains Zoo. Airport courtesy car. 336-0650

Town House. *Moderate.* 400 S. Main Ave. The convenience of downtown location near restaurants and shops. Nicely furnished, this medium-sized motel offers heated pool, color TV, free coffee, restaurant, bar. 336-2740

Train-Motel. *Inexpensive.* 4601 W. 12th St., W on US 16 at jct. I–29. A small motel with heated pool, color TV, playground. 24-hour cafe nearby. Horseshoes. Camp and trailer sites, picnic tables. 332-9644

SPEARFISH

Royal Rest. *Moderate.* 444 Main St. A small motel located near the amphitheatre where the Passion Play is performed in summer. Good selection of accommodationss and rates, including family. Color TV. Restaurant across the street. Recreation area. 642-3842

McColley. *Inexpensive.* 135 E. Illinois St. Small downtown motel set around a shaded courtyard. Has nice well-

furnished rooms and a few family units with kitchens. Heated pool. Restaurant nearby. 642-2742

VERMILLION

Lamplighter. *Moderate.* 112 E. Cherry St. Very nice accommodations. TV, heated pool, restaurant next door. Near University of South Dakota campus. 624-4451

WATERTOWN

Plateau Inn. *Moderate.* On US 212, W of jct. with US 81. Extremely nice two-story motel with handsome rooms and oversize beds. Color TV, heated pool, playground, Wedding Chapel, dining room, coffee shop, cocktail lounge. Bowling. Family rates. 886-8011

YANKTON

Kochi Motel. *Expensive.* 2 mi. N on US 81. Medium-size, two-story motel with large rooms, all with balconies. Color TV, heated pool, children's pool, bowling. Coffee shop and supper club, bar, dancing. Set back from highway on impressive grounds. 665-7885

Skyline. *Inexpensive.* 1200 N. Broadway. N on US 81. A small, well-run motel with delightful accommodations. Air-conditioning, color TV, heated pool, sundeck, play area. Restaurant and coffee shop, lounge, dancing. Family rates. 665-7805

DINING OUT. The number of tourists visiting South Dakota has increased dramatically in recent years, and as a result many of the newer restaurants have been built in conjunction with the motels intended to accommodate this influx of visitors. But there remain a number of restaurants, not associated with any lodging establishment, which serve good food, usually at moderate prices.

Restaurant price categories are as follows: *Deluxe* will average $8.50 and up, *Expensive* $5–$7.50, *Moderate* $3–$5, and *Inexpensive* $1.75–$3. These prices are for *hors d'oeuvres* or soup, *entrée*, and dessert. Not included are drinks, tax and tips. For a more complete explanation of restaurant categories refer to THE ROCKIES & PLAINS *Facts at Your Fingertips* at the front of this volume.

CUSTER

Skyway Cafe. *Moderate.* 515 Mt. Rushmore Rd. Serves steaks, seafood and other well-prepared foods and baked goods in pleasant modern surroundings. Cocktail lounge. Open 6 a.m. to 11 p.m., Apr. to Nov.; from 11 a.m. to midnight rest of year. 673-4477

KEYSTONE

Buffalo Room. *Moderate.* 2 mi. W off State 10A. View the Mount Rushmore Memorial in the Black Hills. Cafeteria-style service featuring salad bar, homemade pastries and rolls. Snack bar and gift shop. Open 7:30 to 10 a.m., 10:30 a.m. to 3 p.m., 5 to 8 p.m.; after Labor Day to May, snack bar only 9 a.m. to 4 p.m. 574-2515

MITCHELL

Chef Louie's Steak House. *Expensive.* E on I–90 Business Loop at jct. US 16, State 37. Mitchell's leading steak house and cocktail lounge. Friendly atmosphere. Specialties include pheasant with wild rice, as well as a fine variety of steaks. Open 4 p.m. to 11 p.m. 996-7565

MURDO

Star Restaurant. *Moderate.* On US 16, just W of jct. US 83. Serves wholesome food, with steak the specialty. Children's plates. Open 6:30 a.m. to 10 p.m. Closed Oct. 16 to May 14. 669-2411

RAPID CITY

The Embers. *Expensive.* 2424 W. Main St. Its cozy atmosphere is just right for grilled specialties and the late evening entertainment or dancing. Cocktails. Polynesian and American menu. Open 11:30 a.m. to 2 a.m. Closed Sun. 348-0111

The Chuck Wagon. *Moderate.* 3609 Sturgis Rd., NW on State 79. Western decor includes waitresses in costume. Fun for the children. Chuck Wagon buffet daily, fish fry on Friday. Children's portions available. Open 6 a.m. to 9 p.m. 343-9375

Taylor's. *Moderate.* 2501 Mt. Rushmore Rd. Locally popular this restaurant serves basic fare in an early American decor. Open 6 a.m. to 11 p.m. 342-6886

Westwood. *Moderate.* 516 Mt. Rushmore Rd., on US 16. An attractive modern setting for a variety of popular beef specialties. Children's plates. Open 11 a.m. to 11 p.m. 342-5911

Tally's. *Inexpensive.* 530 6th St., on US 16. The specialties are steak and their own pastries. Open 7 a.m. to 10 p.m. Closed Sun. 342-7621

SIOUX FALLS

Wilson's Town 'N Country Restaurant. *Moderate.* 2104 W. 12th St. W edge on US 16. Serves a variety of home-cooked food including their own pastries and breads. Open 7 a.m. to 10 p.m.; until 9 p.m. Sept. 1 to June 15. 338-6361

Lemonds' Finer Foods. *Inexpensive.* 301 S. Phillips Ave. on US 16. Steak is the specialty but sandwiches and salads are also served. A good restaurant for families. Does its own baking. Open 7 a.m. to 7 p.m. Closed Sun. and hols. 334-5441

VERMILLION

The Prairie. *Moderate.* 1 blk. N of State 50. Coffee shop and dining room, serving steak but with a broad, general menu. Cocktails and bowling on premises also. Open 7 a.m. to 1 a.m. 624-2657

YANKTON

The Black Steer. *Moderate.* 3rd and Pine Sts., S of State 50. Rated highly by people in this corner of the state. Pleasant atmosphere for the charcoal-broiled steaks, chicken. Children's plates. Cocktails. Open 4:30 p.m. to midnight; Sun. 4 to 9 p.m. 665-5771

Kochi Lounge and Supper Club. *Moderate.* On US 81, 3 mi. N. In an impressive Oriental decor this restaurant features prime steaks and a weekly special. Children's servings. Cocktails. Entertainment Fri. and Sat. Open 4:30 p.m. to 1 a.m. Closed Sun. 665-9174

Russo's. *Moderate.* 311 Cedar. Enjoy Italian atmosphere and fine Italian cuisine at this small restaurant specializing in pasta dishes. Also serves pizza and sandwiches. Open 10 a.m. to midnight. 665-9085

NEBRASKA

The Full Larder

by

LOWELL JOHNSON

Lowell Johnson is the editor of NEBRASKAland Magazine, *the official publication of the Nebraska Game and Parks Commission. In this capacity, he travels every corner of the state, and is familiar with its scenery, wildlife, and people.*

There was a time when the Nebraska Territory consisted of virutally all that was known of the western United States. It stretched from the Missouri River to the Rockies and from Kansas to the Canadian Border. Yet for all its vast expanse the state remained sparsely populated. The first territorial census in 1854 showed only 2,732 whites living within the borders.

The attraction of the real or imagined riches in the west, however, brought thousands of hopeful people pouring across Nebraska's borders on their way to easy fortunes.

A few of these recognized the potentially rich farmland in the territory and remained behind. By 1856 there were over 10,000 white settlers. But it was not until after the Civil War that the stage was truly set for Nebraska settlement. The Homestead Act of 1862 made free land available to those who would work it for five years and soldiers, at loose ends following the war, and Europeans, attracted by democracy and the lure of free land, came by the thousands.

There was nothing easy in the life of these early pioneers. The harsh climate could deliver freezing blizzards in winter and dust storms in summer, and these early settlers had to be necessarily hardy and hard working. But there were also years of milder weather when their labors were repaid with bountiful crops. More people came, attracted by the success of those already there. In 1867, they voted to join the Union and it was at this time that Nebraska was trimmed down to her present size and made the 37th state.

What we know as Nebraska today is topographically diverse. It is a plain which slowly rises from east to west changing in elevation from 825 feet to 5,340 feet. In the south and east are river-bottom farmlands which contrast with the flat wheat lands of the west, the high grasslands of the northwest and the rugged canyon country of the southwest.

The state is heavily agricultural, producing grains and livestock in particular. An extensive network of reservoirs for flood control and irrigation has been a major factor in her success.

From Desert Wasteland to Garden Spot

Where herds of buffalo formerly roamed in the millions, growing ponderous on the prairie grasses, now there are cattle. The grassy expanse of the Sand Hills, whose twenty thousand square miles of light sandy soil were once thought to be a desert wasteland, has become one of the prime cattle-producing regions of the nation. Crisscrossed by clear streams and dotted with natural lakes, the area has proven to be an unplowed garden spot.

The great number of cattle, both in the Sand Hills and on feedyards in the cropland areas, has made Omaha the largest livestock and meat-packing center in the nation, and has contributed to its becoming the fourth largest rail center. With a population of 350,000, Omaha is the largest city in the state, and its location beside the Missouri River makes it a gateway in the east. Omaha, and the capital city of Lincoln just fifty miles away, are the cultural centers for the state. Two-thirds of the state's 1½ million people live in the eastern one-third of the state.

The population of the state as a whole is ethnically diverse, and the customs and culture of many of the Europeans who were attracted to the state by the promise of free land still survive. Such annual celebrations as the Czech Festivals in Wilber and Clarkson or the St. Patrick's Day festivities in O'Neill attract thousands of visitors who come to enjoy the color and gaiety.

Nebraska's earliest inhabitants also have their special observances: Indian powwows are held each year at Winnebago and Macy on the Winnebago and Omaha reservations. Lasting a week or more, these powwows feature dances in the old tradition performed in impressive ceremonial dress.

In all these respects Nebraska appears to be closely linked to the past: her primary industry remains agricultural as it was for the earliest pioneers and she has not forgotten the old traditions and customs. Yet it would be unfair to suggest that the state has failed to keep pace with modern developments. Hundreds of manufacturing firms have established main or branch plants throughout the state to take advantage of the available resources. The same dams which control flooding and provide irrigation generate electric power. The Strategic Air Command Headquarters with its sophisticated aircraft and missiles is unmistakably 20th century.

Yet in many ways the frenzy of the space age seems to have left Nebraska untouched. It is still largely free of air and water pollution. The comparative peace and serenity of rural living remains readily accessible here. To see this land as the first explorers saw it and as the early settlers saw it, one need only stroll through the picturesque openness that is Nebraska.

GENERAL AND PRACTICAL INFORMATION FOR NEBRASKA

 FACTS AND FIGURES. Nebraska derives its name from several very similar Indian words, generally accepted to have been Nibrathka, which meant "flat water." That term described the famous Platte River, and also possibly the Missouri River, both of which have been credited with being "a mile wide and a foot deep." Its nickname is the *Cornhusker State,* and the fabled football team of the University of Nebraska partially adopted the name—the "Huskers."

The state tree, formerly the American elm, is now more appropriately the cottonwood, which grows in abundance in most parts of the state. State flower is the goldenrod, the state bird the western meadowlark, and the state gemstone is the blue agate, found primarily in the northwest portion of the state. "Equality Before the Law" is the state motto.

Lincoln is the capital. The population is 1,539,000.

 HOW TO GET THERE. *By air:* the major airport for flights originating outside the state is Omaha which is served by North Central, United, Frontier, Braniff International, and Ozark. Frontier also flies from Denver into Scottsbluff and Sidney in western Nebraska.

By train: Amtrak has passenger service to Lincoln and Omaha through Denver and Chicago.

By bus: Continental Trailways and Greyhound are the principal bus lines into

Nebraska reaching Omaha from the east and Sidney or North Platte from the west.

By car: I–80 is the principal access route from the east crossing into Nebraska from Iowa near Omaha. The major highways from the west are I–80 through northeastern Colorado, US 26 and US 20 from Wyoming. I–29 reaches Omaha from the north. US 83 and US 81 enter from South Dakota in the north and from Kansas in the south.

 HOW TO GET AROUND. *By air:* Frontier serves Sidney, Scottsbluff, Alliance, Chadron, McCook, North Platte, Kearney, Hastings, Grand Island, Columbus,- Lincoln, Omaha, and Norfolk. United has flights between Omaha and Lincoln; North Central flies between Omaha and Norfolk.

By train: Amtrak has passenger service between Omaha and Lincoln.

By bus: Arrow and Black Hills Stage Lines serves Lincoln, Omaha, Fremont, West Point, Norfolk, Wayne, O'Neill, Ainsworth, Valentine, Gordon, and Chadron. Star Bus Line stops at many towns between Chadron and Sidney and Sidney and Omaha. Wade Bus Lines runs between Ogallala and Scottsbluff with several stops in between. Continental stops at Sidney, North Platte, Lincoln and Omaha. Greyhound has service to many towns between Kimball and Omaha.

By car: the major east–west routes across the state are I–80 from Omaha through Lincoln, Grand Island and North Platte and US 20 from South Sioux City through O'Neill, Valentine and Chadron. Highways running north–south include US 385 through Sidney, Bridgeport, Alliance and Chadron; US 83 through McCook, North Platte and Valentine; US 281 through Hastings, Grand Island and O'Neill; and US 81 through Columbus and Norfolk.

 TOURIST INFORMATION. For information about touring the state or about convention facilities or business opportunities, contact Dept. of Economic Development, Box 94666, Lincoln 68509. Specific information about recreation activities and events is available from NEBRASKAland, Dept. T, State Capitol, Lincoln 68509. "NEBRASKAland," the monthly magazine of the Nebraska Game and Parks Commission, is available by subscription at $3/year. Box 30370, Lincoln 68503.

 SEASONAL EVENTS. *January:* Big Eight Basketball, University of Nebraska at Lincoln. *February:* Horse racing opens at Grand Island. *March:* Omaha Area Square Dance Festival, Omaha. *April:* National Arbor Day Awards in Nebraska City. Activities include tree-planting ceremonies at Arbor Lodge State Historical Park. Horse racing season begins in Omaha. *May:* There are German Heritage Days festivities at McCook and Danish Festival at Blair. McCook is also the site of an annual fishing derby. *June:* Omaha hosts the NCAA Baseball World Series. There are canoe races at Valentine. For a week at mid-month is NEBRASKAland Days at North Platte when entertainment typical of Nebraska's pioneer days and western heritage includes rodeos barbecues, ceremonial Oglala-Sioux Indian dancing, frontier musicals, and western art exhibits. *July:* Buffalo Bill Wild West Show begins a 5–week run in North Platte at mid-month. There is the RCA Rodeo at Crawford and the Little Britches Rodeo at Chadron. Late in the month is the Old Fiddlers' Contest at Crawford. *August:* Fremont is the site of the 7–County 4–H Fair. Nebraska's Big Rodeo takes place at mid-month in Burwell. The Czech Festival is held in Wilber. *September:* The Nebraska State Fair takes place at the Fairgrounds in Lincoln during the first week. In Omaha is the Livestock Show and Rodeo during the last week. Big Eight Football season begins and continues through the fall with the

University of Nebraska competing. *October:* Horse racing begins in South Sioux City. There is a Czech Hobby Show at Wilber and a Swedish Smorgasbord at Wause. *November:* Omaha hosts the Holiday on Ice. *December:* Minden offers the Annual Light of the World Pageant.

NATIONAL FORESTS. The *Nebraska National Forest* is located in three areas of north central Nebraska. The Forest covers over 300,000 acres of lake and river country. State 97 south from Nezel leads to the Samuel R. McKelvie National Forest (formerly Niobrara Division). The Bessey Division, 15 mi. E of Thedford on State 2, then 2 mi. S on an unnumbered road, was the site of a disastrous 20,000-acre fire in 1965 and is now the largest man-planted forest in the world. It offers hunting, camping, hiking, picnicking, pool and lookout tower. The Pine Ridge Division lies 8 mi. S of Crawford on State 2 and has picnicking, hunting, fishing and camping.

Valentine National Wildlife Refuge, 17 mi. S of Valentine on US 83, then 13 mi. W on State 16B, consists of nine lakes. These are closed to fishing during waterfowl hunting season, but the area also offers nature study, birdwatching, picnicking, upland game bird and deer hunting. Free. Headquarters are open Mon. to Fri. 8 to 5.

STATE PARKS. *Indian Cave* is the newest of the Nebraska state parks. It borders the Missouri River and includes some of the finest of that scenic territory. Rich in wildlife and native plants this park is one of the most varied in the state because of the relatively high rainfall and diverse habitats. The park is accessible from the main county road just north of Shubert on State 67. Facilities include hiking, fishing, hunting, picnicking, drinking water, and primitive camping.

Fort Robinson, 3 mi. W of Crawford on US 20, surrounds the fort established in 1874 in the midst of Indian fighting. Crazy Horse, the Sioux Indian chief, was killed here. Today this 11,000-acre park offers hiking, fishing, picnicking, horseback riding, non-power boating, and trailer, camping and sanitary facilities. There are also a lodge, restaurant, rides and museums.

Chadron, 9 mi. S of Chadron on US 385, is a modern recreation complex amidst streams and ponderosa pine. Hiking, fishing, picnicking, power boating, horseback riding, camping, trailer, and sanitary facilities are all available.

Ponca, 2 mi. N of Ponca on State 12, overlooks the Missouri River Valley. Here campgrounds include paved pads for trailers with electrical hookups and sewage dump facilities. Hiking, fishing, river boating, a pool for swimming, and complete camping and sanitary facilities are available.

Niobrara, 1 mi. W of Niobrara on State 12, includes a portion of the Lewis and Clark Trail through hardwood forests and across sandy bottoms. The park offers hiking, fishing, picnicking, camping, boating, swimming pool, and trailer and sanitary facilities.

CAMPING OUT. Nebraska has more than fifty recreation areas in addition to other special use and wayside sites. Camping is generally limited to only two days in wayside areas and to fourteen days in state-run recreation areas. The following are some of the larger campgrounds. "Complete facilities" as used here means sanitary facilities, drinking water, picnic tables, fireplaces, hiking, fishing, and hunting.

Bridgeport, in Bridgeport, offers complete facilities (except hunting) and boating and swimming.

Branched Oak Lake, 3 mi. N of Malcolm or 4 mi. W of Raymond, is the largest lake in the Salt Valley complex. The recreation area offers complete facilities and boating, swimming, and shelter houses.

Fremont Lakes, 3 mi. W of Fremont, has complete facilities (except hunting) plus boating, swimming, showers, and trailer sanitary hookups.

Lake McConaughy, northwest of Ogallala, has five campgrounds with complete or nearly complete facilities plus boating and swimming.

Lewis and Clark, 15 mi. N of Crofton, has seven campgrounds with complete facilities along with boating and swimming. Most have shelter houses.

Medicine Creek, 2 mi. W and 7 mi. N of Cambridge, has complete facilities and shelters, boating, and swimming.

Two Rivers, 1 mi. S and 1 mi. W of Venice, has complete facilities, supervised swimming, showers, trailer parking and sanitary dump.

 TRAILER TIPS. In addition to the state parks and recreation areas already mentioned, Nebraska has a number of county or civic trailer sites. Those listed below are among the more complete.

Sutherland Reservoir Park, ½ mi. S of US 80 at Sutherland, has water and electric hookups and sanitary station. The area is open May 15 to Sept. 15 and a $1 minimum fee is charged.

Riverside Park, 1 mi. W of Broadway on S Beltline US 26 truck bypass, has water, electric, and sewer hookups and sanitary dump facilities. Open May to Oct.; there is a $2 minimum charge.

Fairgrounds Trailer Park, on the S side of US 30, 1½ mi. W of Sidney, has water and electric hookups and sanitary dump facilities. It is open all year and there is no minimum fee.

Crystal Springs Park, in Fairbury, has water and electric hookups and sanitary dump facilities. Open all year; there is no fee.

 FARM VACATIONS AND GUEST RANCHES. At *Deer Lawn Guest Ranch,* a 4,500-acre cattle spread, you can ride out on a roundup and help check fences and windmills. It's in the Sand Hills of the beautiful Snake River Canyon. Water sports activities, golf, rodeos and museums are nearby. Up to 6 can be accommodated in a new cabin. Contact Bill and Pat Powell, S.R.1, Valentine 69201.

Pine Hills Ranch is in the scenic pine country of northwestern Nebraska. This is a cattle ranch which also grows wheat and alfalfa. You may join in the ranch activities, hunt rocks and Indian artifacts, or tour the Black Hills. Up to 10 can be accommodated. Contact Sherman and Mary Grace Harris, Rte. 1, Box 30, Rushville 69360.

Tee Pee Ranch is 2,800 acres of grassland at the edge of the Sand Hills which produces hay, grain, and alfalfa. You can ride, fish, milk cows and gather eggs. Agate Fossil Beds and Scotts Bluff National Monument are nearby. Up to 10 can be accommodated. Contact Bill and Beverly Lore, P.O. Box 94, Alliance 69301.

MUSEUMS AND ART GALLERIES. The *Stuhr Museum of the Prairie Pioneer,* located on the outskirts of Grand Island 3½ mi. N of the Grand Island Interchange at the intersection of US 281 and 34, consists of a building on an island in a man-made lake, an outdoor museum, and a collection of farm machinery. Designed by Edward Durell Stone, the main building houses displays and historical exhibits relating to pioneer life in Nebraska including agricultural implements, Harness Shop and Blacksmith. There are also facilities for displaying art work. The outdoor museum is a late 19th-century railroad town with log cabins, school house, railroad station and many others. Most of the farm machinery exhibited is in running condition including many steam engines. Open Mon. to Sat., Memorial Day to Labor Day, 9 a.m. to 7 p.m.; rest of year to 5 p.m.; Sun. all year from 1 p.m. Adults $1, students 50¢, children 35¢. Lower rates in winter.

The *Museum of the Fur Trade*, 3½ mi. E of Chadron on US 20, traces American fur trading. Frontier weapons, trade goods, Indian exhibits and relics of the frontier past are displayed. There is also a restored trading post. Open June to Labor Day, daily, 8 a.m. to 6 p.m.; rest of year by appointment, phone 432-3843. Adults 50¢; children under 18 free with parents.

The *Hastings Museum*, at 1330 N. Burlington at 14th St. on US 34, 281 in Hastings, has wildlife, Indian, and natural history exhibits and pioneer displays including an extensive Smith and Wesson gun collection. Open Mon. to Sat., June to Aug., 8 a.m. to 8 p.m.; rest of year to 5 p.m.; Sun. all year 1 to 5 p.m. Adults, 75¢; children under 12, 25¢; children under 6, free.

Joslyn Art Museum, 2200 Dodge St. in Omaha, is a magnificent marble structure which houses collections of art from ancient to modern times. Particularly impressive are the paintings and documents from Prince Maximilian's 1833–34 Upper Missouri River Expedition. Concerts, lectures, and classes are offered. Open Tues. to Sat., 10 to 5; Sun. from 1 p.m. Adults $1, children under 12, 50¢.

Also in Omaha are the *Union Pacific Historical Museum* at 1416 Dodge St. where there are thousands of interesting artifacts from the railroad's past including a replica of Lincoln's funeral car. Open Mon. to Fri., 9 to 5; Sat. to 1 p.m. Free. The *Strategic Aerospace Museum*, 12 mi. S of Omaha on US 73, 75 near Bellevue displays bombers, fighters, and missiles used by the Strategic Air Command. Open daily 8 to 5. Adults, $1; children 6 to 15, 50¢; under 6, free.

On the campus of the University of Nebraska at Lincoln are several significant museums including the *University of Nebraska State Museum* at 14th and U Sts. in Morrill Hall. Displays include geology and wildlife of the Great Plains and the world's largest mammoth. Open Mon. to Sat., 8 to 5; Sun. from 1:30 p.m. Adults 50¢, students 25¢. Also on campus, the *State Historical Society Museum* at 15th and R Sts. summarizes Nebraska history with exhibits covering the early days of the pioneers and Indians. Open Mon. to Sat., 8 to 5; Sun. from 1:30. Free. The *Sheldon Memorial Art Gallery and Sculpture Garden*, at 12th and R Sts., houses over 1,100 paintings and offers rotating exhibits. Open Tues., 10 a.m. to 10 p.m.; Wed. to Sat., to 5 p.m.; Sun., 2 to 5 p.m. Free.

Harold Warp Pioneer Village, on US 6, 34, State 10 in Minden, re-creates the country's pioneer heritage with original buildings, including a sod house, pony express station, and more than 30,000 historic and antique items. Open daily 8 a.m. to sundown. Adults, $1.50; children 6 to 16, 50¢; under 6, free.

Willa Cather Pioneer Memorial and Museum, 38 mi. S of Hastings on US 281 on Webster St. in Red Cloud, contains her letters, first editions of her books, and family memorabilia. Open May to Sept., daily, 1 to 5 p.m.; rest of year by appointment. Free. Also here is her *Childhood Home* which has been restored and contains some of the original furnishings. Open by appointment only, phone 746-2653. Adults, $1; students, 50¢; children under 12, 25¢.

The *State Capitol Building* in Lincoln has long been recognized as one of the world's architectural masterpieces. Designed by Bertram Grosvenor Goodhue, the building combines sculpture, paintings, mosaics and inscriptions. Atop the dome is a bronze statue, The Sower, symbolically sowing the seeds of good will. Around the dome are symbolic Indian Thunderbirds. Inside are murals and paintings, carved doors and mosaic floors. The capitol is open at 9 a.m. Mon. to Sat. and at 2 p.m. Sun.

HISTORIC SITES. *Scotts Bluff National Monument,* 2 mi. W of Gering on State 92, is a massive promontory rising 800 feet above the valley floor. It served as a major landmark on the Oregon and Mormon Trails. Exhibits at the Oregon Trail Museum in the visitor's center tell the story of this westward migration, and paintings by William Henry Jackson, the famous pioneer photographer and artist who followed the trail in 1866, are also on display. Open daily, Memorial Day to Labor Day, 7 a.m. to 8:30 p.m.; rest of year, 8 a.m. to 4:30 p.m.

Homestead National Monument, 4 mi. NW of Beatrice, just off State 4, is on the site of the claim of Daniel Freeman, one of the first applicants to file for land under the Homestead Act. Signed in 1862, this act permitted every citizen or anyone who declared his intention to become a citizen, to file claim to 160 acres of unappropriated Government land. The visitor's center near the monument entrance exhibits historical objects of pioneer days and presents graphic accounts of life during settlement of the public domain. There is a 1½-mi. self-guiding tour of the area. The museum is open daily, Memorial Day to Labor Day, 8 a.m. to 7 p.m.; rest of year to 5 p.m. Free.

Chimney Rock National Historical Site, 16 mi. W of Bridgeport off US 26, State 92, is a landmark of the Oregon Trail, marking the end of the prairies. The cone-shaped mound narrows to a 150-foot column rising 500 feet above the North Platte River. From June to Aug. a State Historical Society Information Trailer is located in the area and open from 8:30 a.m. to 4:30 p.m.

Agate Fossil Beds National Monument, 9 mi. NW of Scottsbluff on US 26 to Mitchell, then 34 mi. N on State 29, is an area where the fossils of animals alive 20 million years ago are concentrated. The site is still under development but offers a self-guiding nature trail and temporary visitors' center whose exhibits explain the story of the fossils found here and of the animals who once roamed this region. Open 8:30 a.m. to 4:30 p.m., Memorial Day to Labor Day, daily; rest of year, Sat. and Sun. only. Free.

John Brown's Cave on State 2 near 20th St. in Nebraska City. This was a major station of the famed "Underground Railroad" which helped slaves to escape from captivity in the South. It was run by John Brown, the Great Abolitionist who later became famous at Harpers Ferry, W. Va. Open all year, weather permitting. Adults $1, children 15 years and under 35¢.

Arbor Lodge State Historical Park, 1 mi. NW of Nebraska City on US 73, is Nebraska's oldest state historical park. Once the home of J. Sterling Morton, founder of Arbor Day, Arbor Lodge is a 52–room mansion furnished with period decor. An arboretum with hundreds of varieties of trees surrounds the home. The mansion is open June 15 to Sept. 15, Mon. to Sat., 10 a.m. to 5:30 p.m.; Sept. 16 to Oct., daily, 1 to 5:30 p.m.; closed rest of year. Adults 25¢, children 10¢. The park is open all year.

Fort Kearny State Historical Park, 8 mi. SE of Kearney on State 10, re-creates the frontier outpost as it was a century ago. The fort, originally in Nebraska City, was moved here in 1848 to protect the Oregon Trail. The stockade has been reconstructed as well as a replica of the sod blacksmith-carpenter shop.

Buffalo Bill Ranch State Historical Park, at North Platte, 1½ mi. N on Buffalo Bill Ave., was William F. Cody's ranch and winter quarters. Buildings are open to visitors Memorial Day to Labor Day, daily, 8 a.m. to 9 p.m.; inquire rest of year.

Fort Hartsnuff State Historical Park, 2½ mi. NW of Elyria on State 11, is still under development. Fort Hartsnuff was established to protect pioneers in the Loup Valley from the Sioux. It is still being restored.

Champion Mill State Historical Park at Champion and *Ash Hollow State Historical Park,* 2½ mi. S of Lewellen on US 26, are being developed. Champion Mill is the last working water-powered mill in Nebraska. Ash Hollow still shows evidence of the passage of the Conestogas. Ruts, chiseled by the wheels of the prairie schooners over 100 years ago, are visible yet today.

 TOURS. The *Belle of Brownville*, the largest excursion boat on the Missouri River, offers 2–hour scenic cruises on the river Sun. afternoons during June, July, and Aug. leaving from the Brownville dock at 1:30, 2:30, and 3:30 p.m. Adults $2.50, children $1.75.

Stardust River Cruises leave from the Marina Inn at 4th and B Sts. in South Sioux City from July to Labor Day, Sat. at 10:15 p.m. and Sun. at 8:15 p.m. Cruise lasts 1½ hours. Adults $2.50; children under 12, $1.25. Phone 755-2511 for further information.

Free guided tours of the *State Capitol Building* in Lincoln are given every day of the week. Mon. to Fri. tours begin at 9, 10, 11 a.m., 1, 2, 3, 3:45 p.m.; Sat. the same schedule applies from 10 a.m. to 2 p.m. then 2:45 and 3:30; Sun. at 2, 2:45, and 3:30 p.m.

 INDUSTRIAL TOURS. The *Good Year Tire and Rubber Company* at 4021 N. 56th St. in Lincoln has tours of their plant operations. A minimum 1 day's advance notice is required for these 1½-hour tours given at 9 a.m. or 1 p.m. Mon. to Fri. For safety reasons children under 12 are not allowed. Contact the office, 466-2311.

Bausch and Lomb, Inc. at 218½ N. Locust in Grand Island gives tours of their optical plant by appointment.

Norfolk Livestock Market, Inc. at 1601 S. 1st St. in Norfolk gives tours of their operation Thurs. 9 a.m. to 5 p.m. and Fri. 9 a.m. to noon. Phone 371-0500.

 SPECIAL INTEREST TOURS. *Boys Town*, 10 mi. W of Omaha on Dodge St., US 6. Father Flanagan founded this institution for homeless and underprivileged boys in 1917. Now there are over 900 boys living here. The administration of the government in this community is in the hands of those who live there including the management of the post office, library, and bank. A map with an outlined tour is available at the entrance. Open Mon. to Sat., 8 to 4; Sun., 9 to 5. Free.

The *U.S.S. Hazard*, which ran antisubmarine patrol sweeps during World War II, is now permanently berthed in the N.P. Dodge Park at 11000 N. River Dr. in Omaha. Virtually intact the ship has most systems in operating condition. Adults, $1.25; children over 5, 75¢; children 5 and under, free.

 STAGE AND REVUES. From July to mid-Aug. the Nebraska Wesleyan University students give theatrical performances in the Village Theatre in Brownville at 8 p.m., Thurs. to Sun. There is also a Sun. matinee at 2 p.m. Adults $2.50, children $1. Reservations advised, phone 825-4121.

A number of Nebraska towns have theaters where touring companies give performances and several have community theatres which draw on local talent.

Lincoln has a *Children's Theatre* which gives performances and puppet shows of special interest to children.

MUSIC. Omaha has an *opera company* and both Omaha and Lincoln have *symphony orchestras* which provide musical fare throughout the season. Lincoln also has the *Czech Chamber Orchestra*. A number of Nebraska towns host touring symphonies and operas.

DRINKING LAWS. Liquor is sold by the drink or the bottle from 6 a.m. to 1 a.m. Sun. no package liquor sales may be made except beer. Liquor sale is subject to local option. The minimum drinking age is 19.

SUMMER SPORTS. *Fishing.* Game fish are so abundant in Nebraska that a fisherman may indulge himself all year and catch black bass, trout, crappie, northern pike, walleye, catfish and sauger. There are 2,300 lakes and some 11,000 miles of streams which provide ample opportunity for sports fishing. The state stocks many of these lakes.

Hunting. The ring-necked pheasant is the prime target in Nebraska. In addition there are seasons on rabbits, geese, ducks, squirrels, grouse, quail, and prairie chickens. For bow and arrow hunters there are seasons for turkey, deer, and antelope. The State Game and Parks Commission in Lincoln has information regarding seasons and licenses.

Boating, swimming, and *water-skiing.* Dams associated with conservation projects have backed up such rivers as the Missouri, Platte, Loup, Republican, and Frenchman and formed large lakes well-suited to water sports. Power boats are not permitted on some of the smaller lakes in the state so check first to avoid disappointment.

WINTER SPORTS. *Ice skating* and *ice boating.* When weather conditions permit, many of the same lakes that serve summer sports enthusiasts can provide activity for the winter months.

SPECTATOR SPORTS. *Rodeo.* These events take place all over Nebraska during the summer and fall. The largest event is the rodeo at Burwell around mid-Aug.

Hockey. Although limited to Omaha, hockey is a very popular sport. There is a season of about 35 games from October to March at the Ak-Sar-Ben Coliseum, 63rd and Shirley, Omaha.

Horse Racing. Pari-mutuel thoroughbred racing starts off in Grand Island in late March, then moves to Ak-Sar-Ben in Omaha in May. The state fairgrounds in Lincoln begin in early July, followed by Madison in Sept., and South Sioux City in late Sept.

Football, basketball, baseball. The University of Nebraska competes in Big Eight football and basketball in the fall and winter. The NCAA World Series of Baseball is held in Omaha in June.

WHAT TO DO WITH THE CHILDREN. *Buffalo Bill's Wild West Show,* 2 mi. W of North Platte on US 30, is a reenactment of the 19th-century show with Indian dances, stagecoach holdups, trick riding and roping. Shows mid-July to Aug., Mon. to Sat., 8 p.m.; Sun. 6 p.m. Adults $2.75–$3.75; children 3 to 12, $1 less. Phone 532-5450.

At Front Street in Ogallala children can take a stagecoach ride for 60¢. There is also a free cowboy museum.

INDIANS. Nebraska has three Indian reservations: the Santee Reservation in the north bordering Lewis and Clark Lake and the adjacent Winnebago and Omaha Reservations just below South Sioux City. The annual Winnebago Indian Powwow at Winnebago in July and the Omaha Indian Powwow at Macy in August are major events on the Nebraska calendar and feature the traditional ceremonial dances of these tribes.

301

RECOMMENDED READING. Mari Sandoz is considered the chronicler of pioneer history on the Plains with such works as *Hostiles and Friendlies, Old Jules,* and *Crazy Horse: The Strange Man of the Oglalas.* There are also the writings of Willa Cather. *The World of Willa Cather* by Mildred R. Bennett is a good introduction. John G. Neihardt, whose office in Bancroft is open to visitors, has written about the Indians of the state in *A Cycle of the West* and *Dreams Are Wiser Than Men.*

EXPLORING NEBRASKA

A vast array of sights awaits visitors to Nebraska, from the timbered bluffs along the Missouri River to the pine-studded buttes of the Pine Ridge country of the northwest. There are miles of perfectly level farmland interspersed with streams. There are mighty buttes and canyons in the southwest where oil derricks pump black gold from far below. There has been no extensive mining in the state, but riches are found beneath the surface in perhaps the world's largest underground reservoirs of water.

The vast Sand Hills region, unlike any other area of the world, is still of largely uncertain history. Some believe it was totally avoided by the herds of buffalo which migrated through the state in numbers estimated into the hundreds of millions, and equally avoided by the Plains Indians. Others claim it was a rich hunting ground even in the earliest times, just as it now sustains extensive cattle herds.

Nebraska has long been known as a corridor to the west, for the Mormon Trail, Oregon Trail, Lewis and Clark trail and Pony Express route all crossed through the state.

The railroad was a vital force in Nebraska's settlement and expansion, and the Union Pacific was of primary importance. It was in Omaha in 1863 that ground was broken for the eventual joining of rails to the West Coast. Headquarters for the Union Pacific are in Omaha, and a museum operated by the company houses many souvenirs from the railroad's history, including documents of Abraham Lincoln and other Civil War memorabilia.

Interstate 80's twin ribbons of concrete now carry the bulk of traffic to and through Nebraska. It closely parallels the old Oregon Trail, and modern travelers pass the guideposts which served the earlier migrations. Chimney Rock near Bayard was probably the most-mentioned land feature in pioneer journals, since it signaled the approach to the mountains. Scotts Bluff National Monument is on Rte. 92, two miles west of Gering. A museum and road to the top of the bluff are among highlights there, but many other rock formations are of nearly equal importance and interest. Indian legend says one of the formations was used by one tribe to escape another. However, once up there, they could not come down without exposing themselves, so they became prisoners. Only a daring nighttime descent by rope down the back side allowed them to escape.

A modern addition to the landscape is the "Chain of Lakes," pleasant lakes built along the interstate and open to the public.

Omaha Livestock Market and Art Center

As far as Nebraska is concerned, I–80 begins in Omaha where a number of sites should not be missed. Omaha is the biggest livestock market and meat-packing center in the world. The Joslyn Art Museum, a pink marble palace, is considered by many authorities to be the foremost center in America of early West documentation in various art forms, although it also exhibits modern art. The popular Union Pacific Historical Museum's many exhibits have to do with railroad history, including a replica of the funeral car which bore Lincoln. Father Flanagan's Boys' Town, long an institution of national fame, was founded by the kindly priest as a home and school for boys, and based on his belief that there was no such thing as a "bad boy." Outside Omaha is the headquarters of the Strategic Air Command with its underground control center with world-wide communications and the Aerospace Museum, presently undergoing developments that will eventually entail millions of dollars.

Lincoln, fifty miles west of Omaha along I–80, has the state capitol, a building which should not be missed. Visible for miles, this landmark rises 400 feet. The statue at the top of the dome is Lee Lawrie's *The Sower* and the base of the dome is decorated with the symbolic Indian Thunderbird.

At the University of Nebraska at Lincoln is the State Museum, which has geology displays, fossils, natural history dioramas and the world's largest mammoth. The State Historical Society Museum has outstanding pioneer and Indian exhibits. And Sheldon Art Galleries offers permanent and traveling art exhibits.

The home of the famous orator William Jennings Bryan is here on the grounds of Bryan Hospital and contains original furnishings and memorabilia.

All across the state, towns adjacent to the interstate have links with the frontier, and have something special to offer. In North Platte, toward the western portion of the state, rodeo was born on July 4, 1882, when Buffalo Bill Cody staged his Old Glory Blowout. This was later expanded into his original Wild West Show and Congress of Rough Riders, a true western extravaganza which gained world-wide fame with tours in Europe. That show has been re-created, and each year plays during much of the summer in North Platte, still thrilling thousands with its pageantry and excitement.

Buffalo Bill's home, Scout's Rest Ranch, is now operated as a State Historical Park, with many curios and mementoes on display in the house and barn.

Pioneer Village

Heading west from Lincoln, one gets the feeling of the Old West at such places as Pioneer Village in Minden. One of the top attractions in the nation, the village contains over thirty thousand historic items in twenty-two buildings, including a sod house, a pioneer school, and log pony express station. There is an old steam locomotive and tender, a full-scale Indian stockade, plus artisans at work on loom and spinning wheel and in a broom factory. More than one million tourists annually visit the village, which contains one of the largest collections of antique cars, airplanes, and wagons in the nation.

Near Minden is the town of Hastings, whose museum, the House of Yesterday, contains mementoes of yesteryear, dioramas, collections, a natural history section, and planetarium. Exhibits provide insights into the hardships of the courageous pioneers and demonstrate their way of life.

Grand Island, only a few miles north of Minden on Interstate 80, is the third largest city in the state. Its Stuhr Museum is becoming one of the most ambitious projects of its type in the world. Not only does it include a large antique vehicle collection and a beautiful, unique main building surrounded by a moat, but outlying areas are being developed into authentic sites devoted to such things as a 19th-century prairie town, a log cabin settlement, trapper's camp, and Indian village. The town is nearly complete with depot, train, early post office, and refurbished homes.

Many early military forts were established in the state, and many have either been preserved or restored, including Fort Kearny near the town of Kearney. Located just south of the Platte River in the central part of the state, the fort was an important deterrent to Indian troubles, and provided protection for wagon trains. Fort Hartsuff near Ord is undergoing a face lifting, and Fort McPherson near Maxwell has been declared a National Cemetery. Fort Robinson, one of the major state parks, remained an active military post until after World War I. At Fort Robinson, the aura of the Old West survives despite the more modern facilities now there. It was here that the great Sioux chief Crazy

Horse was mortally wounded. After surrendering himself and his people to the reservation life, he learned that he was about to be imprisoned and in an attempted escape was stabbed by a trooper.

Crazy Horse planned the attack on General Custer at the Battle of Little Big Horn, and he was the first to break Custer's lines there. Even now, Crazy Horse is considered to have been the greatest strategist and military genius of the Plains Indians.

The fort lies in a deep valley of the Pine Ridge with sheer cliffs rising in a long wall behind it. Trout fishing, some of the best deer, antelope, and turkey hunting in the state, trail rides and other recreation make it one of the most popular parks in the state. Only a few miles away on US 20 is Chadron whose Museum of the Fur Trade has a gun collection, Indian exhibits and relics of the fur traders who first penetrated the area. The Pine Ridge Division of the Nebraska National Forest extends north to Chadron.

Farther east on US 20, at Valentine, is still another fort, although it was never the scene of any serious conflict or confrontation. Fort Niobrara, considered rough duty for military personnel because of its isolation and weather extremes, is now a National Wildlife Refuge. Although it lies on the northern fringes of the Sand Hills, it also fronts on the scenic Niobrara River, which runs along the edge in a deep valley. During part of the year, the herd of buffalo is moved to this area, and in other seasons they roam the sandy hills to the south. An extensive herd of genuine longhorned steers and another of elk also call the refuge home.

Largest Man-Planted Forest

South of Valentine on US 83 is Thedford. West of Thedford on State 2 is Halsey and the Bessey Division of the Nebraska National Forest, the world's largest man-planted forest. In May of 1965 this was the site of a disastrous 20,000–acre fire. You can take a self-guiding tour through the Bessey Nursery and Plantation.

This loop tour through central and northwestern Nebraska has missed two regions of significant interest. Across the southern portion of the state are numerous reservoirs. Among the more noteworthy is Harlan County Reservoir at Alma. Serious floods in 1939 led to the erection of a dam across the Republican River and the formation of this 16,000–acre lake which now provides not only flood control and irrigation but also affords excellent sportsfishing for walleye, catfish and white bass. Similar measures were followed across this region of the state and Medicine Creek Reservoir near Cambridge, Red Willow Reservoir near McCook,

Swanson Reservoir near Trenton, and Enders Reservoir at Enders were formed as a result. US 34 and US 6 provides easy access to these recreation areas.

Downstream from Harlan Reservoir is Red Cloud, near the Kansas Border. It was the home of Pulitzer Prize winner Willa Cather and the inspiration and setting for many of her novels, including *O Pioneers!* and *My Antonia,* and a posthumous volume of novelettes and short stories. The Willa Cather Pioneer Memorial Museum and many of the places made famous in her books can be visited in a self-guiding tour. The Childhood Home of Willa Cather has been restored and contains some of the original furnishings.

Homestead on the Range

East of Red Cloud on US 136 is Beatrice, site of the Homestead National Monument. More than 100,000 settlers came to Nebraska as a result of the Homestead Act of 1862 that provided for distribution of public lands, free of charge, to those who settled on them, cultivated and inproved them, and remained for a period of five years. The Homestead Monument marks the site of one of the first homesteads: Daniel Freeman filed Application No. 1 under the Act for this land, built first a log cabin and later a brick house. A Visitor Center museum has exhibits explaining the homestead story.

Further west from Beatrice on US 136 then north on US 73, 75 leads to Nebraska City and Arbor Lodge State Historical Park. J. Sterling Morton, the founder of Arbor Day and later Secretary of Agriculture under Grover Cleveland, settled in Nebraska City in 1855 and built a house overlooking the Missouri River. Because there were no trees near his home, he planted his own—shade trees, evergreens, ornamentals, and an orchard. Eventually he became so enthused about the need for such planting that he dedicated most of his life to that pursuit, and in 1874 the state set aside April 10, Morton's birthday, as a special tree-planting day. Now, his former mansion is a State Historical Park, with the acres of trees open year round to visitors. Tree-planting ceremonies take place annually in the park in late April.

Also in Nebraska City is John Brown's Cave, a major station on the Underground Railroad which helped slaves to escape from captivity in the South.

This leaves one major point of interest unexplored. US 73 north from Nebraska City passes through the Winnebago and Omaha Indian Reservations in the northeast corner of the state. At Winnebago and Macy in July and August, these Indian tribes hold powwows and perform their traditional ceremonial dances in full tribal dress.

Whether you choose to explore Nebraska for history or recreation, the state has a great deal to offer. There are bountiful lakes and forests for camping and sports and abundant reminders in museums and historical sites of the pioneer heritage. In either case you will discover the friendliness and well-being of the people who live there.

For those who are seeking the peace and serenity of rural living, or the legacy, saga, and pageantry of the Old West, or just a picturesque and elegant jaunt in the wide-open spaces, Nebraska is the place.

AROUND THE STATE

HOTELS AND MOTELS. Omaha and Lincoln offer a good selection of hotels and motor inns. Elsewhere in the state, motels are usually chosen for their proximity to tourist sites. There are definite summer and winter seasons so rates may be slightly higher or lower in or out of season. Listings are in order of price category.

The price categories in this section, for double occupancy, will average as follows: *Deluxe* $24, *Expensive* $20, *Moderate* $16, and *Inexpensive* $12. For a more complete description of these categories see the *Hotels & Motels* part of THE ROCKIES & PLAINS *Facts at Your Fingertips* at the front of this volume.

AURORA

Ken's. *Inexpensive.* 1515 11th St. Small but roomy motel which features large guest lobby and tastefully furnished rooms. Color TV. Restaurant nearby. City park, pool and playground opposite. 694-3141

BROKEN BOW

Gateway. *Inexpensive.* 1 mi. E on State 2, 70, 92. TV. Sauna, playground, 24-hour cafe, municipal pool, and bowling nearby. 872-2478

CHADRON

Roundup. *Inexpensive.* 901 E. 3rd St. Small pleasant motel with family units, color TV. Restaurant across road. 432-5591

COLUMBUS

Country Club Inn. *Moderate.* 1 mi. SW at jct. US 30, 81. Medium-sized facility with elegant yet relaxing atmosphere. Well-furnished rooms surround large

pool area. TV, free coffee; 24-hour cafe nearby. 564-2886

Gembol's. *Inexpensive.* 3224 8th St. Small, pleasant motel with family units, color TV. Restaurant nearby. Centrally located near municipal park and swimming pool. 563-3150

Keen Korner. *Inexpensive.* 3221 23rd St. at 33rd Ave. Medium-sized motel with some kitchen units. TV. Restaurant, cocktail lounge. Very pleasant grounds with play area. 564-6332

X-L. *Inexpensive.* 2222 23rd St. Comfortable small motel with large lounge area. Heated pool with play area. Color TV. Quiet in-the-country atmosphere. 24-hour cafe nearby. 564-9180

FREMONT

Modern-Aire. *Moderate.* 2 mi. E on US 30. Small, comfortable motel with pleasant, guest lounge. Color TV, pool, free coffee. Restaurant nearby. 721-2713

Erin Manor. *Inexpensive.* 239 W. 23rd St. at jct. US 30, 77, 275. Well-furnished, medium-sized motel with some family units. TV, playground. Restaurant across the road. 721-1310

Midwestern. *Inexpensive.* 424 W. 23rd St. on US 30, 2 blks. W of jct. US 77, 275. Small, tastefully furnished motel with comfortable guest lounge, TV. pool. Restaurant nearby. 721-7100

GRAND ISLAND

Conoco. *Moderate.* 2107 W. 2nd St. on US 30. Popular, medium-sized motel with TV, heated pool, family units, and restaurant. 384-2700

Erin Rancho. *Moderate.* 2114 W. 2nd St. on US 30W. Large motor hotel, with TV, indoor heated pool, sauna, playground, free coffee. Restaurant and cocktail lounge. 384-2240

Grand Island TraveLodge. *Moderate.* 507 W. 2nd St. on US 30. This downtown, comfortable member of chain features color TV, heated pool, free coffee. Restaurant nearby. 384-1000

Holiday Inn. *Moderate.* 2503 S. Locust St. on State 2. Large chain member with spacious rooms. Color TV, heated pool, playground, restaurant, cocktail lounge, entertainment. Free airport bus. 384-1330

Yancey Hotel. *Moderate.* 2nd and Locust Sts. A large, comfortable downtown hotel with a wide choice of accommodations. TV, restaurant, cocktail lounge. This establishment is well-run and remains the meeting place in town. 382-5800

HASTINGS

Midlands Lodge. *Moderate.* 1 mi. S at jct. US 6, 34, 281. Modern, handsomely furnished downtown hotel with color TV, heated pool, playground, restaurant, cocktail lounge. 463-2428

Clarke Hotel. *Inexpensive.* 223 N. Hastings Ave. Large, comfortable downtown hotel with TV, restaurant, cocktail lounge, barber and beauty shops. Civic and social groups frequently use this hotel's meeting facilities. 462-5161

Redondo. *Inexpensive.* 907 E. South St. Small, comfortable motel with connecting units. TV. Restaurant across the street. Centrally located. 462-2404

Wayfair. *Inexpensive.* Jay and Wabash Sts. Conveniently located small motel with color TV, heated pool, playground. Restaurant nearby. 463-2434

HOLDREGE

Plains. *Inexpensive.* 519 W. 4th Ave. on US 6, 34. Small motel has nicely decorated rooms with TV, free coffee. Playground. 24–hour restaurant next door. 995-8646

KEARNEY

Fort Kearny Inn. *Expensive.* 2 mi. S at jct. State 10, 44, I–80. Large motel has color TV, heated pool, restaurant, and cocktail lounge. Horses can be boarded. Stocked pond available for fishing. 234-2541

Holiday Inn. *Expensive.* 1½ mi. S on State 44. This large member of the chain has color TV, heated pool, sauna, playground. Free coffee. Restaurant, cocktail lounge, entertainment, dancing. 237-3141

Shady Lane. *Moderate.* 1 mi. W on US 30. Another of the small attractive motels offering TV, playground. Cafe next door. 237-5161

Tel-Star. *Moderate.* S. 2nd Ave. on State 10, 44. Medium-sized motel which offers color TV, heated pool, playground, sundeck, restaurant. 237-5185

Hammer. *Inexpensive.* 1 mi. W on US 30. This medium-sized motel has color TV, heated pool, playground. Free coffee. Horses boarded. Restaurant nearby. 237-2123

St. John's Motor Court. *Inexpensive.* 1 mi. W on US 30. For the traveler who wants to stretch his legs, this medium-sized facility offers nicely landscaped grounds. TV, heated pool, playground, free coffee. Horses boarded. Cafe nearby. Also campsites. 237-5131

LEXINGTON

Hollingsworth. *Inexpensive.* 4 blks. E on US 30. A pleasant stop for families. This small motel has family units, TV, playground. Restaurant nearby. 324-2388

LINCOLN

Villager. *Expensive.* 5200 O St. This large motel offers color TV, heated pool, 24-hour cafe, cocktail lounge, dancing, entertainment, putting green. 434-9111

Buffalo. *Moderate.* 347 N. 48th St. This medium-sized motel has TV, heated pool, playground. Cafe nearby. 466-1931

Clayton House. *Moderate.* 10th and O Sts. This medium-sized hotel has color TV, rooftop pool, sundeck. Restaurant and cocktail lounge. Conveniently located. 432-0333

Colonial Inn. *Moderate.* 5600 Cornhusker Hwy. A fine, medium-sized motel, somewhat on the outskirts of town. It has TV, heated pool, sauna, restaurant, cocktail lounge. 434-5971

Holiday Inn-Northeast. *Moderate.* 5250 Cornhusker Hwy. This large member of the chain has color TV, indoor heated pool, sauna, recreation room, and putting green. Restaurant, cocktail lounge. 434-3171

Radisson Cornhusker. *Moderate.* 13th and M Sts. This large hotel has color TV, barber and beauty shops. Restaurant and cocktail lounge. Airport bus available. 432-4471

Sleepy Hollow. *Moderate.* 4848 O St. One of the older motels in this area which has been kept up-to-date. Has color TV, heated pool. Restaurant nearby. 434-3166

Congress Inn. *Inexpensive.* 2001 W. O St. This motel has TV, heated pool, playground, shuffleboard, and free coffee. Restaurant and cocktail lounge. 477-4488

Motel 6. *Inexpensive.* 3001 N.W. 12th St. at I-80 Municipal Airport exit. This motel has TV, heated pool. Restaurant next door. 475-9502

McCOOK

Chief. *Moderate.* 612 W. B St. A medium-sized motel located downtown but the pleasant grounds give it a country atmosphere. Family units, color TV, restaurant. Free passes to city pool. 345-3700

Cedar. *Inexpensive.* 1300 E. C St. A delightful small motel with a stream running through its back yard. Rooms are nicely furnished. Family units with TV, free coffee. Cafe nearby. 345-1896

Royal. *Inexpensive.* 202 E. 10th St. on US 6, 34. For the traveler who likes music, this medium-sized motel offers organ music in the lobby. TV, recreation room. Restaurant ½ mi. 345-6420

NORFOLK

Villa Inn. *Moderate.* 1227 Omaha Ave. This large motel offers color TV, indoor heated pool, 24-hour cafe, cocktail lounge, entertainment, dancing. 371-7000

Capri. *Inexpensive.* 211 E. Norfolk Ave. This small modern downtown motor hotel has rooms overlooking the North Fork River. TV, free complimentary breakfast. Restaurant nearby. 371-4550

Sey-Crest. *Inexpensive.* 721 E. Norfolk Ave. A medium-sized comfortable motel with well-maintained beautiful grounds. Family units with TV. Playground. Restaurant next door. 371-2750

NORTH PLATTE

Howard Johnson's. *Expensive.* At. jct. US 83, I–80. This medium-sized chain member offers color TV, heated pool, cafe, cocktail lounge. 534-3120

Ramada Inn. *Expensive.* 1402 S. Jeffers. This member of the chain has color TV, heated pool, playground, restaurant, bar, entertainment, dancing. Free airport bus. 534-3630

Circle C South. *Moderate.* 1211 S. Dewey St. This moderately large motel has color TV, two heated pools, sauna, restaurant, cocktail lounge, and free airport bus. 532-0130

Rambler Court. *Moderate.* 1420 W. Rodeo Rd. A small comfortable motel with pleasant restful surroundings. Some family units. TV, heated pool, playground. Restaurant and cocktail lounge adjacent. 532-9290

Sands. *Moderate.* 2 mi. S at jct. US 83, I–80. A two-story motel featuring color TV, heated pool, restaurant, cocktail lounge. Free airport bus. 532-0151

Stanford Lodge. *Moderate.* 1400 E. 4th St. An attractive medium-sized facility with large comfortable rooms. TV, heated pool, playground, free coffee. Cafe nearby. 532-9380

Capri. *Inexpensive.* 1402 Rodeo Rd., W on US 30. This small motel has restaurant and cocktail lounge, TV, playground. Family size rooms. 532-3477

El Rancho. *Inexpensive.* 615 Rodeo Rd. Another medium-sized comfortable motel with heated pool, playground, TV, some kitchenettes. 24–hour cafe nearby. 532-0490

North Platte TraveLodge. *Inexpensive.* 602 E. 4th St. A medium-sized chain member features in-room coffee, heated pool, color TV. Restaurant nearby. 532-7705

OGALLALA

Chieftain Tourist Village. *Inexpensive.* 909 W. 1st St. A small pleasant motel, which has a few family units with kitchens. Free coffee, TV, playground. Restaurant ½ mi. 284-3661

Erin Plaza. *Inexpensive.* 1st and E. B Sts. A medium-sized modern motor hotel. Heated pool, playground, TV, restaurant opposite. 284-3651

OMAHA

Omaha Hilton. *Deluxe.* 16th and Dodge Sts. A very large hotel with color TV, year-round heated pool, barber and beauty shops. Restaurant and cocktail lounge. 346-7600

Howard Johnson's. *Expensive.* 72nd St. and Grover. A large member of the chain offering color TV, indoor heated pool, sauna, barber. Restaurant and cocktail lounge. 397-3700

Commodore Motor Inn. *Moderate.* 24th St. at Dodge. This moderately large motor inn has color TV, free coffee, barber, restaurant and cocktail lounge. Airport bus available. 342-7755

Omaha TraveLodge. *Moderate.* 3902 Dodge St. A large member with family units. Comfortable rooms with color TV. 24–hour cafe adjacent. 558-4000

Prom-Town House Motor Inn. *Moderate.* 7000 Dodge. This large, rambling facility has the *Fish Pier West*, one of the better restaurants in Omaha. Other features include indoor heated pool, playground, color TV, barber and beauty shops, sauna, putting green, winter ice rink. Airport bus available. 556-5161

Radisson Blackstone. *Moderate.* 36th and Farnam Sts. This large midtown hotel is handsomely furnished. Color TV, restaurant and cocktail lounge, barber and beauty shops. Airport bus available. 348-0111

Ramada Inn-South. *Moderate.* 1811

Hillcrest Rd. in Bellevue. A large member of the chain offering indoor heated pool, playground, sauna, color TV, restaurant, cocktail lounge, entertainment, dancing, barber and beauty shops, indoor putting green, ping-pong and pool tables. 292-3800

Castle. *Inexpensive.* 632 S. 16th St. A large, well-maintained downtown hotel offering TV, restaurant, cocktail lounge. Airport bus available. 341-8750

Sandman. *Inexpensive.* 105 S. Ft. Crook Rd., Bellevue. A small motel with TV back from the highway on a hill. Restaurant nearby. 291-4990

O'NEILL

Town House Inn. *Moderate.* 725 E. Douglas. A small nicely furnished motel with color TV, heated pool, restaurant, cocktail lounge. Free airport bus. 336-1640

SCOTTSBLUFF

Lamplighter. *Moderate.* 606 E. 27th St. This modern, well-designed motel is very popular with color TV, indoor heated pool, sauna, restaurant, cocktail lounge. 632-7108

Park. *Inexpensive.* 209 W. 27th St. A conveniently located motel near shopping center and restaurants. This medium-sized facility has color TV, free coffee. Comfortable rooms. 632-6176

SIDNEY

Fort Sidney. *Moderate.* 935 9th Ave. The traveler will find this medium-sized motor hotel offers many guest conveniences including family units, color TV, heated pool, restaurant and cocktail lounge. 254-5863

SOUTH SIOUX CITY

Marina Inn. *Expensive.* 4th and B Sts. This large motel offers color TV, year-round heated pool, sauna, restaurant, cocktail lounge, dancing, beauty shop. On the Missouri River with marina, boat ramp, dock. 494-2441

Ramada Inn. *Moderate.* 217 W. 29th St. A very fine motel with attractive accommodations including color TV. Pool, restaurant, cocktail lounge. Exercise room, sauna. 494-3023

South Sioux City TraveLodge. *Moderate.* 400 Dakota Ave. This chain member is quite attractive and has a restaurant and cocktail lounge, heated pool. Color TV in rooms. 494-3046

VALENTINE

Raine. *Moderate.* ½ mi. W on US 20. A small motel with large comfortable rooms. TV, 24-hour cafe nearby. 376-2030

Valentine Motel. *Moderate.* ½ mi. SE on US 20, 83. Small, well-equipped motel with color TV, playground, 24-hour cafe nearby. Camper-trailer facilities for 20. 376-2450

DINING OUT in Nebraska usually means eating at a restaurant connected or adjacent to a hotel or motel. Distances are great in this state, and there are few good, independent restaurants outside the two major cities, Omaha and Lincoln. There are plenty of bus stop cafes and gas station diners though, and most are clean and pleasant and serve good, wholesome food. A few of the state's outstanding establishments are listed below.

Restaurant price categories are as follows: *Deluxe* will average $9, *Expensive* $5.50–$7.50, *Moderate* $3.50–$5.50, and *Inexpensive* $2–$3.50. These prices are for *hors d'oeuvres* or soup, *entrée* and dessert. Not included are drinks, tax and tips. For a more complete explanation of restaurant categories, refer to THE ROCKIES & PLAINS *Facts at Your Fingertips* at the front of this volume.

GRAND ISLAND

Dreisbach's. *Moderate.* 1137 S. Locust. An attractive restaurant that serves really hearty portions of food and great steaks and seafood. Family style dinners are available for 4 or more. Open 5 p.m. to midnight. 382-5450

KEARNEY

Grandpa's Steak House. *Moderate.* 2 mi. S on State 10, 44. This is a cozy place, red tapestry wallpaper gives it an elegant touch, but it is very much a family spot. Steaks, seafood, and chicken are specialties. Open 5 p.m. to 1 a.m. 237-2882

LINCOLN

Tony & Luigi's. *Moderate.* 5140 O St. A locally popular restaurant featuring steak and Italian dishes. Dinner music and entertainment add to your enjoyment. Open 5 p.m. to midnight. Closed Sun. 466-2351

Miller & Paine Tea Room. *Inexpensive.* 13th and O Sts. Nebraska beef and chicken pot pie are the specialties here. They make their own pastries. Located on the 5th floor. Open 11 a.m. to 2 p.m.; tea, 2 to 4:45 p.m.; Thurs., also 4:45 to 7:30 p.m. Closed Sun. 432-8511. Also at Gateway Center, 61st and O Sts. on US 6, 34. Open 11 a.m. to 8 p.m., Sat. to 5 p.m. Closed Sun. 434-7451

NORFOLK

Prenger's. *Moderate.* 116 E. Norfolk Ave. Specialties are steak and prime ribs and seafood. Background organ music enhances this pleasant atmosphere. Open 8:30 a.m. to midnight. Closed Sun. 371-0422

NORTH PLATTE

Tucker's. *Moderate.* 509 Jeffers St. on US 30. A bar and restaurant with cowboy atmosphere, this place offers good steaks, chicken and seafood. Open 11 a.m. to 10 p.m. 532-3922

OMAHA

Le Versailles. *Expensive.* 6311 Center St. Specialties in this fine restaurant are steak Diane, feuilletage de homard, roast duck. The atmosphere amid the French decor is intimate. Open 6 to 11 p.m.; Fri. and Sat. to midnight. Closed Sun. 558-6912

Orleans Room. *Expensive.* At 36th and Farnam Sts. in the Radisson Blackstone. A varied French and American menu includes crepes à la reine and sole Marguery. There is a luncheon smorgasbord. The decor is French. Open 11:30 a.m. to 2:30 p.m., 5:30 to 11 p.m. 348-0111

Domenico's. *Moderate.* 707 S. 72nd St. An Italian and American menu includes steak and seafood. Background music adds to the intimate relaxed dining. Open 5 p.m. to 1 a.m. 397-2300

Gorats Steak House. *Moderate.* 4917 Center St. Another Italian and American menu but the emphasis is on steak, seafood and chicken. The fireplace is a feature of the relaxed atmosphere. Open 11 a.m. to 2 p.m., 5 p.m. to 1 a.m. Closed Sun. 551-3733

Bishop Buffet. *Inexpensive.* 7 mi. W on US 6, 30A in Westroads Shopping Center; I-680 Dodge exit. A cafeteria with a large selection of salads, pastries. Special children's portions are available. Open 11 a.m. to 8 p.m.; Sun. to 7:30 p.m. 397-3101

INDEX

INDEX

In the *Geographical Index*, the H in front of the number indicates the page on which *hotels or motels* for the town or city are listed: the letter R indicates the page for *restaurant* listings.

COLORADO

GENERAL AND PRACTICAL INFORMATION

GEOGRAPHICAL

UTAH

GENERAL AND PRACTICAL INFORMATION

GEOGRAPHICAL

WYOMING

GENERAL AND PRACTICAL INFORMATION

GEOGRAPHICAL

MONTANA

GENERAL AND PRACTICAL INFORMATION

GEOGRAPHICAL

NORTH DAKOTA

GENERAL AND PRACTICAL INFORMATION

GEOGRAPHICAL

SOUTH DAKOTA

GENERAL AND PRACTICAL INFORMATION

GEOGRAPHICAL

NEBRASKA

GENERAL AND PRACTICAL INFORMATION

GEOGRAPHICAL